MARVEL

GUARDIANS
OF THE GALAXY

PRELUDE

MARVEL

GUARDIANS OF THE GALAXY

PRELUDE

MARVEL'S GUARDIANS OF THE GALAXY PRELUDE #1-2
WRITERS: **DAN ABNETT & ANDY LANNING**
PENCILER: **WELLINTON ALVES**
INKER: **MANNY CLARK**
COLORIST: **JAY DAVID RAMOS**

MARVEL'S GUARDIANS OF THE GALAXY: DANGEROUS PREY
PLOT: **ANDY LANNING**
SCRIPT: **DAN ABNETT**
STORYBOARDS/PRINT ADAPTATION: **DANIEL GOVAR**
ARTIST: **ANDREA DI VITO**
COLORIST: **LAURA VILLARI**
PRODUCTION: **ARLIN ORTIZ & LARISSA LOUIS**
PRODUCTION MANAGER: **TIM SMITH 3**

LETTERER: **VC'S CLAYTON COWLES**
ASSISTANT EDITOR: **MARK BASSO**
EDITOR: **BILL ROSEMANN**

MARVEL STUDIOS
CREATIVE MANAGER: **WILL CORONA PILGRIM**   VP PRODUCTION & DEVELOPMENT: **JONATHAN SCHWARTZ**
SVP PRODUCTION & DEVELOPMENT: **JEREMY LATCHAM**   PRESIDENT: **KEVIN FEIGE**

COLLECTION EDITOR: JENNIFER GRÜNWALD   ASSISTANT EDITOR: SARAH BRUNSTAD
ASSOCIATE MANAGING EDITOR: ALEX STARBUCK   EDITOR, SPECIAL PROJECTS: MARK D. BEAZLEY
SENIOR EDITOR, SPECIAL PROJECTS: JEFF YOUNGQUIST   SVP PRINT, SALES & MARKETING: DAVID GABRIEL

EDITOR IN CHIEF: AXEL ALONSO   CHIEF CREATIVE OFFICER: JOE QUESADA   PUBLISHER: DAN BUCKLEY   EXECUTIVE PRODUCER: ALAN FINE

MARVEL'S GUARDIANS OF THE GALAXY PRELUDE. Contains material originally published in magazine form as MARVEL'S GUARDIANS OF THE GALAXY PRELUDE #1-2, MARVEL'S GUARDIANS OF THE GALAXY INFINITE COMIC #1, IRON MAN #55, STRANGE TALES #181, INCREDIBLE HULK #271, TALES TO ASTONISH #13 and GUARDIANS OF THE GALAXY #0.1. Second printing 2014. ISBN# 978-0-7851-5410-5. Published by MARVEL WORLDWIDE, INC., a subsidiary of MARVEL ENTERTAINMENT, LLC. OFFICE OF PUBLICATION: 135 West 50th Street, New York, NY 10020. Copyright © 1960, 1973, 1975, 1982, 2013 and 2014 Marvel Characters, Inc. All rights reserved. All characters featured in this issue and the distinctive names and likenesses thereof, and all related indicia are trademarks of Marvel Characters, Inc. No similarity between any of the names, characters, persons, and/or institutions in this magazine with those of any living or dead person or institution is intended, and any such similarity which may exist is purely coincidental. **Printed in the U.S.A.** ALAN FINE, EVP - Office of the President, Marvel Worldwide, Inc. and EVP & CMO Marvel Characters B.V.; DAN BUCKLEY, Publisher & President - Print, Animation & Digital Divisions; JOE QUESADA, Chief Creative Officer; TOM BREVOORT, SVP of Publishing; DAVID BOGART, SVP of Operations & Procurement, Publishing; C.B. CEBULSKI, SVP of Creator & Content Development; DAVID GABRIEL, SVP Print, Sales & Marketing; JIM O'KEEFE, VP of Operations & Logistics; DAN CARR, Executive Director of Publishing Technology; SUSAN CRESPI, Editorial Operations Manager; ALEX MORALES, Publishing Operations Manager; STAN LEE, Chairman Emeritus. For information regarding advertising in Marvel Comics or on Marvel.com, please contact Niza Disla, Director of Marvel Partnerships, at ndisla@marvel.com. For Marvel subscription inquiries, please call 800-217-9158. **Manufactured between 9/17/2014 and 10/20/2014 by R.R. DONNELLEY, INC., SALEM, VA, USA.**

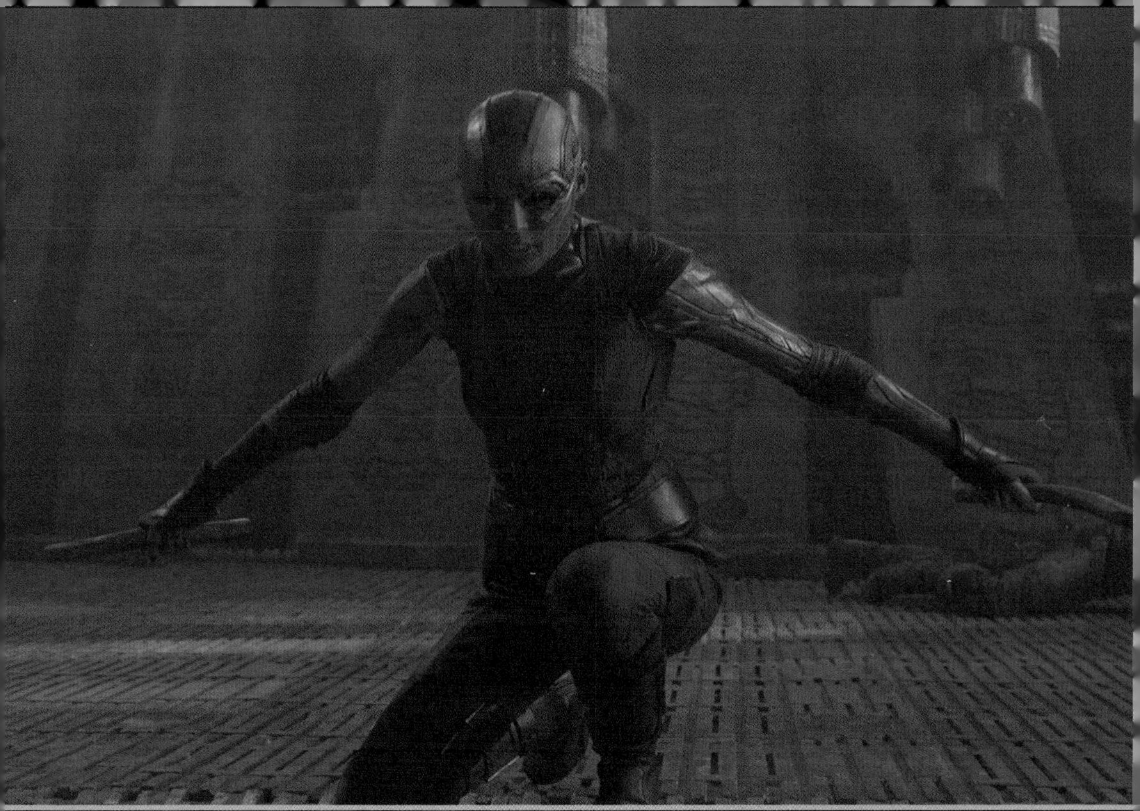

MARVEL'S GUARDIANS OF THE GALAXY PRELUDE #1

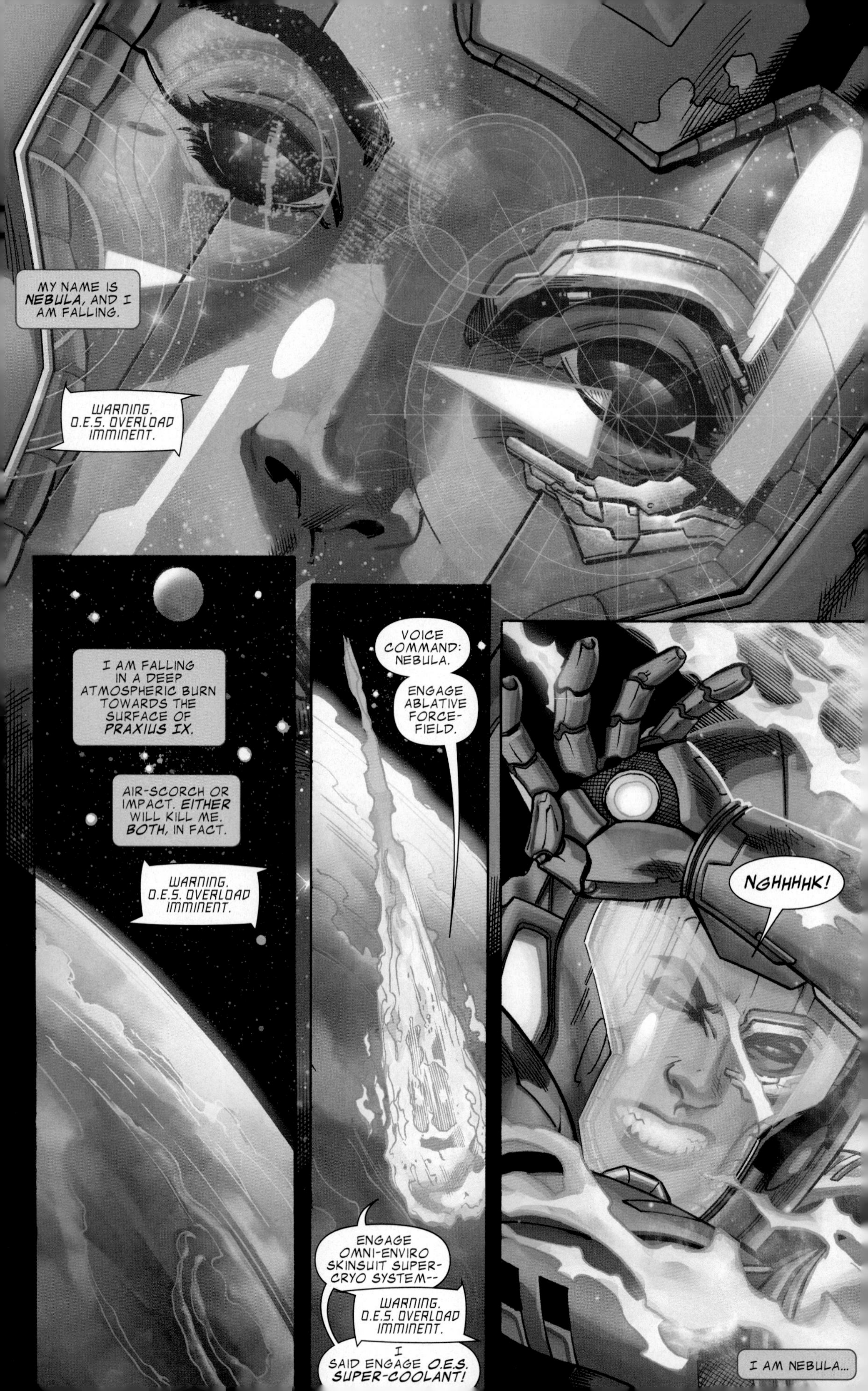

MY NAME IS NEBULA, AND I AM FALLING.
WARNING. O.E.S. OVERLOAD IMMINENT.
I AM FALLING IN A DEEP ATMOSPHERIC BURN TOWARDS THE SURFACE OF PRAXIUS IX.
AIR-SCORCH OR IMPACT. EITHER WILL KILL ME. BOTH, IN FACT.
WARNING. O.E.S. OVERLOAD IMMINENT.
VOICE COMMAND: NEBULA.
ENGAGE ABLATIVE FORCE-FIELD.
ENGAGE OMNI-ENVIRO SKINSUIT SUPER-CRYO SYSTEM--
WARNING. O.E.S. OVERLOAD IMMINENT.
I SAID ENGAGE O.E.S. SUPER-COOLANT!
NGHHHHK!
I AM NEBULA...

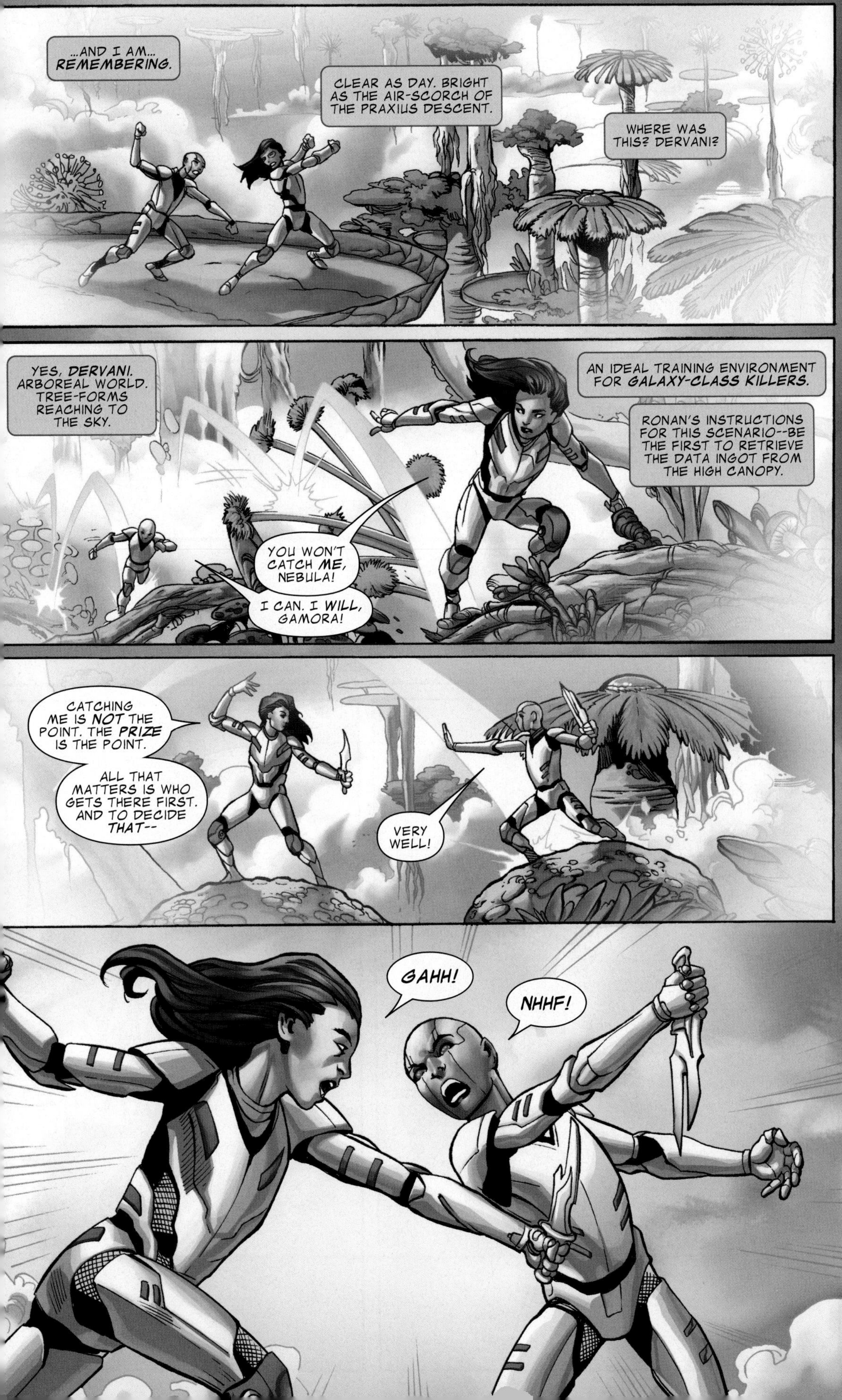
...AND I AM... REMEMBERING.
CLEAR AS DAY. BRIGHT AS THE AIR-SCORCH OF THE PRAXIUS DESCENT.
WHERE WAS THIS? DERVANI?
YES, DERVANI. ARBOREAL WORLD. TREE-FORMS REACHING TO THE SKY.
AN IDEAL TRAINING ENVIRONMENT FOR GALAXY-CLASS KILLERS.
RONAN'S INSTRUCTIONS FOR THIS SCENARIO--BE THE FIRST TO RETRIEVE THE DATA INGOT FROM THE HIGH CANOPY.
YOU WON'T CATCH ME, NEBULA!
I CAN. I WILL, GAMORA!
CATCHING ME IS NOT THE POINT. THE PRIZE IS THE POINT.
ALL THAT MATTERS IS WHO GETS THERE FIRST. AND TO DECIDE THAT--
VERY WELL!
GAHH!
NHHF!

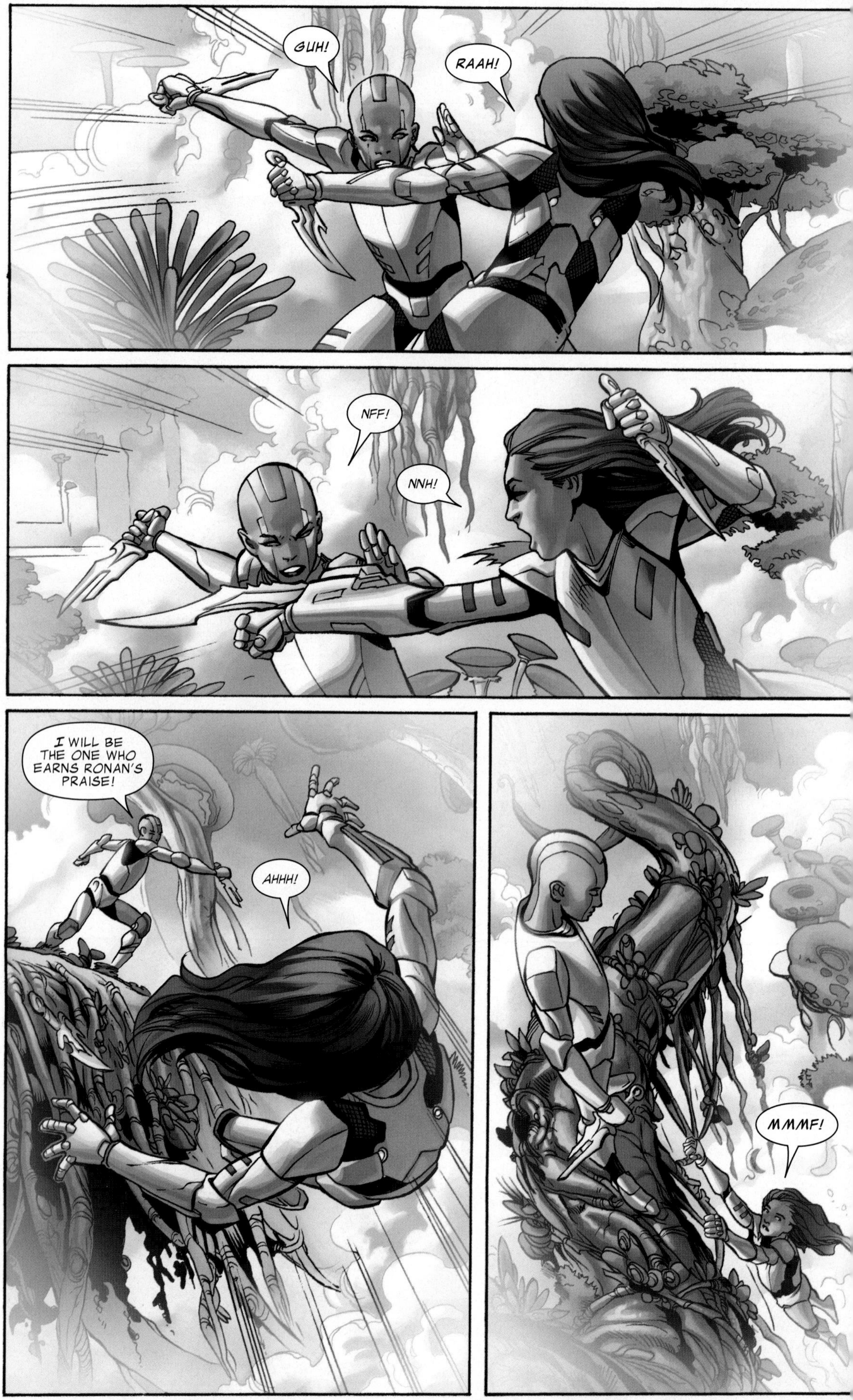
GUH!
RAAH!
NFF!
NNH!
I WILL BE THE ONE WHO EARNS RONAN'S PRAISE!
AHHH!
MMMF!

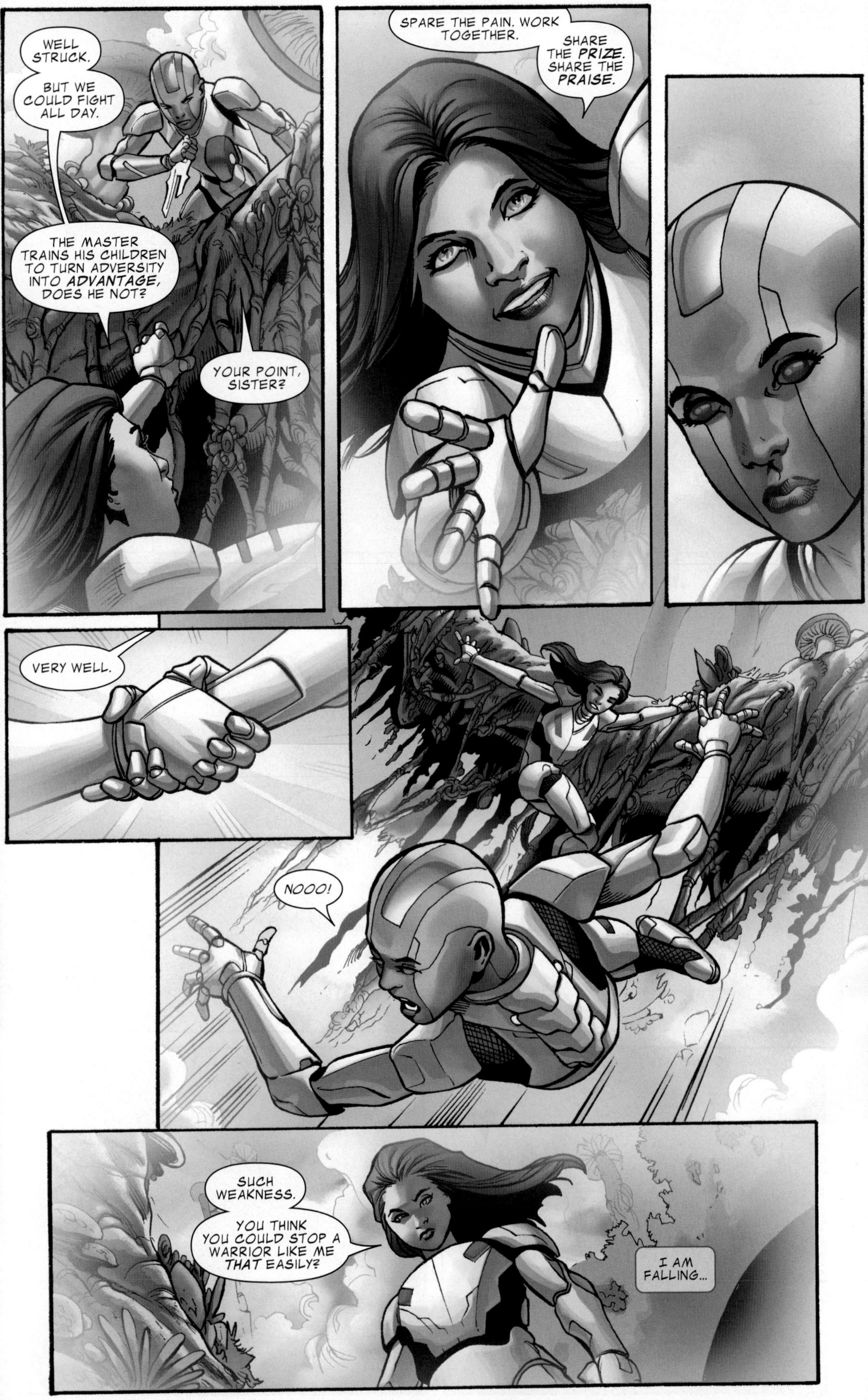
WELL STRUCK.
BUT WE COULD FIGHT ALL DAY.
THE MASTER TRAINS HIS CHILDREN TO TURN ADVERSITY INTO *ADVANTAGE*, DOES HE NOT?
YOUR POINT, SISTER?
SPARE THE PAIN. WORK TOGETHER.
SHARE THE *PRIZE*. SHARE THE *PRAISE*.
VERY WELL.
NOOO!
SUCH WEAKNESS.
YOU THINK YOU COULD STOP A WARRIOR LIKE ME *THAT* EASILY?
I AM FALLING...

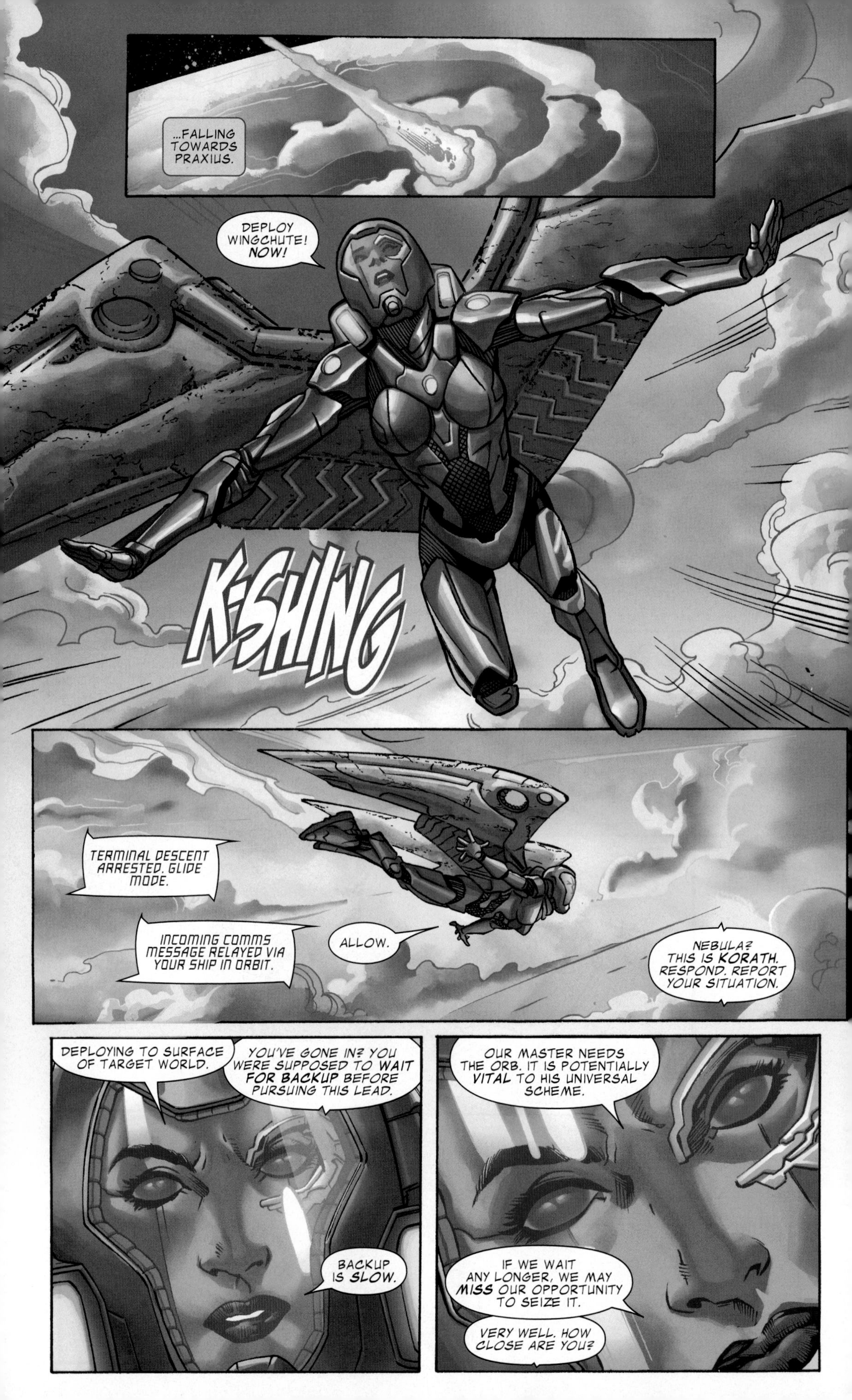
...FALLING TOWARDS PRAXIUS.
DEPLOY WINGCHUTE! NOW!
K-SHING
TERMINAL DESCENT ARRESTED. GLIDE MODE.
INCOMING COMMS MESSAGE RELAYED VIA YOUR SHIP IN ORBIT.
ALLOW.
NEBULA? THIS IS KORATH. RESPOND. REPORT YOUR SITUATION.
DEPLOYING TO SURFACE OF TARGET WORLD.
YOU'VE GONE IN? YOU WERE SUPPOSED TO WAIT FOR BACKUP BEFORE PURSUING THIS LEAD.
BACKUP IS SLOW.
OUR MASTER NEEDS THE ORB. IT IS POTENTIALLY VITAL TO HIS UNIVERSAL SCHEME.
IF WE WAIT ANY LONGER, WE MAY MISS OUR OPPORTUNITY TO SEIZE IT.
VERY WELL. HOW CLOSE ARE YOU?

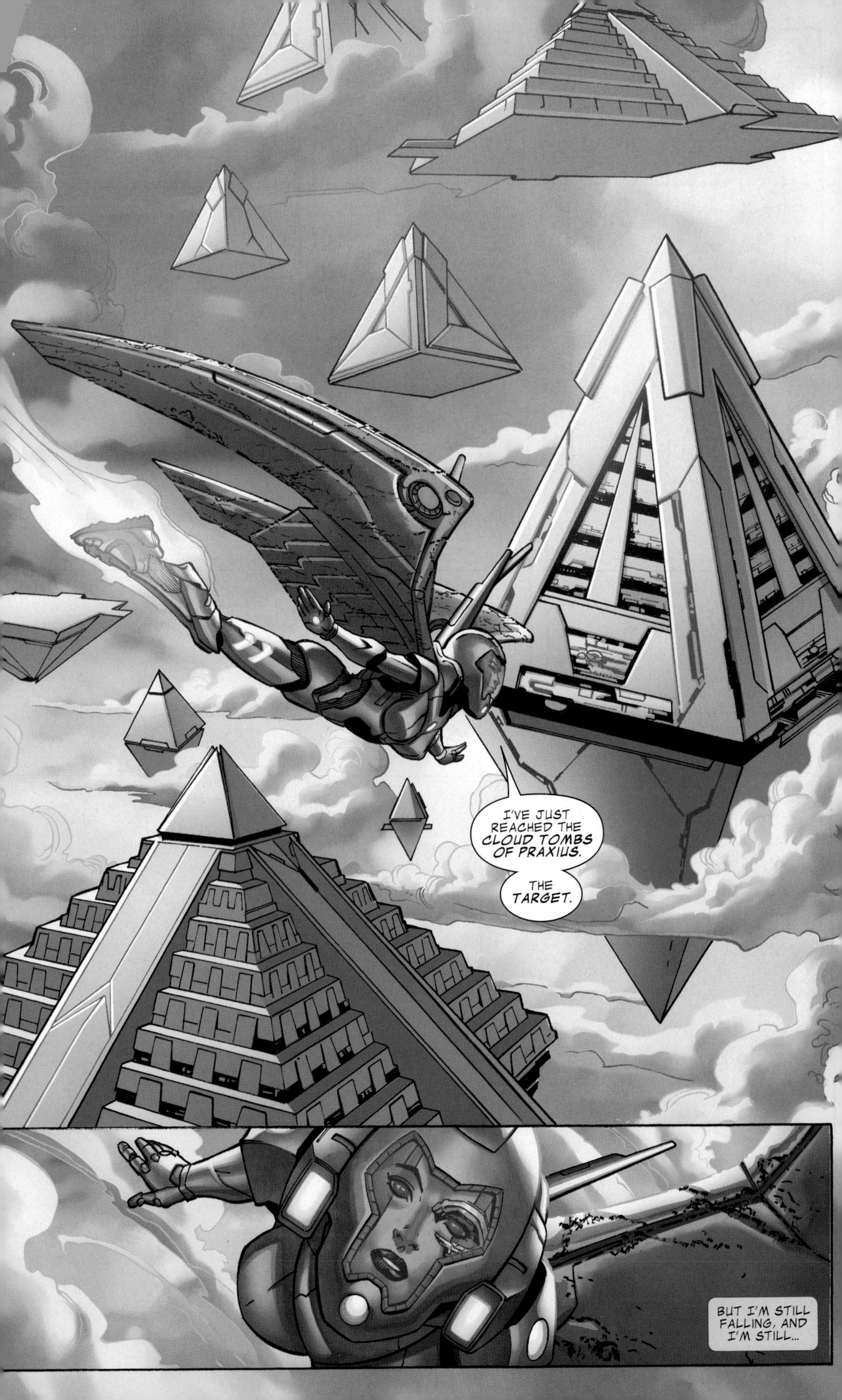
I'VE JUST REACHED THE CLOUD TOMBS OF PRAXIUS.
THE TARGET.
BUT I'M STILL FALLING, AND I'M STILL...

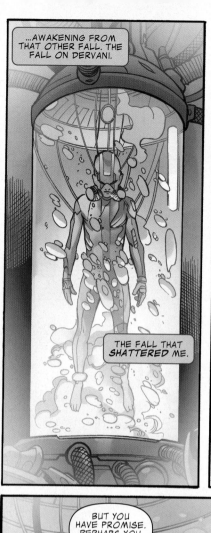

...AWAKENING FROM THAT OTHER FALL. THE FALL ON DERVANI.

THE FALL THAT *SHATTERED* ME.

IN THE HEALING TANK, PARTS OF MY BODY ALREADY REPLACED WITH TECH-MECHANISM, I HEARD THANOS'S VOICE...

NEBULA.

DO NOT *ACCEPT* WEAKNESS.

I SHOULD HAVE YOU KILLED FOR YOUR FAILURE.

BUT YOU HAVE PROMISE. PERHAPS YOU WILL LEARN.

NEXT TIME YOU FIGHT, YOUR METAL IMPLANTS WILL *BREAK* THE WEAPON THAT TRIES TO SEVER THEM.

FLESH IS *WEAK*. WEAKNESS MUST BE CAST ASIDE FOR THE SAKE OF *POWER*.

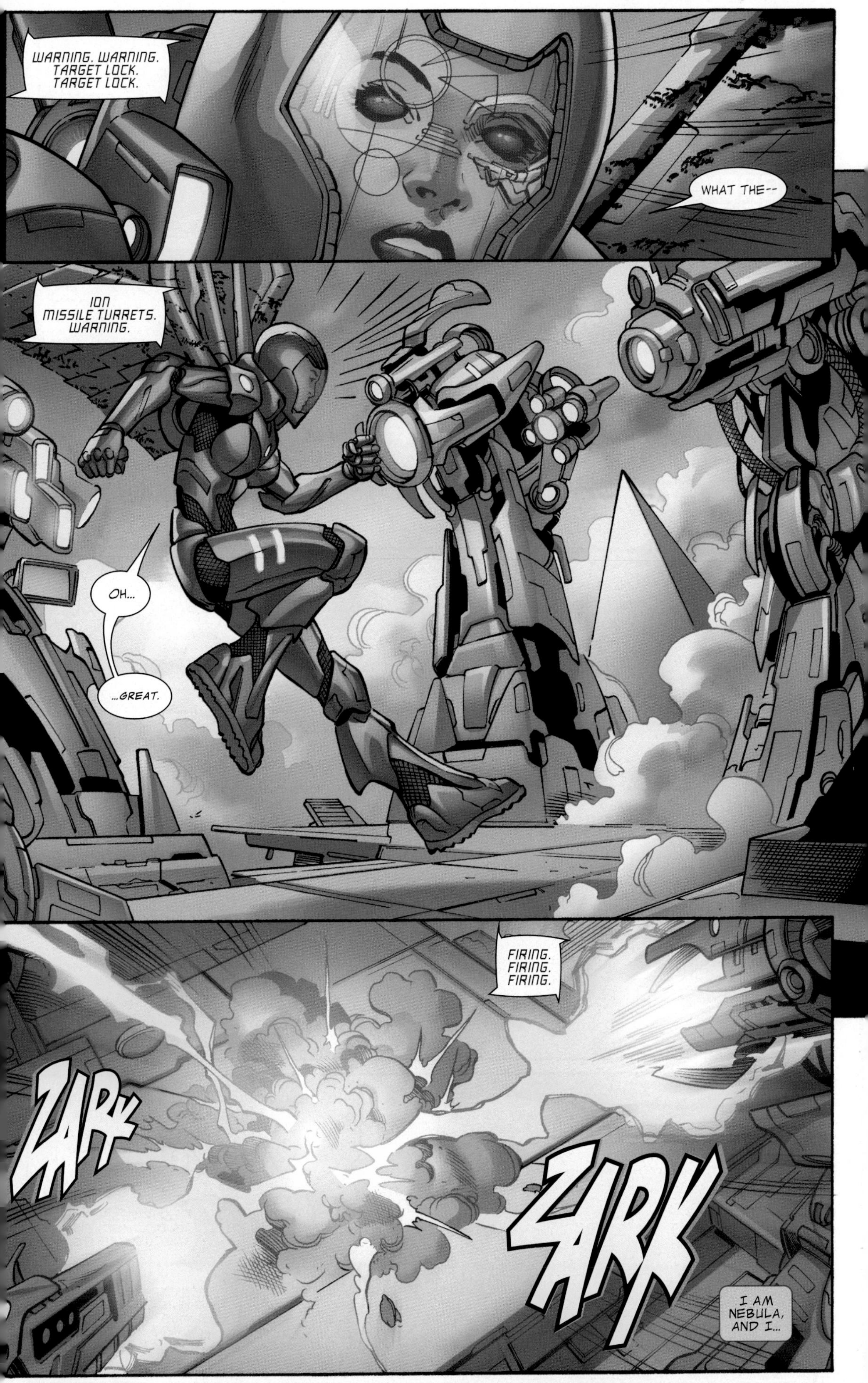
WARNING. WARNING.
TARGET LOCK.
TARGET LOCK.
WHAT THE--
ION
MISSILE TURRETS.
WARNING.
OH...
...GREAT.
FIRING.
FIRING.
FIRING.
ZARK
ZARK
I AM
NEBULA,
AND I...

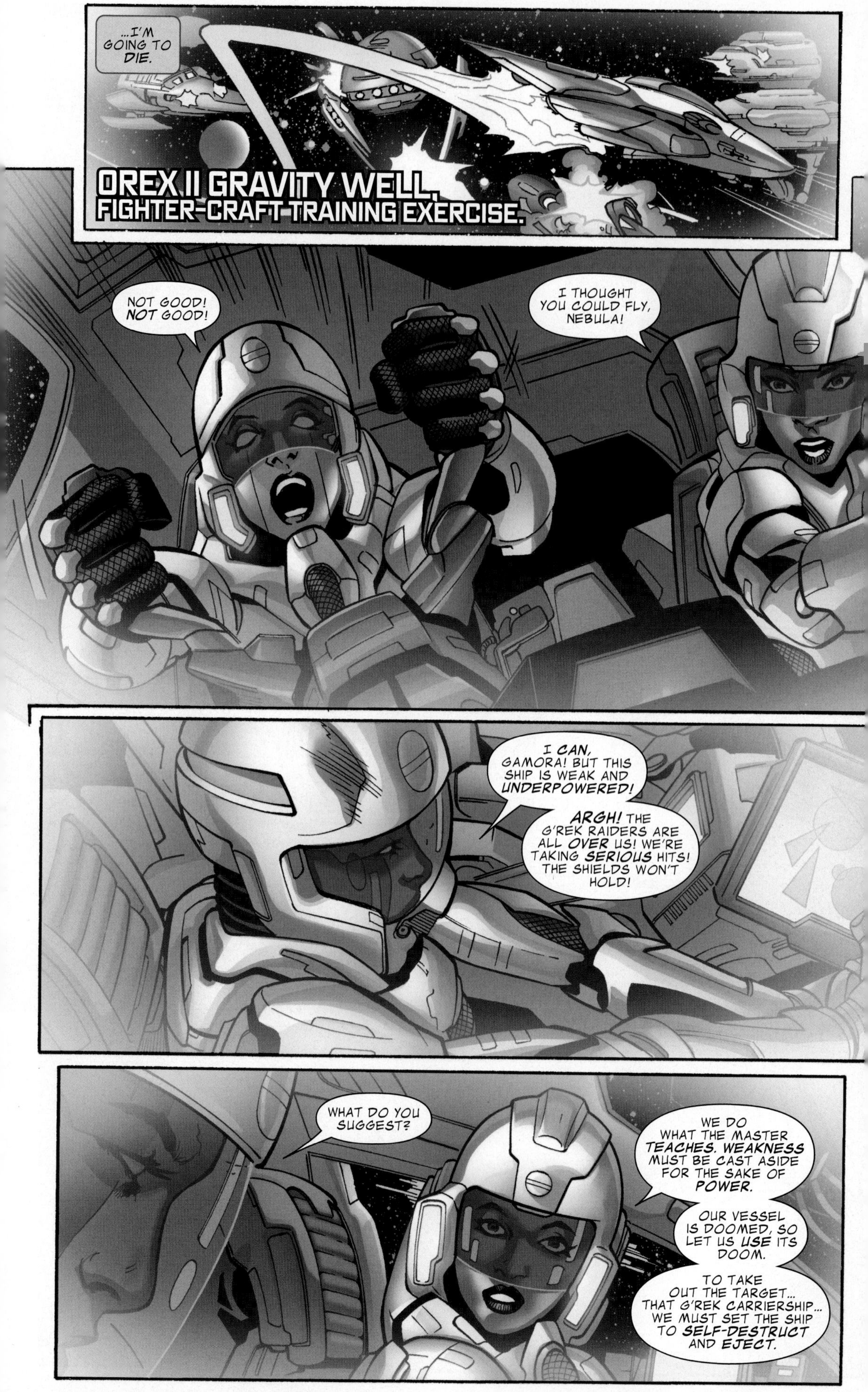
...I'M GOING TO DIE.
OREX II GRAVITY WELL, FIGHTER-CRAFT TRAINING EXERCISE.
NOT GOOD! NOT GOOD!
I THOUGHT YOU COULD FLY, NEBULA!
I CAN, GAMORA! BUT THIS SHIP IS WEAK AND UNDERPOWERED!
ARGH! THE G'REK RAIDERS ARE ALL OVER US! WE'RE TAKING SERIOUS HITS! THE SHIELDS WON'T HOLD!
WHAT DO YOU SUGGEST?
WE DO WHAT THE MASTER TEACHES. WEAKNESS MUST BE CAST ASIDE FOR THE SAKE OF POWER.
OUR VESSEL IS DOOMED, SO LET US USE ITS DOOM.
TO TAKE OUT THE TARGET... THAT G'REK CARRIERSHIP... WE MUST SET THE SHIP TO SELF-DESTRUCT AND EJECT.

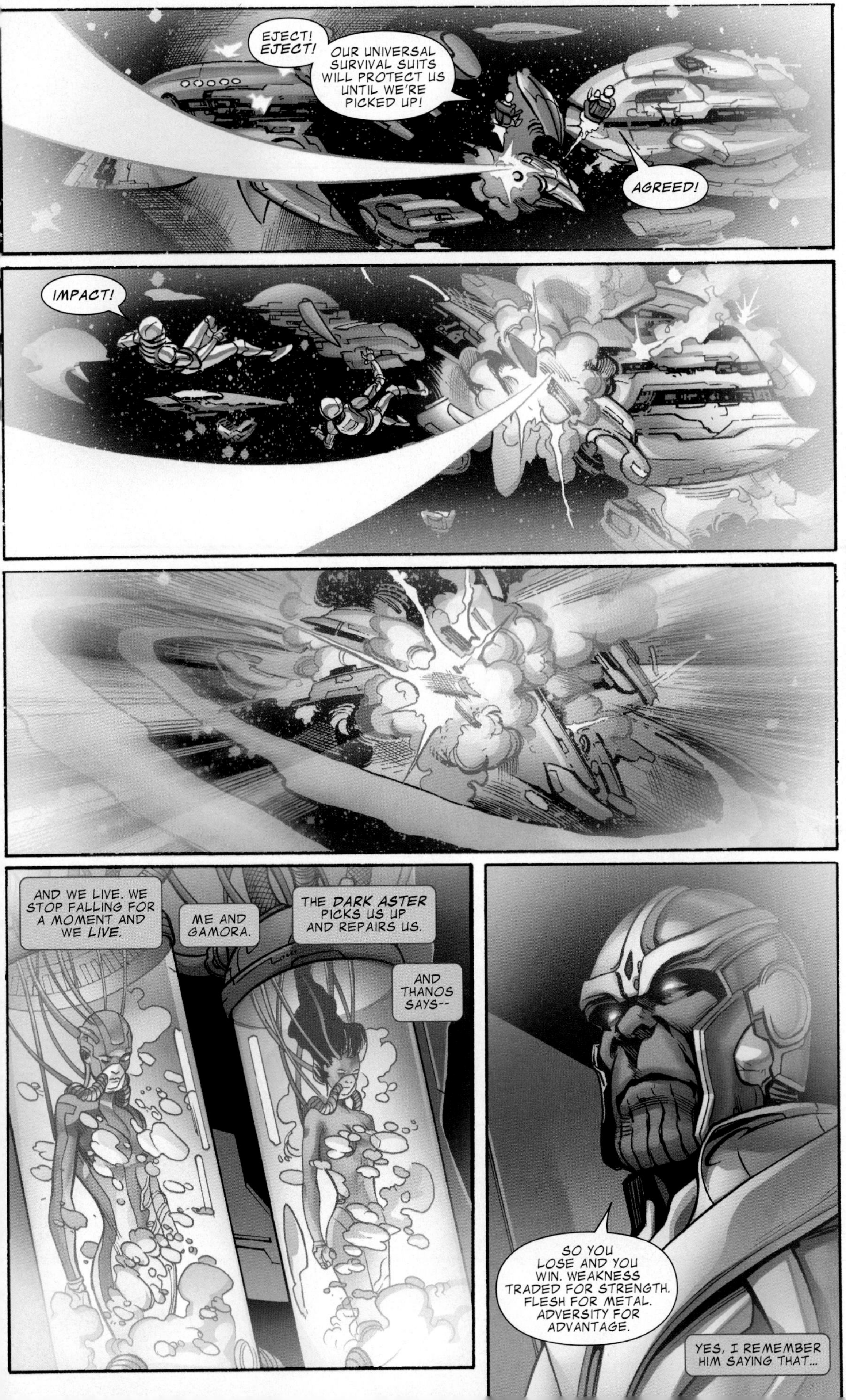
EJECT! EJECT!
OUR UNIVERSAL SURVIVAL SUITS WILL PROTECT US UNTIL WE'RE PICKED UP!
AGREED!
IMPACT!
AND WE LIVE. WE STOP FALLING FOR A MOMENT AND WE LIVE.
ME AND GAMORA.
THE DARK ASTER PICKS US UP AND REPAIRS US.
AND THANOS SAYS--
SO YOU LOSE AND YOU WIN. WEAKNESS TRADED FOR STRENGTH. FLESH FOR METAL. ADVERSITY FOR ADVANTAGE.
YES, I REMEMBER HIM SAYING THAT...

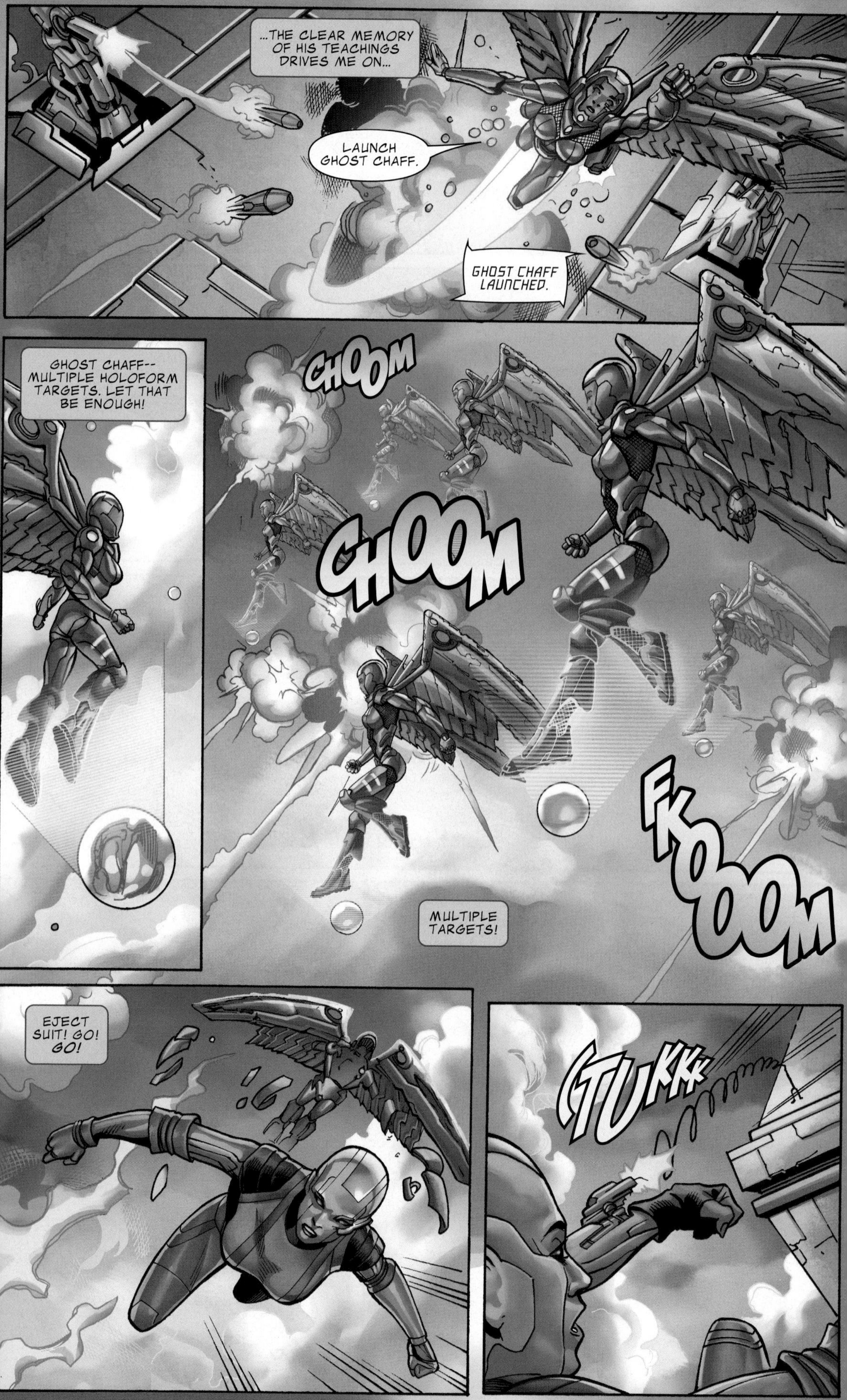

...THE CLEAR MEMORY OF HIS TEACHINGS DRIVES ME ON...
LAUNCH GHOST CHAFF.
GHOST CHAFF LAUNCHED.
GHOST CHAFF-- MULTIPLE HOLOFORM TARGETS. LET THAT BE ENOUGH!
CHOOM
CHOOM
FKOOOM
MULTIPLE TARGETS!
EJECT SUIT! GO! GO!
CTUKKK

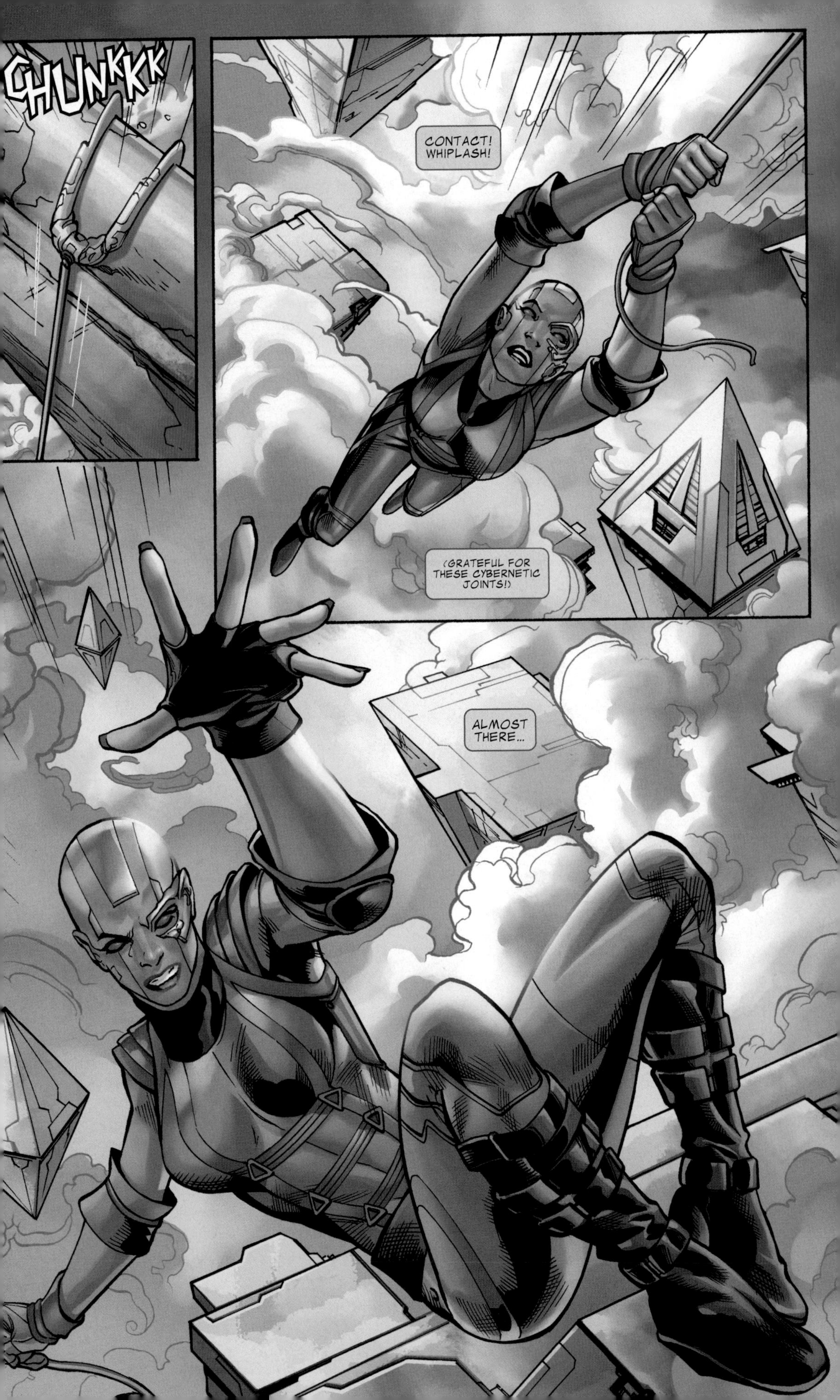
CHUNKKK
CONTACT! WHIPLASH!
(GRATEFUL FOR THESE CYBERNETIC JOINTS!)
ALMOST THERE...

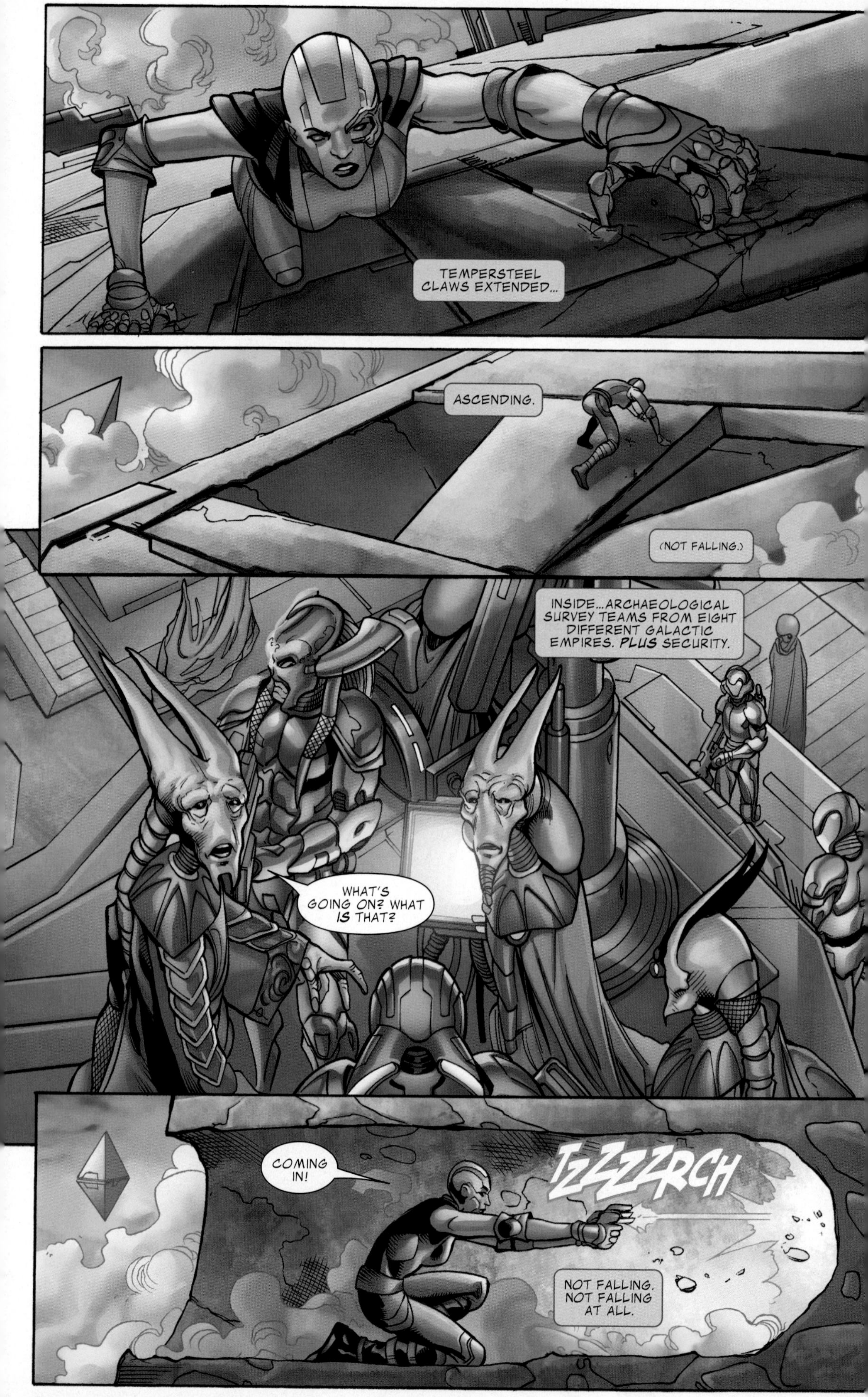
TEMPERSTEEL CLAWS EXTENDED...
ASCENDING.
(NOT FALLING.)
INSIDE...ARCHAEOLOGICAL SURVEY TEAMS FROM EIGHT DIFFERENT GALACTIC EMPIRES. PLUS SECURITY.
WHAT'S GOING ON? WHAT IS THAT?
COMING IN!
TZZZZRCH
NOT FALLING. NOT FALLING AT ALL.

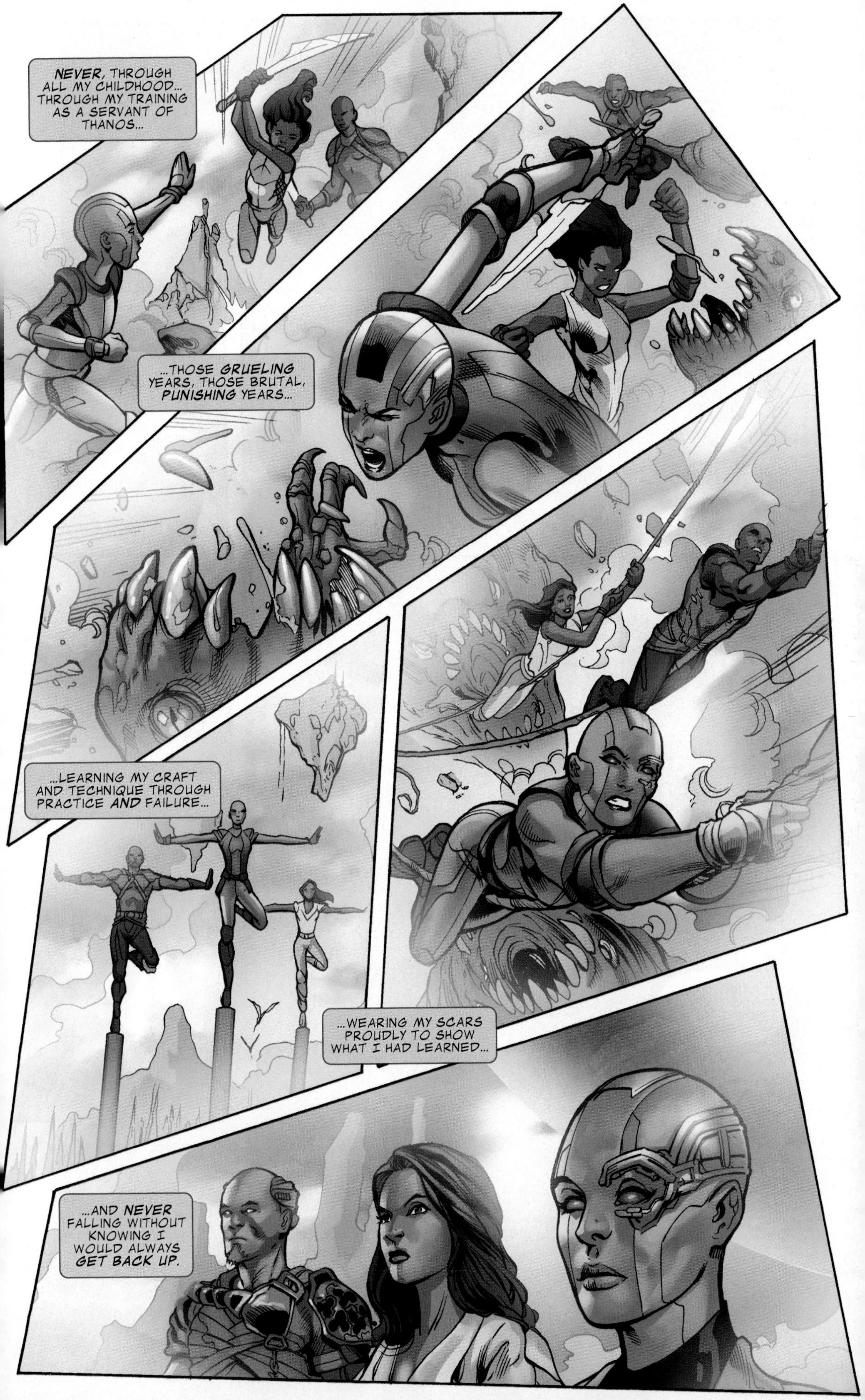
NEVER, THROUGH ALL MY CHILDHOOD... THROUGH MY TRAINING AS A SERVANT OF THANOS...
...THOSE GRUELING YEARS, THOSE BRUTAL, PUNISHING YEARS...
...LEARNING MY CRAFT AND TECHNIQUE THROUGH PRACTICE AND FAILURE...
...WEARING MY SCARS PROUDLY TO SHOW WHAT I HAD LEARNED...
...AND NEVER FALLING WITHOUT KNOWING I WOULD ALWAYS GET BACK UP.

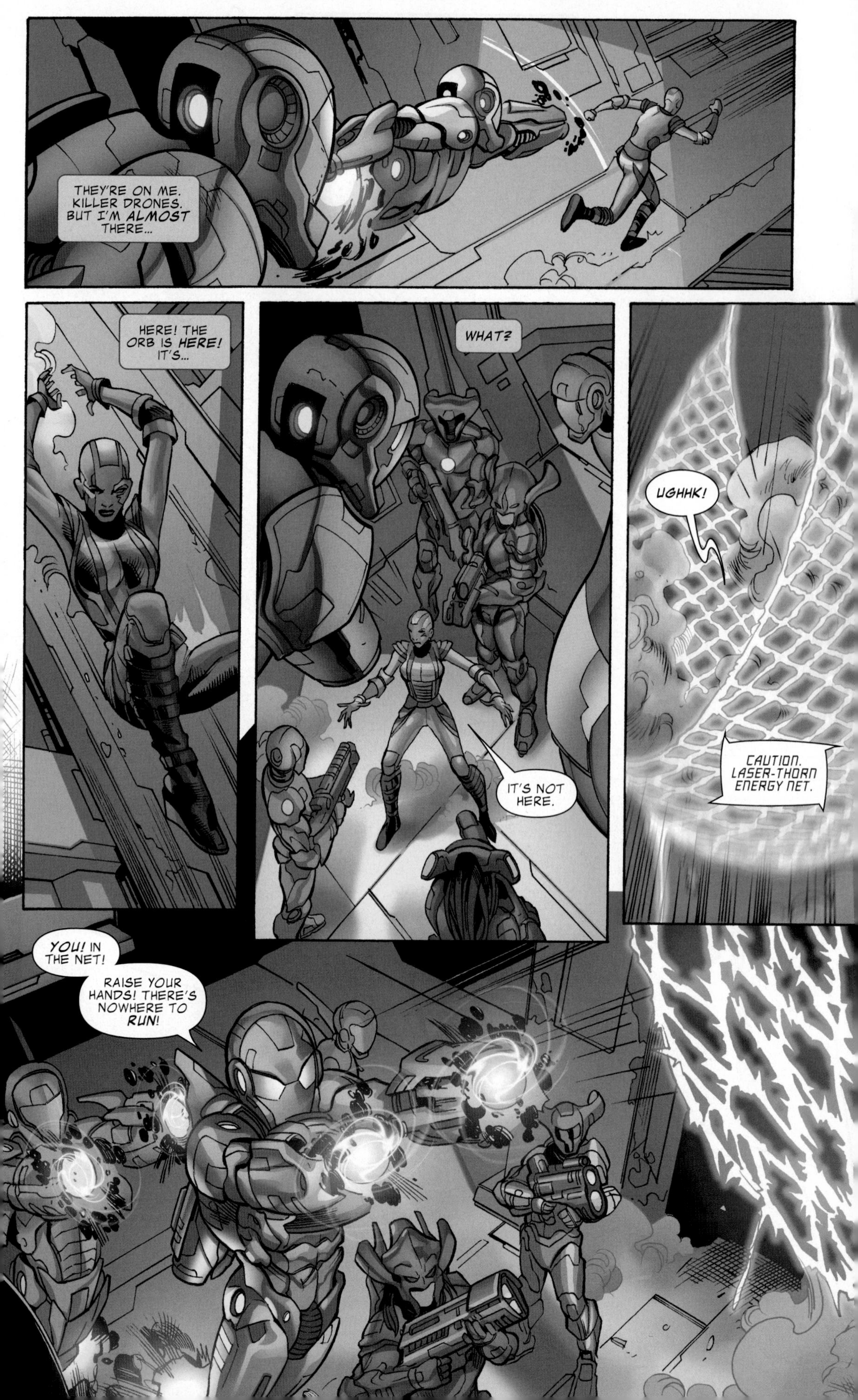
THEY'RE ON ME. KILLER DRONES. BUT I'M ALMOST THERE...
HERE! THE ORB IS HERE! IT'S...
WHAT?
IT'S NOT HERE.
UGHHK!
CAUTION. LASER-THORN ENERGY NET.
YOU! IN THE NET!
RAISE YOUR HANDS! THERE'S NOWHERE TO RUN!

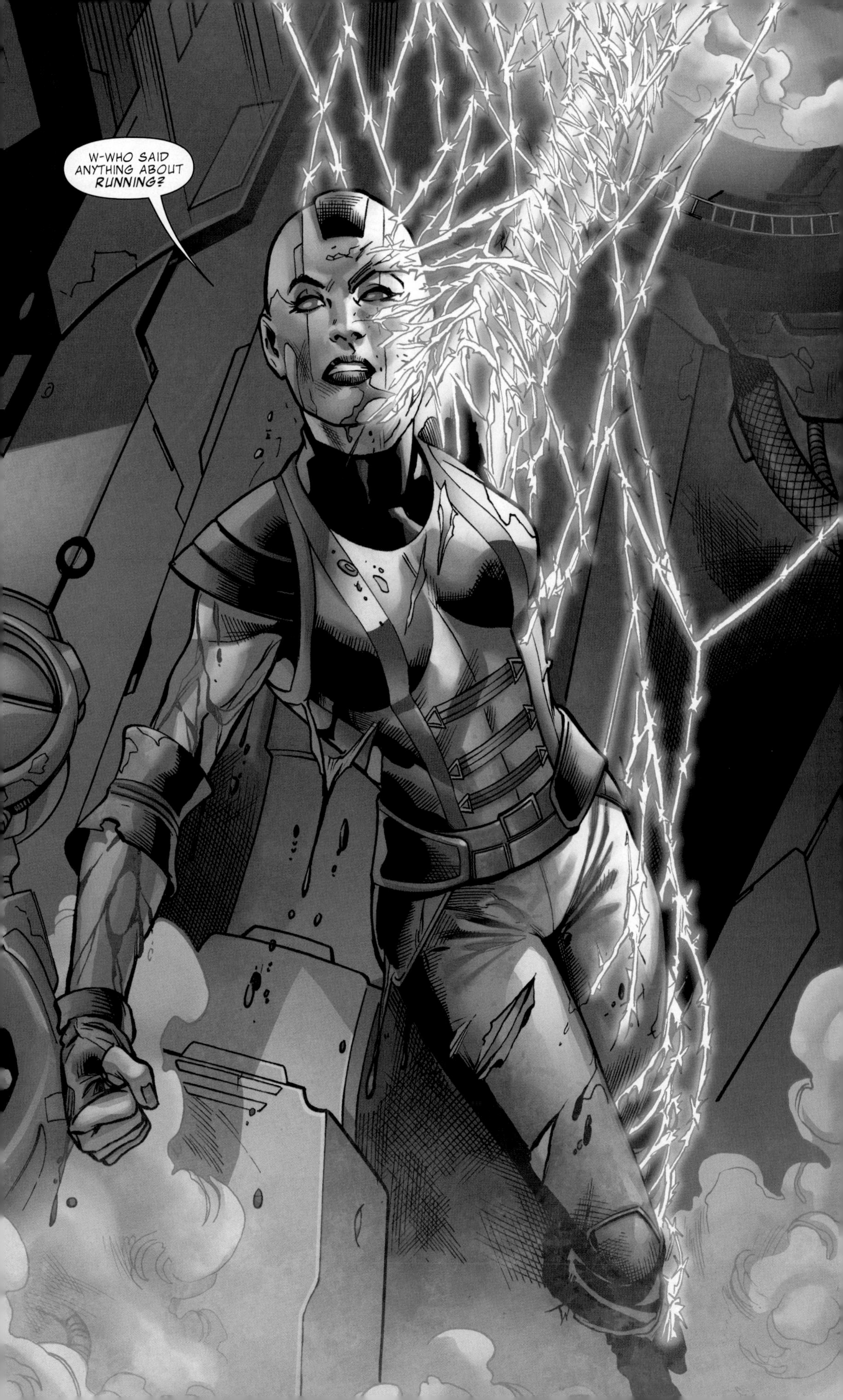
W-WHO SAID ANYTHING ABOUT RUNNING?

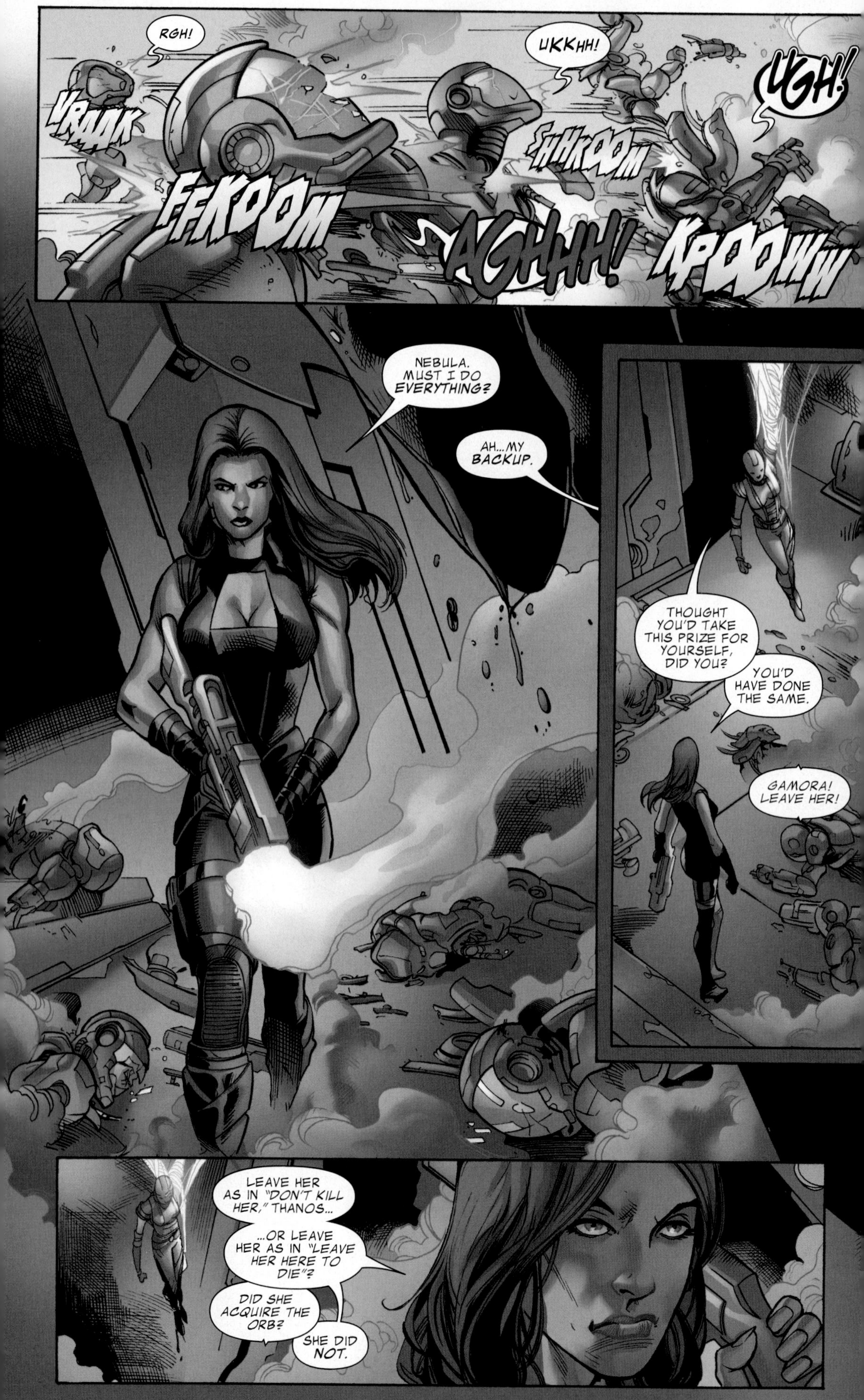
RGH!
VRAAK
FFKOOM
UKKHH!
SHHKOOM
UGH!
AGHHH!
KPOOWW
NEBULA. MUST I DO EVERYTHING?
AH...MY BACKUP.
THOUGHT YOU'D TAKE THIS PRIZE FOR YOURSELF, DID YOU?
YOU'D HAVE DONE THE SAME.
GAMORA! LEAVE HER!
LEAVE HER AS IN "DON'T KILL HER," THANOS...
...OR LEAVE HER AS IN "LEAVE HER HERE TO DIE"?
DID SHE ACQUIRE THE ORB?
SHE DID NOT.

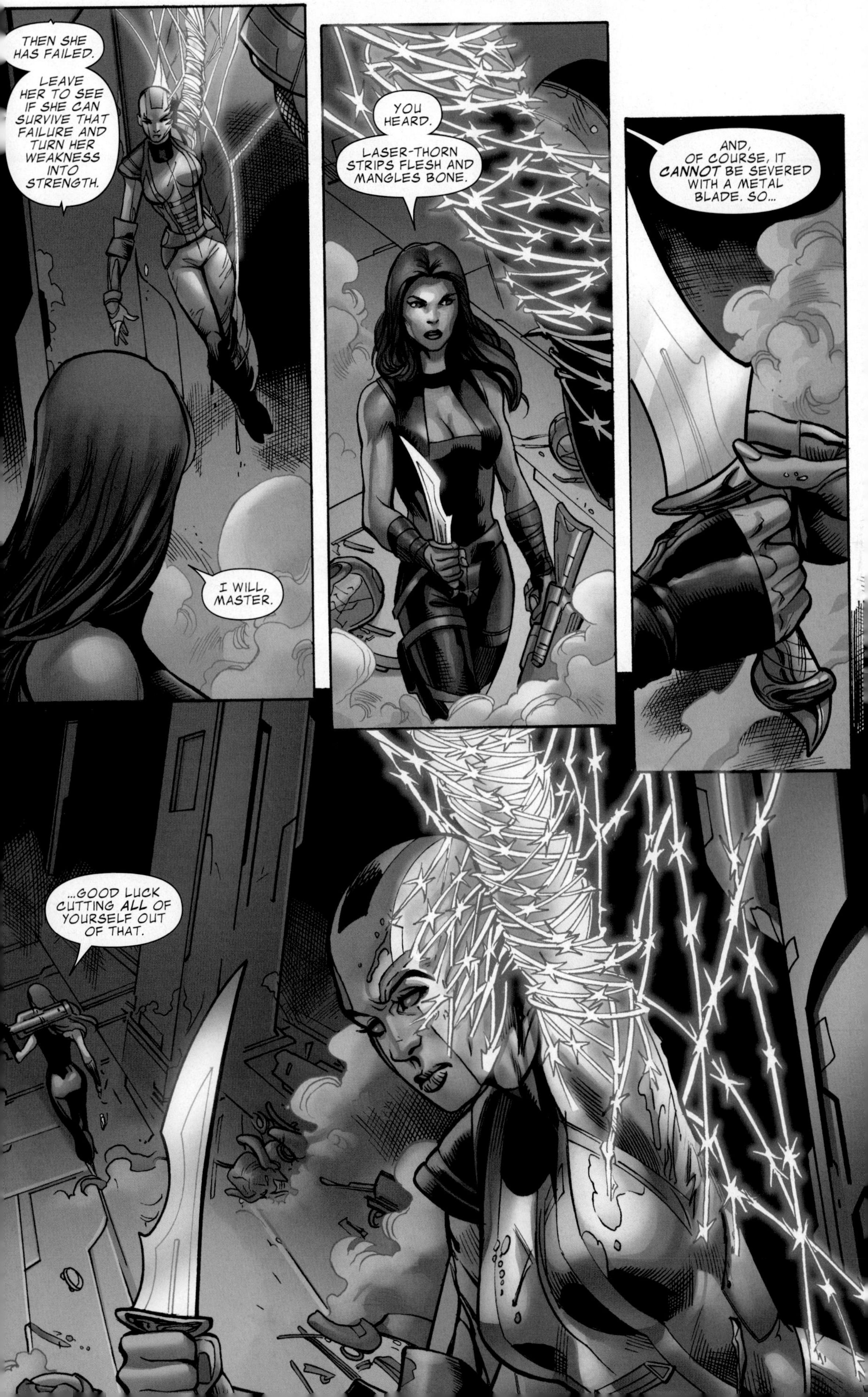
THEN SHE HAS FAILED.
LEAVE HER TO SEE IF SHE CAN SURVIVE THAT FAILURE AND TURN HER WEAKNESS INTO STRENGTH.
I WILL, MASTER.
YOU HEARD.
LASER-THORN STRIPS FLESH AND MANGLES BONE.
AND, OF COURSE, IT CANNOT BE SEVERED WITH A METAL BLADE. SO...
...GOOD LUCK CUTTING ALL OF YOURSELF OUT OF THAT.

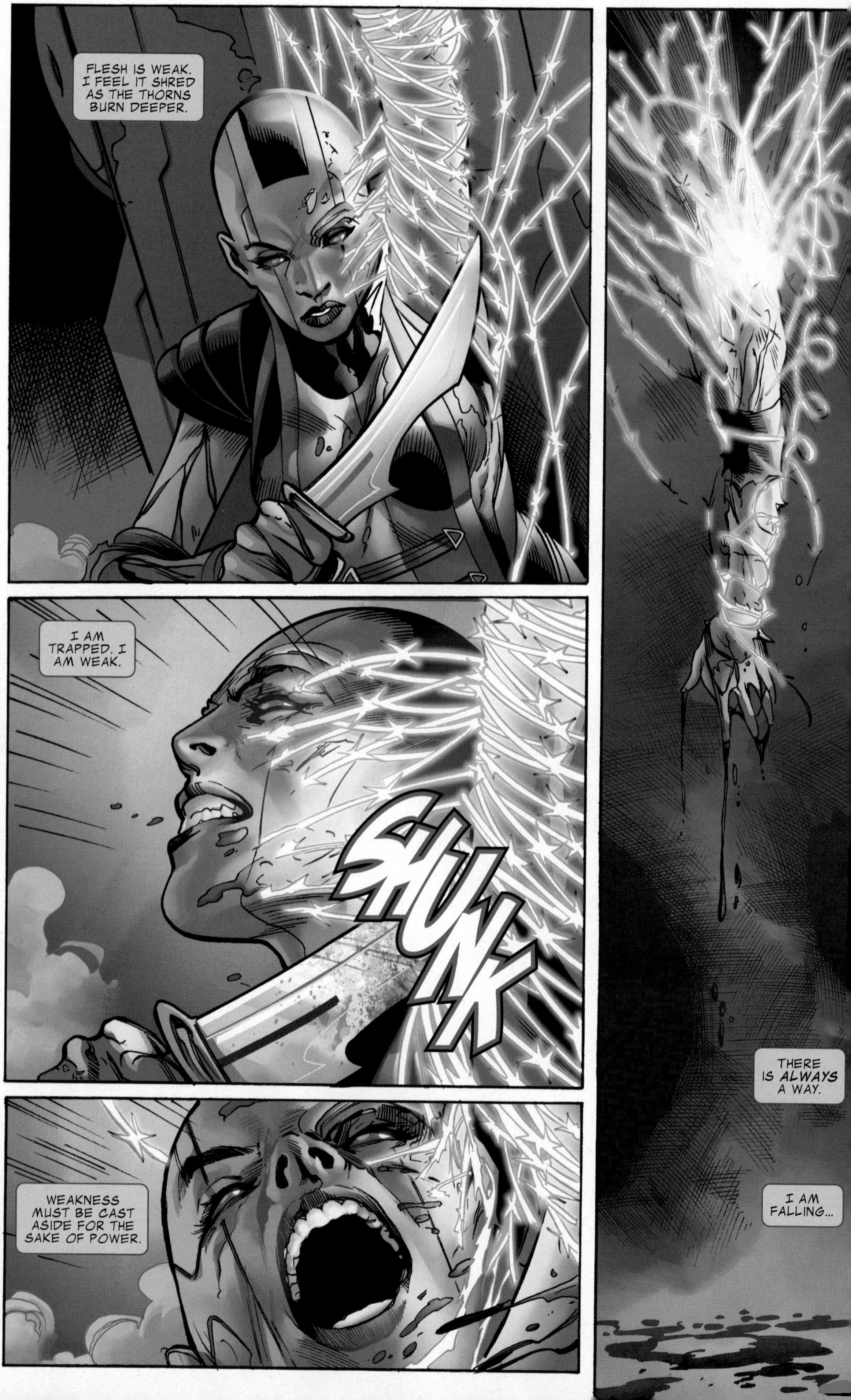
FLESH IS WEAK. I FEEL IT SHRED AS THE THORNS BURN DEEPER.
I AM TRAPPED. I AM WEAK.
SHUNK
WEAKNESS MUST BE CAST ASIDE FOR THE SAKE OF POWER.
THERE IS ALWAYS A WAY.
I AM FALLING...

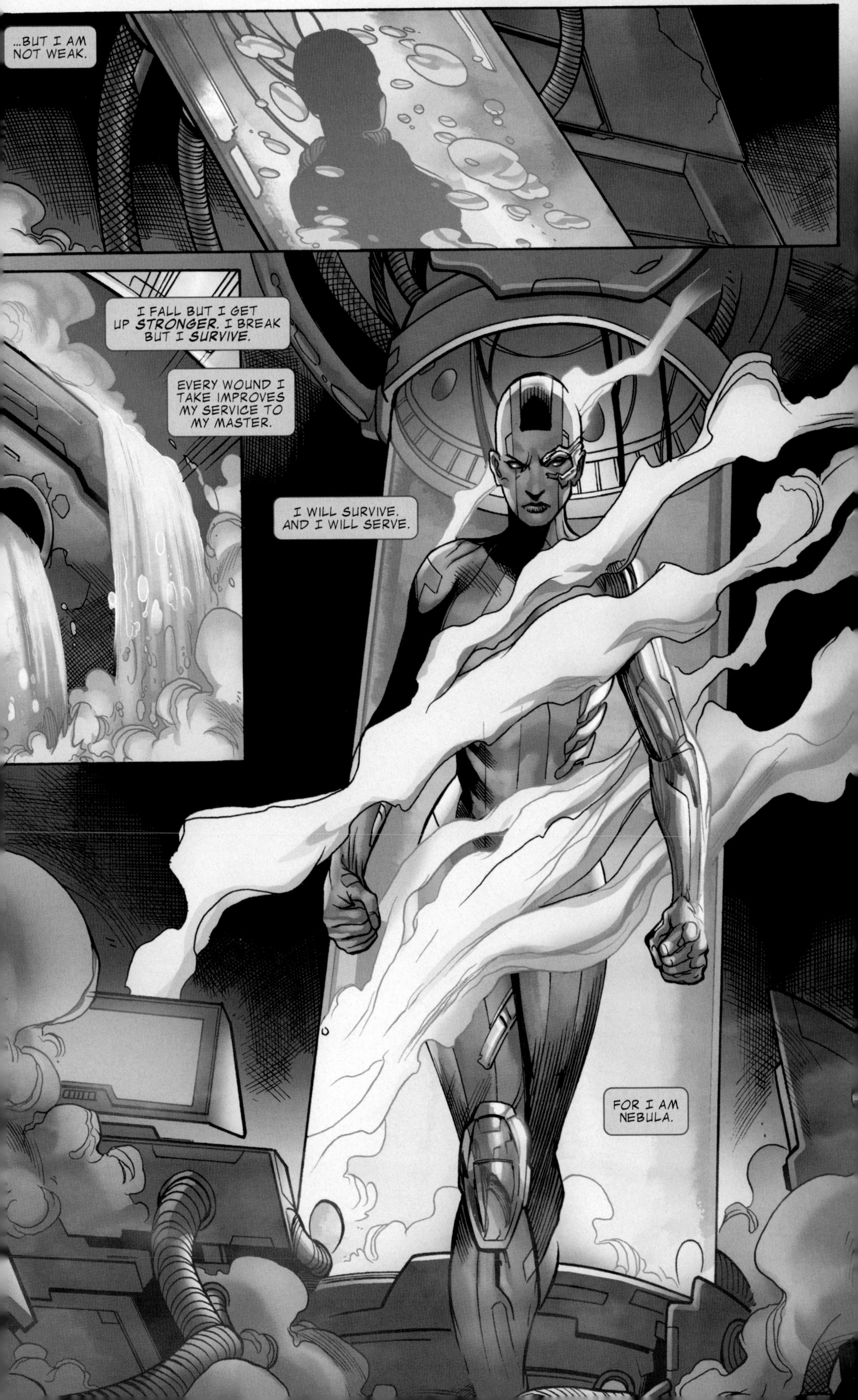
...BUT I AM NOT WEAK.
I FALL BUT I GET UP STRONGER. I BREAK BUT I SURVIVE.
EVERY WOUND I TAKE IMPROVES MY SERVICE TO MY MASTER.
I WILL SURVIVE. AND I WILL SERVE.
FOR I AM NEBULA.

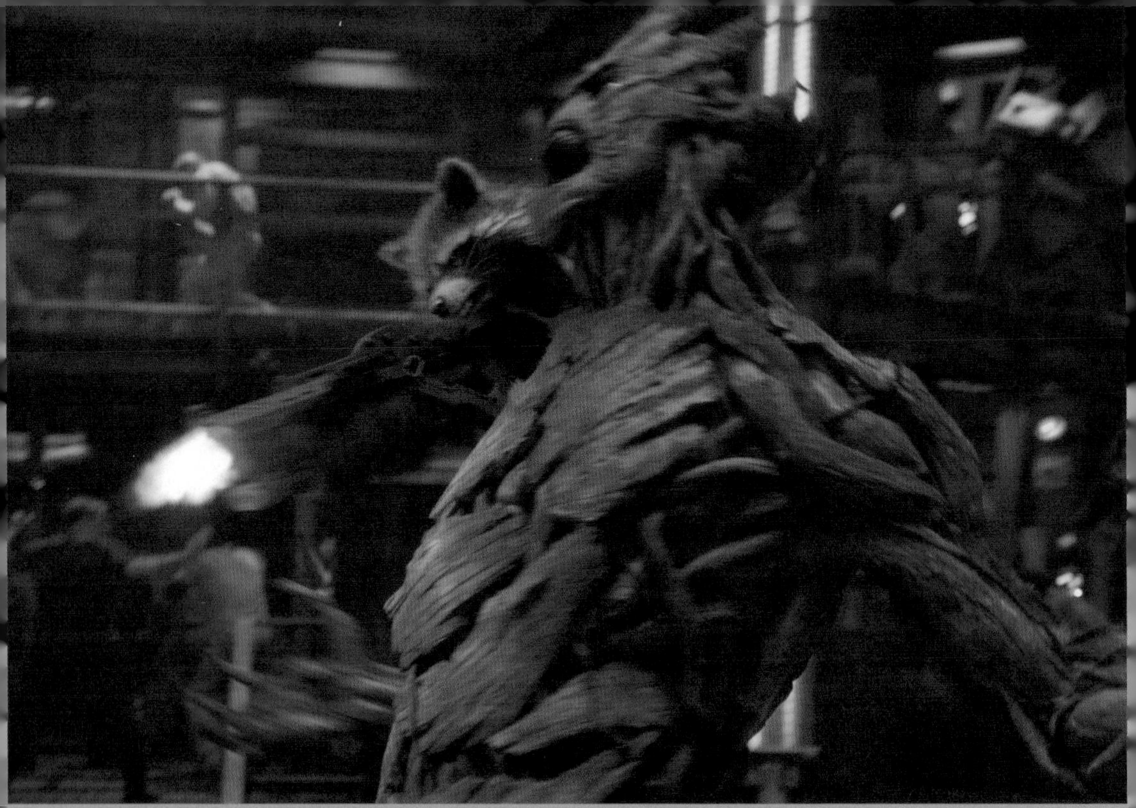

MARVEL'S GUARDIANS OF THE GALAXY PRELUDE #2

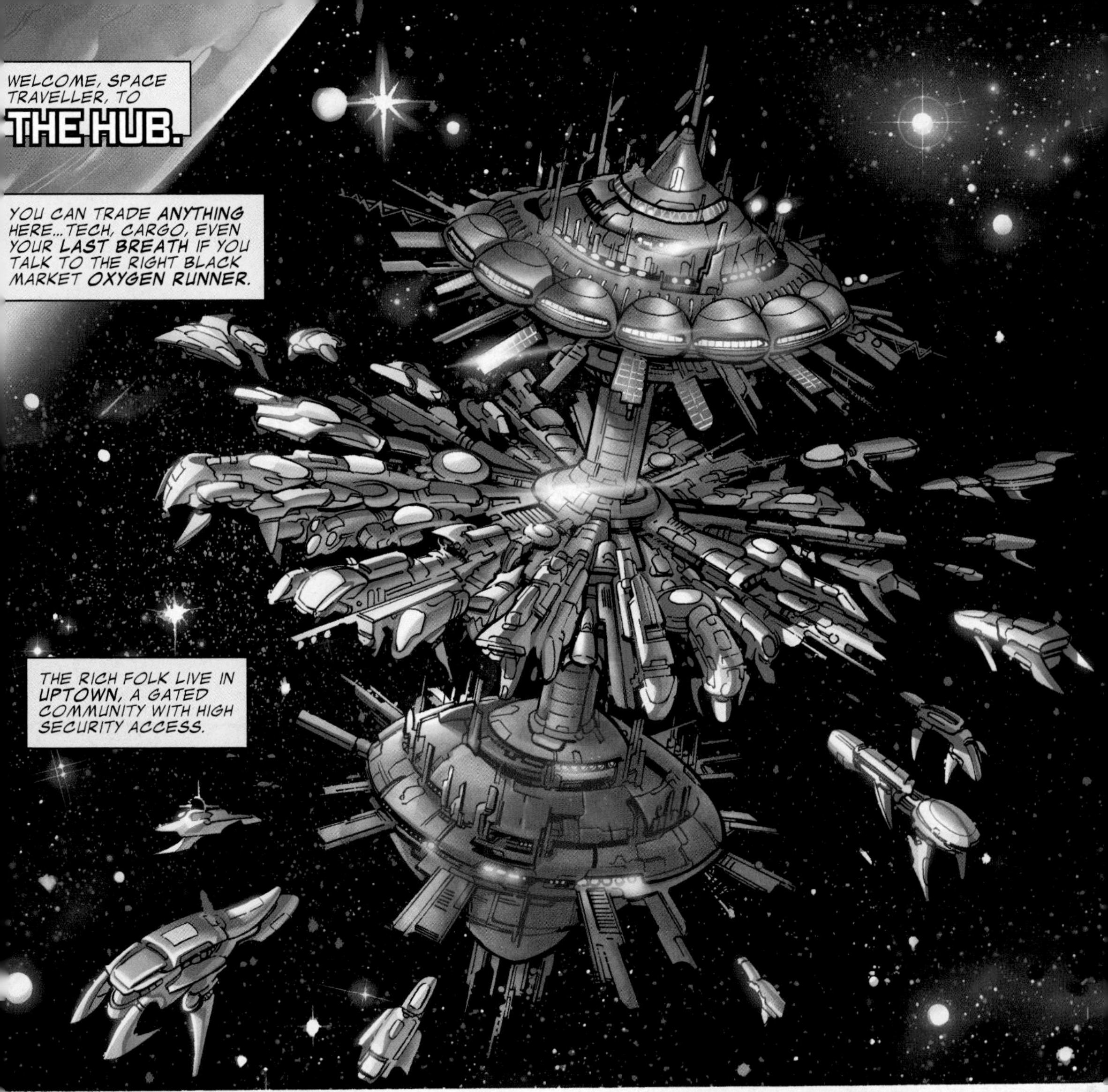
WELCOME, SPACE TRAVELLER, TO
THE HUB.
YOU CAN TRADE ANYTHING HERE...TECH, CARGO, EVEN YOUR LAST BREATH IF YOU TALK TO THE RIGHT BLACK MARKET OXYGEN RUNNER.
THE RICH FOLK LIVE IN UPTOWN, A GATED COMMUNITY WITH HIGH SECURITY ACCESS.

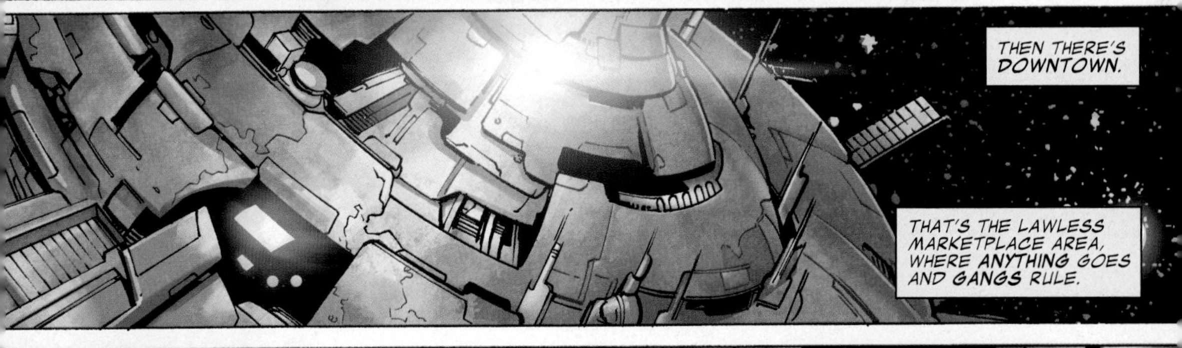
THEN THERE'S DOWNTOWN.
THAT'S THE LAWLESS MARKETPLACE AREA, WHERE ANYTHING GOES AND GANGS RULE.

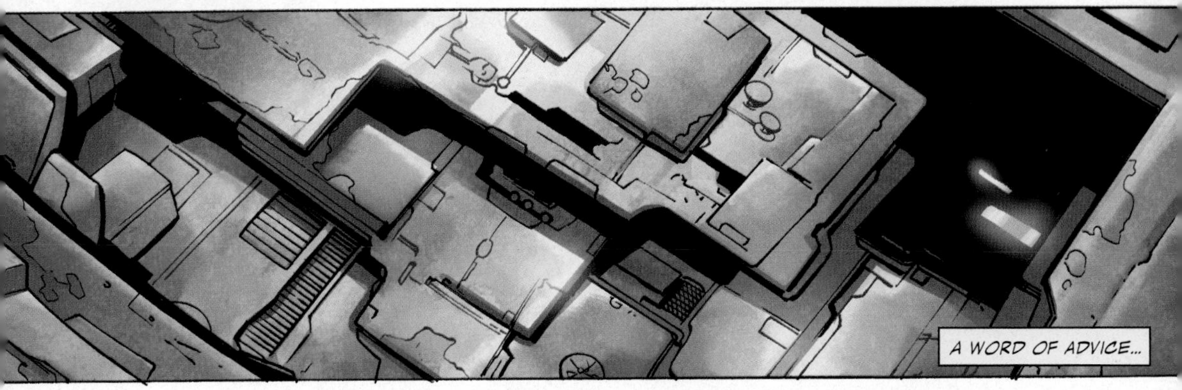
A WORD OF ADVICE...

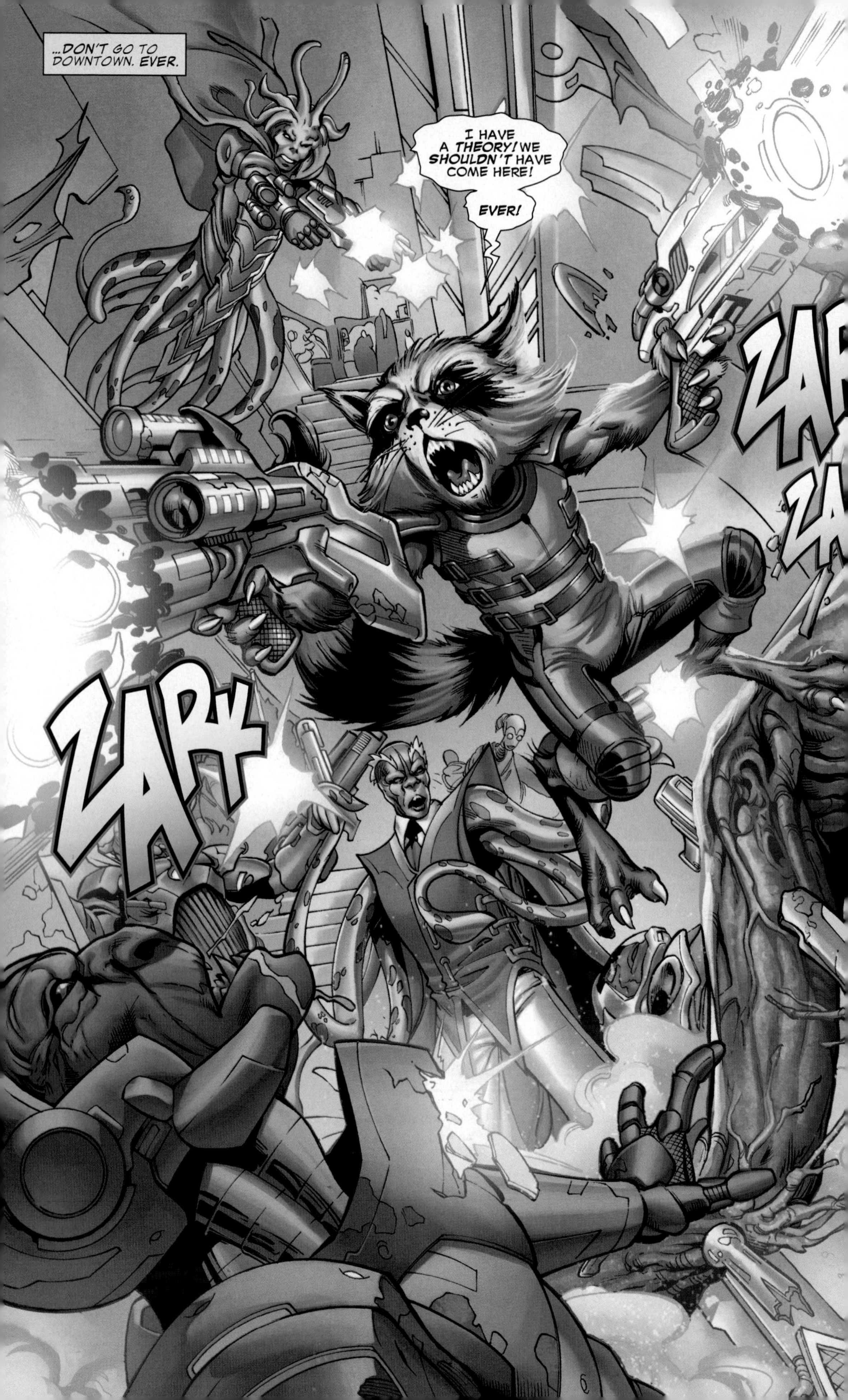
...DON'T GO TO DOWNTOWN. EVER.
I HAVE A THEORY! WE SHOULDN'T HAVE COME HERE!
EVER!
ZARK
ZARK

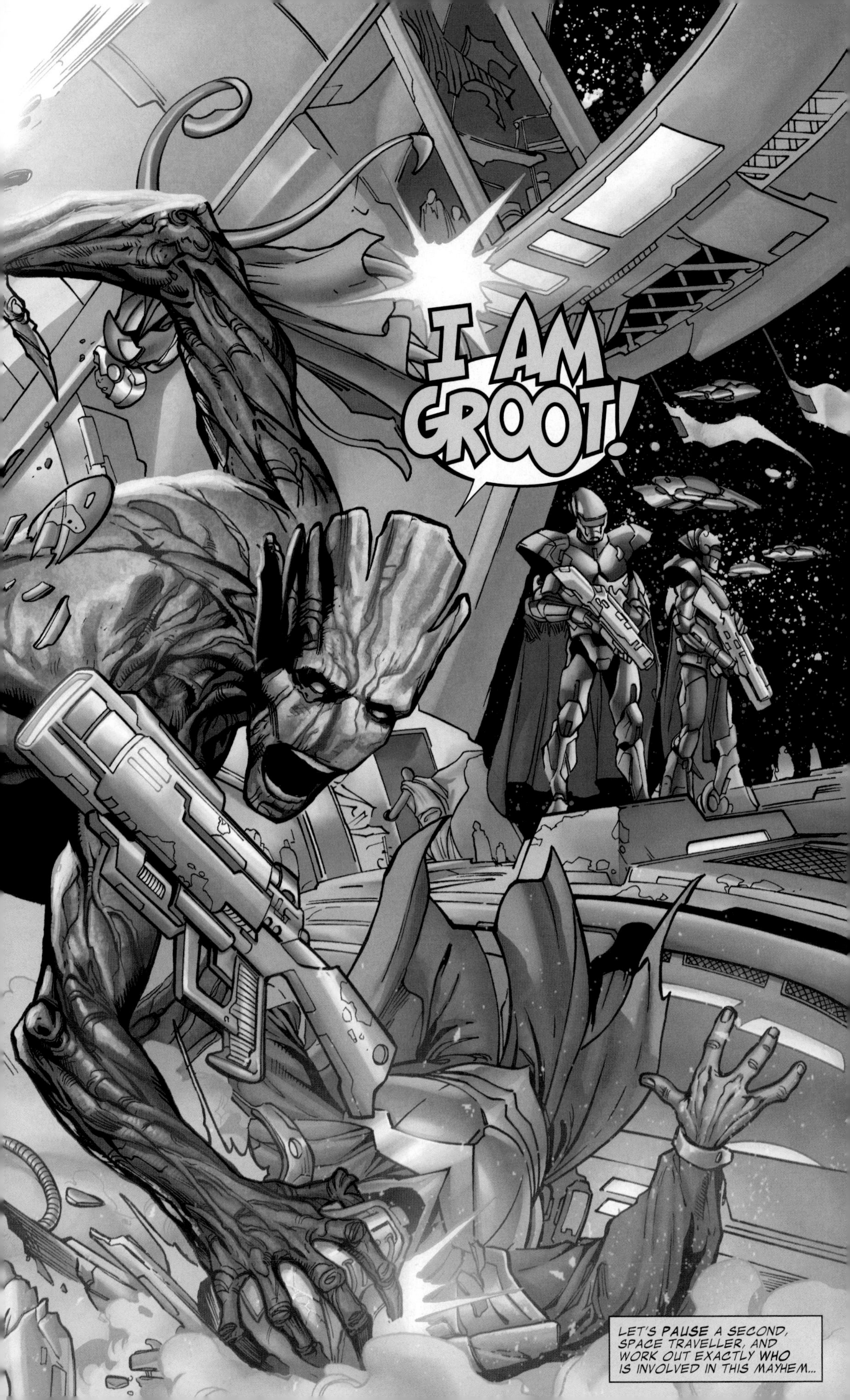
I AM GROOT!
LET'S PAUSE A SECOND, SPACE TRAVELLER, AND WORK OUT EXACTLY WHO IS INVOLVED IN THIS MAYHEM...

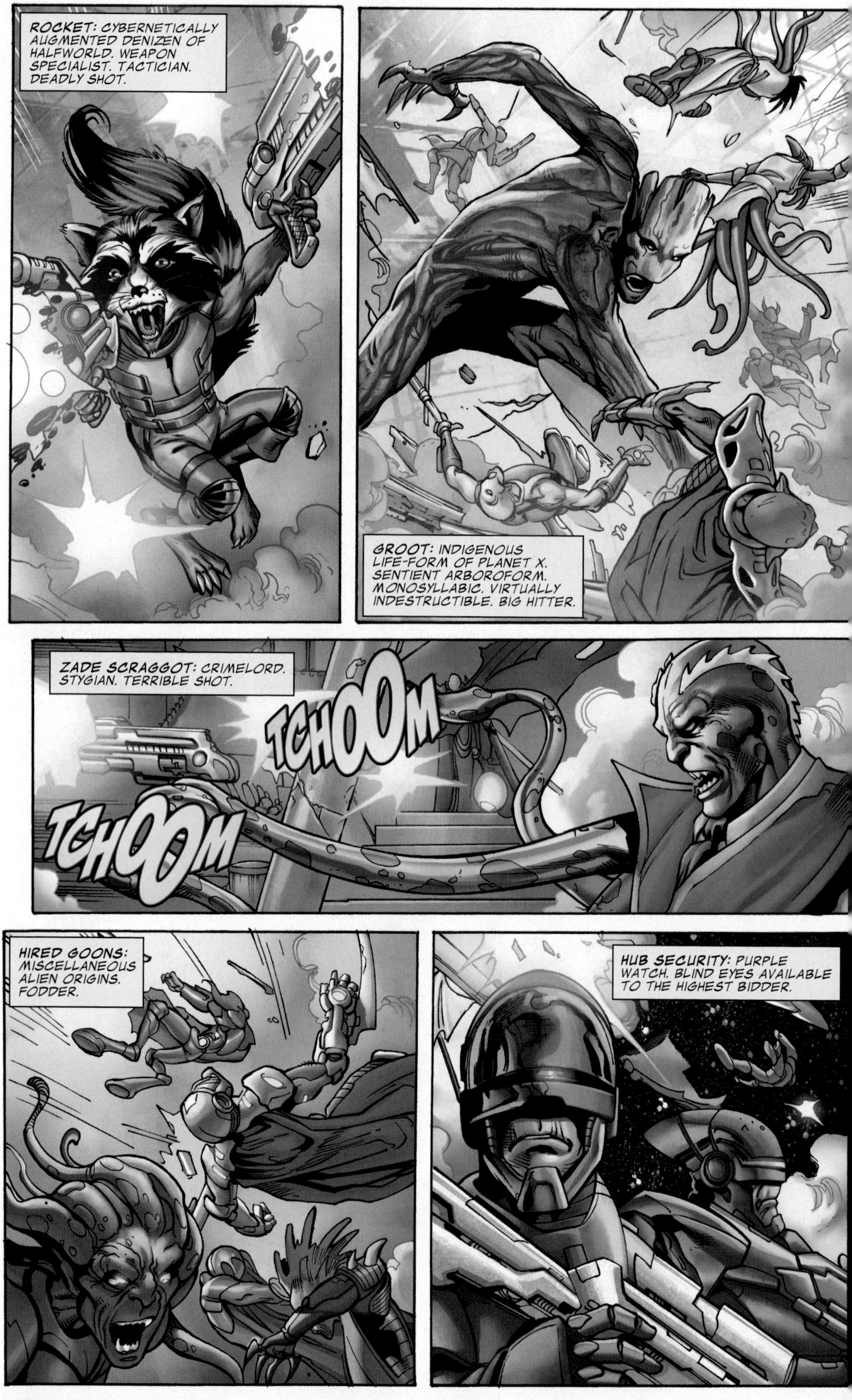

ROCKET: CYBERNETICALLY AUGMENTED DENIZEN OF HALFWORLD. WEAPON SPECIALIST. TACTICIAN. DEADLY SHOT.
GROOT: INDIGENOUS LIFE-FORM OF PLANET X. SENTIENT ARBOROFORM. MONOSYLLABIC. VIRTUALLY INDESTRUCTIBLE. BIG HITTER.
ZADE SCRAGGOT: CRIMELORD. STYGIAN. TERRIBLE SHOT.
TCHOOM
TCHOOM
HIRED GOONS: MISCELLANEOUS ALIEN ORIGINS. FODDER.
HUB SECURITY: PURPLE WATCH. BLIND EYES AVAILABLE TO THE HIGHEST BIDDER.

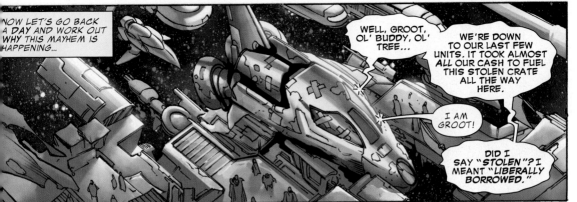

NOW LET'S GO BACK A *DAY* AND WORK OUT WHY THIS MAYHEM IS HAPPENING...

WELL, GROOT, OL' BUDDY, OL' TREE...

WE'RE DOWN TO OUR LAST FEW UNITS. IT TOOK ALMOST *ALL* OUR CASH TO FUEL THIS STOLEN CRATE ALL THE WAY HERE.

I AM GROOT!

DID I SAY "STOLEN"? I MEANT "LIBERALLY BORROWED."

I'M JUST HOPING THIS HUB PLACE LIVES UP TO ITS *REP*.

WE NEED A BIG SCORE, *FAST*.

WOW! *HOW* MUCH FOR ONE DAY'S DOCKING?

THAT'S IT! WE'RE *OFFICIALLY* BROKE!

IF WE WANT TO MAKE THE UNITS FOR REFUELING, WE'RE GONNA HAVE TO HIT *DOWNTOWN*.

AND I'M GONNA HAVE TO DO SOMETHING I'M GONNA *REGRET* IN THE MORNING.

I AM GROOT.

NO, WE'RE NOT VISITING A *BAR*. WE'RE VISITING A *PAWN-SHOP*.

HOW MUCH? YOU'RE *KIDDING* ME! IT'S MY *FAVORITE* ION CANNON!

TAKE IT OR LEAVE IT, FURBALL. SINCE THE I-EX 50 CAME OUT, *NOBODY'S* BUYING THESE PUMP-ACTIONS.

THIRTY UNITS? A MEASLY *THIRTY* UNITS?

PAL, WE JUST GOT *ROBBED* WITHOUT A SHOT BEING FIRED!

HEY! HEY, LITTLE BUDDY...

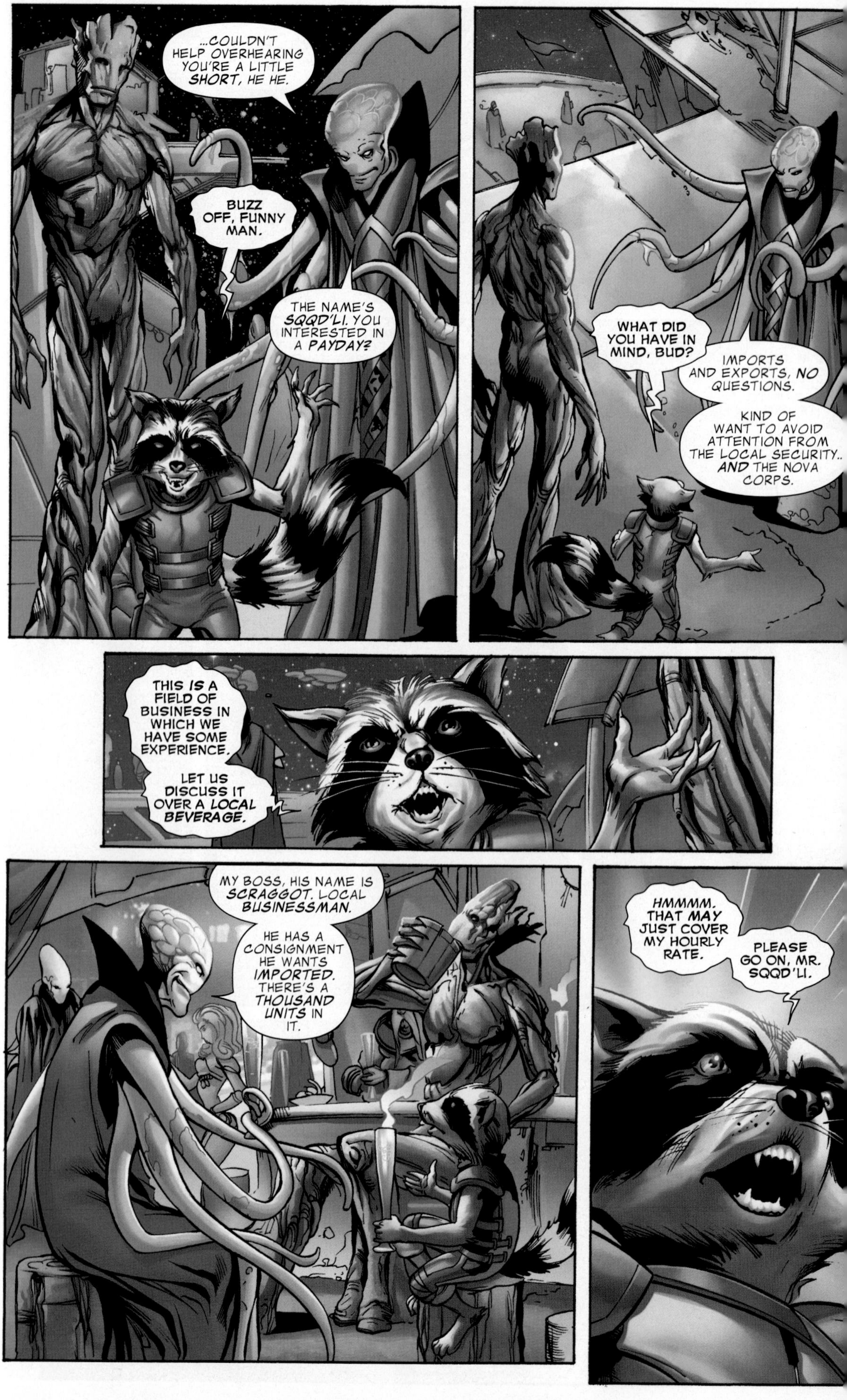
...COULDN'T HELP OVERHEARING YOU'RE A LITTLE SHORT, HE HE.
BUZZ OFF, FUNNY MAN.
THE NAME'S SQQD'LI. YOU INTERESTED IN A PAYDAY?
WHAT DID YOU HAVE IN MIND, BUD?
IMPORTS AND EXPORTS, NO QUESTIONS.
KIND OF WANT TO AVOID ATTENTION FROM THE LOCAL SECURITY.. AND THE NOVA CORPS.
THIS IS A FIELD OF BUSINESS IN WHICH WE HAVE SOME EXPERIENCE.
LET US DISCUSS IT OVER A LOCAL BEVERAGE.
MY BOSS, HIS NAME IS SCRAGGOT. LOCAL BUSINESSMAN.
HE HAS A CONSIGNMENT HE WANTS IMPORTED. THERE'S A THOUSAND UNITS IN IT.
HMMMM. THAT MAY JUST COVER MY HOURLY RATE.
PLEASE GO ON, MR. SQQD'LI.

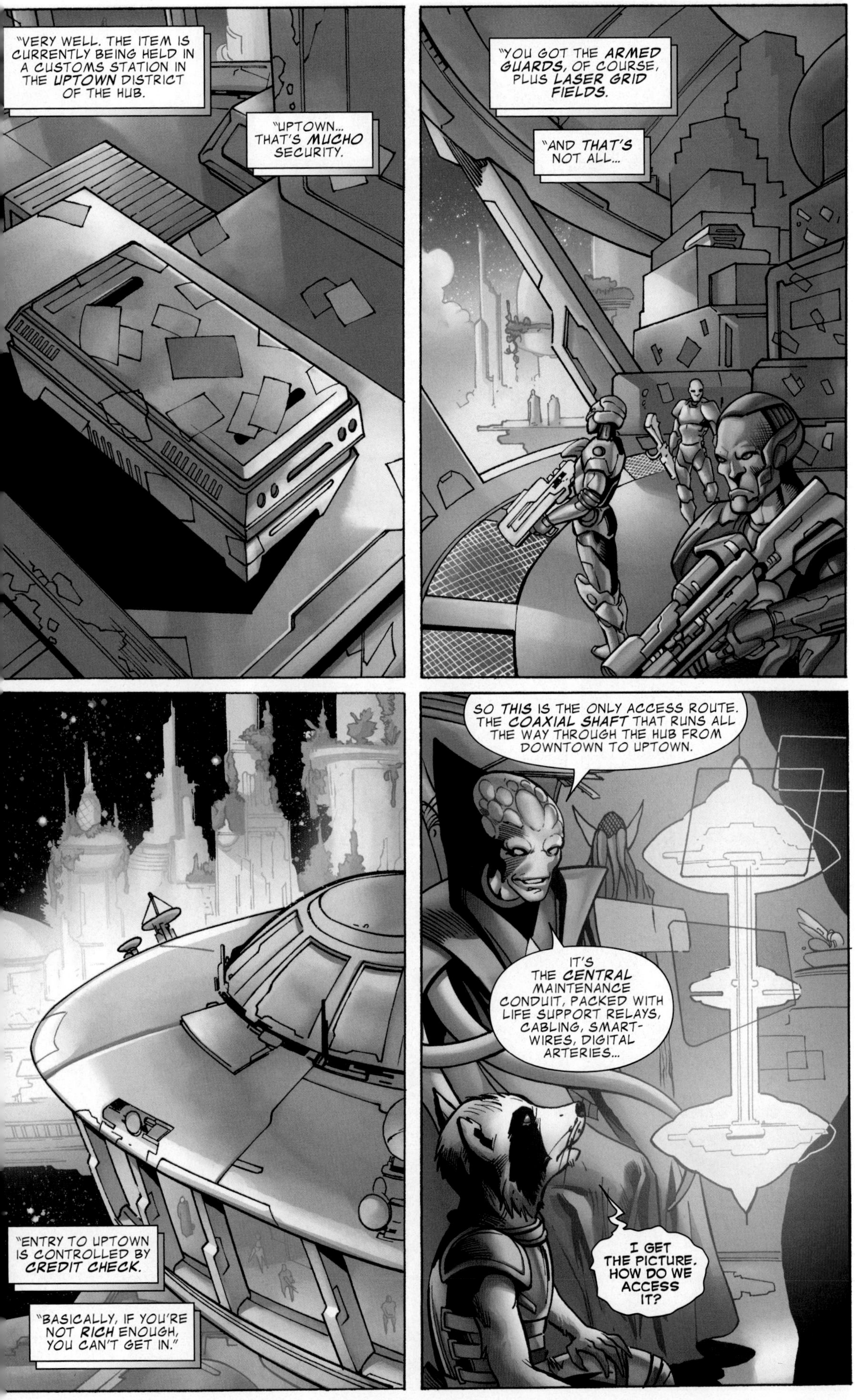
"VERY WELL. THE ITEM IS CURRENTLY BEING HELD IN A CUSTOMS STATION IN THE UPTOWN DISTRICT OF THE HUB.
"UPTOWN... THAT'S MUCHO SECURITY.
"YOU GOT THE ARMED GUARDS, OF COURSE, PLUS LASER GRID FIELDS.
"AND THAT'S NOT ALL...
"ENTRY TO UPTOWN IS CONTROLLED BY CREDIT CHECK.
"BASICALLY, IF YOU'RE NOT RICH ENOUGH, YOU CAN'T GET IN."
SO THIS IS THE ONLY ACCESS ROUTE. THE COAXIAL SHAFT THAT RUNS ALL THE WAY THROUGH THE HUB FROM DOWNTOWN TO UPTOWN.
IT'S THE CENTRAL MAINTENANCE CONDUIT, PACKED WITH LIFE SUPPORT RELAYS, CABLING, SMART-WIRES, DIGITAL ARTERIES...
I GET THE PICTURE. HOW DO WE ACCESS IT?

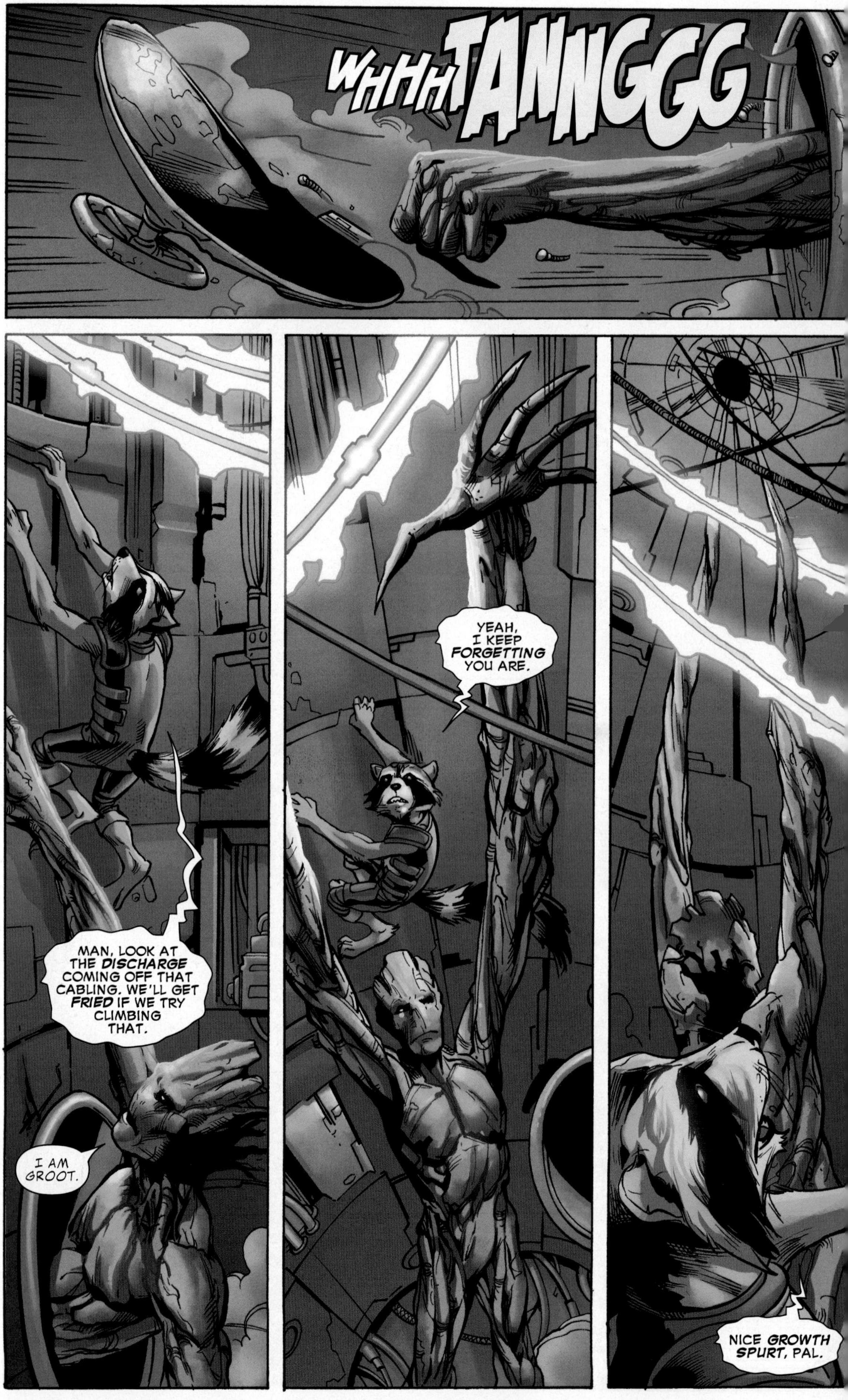
WHHHTANNGGG
MAN, LOOK AT THE DISCHARGE COMING OFF THAT CABLING. WE'LL GET FRIED IF WE TRY CLIMBING THAT.
I AM GROOT.
YEAH, I KEEP FORGETTING YOU ARE.
NICE GROWTH SPURT, PAL.

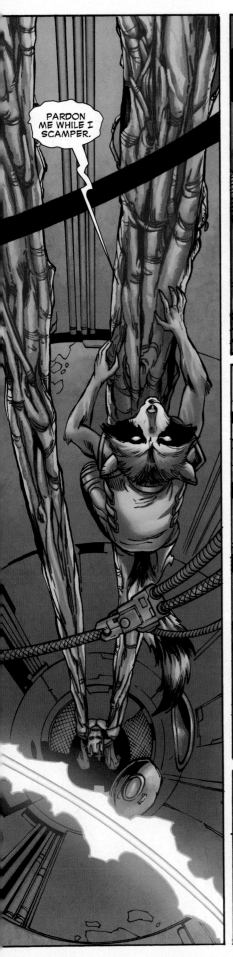

PARDON ME WHILE I SCAMPER.

OKAY, ACCORDING TO SQQD'LI, *THIS* IS THE RIGHT LEVEL FOR THE CUSTOMS STATION.

THIS *IS* THE PLACE, ALL RIGHT, AND I SPY OUR ITEM.

BUDDY, THIS DUCT IS TOO SMALL FOR YOU, BUT GET READY TO *REACH IN.*

SLEEP *TIGHT,* SUCKERS!

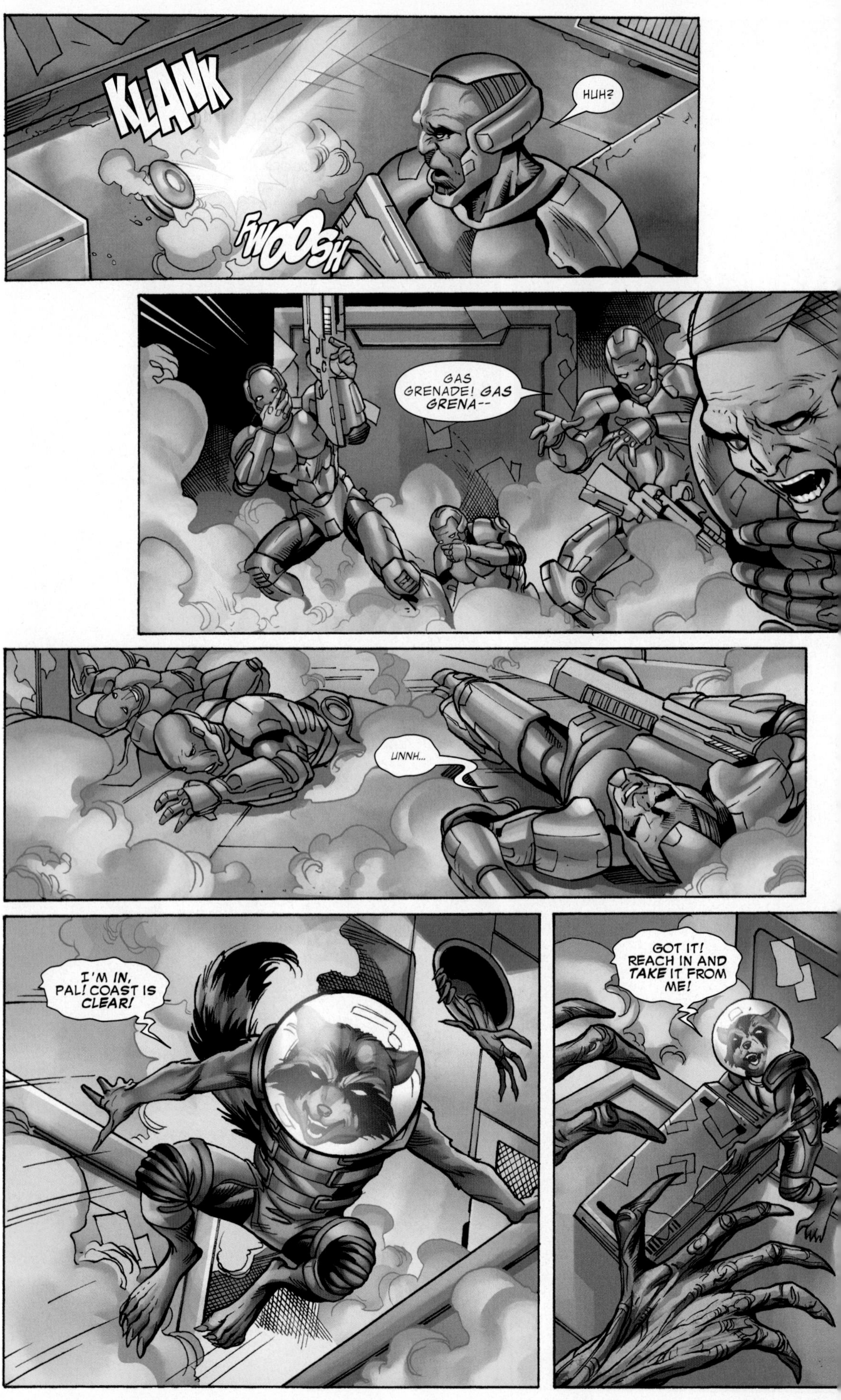
KLANK
HUH?
FWOOSH
GAS GRENADE! GAS GRENA--
UNNH...
I'M IN, PAL! COAST IS CLEAR!
GOT IT! REACH IN AND TAKE IT FROM ME!

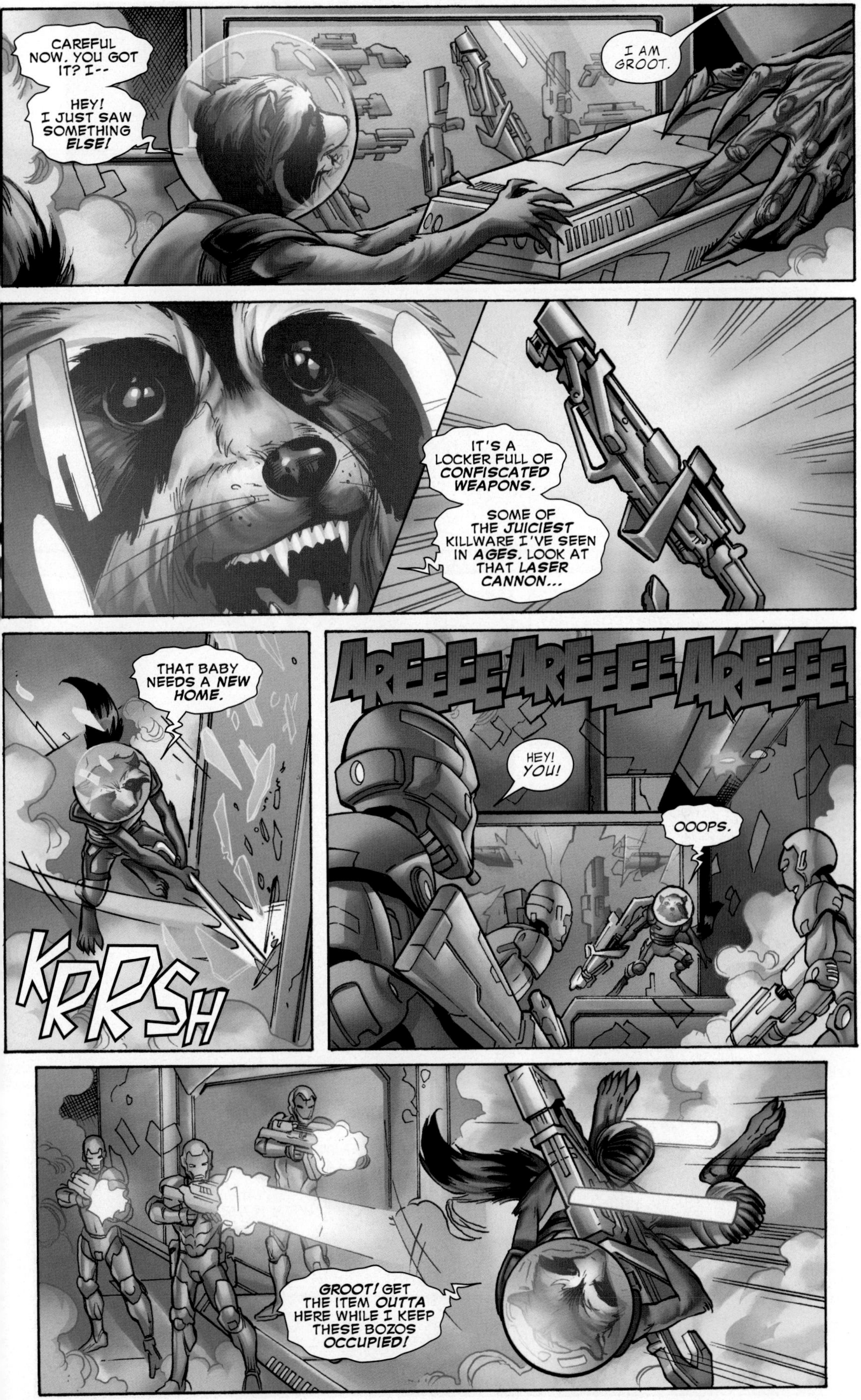
CAREFUL NOW. YOU GOT IT? I--
HEY! I JUST SAW SOMETHING ELSE!
I AM GROOT.
IT'S A LOCKER FULL OF CONFISCATED WEAPONS.
SOME OF THE JUICIEST KILLWARE I'VE SEEN IN AGES. LOOK AT THAT LASER CANNON...
THAT BABY NEEDS A NEW HOME.
KRRSH
AREEEE AREEEE AREEEE
HEY! YOU!
OOOPS.
GROOT! GET THE ITEM OUTTA HERE WHILE I KEEP THESE BOZOS OCCUPIED!

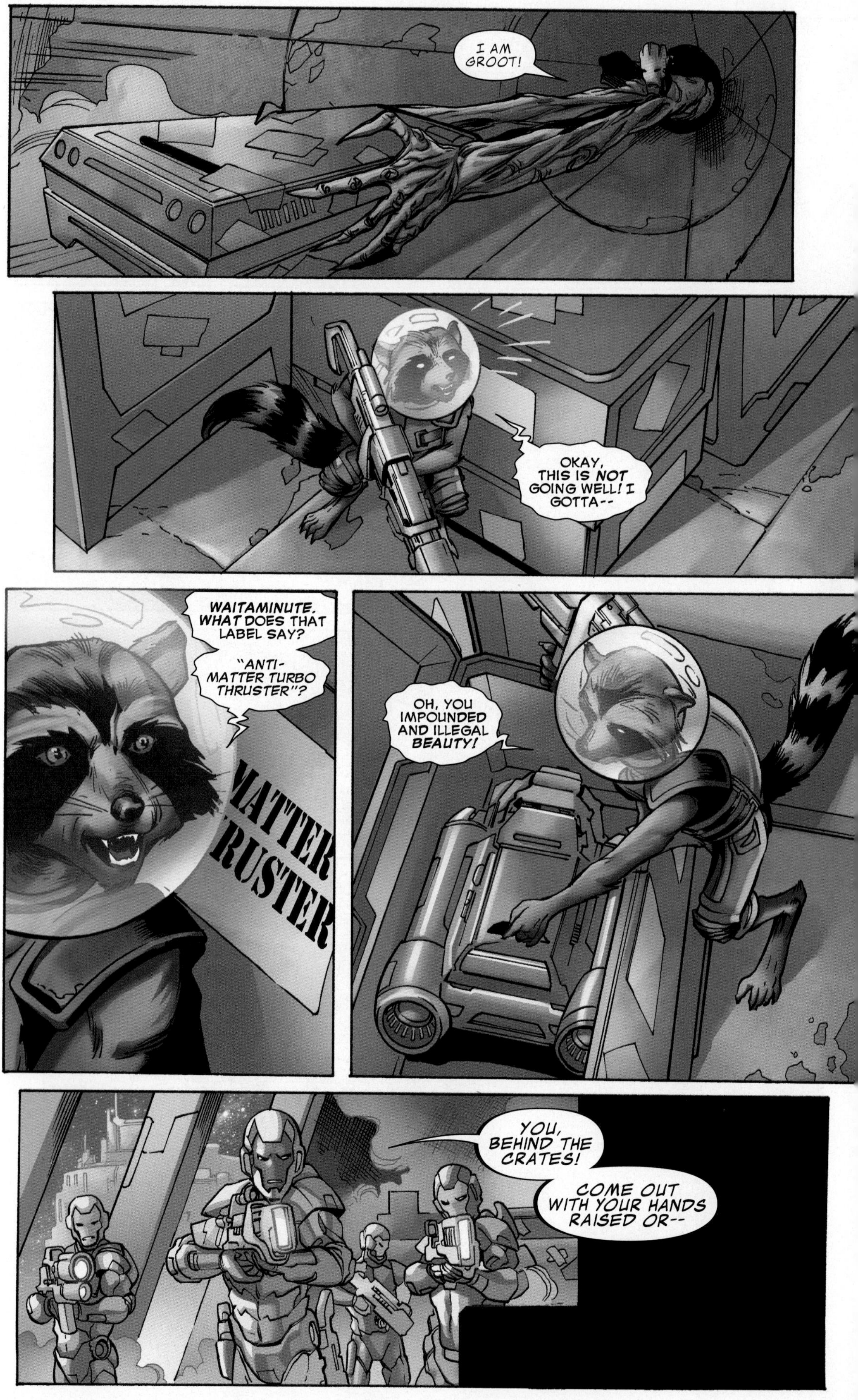
I AM GROOT!
OKAY, THIS IS NOT GOING WELL! I GOTTA--
WAITAMINUTE. WHAT DOES THAT LABEL SAY?
"ANTI-MATTER TURBO THRUSTER"?
MATTER
RUSTER
OH, YOU IMPOUNDED AND ILLEGAL BEAUTY!
YOU, BEHIND THE CRATES!
COME OUT WITH YOUR HANDS RAISED OR--

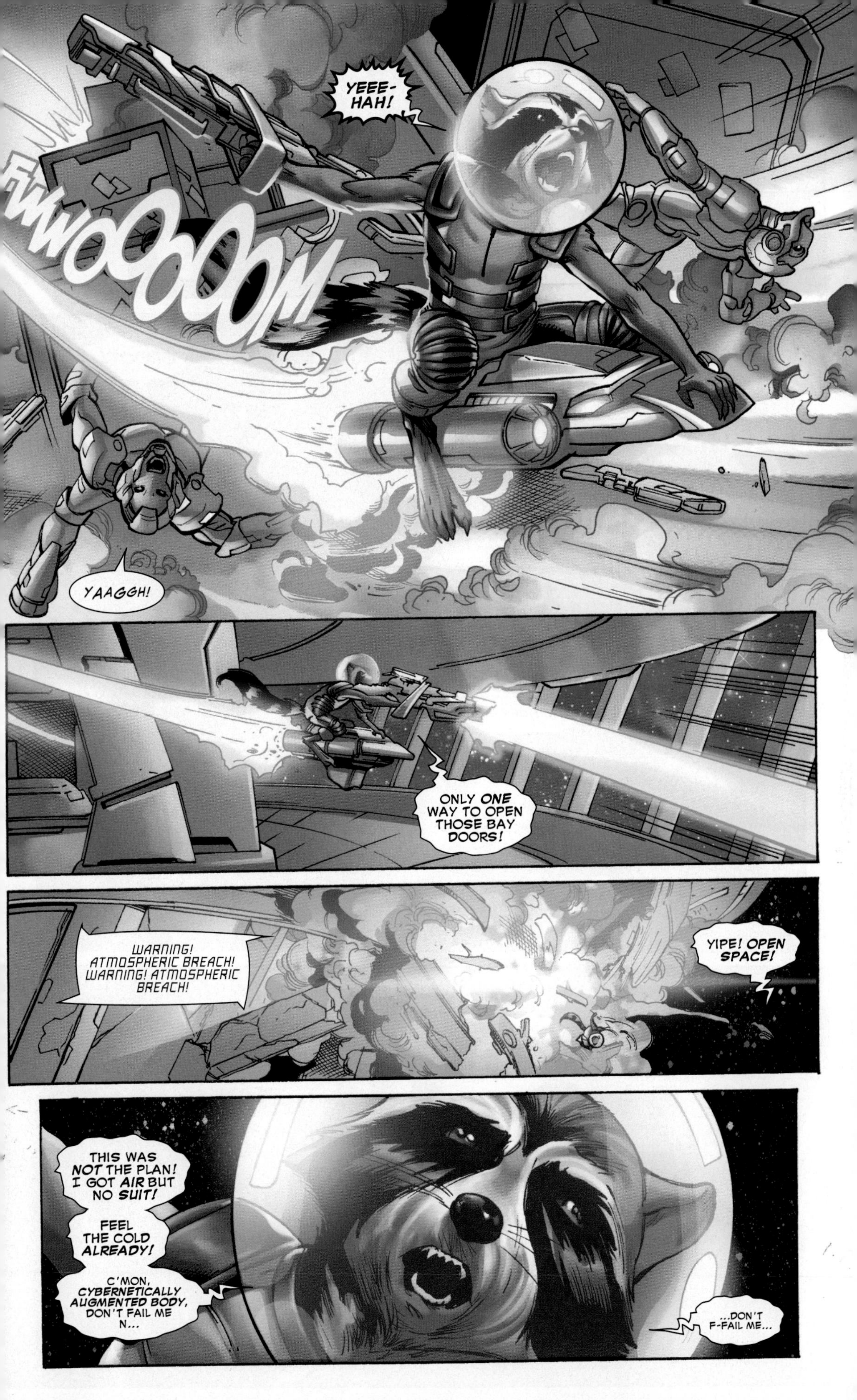
YEEE-HAH!
FWWOOOOOM
YAAGGH!
ONLY ONE WAY TO OPEN THOSE BAY DOORS!
WARNING! ATMOSPHERIC BREACH! WARNING! ATMOSPHERIC BREACH!
YIPE! OPEN SPACE!
THIS WAS NOT THE PLAN! I GOT AIR BUT NO SUIT!
FEEL THE COLD ALREADY!
C'MON, CYBERNETICALLY AUGMENTED BODY, DON'T FAIL ME N...
...DON'T F-FAIL ME...

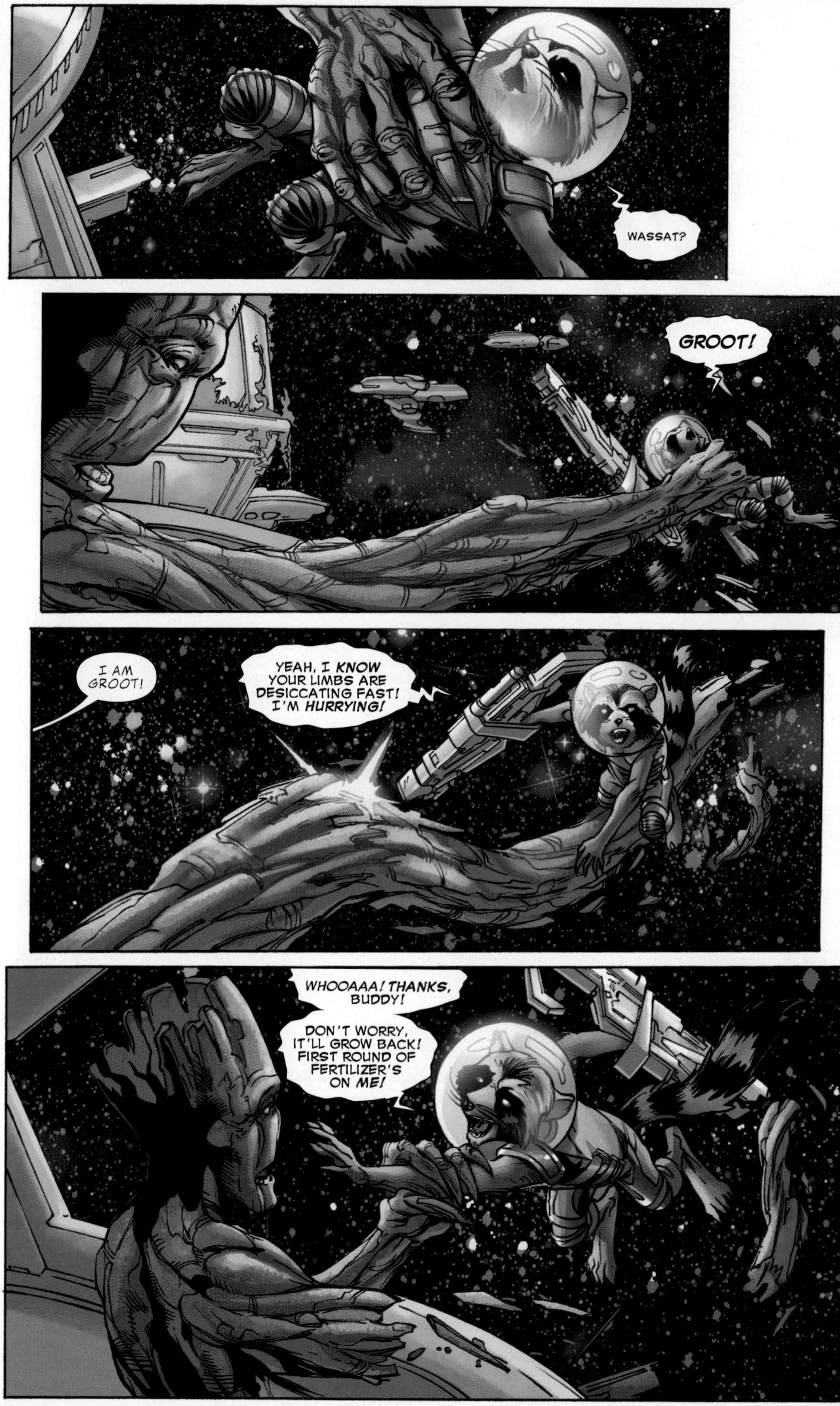
WASSAT?
GROOT!
I AM GROOT!
YEAH, I KNOW YOUR LIMBS ARE DESICCATING FAST! I'M HURRYING!
WHOOAAA! THANKS, BUDDY!
DON'T WORRY, IT'LL GROW BACK! FIRST ROUND OF FERTILIZER'S ON ME!

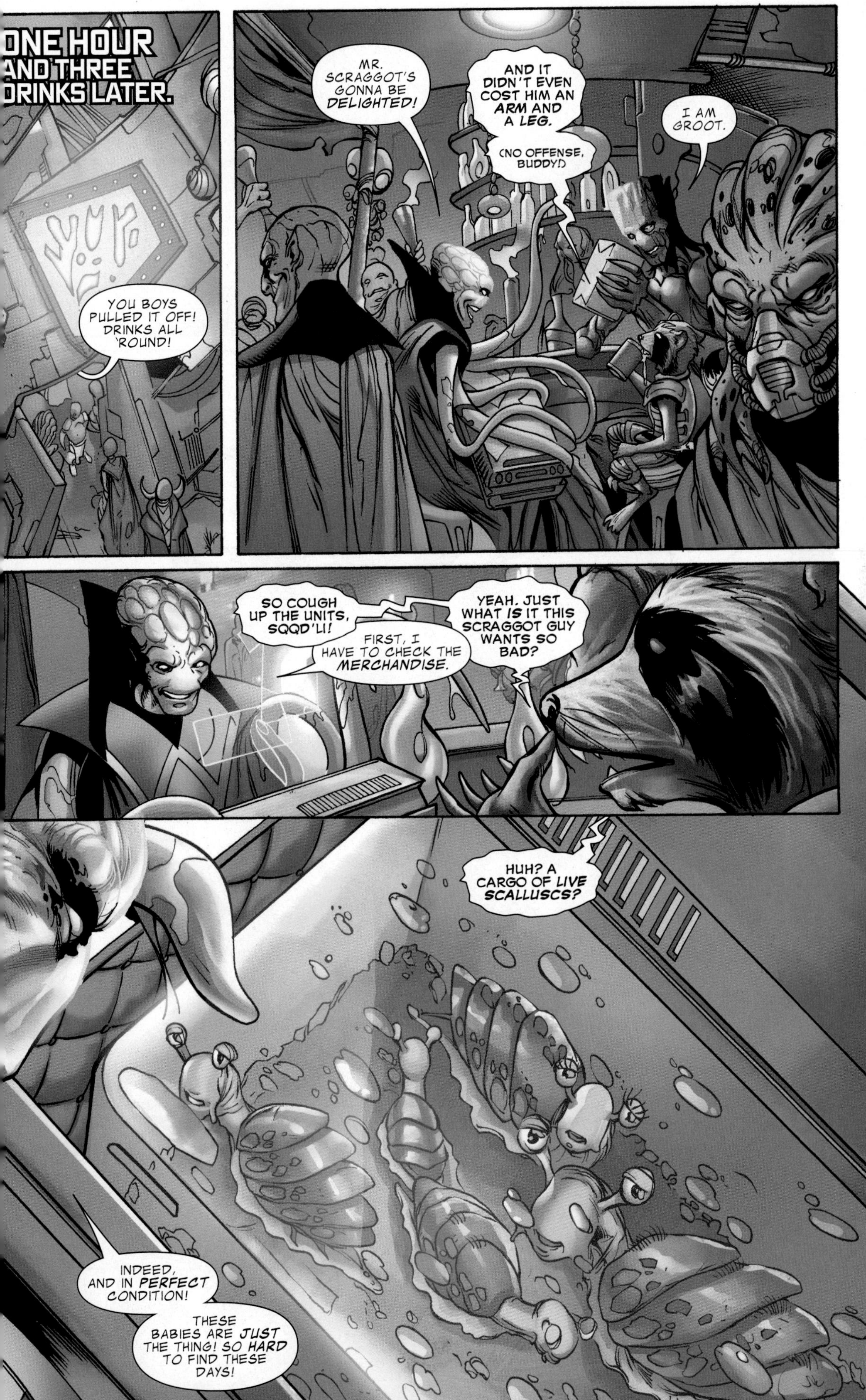
ONE HOUR AND THREE DRINKS LATER.
YOU BOYS PULLED IT OFF! DRINKS ALL 'ROUND!
MR. SCRAGGOT'S GONNA BE DELIGHTED!
AND IT DIDN'T EVEN COST HIM AN ARM AND A LEG.
(NO OFFENSE, BUDDY!)
I AM GROOT.
SO COUGH UP THE UNITS, SQQD'LI!
FIRST, I HAVE TO CHECK THE MERCHANDISE.
YEAH. JUST WHAT IS IT THIS SCRAGGOT GUY WANTS SO BAD?
HUH? A CARGO OF LIVE SCALLUSCS?
INDEED, AND IN PERFECT CONDITION!
THESE BABIES ARE JUST THE THING! SO HARD TO FIND THESE DAYS!

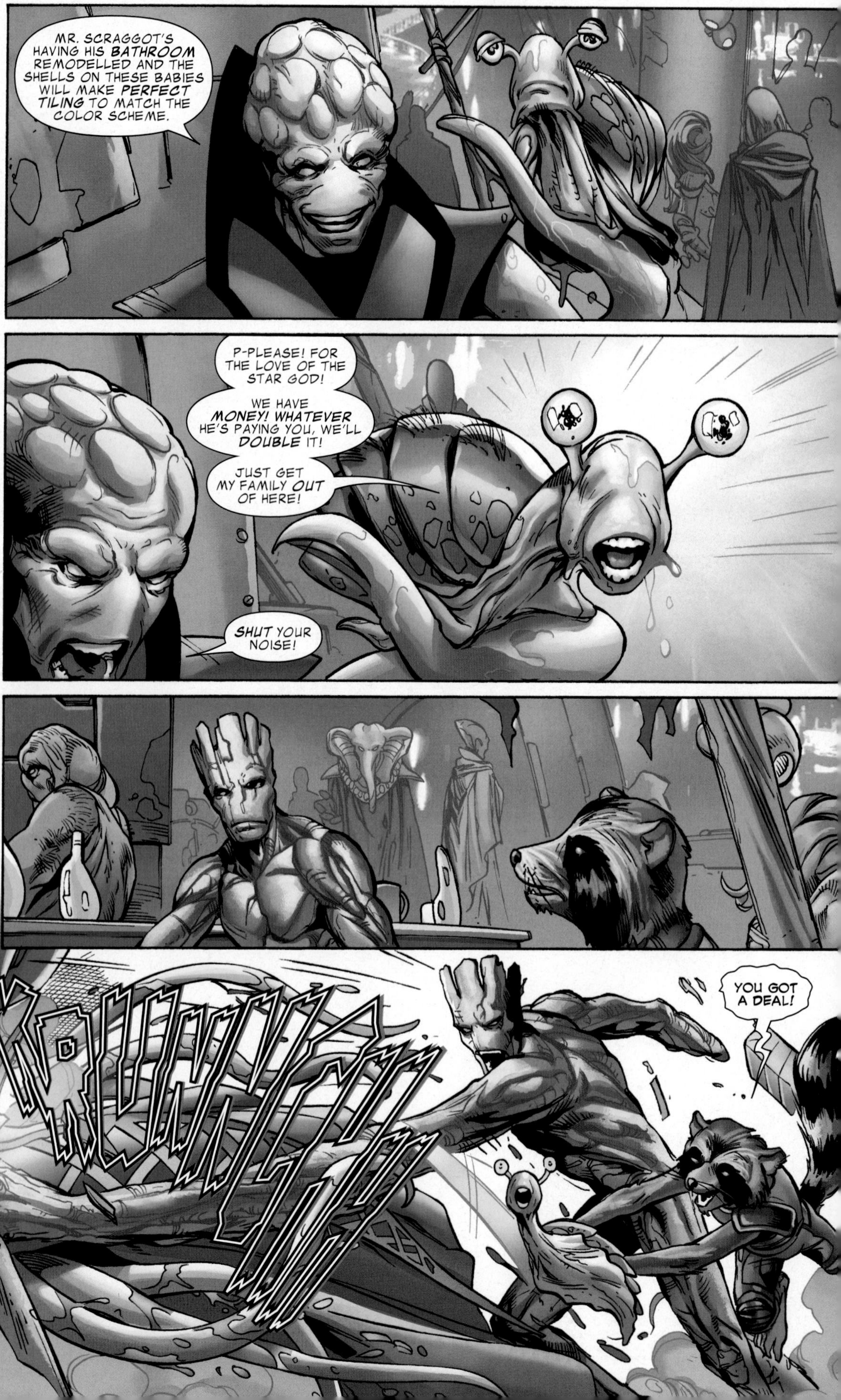
MR. SCRAGGOT'S HAVING HIS BATHROOM REMODELLED AND THE SHELLS ON THESE BABIES WILL MAKE PERFECT TILING TO MATCH THE COLOR SCHEME.
P-PLEASE! FOR THE LOVE OF THE STAR GOD!
WE HAVE MONEY! WHATEVER HE'S PAYING YOU, WE'LL DOUBLE IT!
JUST GET MY FAMILY OUT OF HERE!
SHUT YOUR NOISE!
YOU GOT A DEAL!

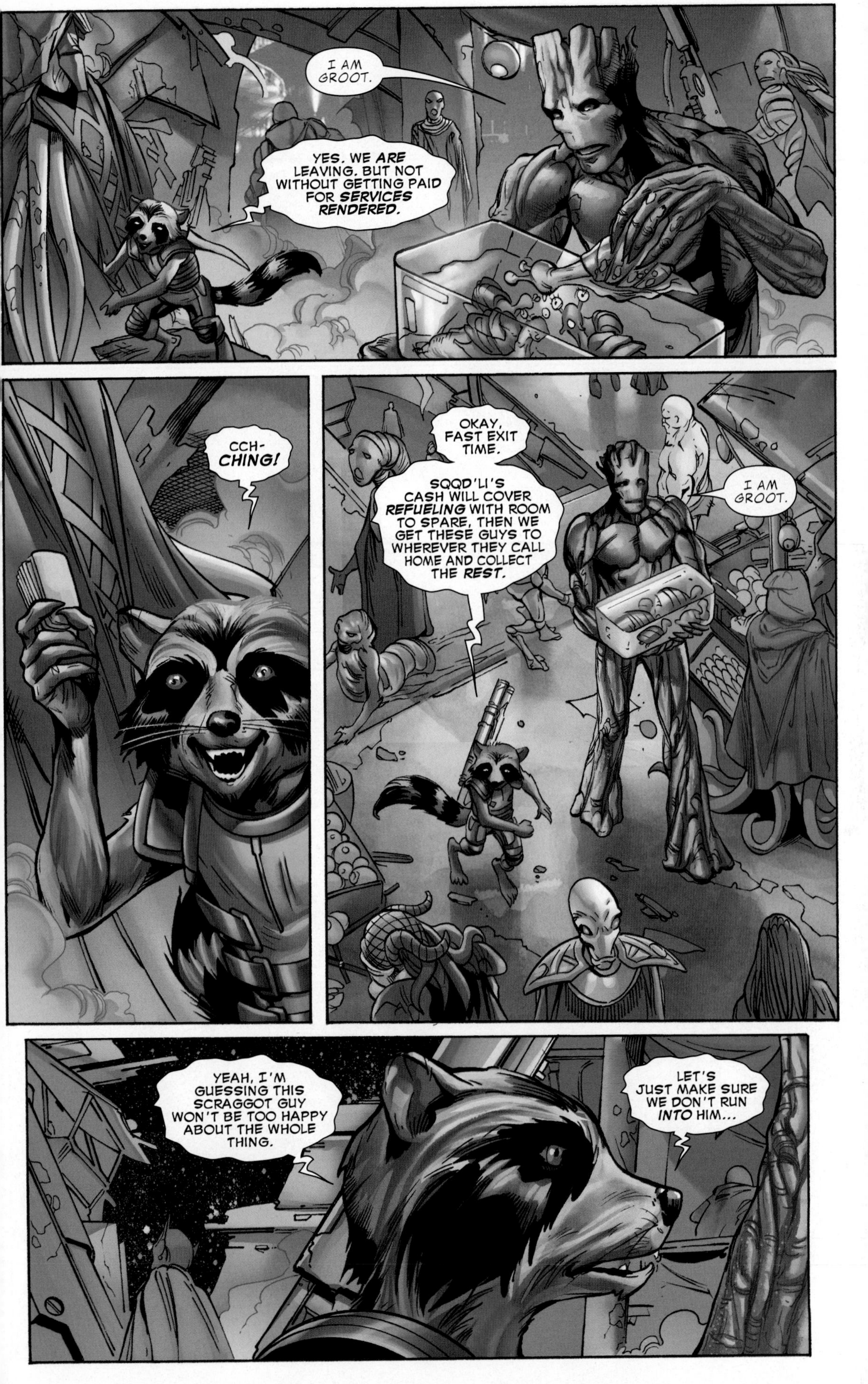
I AM GROOT.
YES. WE ARE LEAVING. BUT NOT WITHOUT GETTING PAID FOR SERVICES RENDERED.
CCH-CHING!
OKAY, FAST EXIT TIME.
SQQD'LI'S CASH WILL COVER REFUELING WITH ROOM TO SPARE, THEN WE GET THESE GUYS TO WHEREVER THEY CALL HOME AND COLLECT THE REST.
I AM GROOT.
YEAH, I'M GUESSING THIS SCRAGGOT GUY WON'T BE TOO HAPPY ABOUT THE WHOLE THING.
LET'S JUST MAKE SURE WE DON'T RUN INTO HIM...

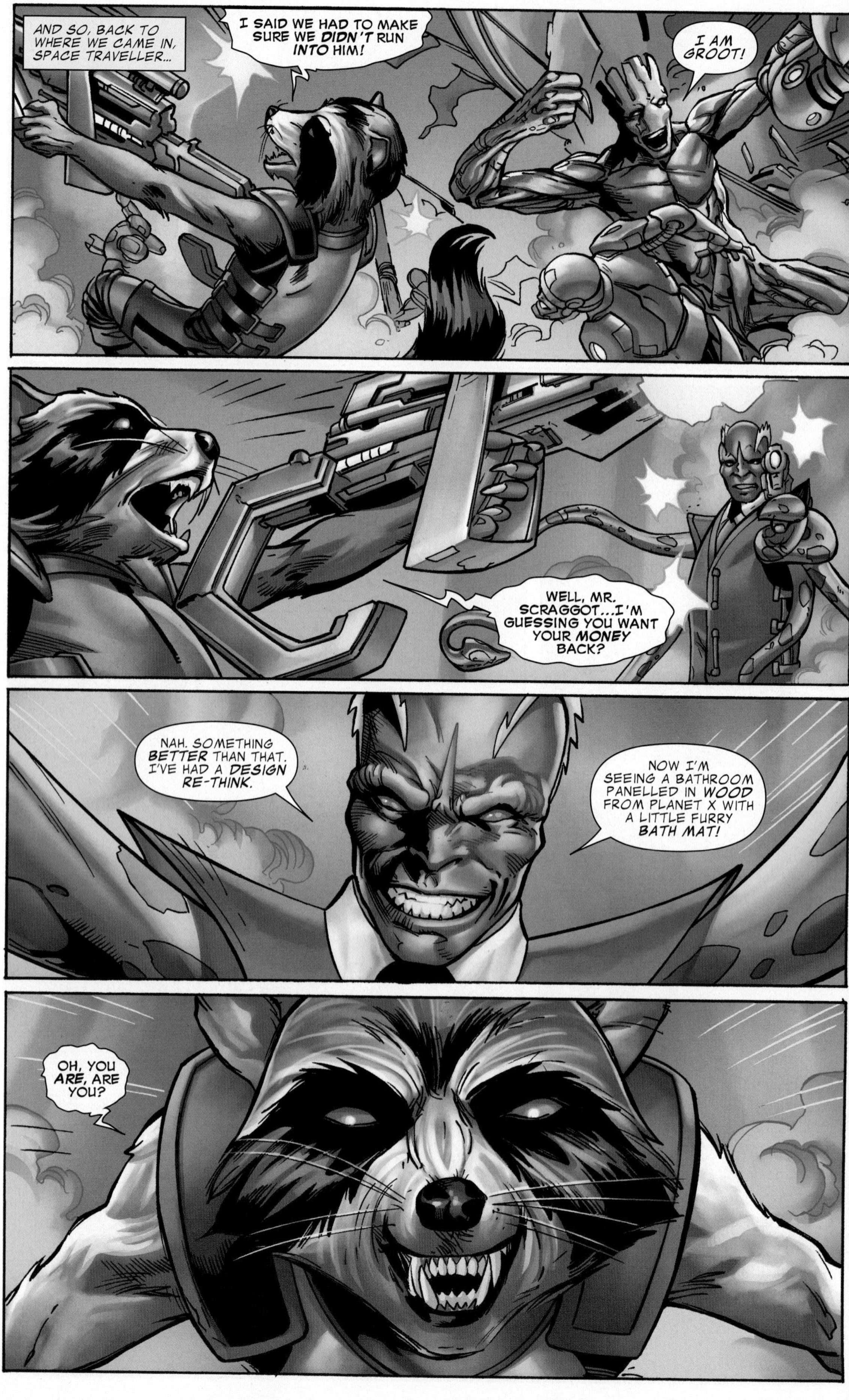
AND SO, BACK TO WHERE WE CAME IN, SPACE TRAVELLER...
I SAID WE HAD TO MAKE SURE WE DIDN'T RUN INTO HIM!
I AM GROOT!
WELL, MR. SCRAGGOT...I'M GUESSING YOU WANT YOUR MONEY BACK?
NAH. SOMETHING BETTER THAN THAT. I'VE HAD A DESIGN RE-THINK.
NOW I'M SEEING A BATHROOM PANELLED IN WOOD FROM PLANET X WITH A LITTLE FURRY BATH MAT!
OH, YOU ARE, ARE YOU?

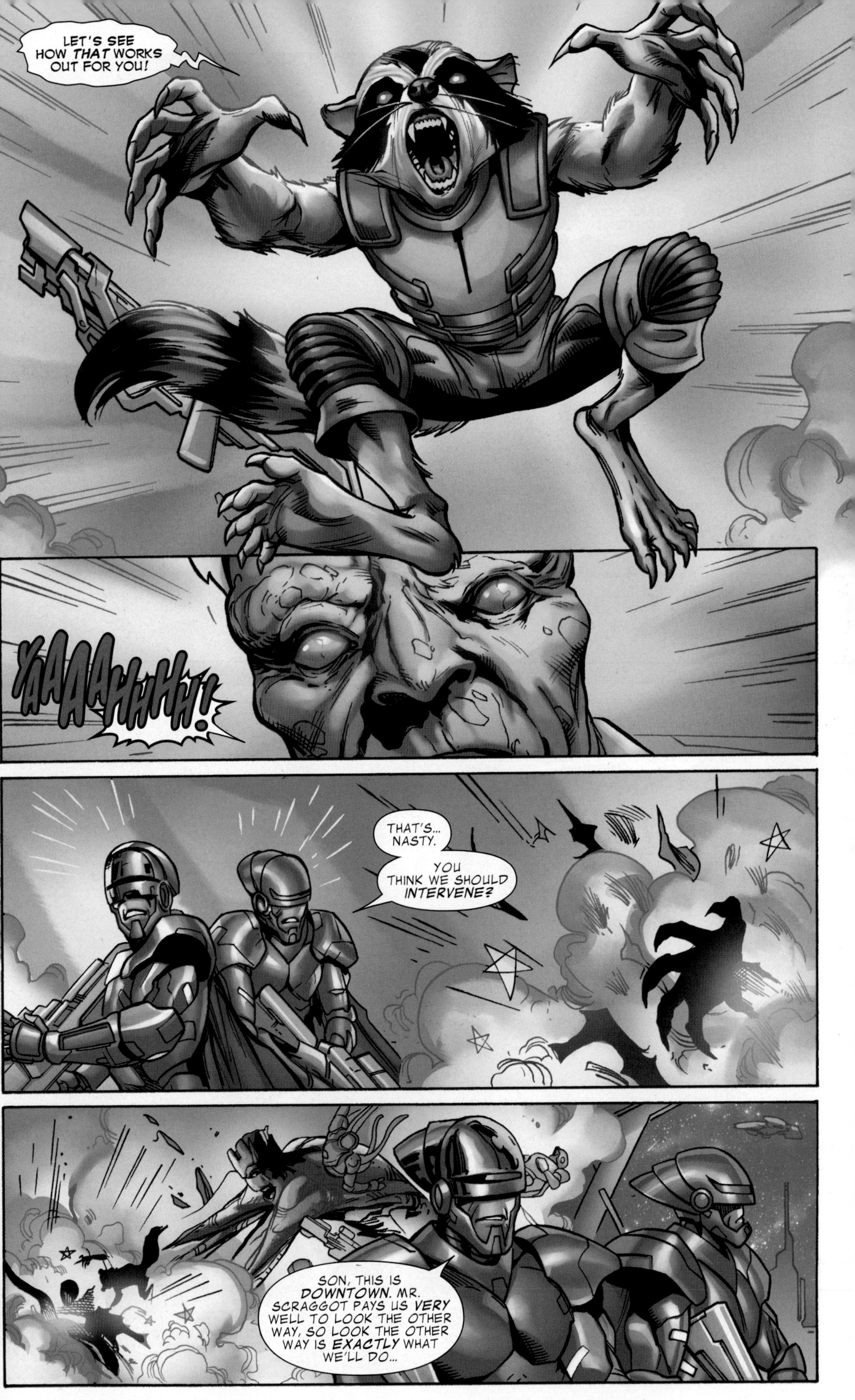
LET'S SEE HOW THAT WORKS OUT FOR YOU!
YAAAAHHHH!
THAT'S... NASTY.
YOU THINK WE SHOULD INTERVENE?
SON, THIS IS DOWNTOWN. MR. SCRAGGOT PAYS US VERY WELL TO LOOK THE OTHER WAY, SO LOOK THE OTHER WAY IS EXACTLY WHAT WE'LL DO...

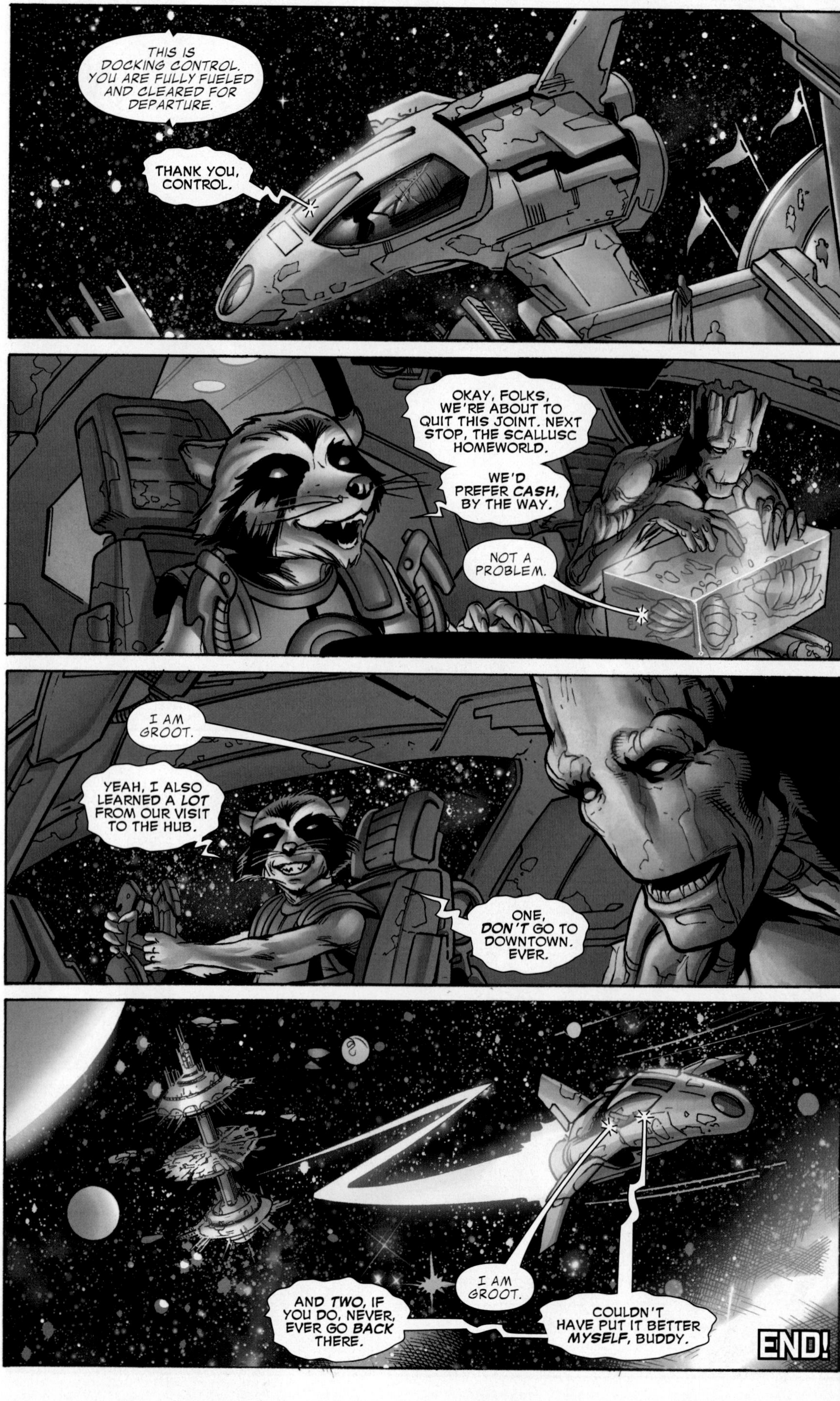
THIS IS DOCKING CONTROL. YOU ARE FULLY FUELED AND CLEARED FOR DEPARTURE.
THANK YOU, CONTROL.
OKAY, FOLKS, WE'RE ABOUT TO QUIT THIS JOINT. NEXT STOP, THE SCALLUSC HOMEWORLD.
WE'D PREFER CASH, BY THE WAY.
NOT A PROBLEM.
I AM GROOT.
YEAH, I ALSO LEARNED A LOT FROM OUR VISIT TO THE HUB.
ONE, DON'T GO TO DOWNTOWN. EVER.
AND TWO, IF YOU DO, NEVER, EVER GO BACK THERE.
I AM GROOT.
COULDN'T HAVE PUT IT BETTER MYSELF, BUDDY.
END!

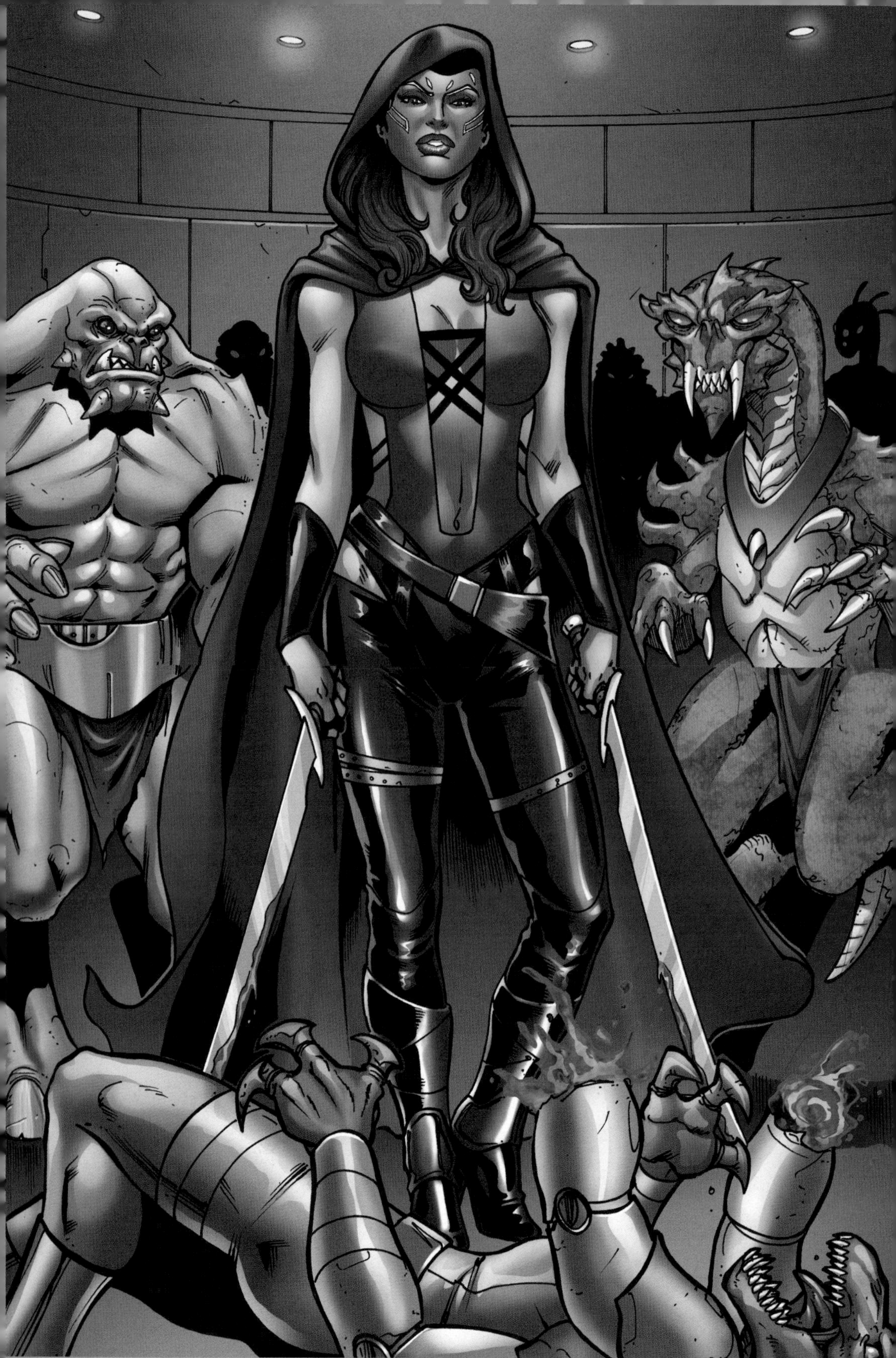

MARVEL'S GUARDIANS OF THE GALAXY: DANGEROUS PREY

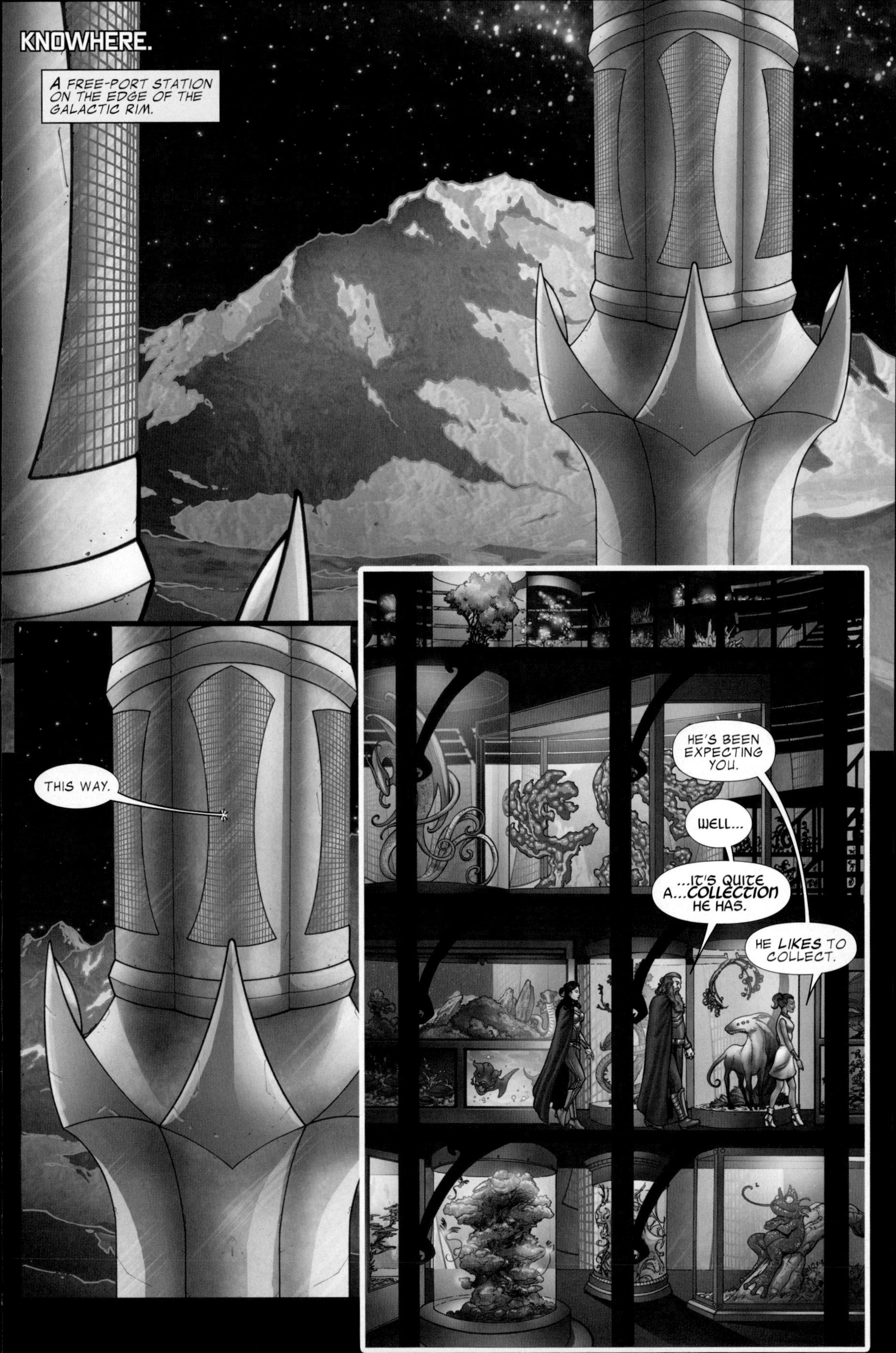
KNOWHERE.
A FREE-PORT STATION ON THE EDGE OF THE GALACTIC RIM.
THIS WAY.
HE'S BEEN EXPECTING YOU.
WELL...
...IT'S QUITE A...COLLECTION HE HAS.
HE LIKES TO COLLECT.

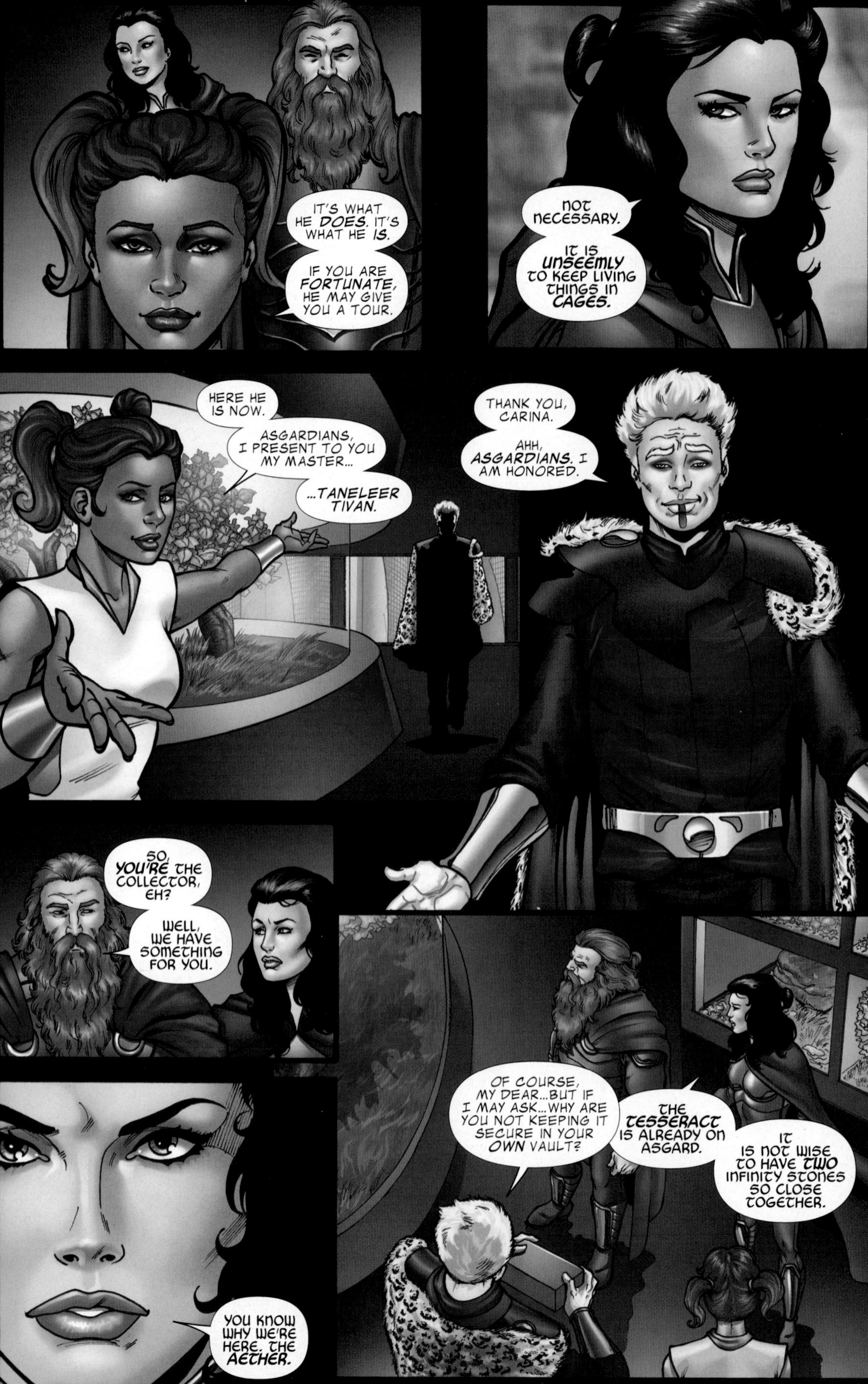

IT'S WHAT HE DOES. IT'S WHAT HE IS.
IF YOU ARE FORTUNATE, HE MAY GIVE YOU A TOUR.
NOT NECESSARY.
IT IS UNSEEMLY TO KEEP LIVING THINGS IN CAGES.
HERE HE IS NOW.
ASGARDIANS, I PRESENT TO YOU MY MASTER...
...TANELEER TIVAN.
THANK YOU, CARINA.
AHH, ASGARDIANS. I AM HONORED.
SO, YOU'RE THE COLLECTOR, EH?
WELL, WE HAVE SOMETHING FOR YOU.
YOU KNOW WHY WE'RE HERE. THE AETHER.
OF COURSE, MY DEAR...BUT IF I MAY ASK...WHY ARE YOU NOT KEEPING IT SECURE IN YOUR OWN VAULT?
THE TESSERACT IS ALREADY ON ASGARD.
IT IS NOT WISE TO HAVE TWO INFINITY STONES SO CLOSE TOGETHER.

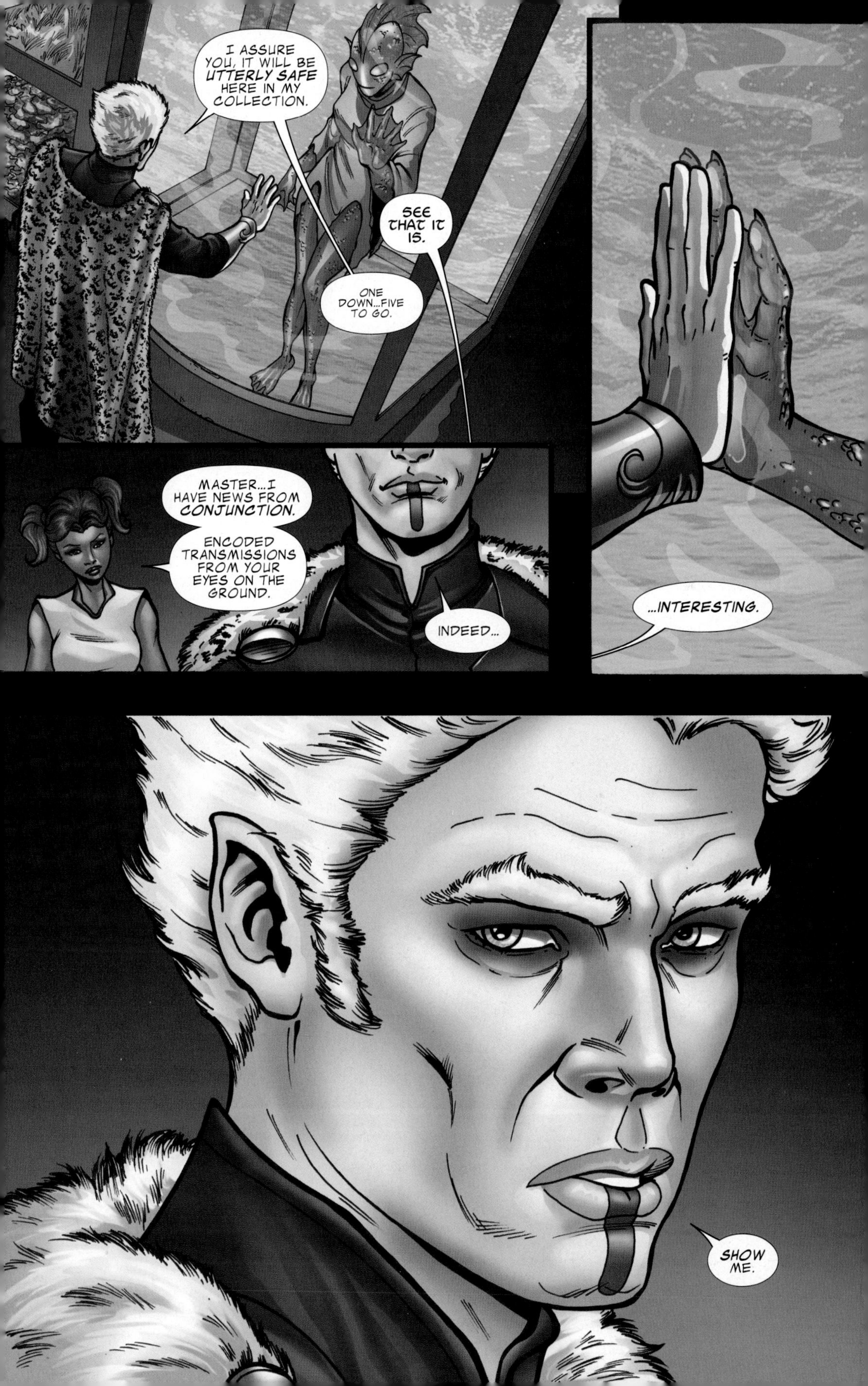
I ASSURE YOU, IT WILL BE UTTERLY SAFE HERE IN MY COLLECTION.
SEE THAT IT IS.
ONE DOWN...FIVE TO GO.
...INTERESTING.
MASTER...I HAVE NEWS FROM CONJUNCTION.
ENCODED TRANSMISSIONS FROM YOUR EYES ON THE GROUND.
INDEED...
SHOW ME.

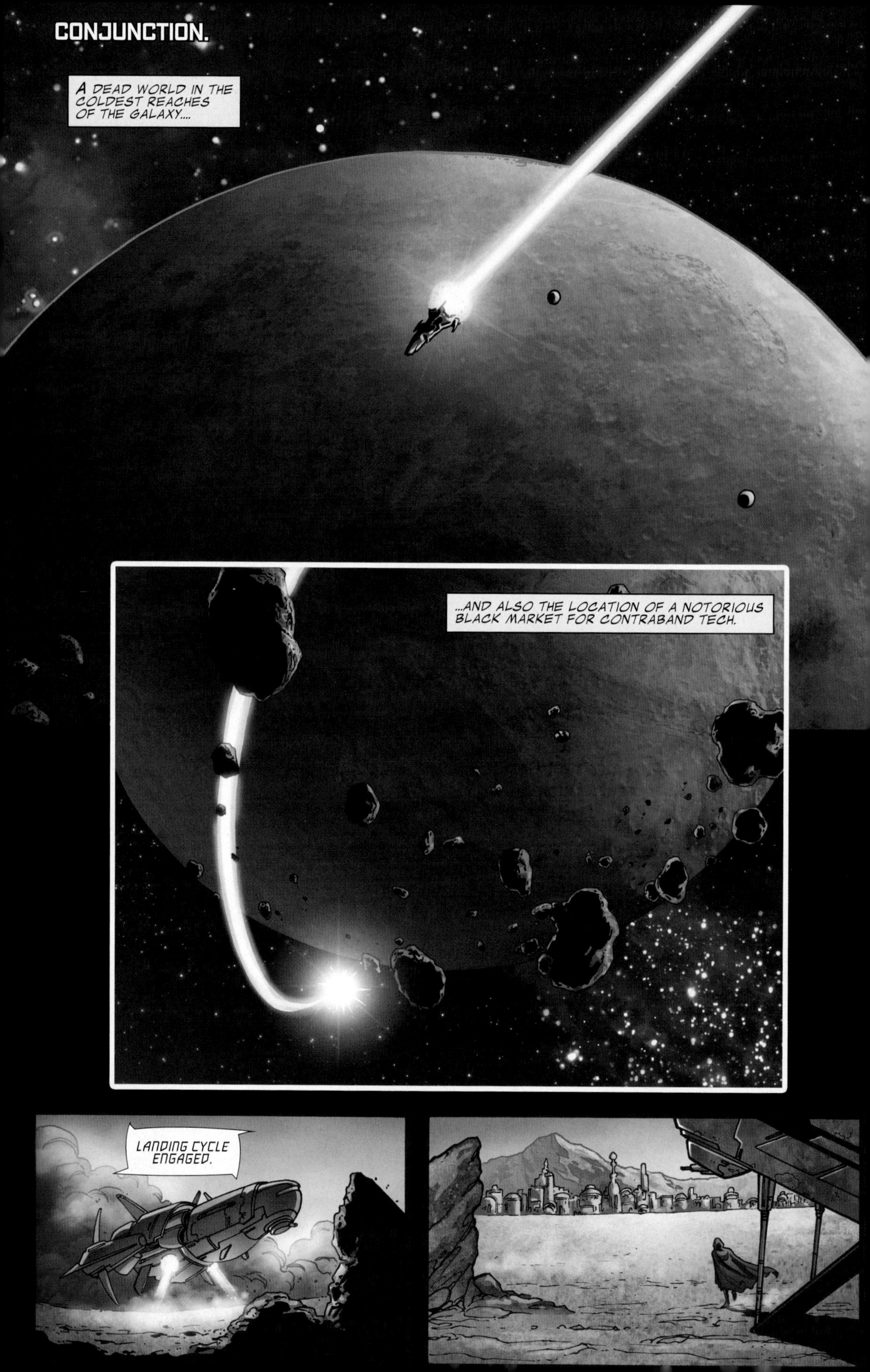
CONJUNCTION.
A DEAD WORLD IN THE COLDEST REACHES OF THE GALAXY....
...AND ALSO THE LOCATION OF A NOTORIOUS BLACK MARKET FOR CONTRABAND TECH.
LANDING CYCLE ENGAGED.

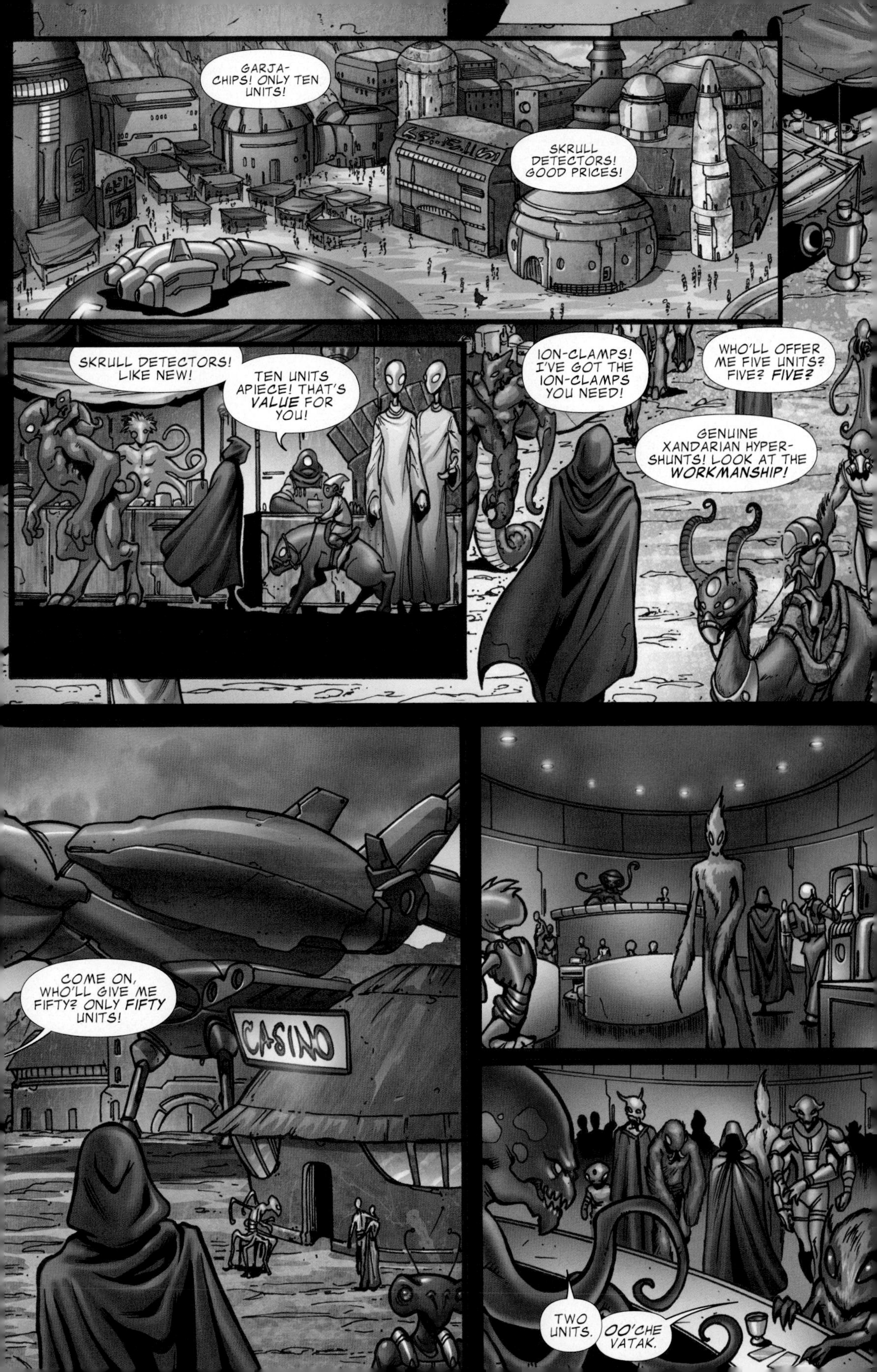
GARJA-CHIPS! ONLY TEN UNITS!
SKRULL DETECTORS! GOOD PRICES!
SKRULL DETECTORS! LIKE NEW!
TEN UNITS APIECE! THAT'S VALUE FOR YOU!
ION-CLAMPS! I'VE GOT THE ION-CLAMPS YOU NEED!
WHO'LL OFFER ME FIVE UNITS? FIVE? FIVE?
GENUINE XANDARIAN HYPER-SHUNTS! LOOK AT THE WORKMANSHIP!
COME ON, WHO'LL GIVE ME FIFTY? ONLY FIFTY UNITS!
CASINO
TWO UNITS.
OO'CHE VATAK.

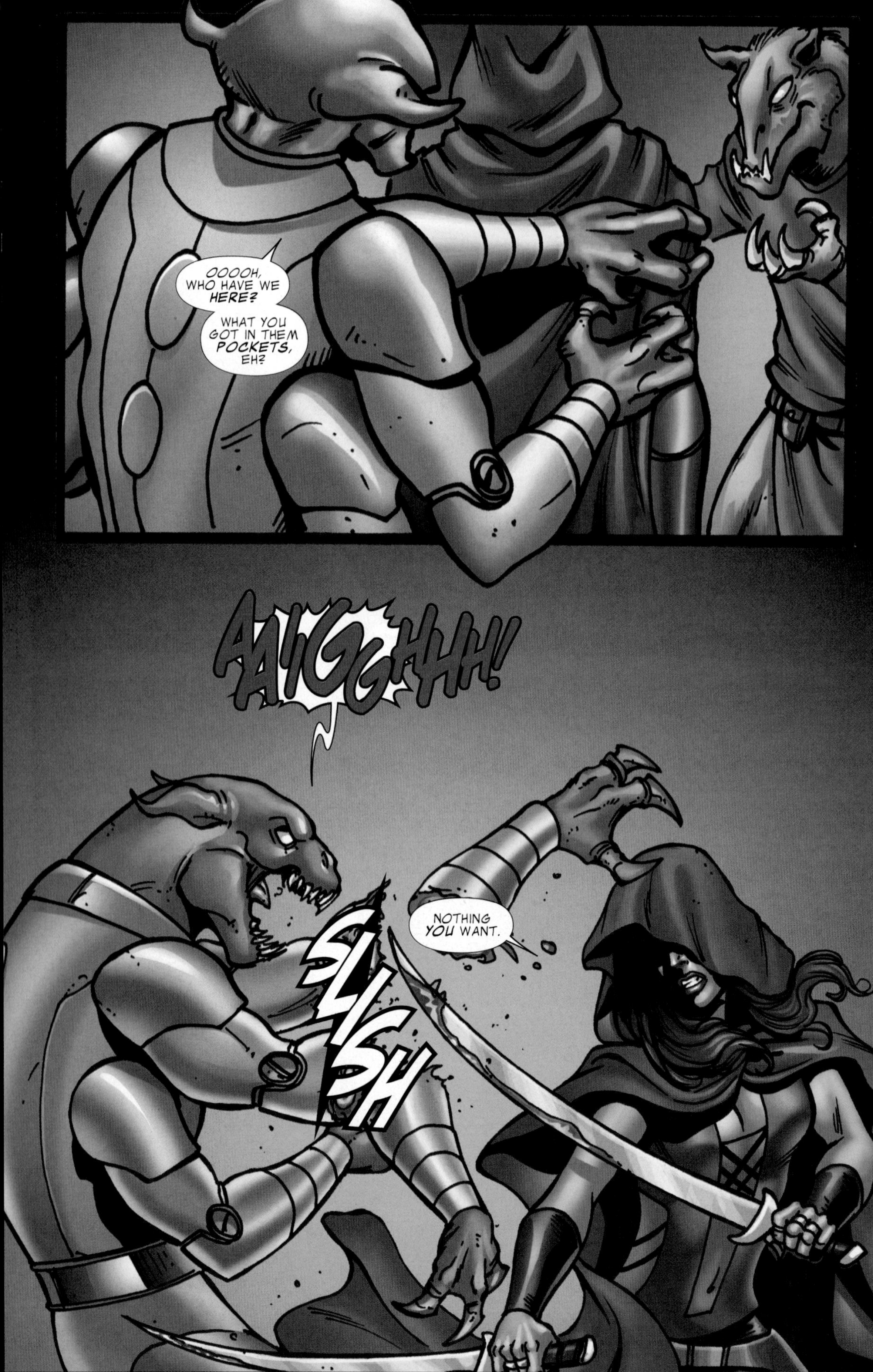
OOOOH, WHO HAVE WE HERE?
WHAT YOU GOT IN THEM POCKETS, EH?
AAIIGGHHH!
NOTHING YOU WANT.
SLISH

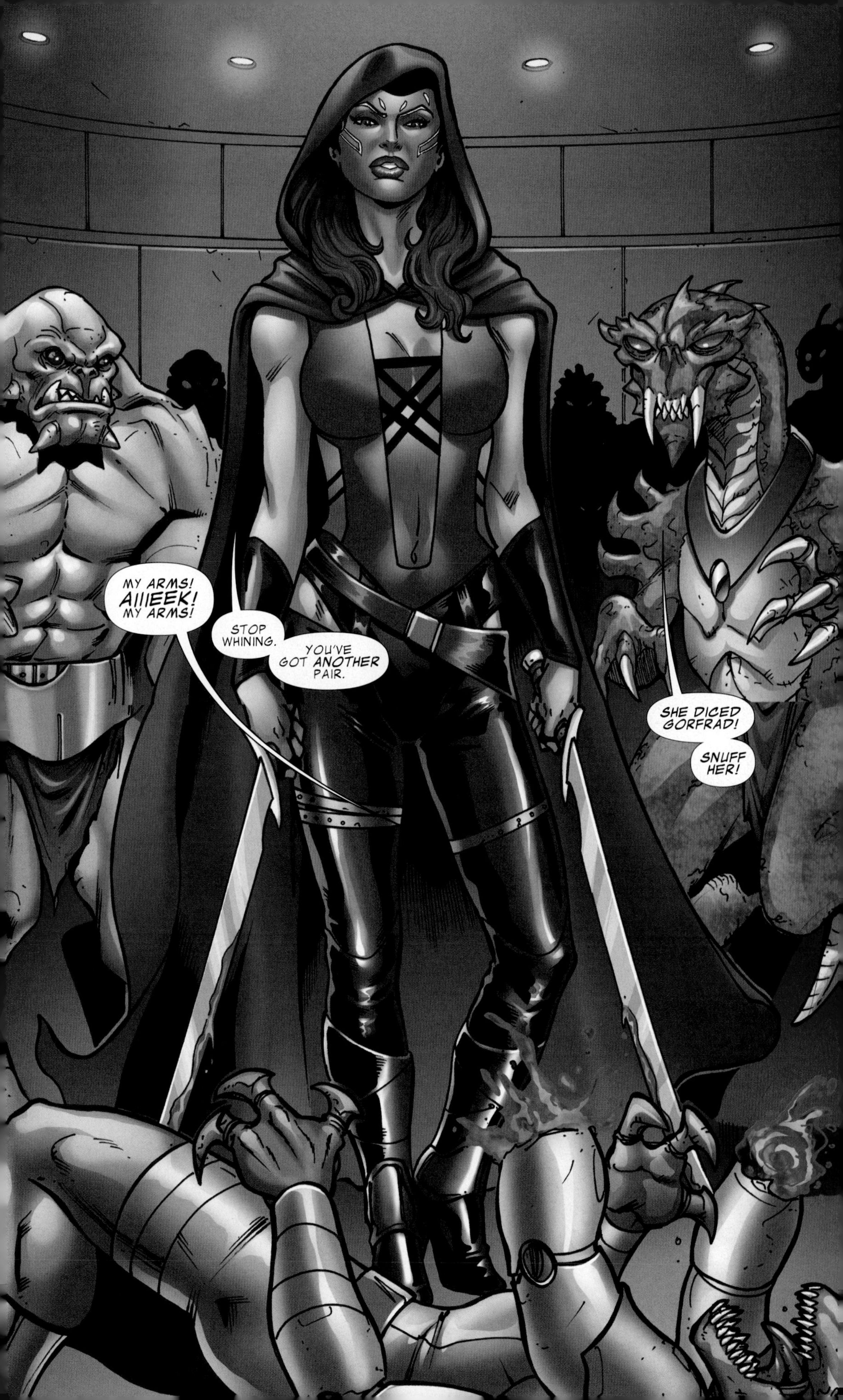

MY ARMS! AIIIEEK! MY ARMS!
STOP WHINING.
YOU'VE GOT ANOTHER PAIR.
SHE DICED GORFRAD!
SNUFF HER!

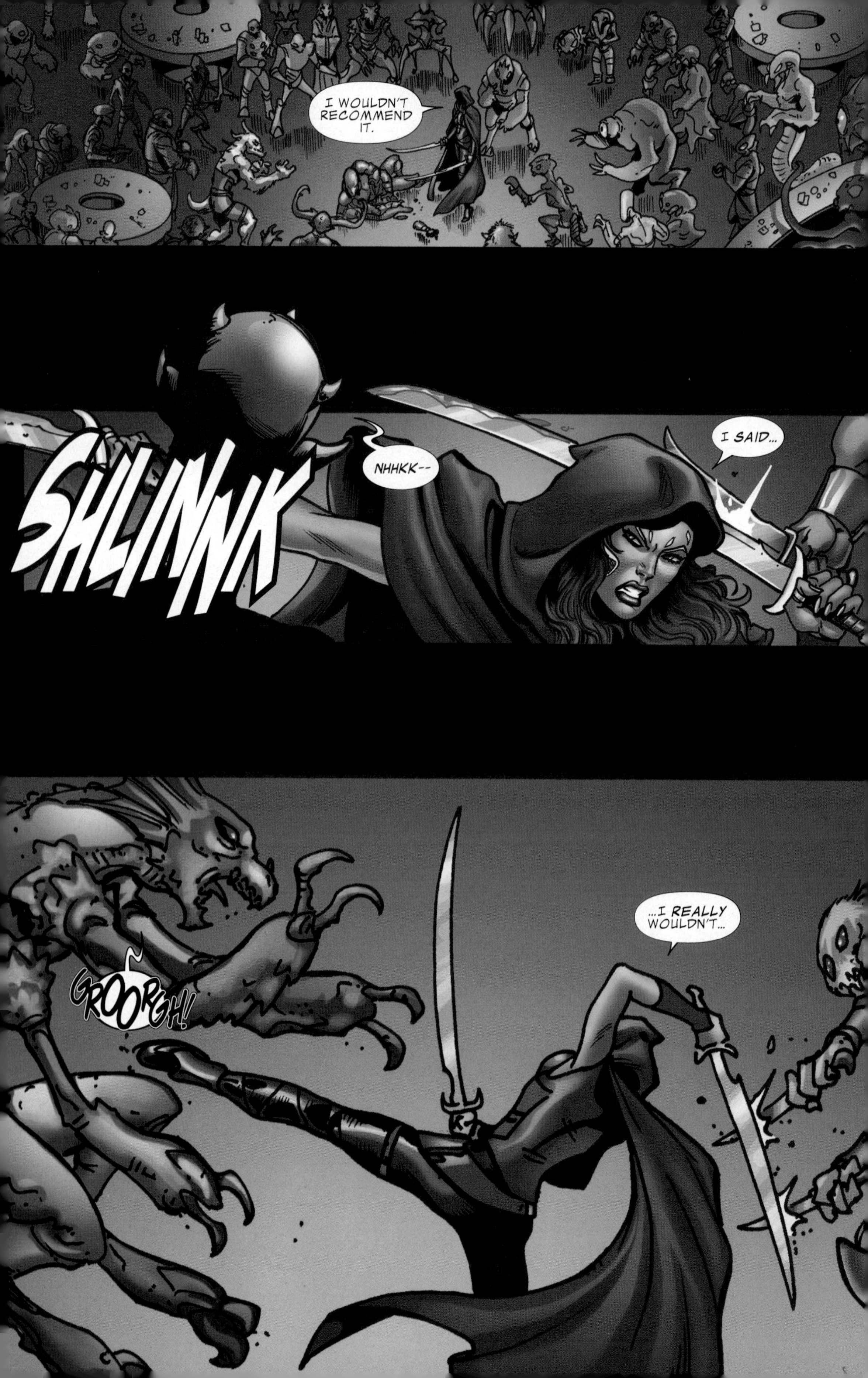
I WOULDN'T RECOMMEND IT.
SHLINNK
NHHKK--
I SAID...
GROORGH!
...I REALLY WOULDN'T...

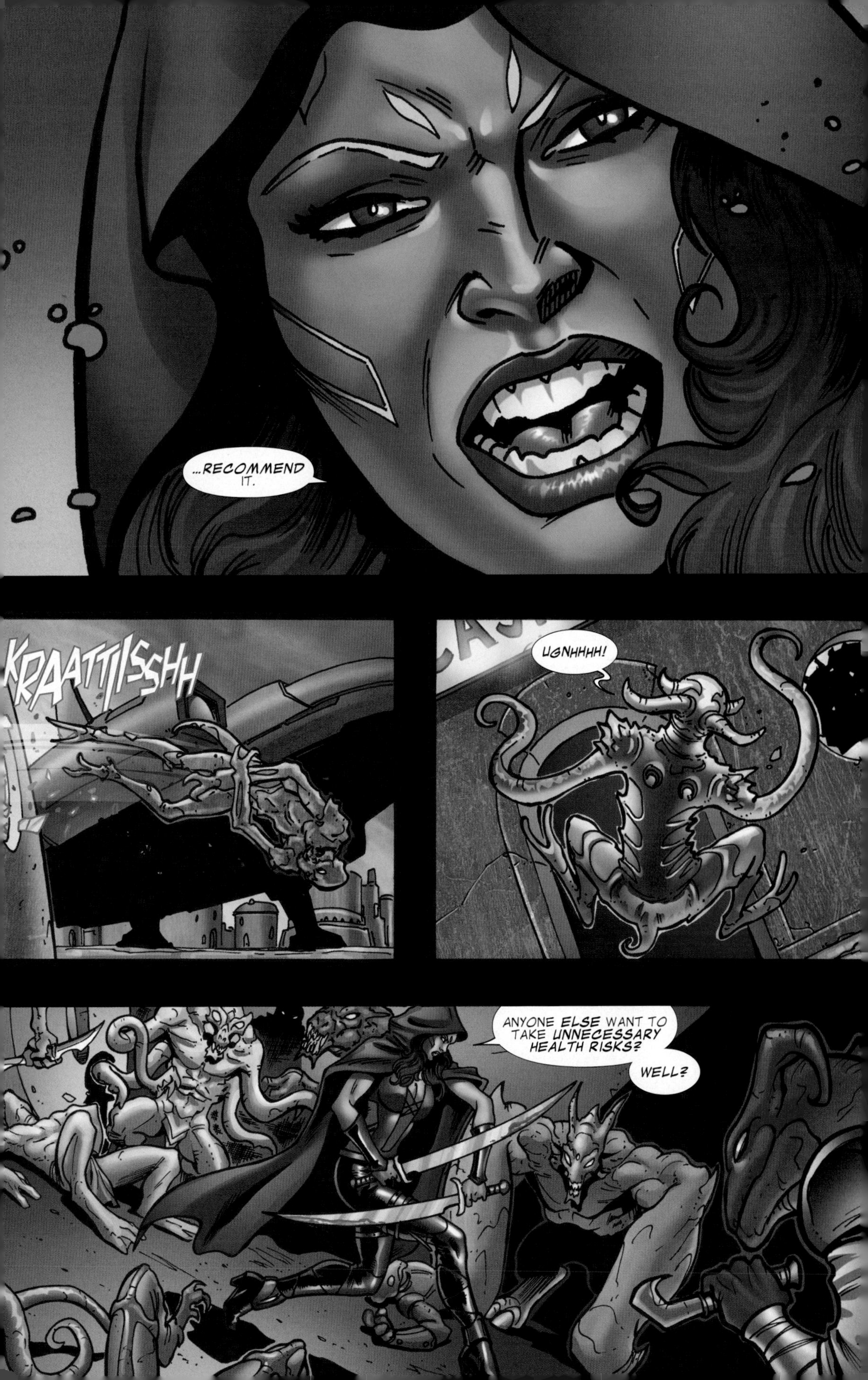
...RECOMMEND IT.
KRAATTIISSHH
UGNHHHH!
ANYONE ELSE WANT TO TAKE UNNECESSARY HEALTH RISKS?
WELL?

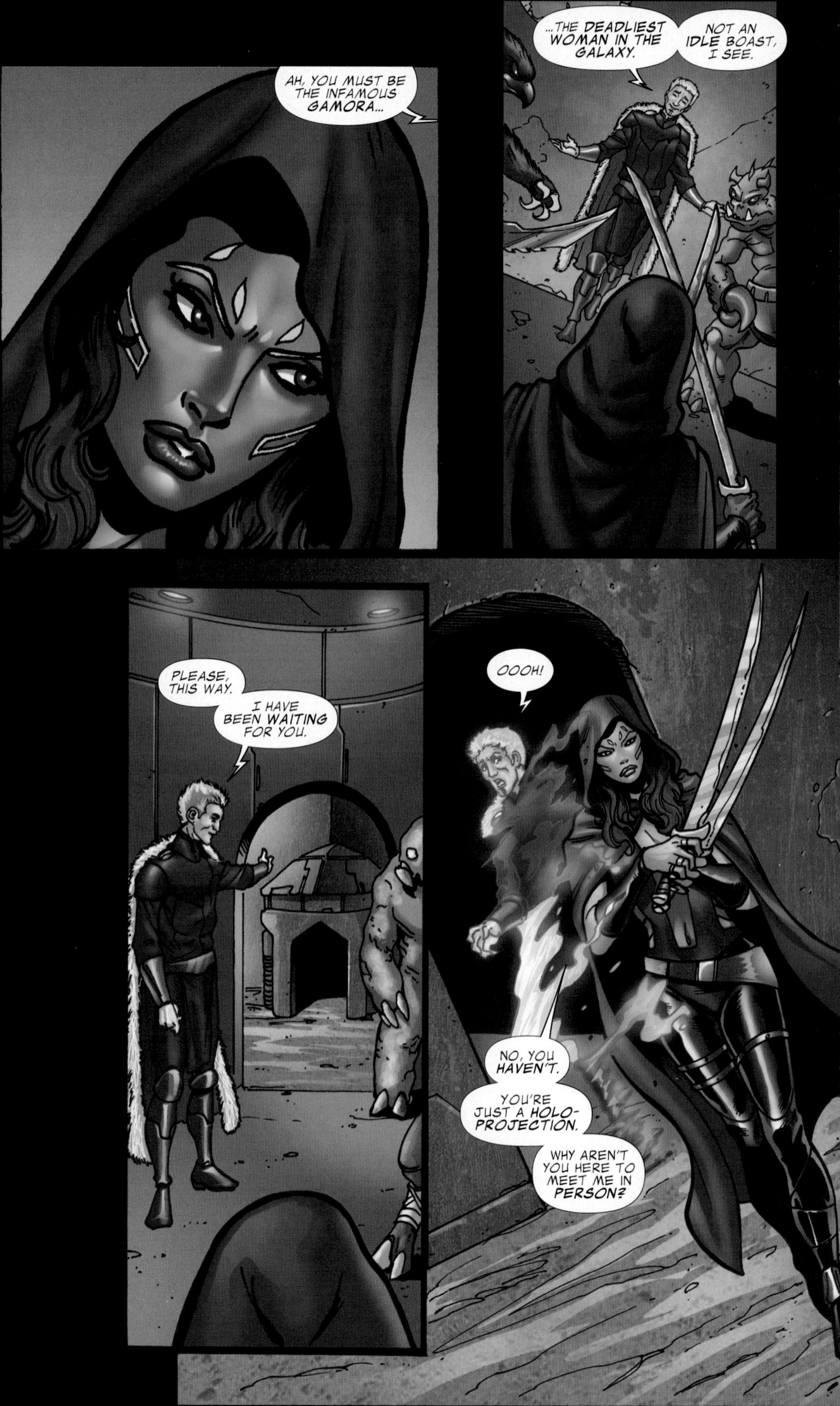
AH, YOU MUST BE THE INFAMOUS GAMORA...
...THE DEADLIEST WOMAN IN THE GALAXY.
NOT AN IDLE BOAST, I SEE.
PLEASE, THIS WAY.
I HAVE BEEN WAITING FOR YOU.
OOOH!
NO, YOU HAVEN'T.
YOU'RE JUST A HOLO-PROJECTION.
WHY AREN'T YOU HERE TO MEET ME IN PERSON?

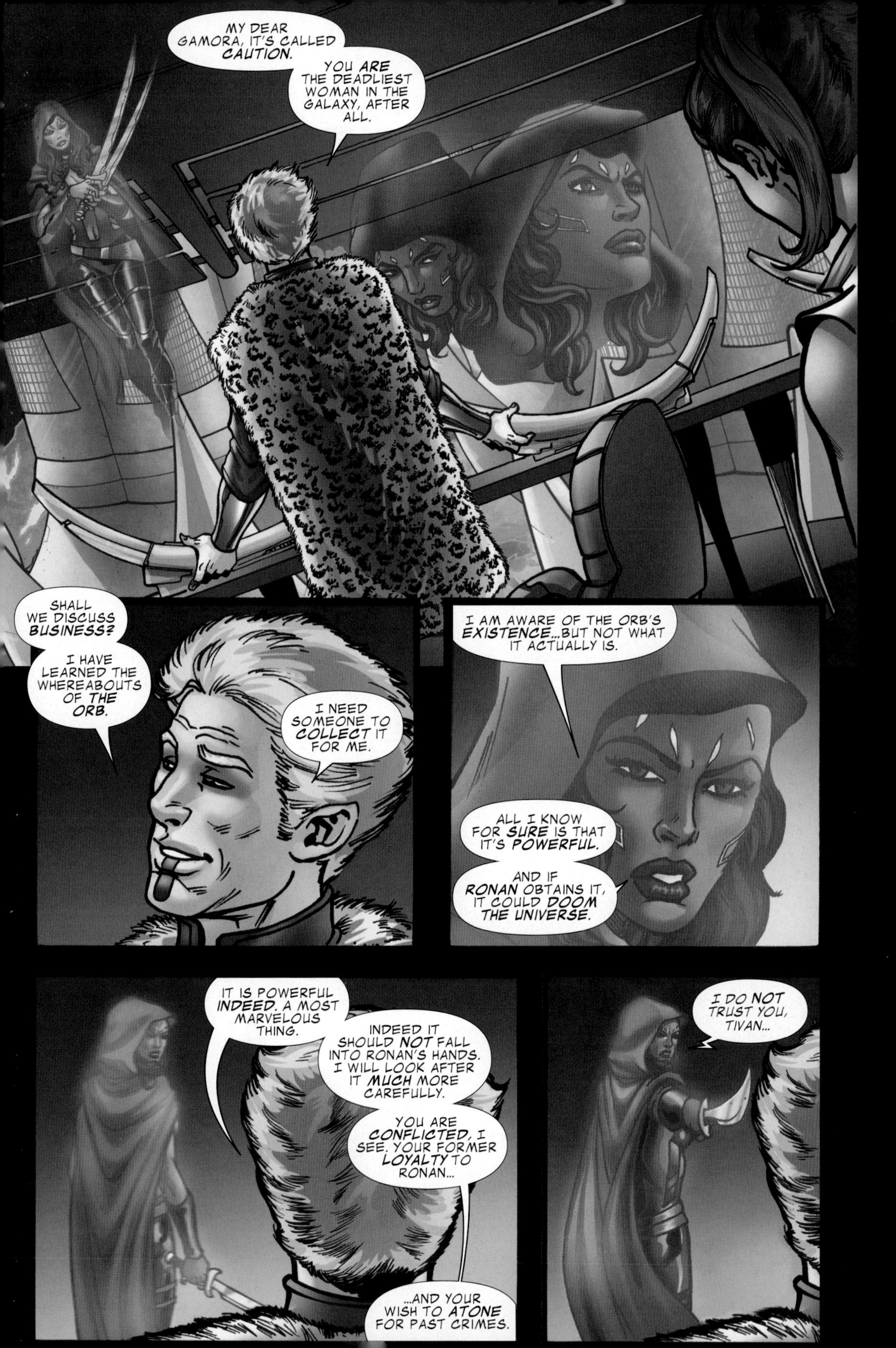
MY DEAR GAMORA, IT'S CALLED CAUTION.
YOU ARE THE DEADLIEST WOMAN IN THE GALAXY, AFTER ALL.
SHALL WE DISCUSS BUSINESS?
I HAVE LEARNED THE WHEREABOUTS OF THE ORB.
I NEED SOMEONE TO COLLECT IT FOR ME.
I AM AWARE OF THE ORB'S EXISTENCE...BUT NOT WHAT IT ACTUALLY IS.
ALL I KNOW FOR SURE IS THAT IT'S POWERFUL.
AND IF RONAN OBTAINS IT, IT COULD DOOM THE UNIVERSE.
IT IS POWERFUL INDEED. A MOST MARVELOUS THING.
INDEED IT SHOULD NOT FALL INTO RONAN'S HANDS. I WILL LOOK AFTER IT MUCH MORE CAREFULLY.
YOU ARE CONFLICTED, I SEE. YOUR FORMER LOYALTY TO RONAN...
...AND YOUR WISH TO ATONE FOR PAST CRIMES.
I DO NOT TRUST YOU, TIVAN...

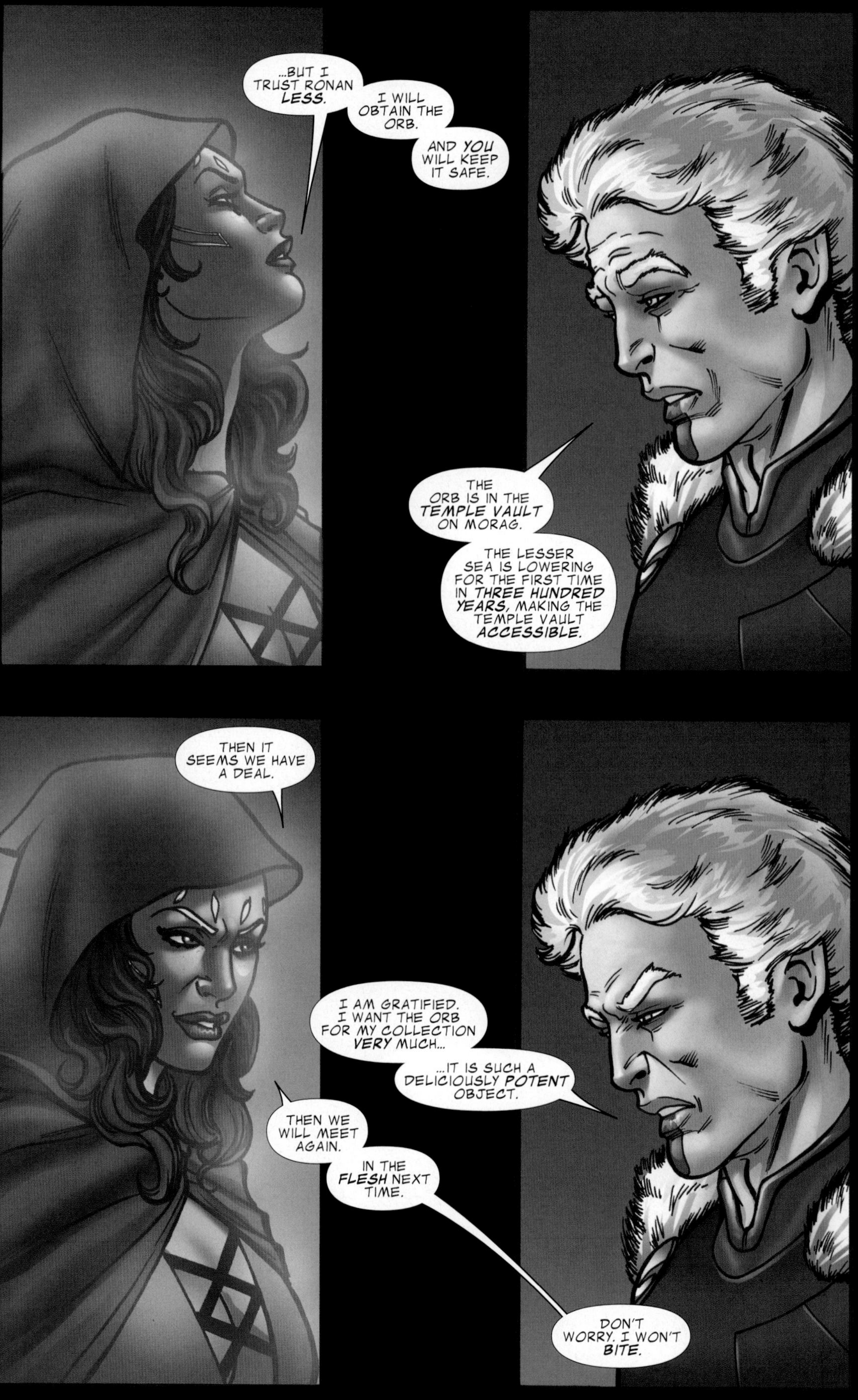
...BUT I TRUST RONAN LESS.
I WILL OBTAIN THE ORB.
AND YOU WILL KEEP IT SAFE.
THE ORB IS IN THE TEMPLE VAULT ON MORAG.
THE LESSER SEA IS LOWERING FOR THE FIRST TIME IN THREE HUNDRED YEARS, MAKING THE TEMPLE VAULT ACCESSIBLE.
THEN IT SEEMS WE HAVE A DEAL.
I AM GRATIFIED. I WANT THE ORB FOR MY COLLECTION VERY MUCH...
...IT IS SUCH A DELICIOUSLY POTENT OBJECT.
THEN WE WILL MEET AGAIN.
IN THE FLESH NEXT TIME.
DON'T WORRY. I WON'T BITE.

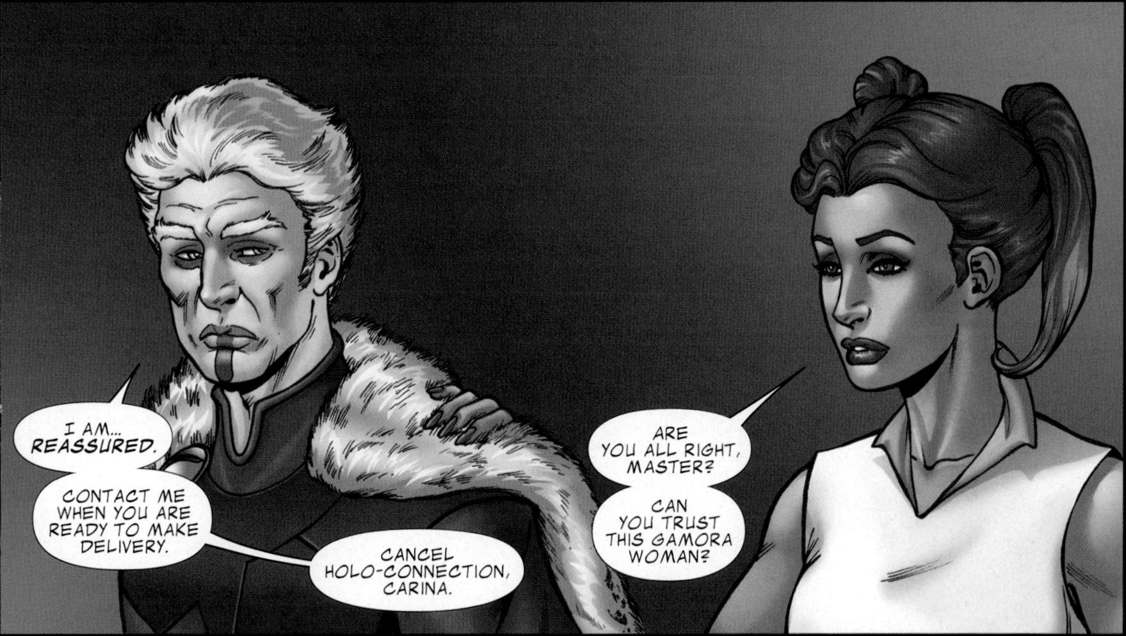
I AM... REASSURED.
CONTACT ME WHEN YOU ARE READY TO MAKE DELIVERY.
CANCEL HOLO-CONNECTION, CARINA.
ARE YOU ALL RIGHT, MASTER?
CAN YOU TRUST THIS GAMORA WOMAN?

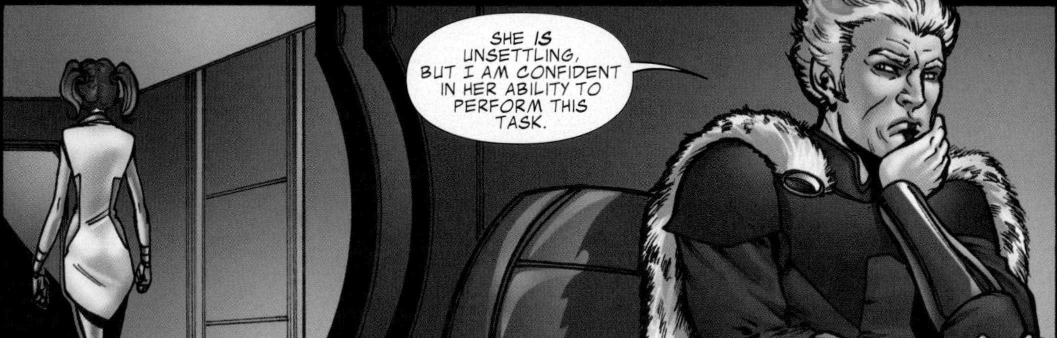
SHE IS UNSETTLING, BUT I AM CONFIDENT IN HER ABILITY TO PERFORM THIS TASK.

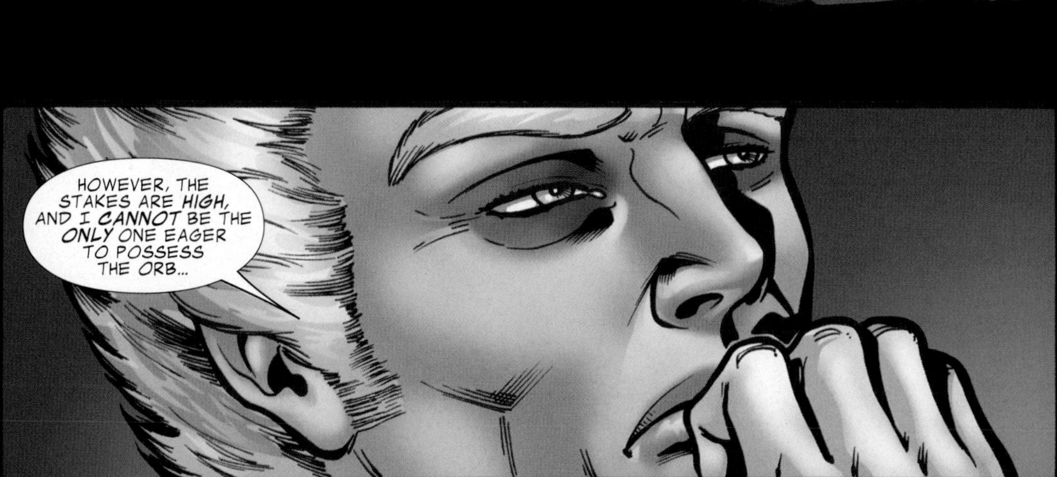
HOWEVER, THE STAKES ARE HIGH, AND I CANNOT BE THE ONLY ONE EAGER TO POSSESS THE ORB...

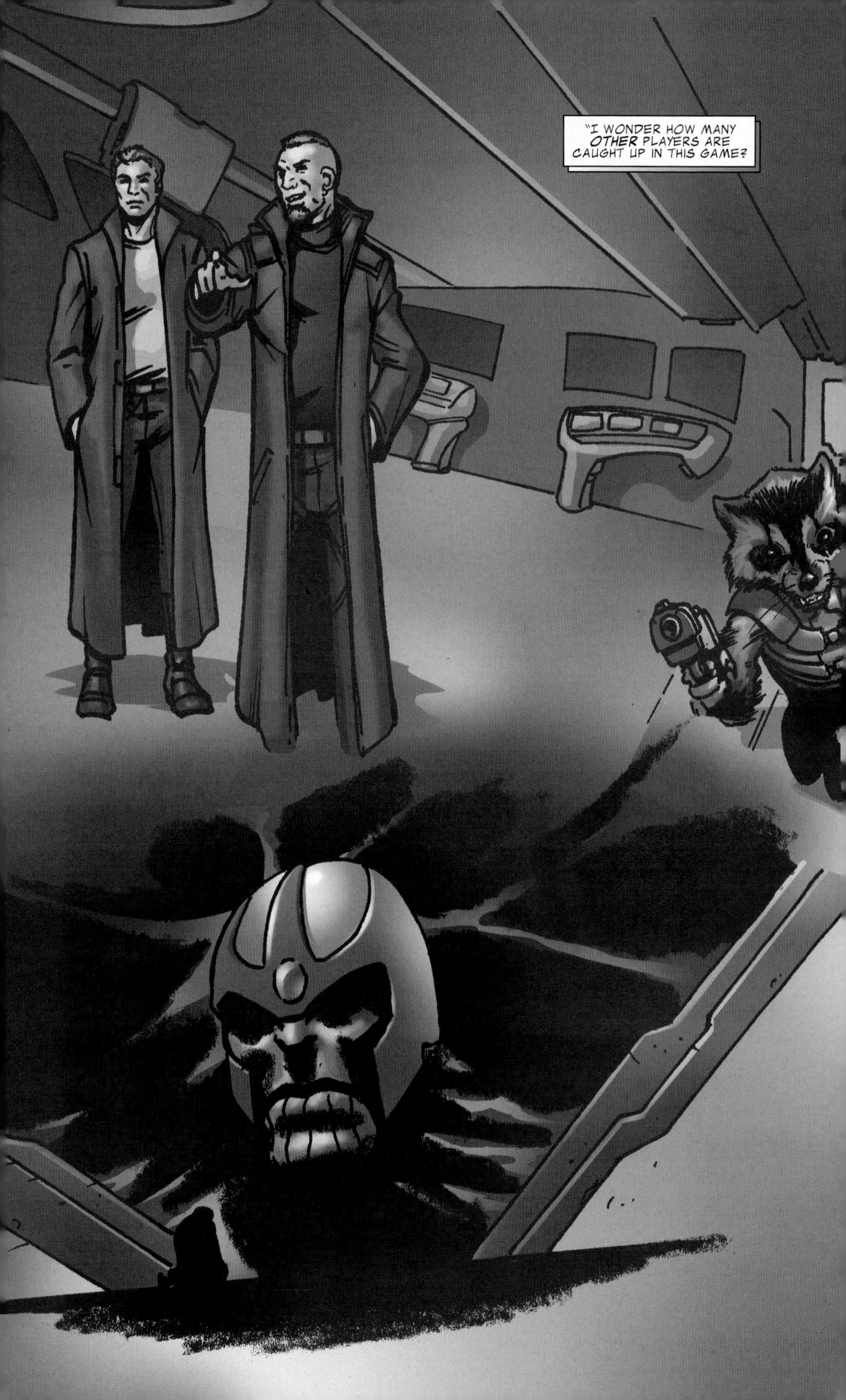
"I WONDER HOW MANY OTHER PLAYERS ARE CAUGHT UP IN THIS GAME?

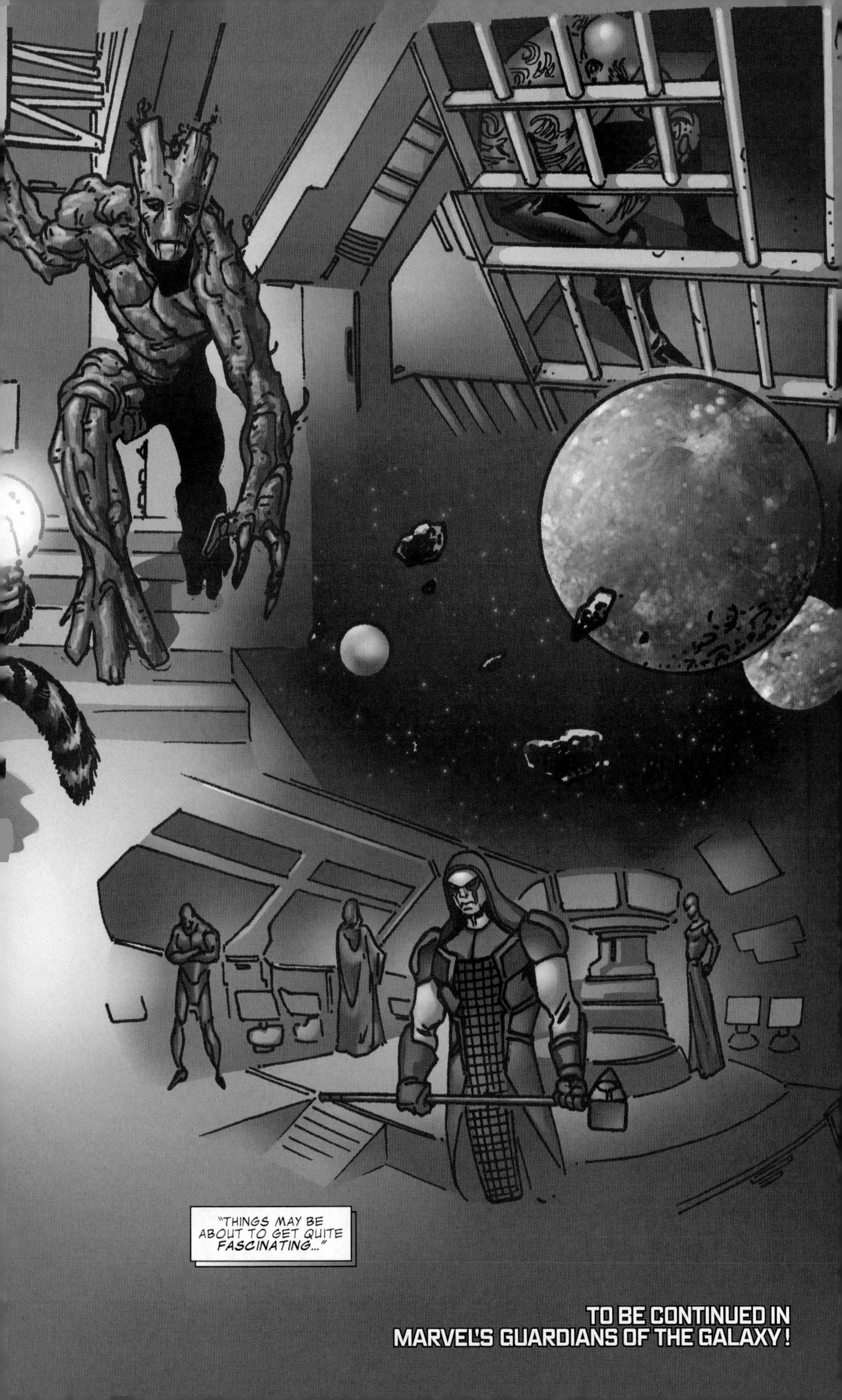
"THINGS MAY BE ABOUT TO GET QUITE FASCINATING..."
TO BE CONTINUED IN MARVEL'S GUARDIANS OF THE GALAXY!

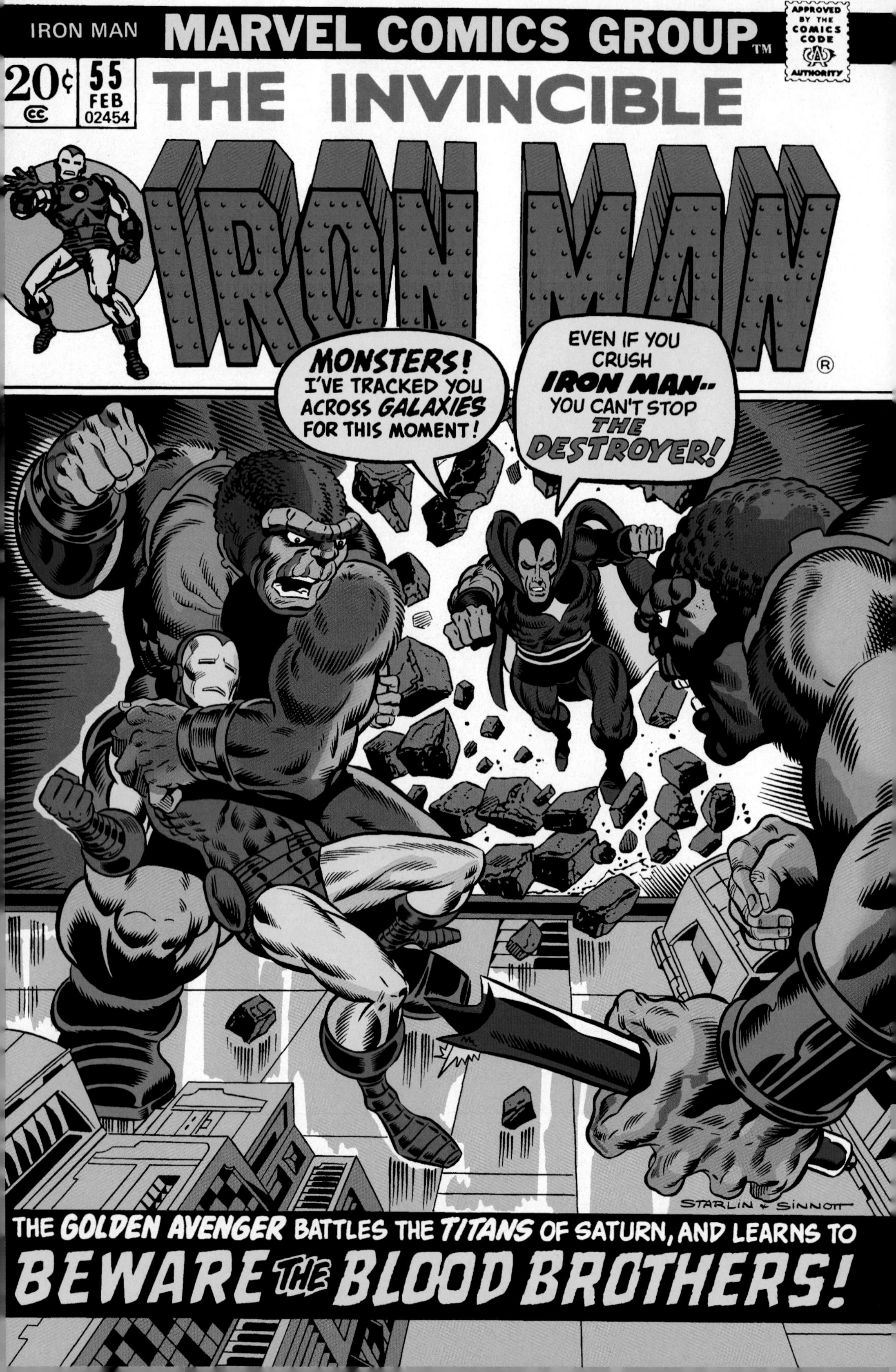
IRON MAN
MARVEL COMICS GROUP™
APPROVED BY THE COMICS CODE AUTHORITY
20¢
CC
55
FEB
02454
THE INVINCIBLE
IRON MAN®
MONSTERS! I'VE TRACKED YOU ACROSS GALAXIES FOR THIS MOMENT!
EVEN IF YOU CRUSH IRON MAN.. YOU CAN'T STOP THE DESTROYER!
STARLIN & SINNOTT
THE GOLDEN AVENGER BATTLES THE TITANS OF SATURN, AND LEARNS TO
BEWARE THE BLOOD BROTHERS!

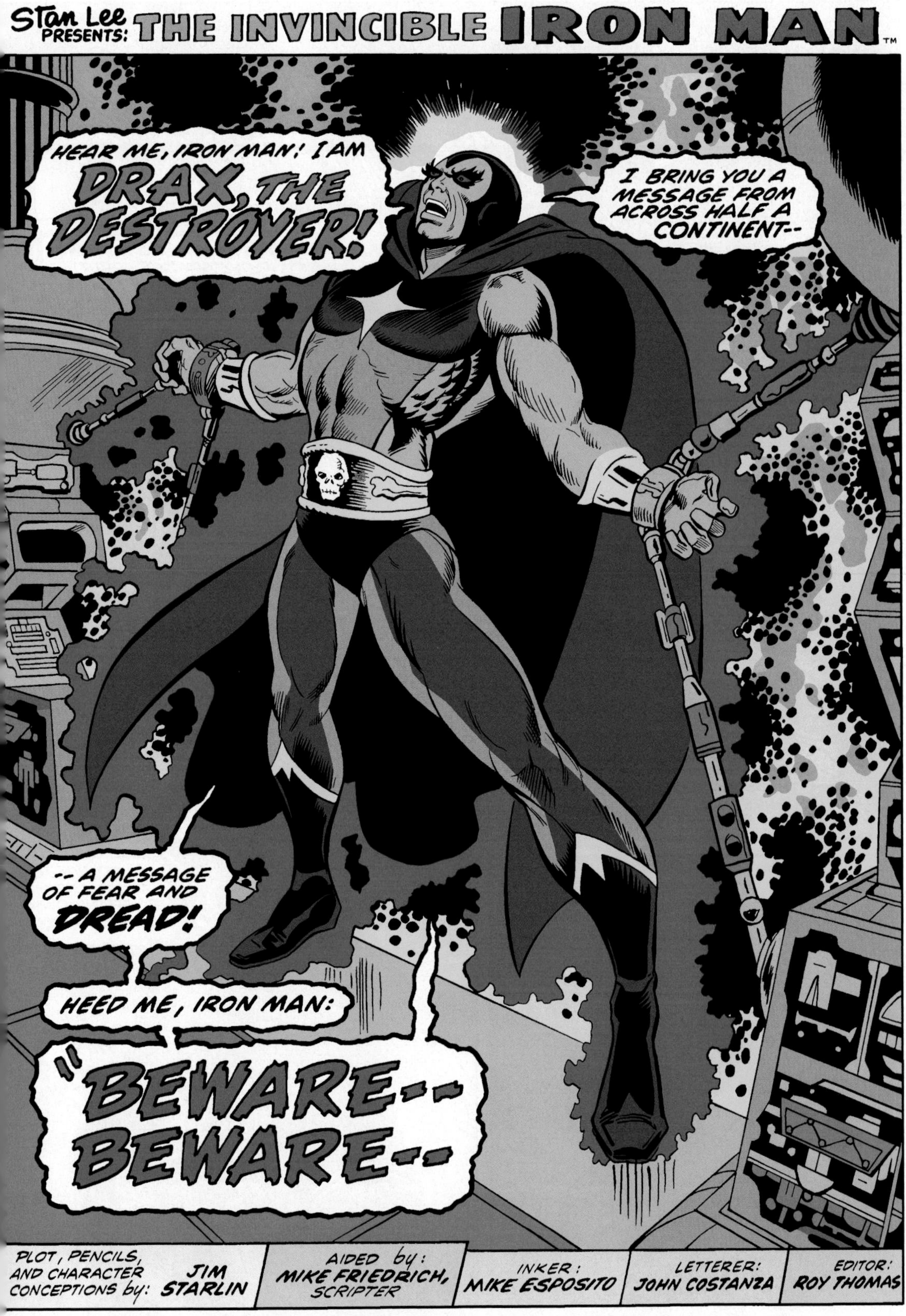
STAN LEE PRESENTS: THE INVINCIBLE IRON MAN™
HEAR ME, IRON MAN! I AM DRAX, THE DESTROYER!
I BRING YOU A MESSAGE FROM ACROSS HALF A CONTINENT--
-- A MESSAGE OF FEAR AND DREAD!
HEED ME, IRON MAN:
"BEWARE-- BEWARE--
PLOT, PENCILS, AND CHARACTER CONCEPTIONS BY: JIM STARLIN
AIDED BY: MIKE FRIEDRICH, SCRIPTER
INKER: MIKE ESPOSITO
LETTERER: JOHN COSTANZA
EDITOR: ROY THOMAS

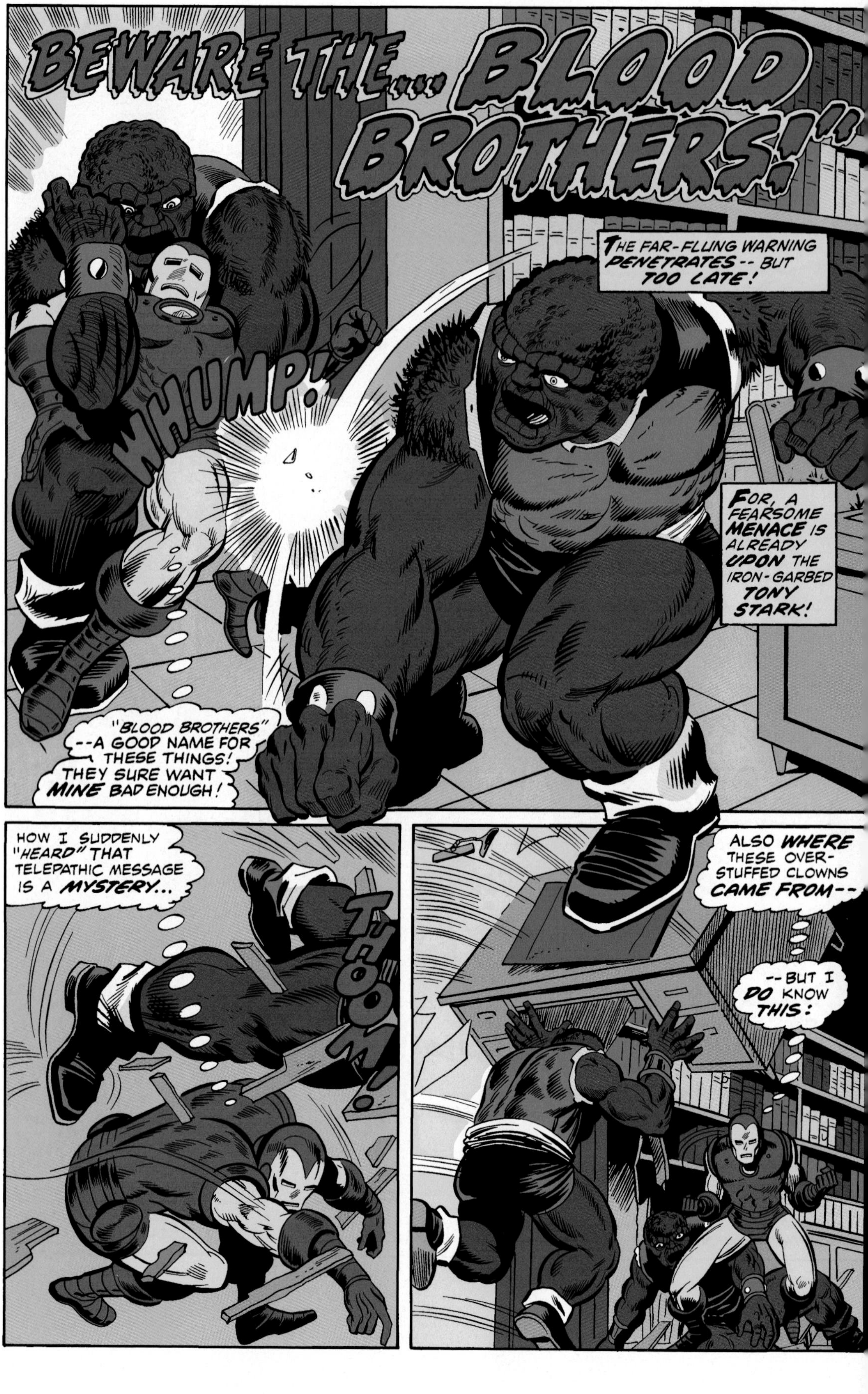
"BEWARE THE... BLOOD BROTHERS!"
THE FAR-FLUNG WARNING PENETRATES -- BUT TOO LATE!
WHUMP!
FOR, A FEARSOME MENACE IS ALREADY UPON THE IRON-GARBED TONY STARK!
"BLOOD BROTHERS" --A GOOD NAME FOR THESE THINGS! THEY SURE WANT MINE BAD ENOUGH!
HOW I SUDDENLY "HEARD" THAT TELEPATHIC MESSAGE IS A MYSTERY...
THOOM!
ALSO WHERE THESE OVER-STUFFED CLOWNS CAME FROM--
--BUT I DO KNOW THIS:

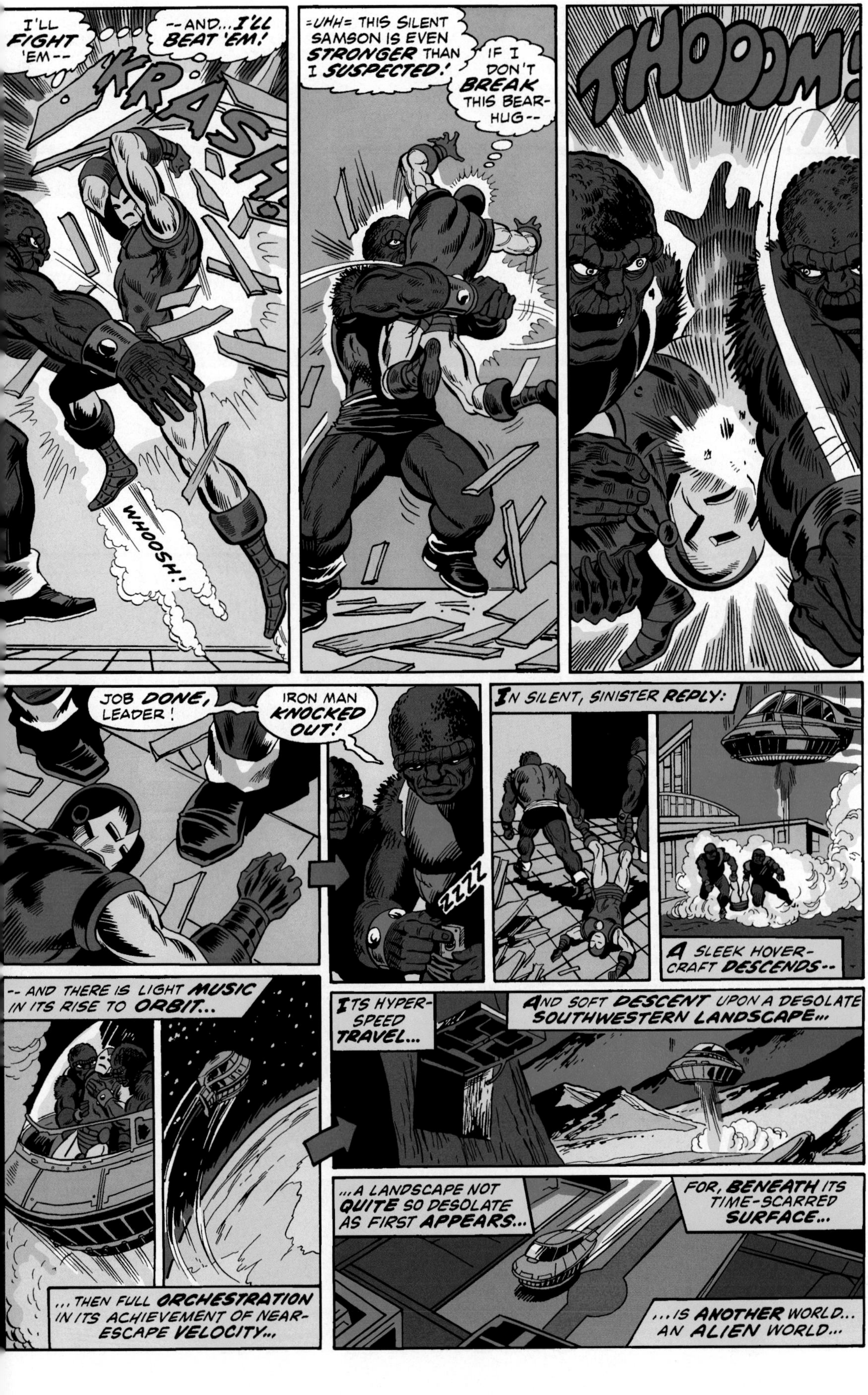

I'LL FIGHT 'EM --
-- AND... I'LL BEAT 'EM!
KRASH!
WHOOSH!
=UHH= THIS SILENT SAMSON IS EVEN STRONGER THAN I SUSPECTED!
IF I DON'T BREAK THIS BEAR-HUG --
THOOOM!
JOB DONE, LEADER!
IRON MAN KNOCKED OUT!
ZZZZ
IN SILENT, SINISTER REPLY:
A SLEEK HOVER-CRAFT DESCENDS --
-- AND THERE IS LIGHT MUSIC IN ITS RISE TO ORBIT...
...THEN FULL ORCHESTRATION IN ITS ACHIEVEMENT OF NEAR-ESCAPE VELOCITY...
ITS HYPER-SPEED TRAVEL...
AND SOFT DESCENT UPON A DESOLATE SOUTHWESTERN LANDSCAPE...
...A LANDSCAPE NOT QUITE SO DESOLATE AS FIRST APPEARS...
FOR, BENEATH ITS TIME-SCARRED SURFACE...
...IS ANOTHER WORLD... AN ALIEN WORLD...

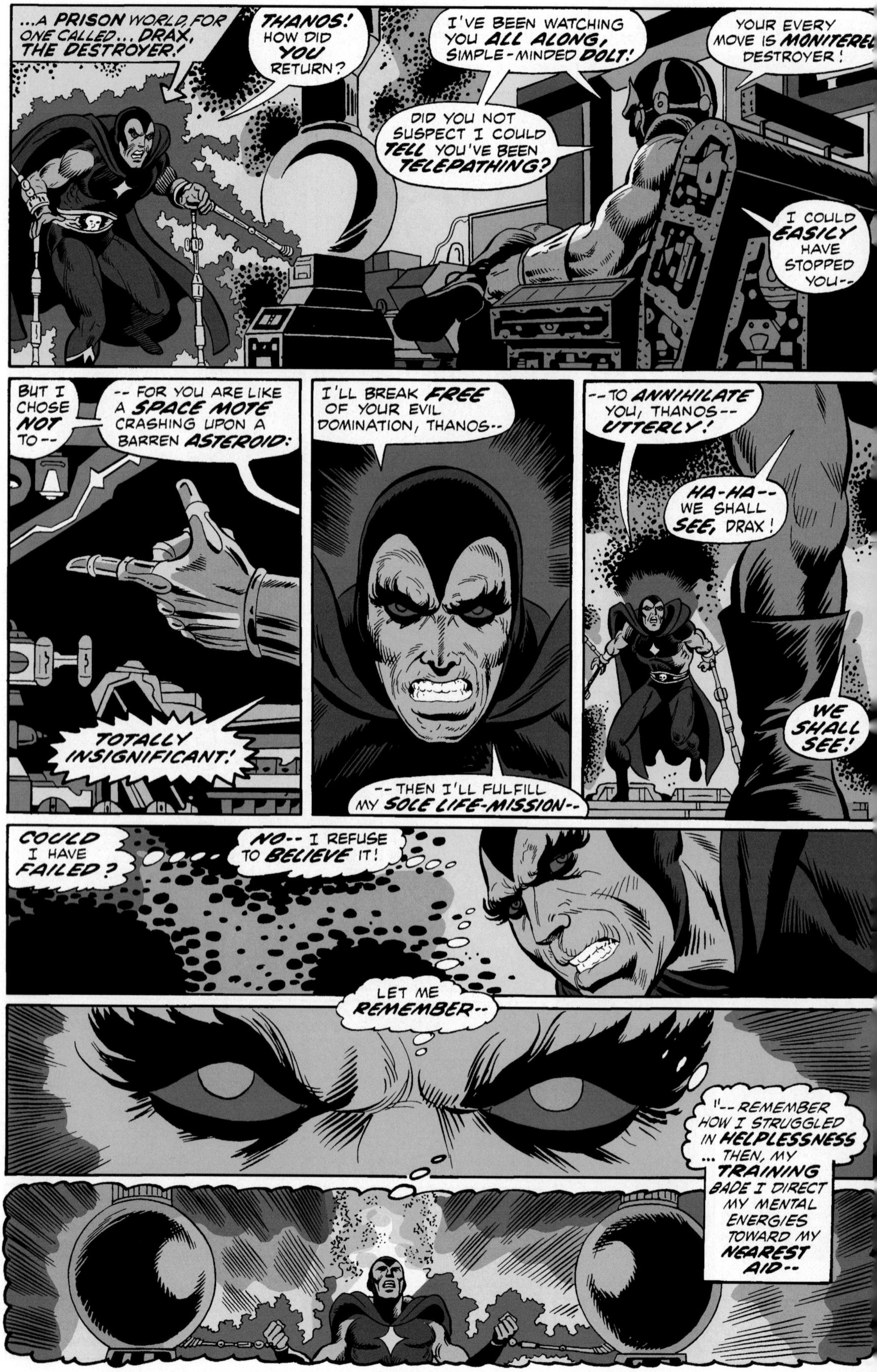
...A PRISON WORLD, FOR ONE CALLED... DRAX, THE DESTROYER!
THANOS! HOW DID YOU RETURN?
I'VE BEEN WATCHING YOU ALL ALONG, SIMPLE-MINDED DOLT!
DID YOU NOT SUSPECT I COULD TELL YOU'VE BEEN TELEPATHING?
YOUR EVERY MOVE IS MONITERED DESTROYER!
I COULD EASILY HAVE STOPPED YOU--
BUT I CHOSE NOT TO--
-- FOR YOU ARE LIKE A SPACE MOTE CRASHING UPON A BARREN ASTEROID:
TOTALLY INSIGNIFICANT!
I'LL BREAK FREE OF YOUR EVIL DOMINATION, THANOS--
--THEN I'LL FULFILL MY SOLE LIFE-MISSION--
--TO ANNIHILATE YOU, THANOS-- UTTERLY!
HA-HA-- WE SHALL SEE, DRAX!
WE SHALL SEE!
COULD I HAVE FAILED?
NO-- I REFUSE TO BELIEVE IT!
LET ME REMEMBER--
"--REMEMBER HOW I STRUGGLED IN HELPLESSNESS ... THEN, MY TRAINING BADE I DIRECT MY MENTAL ENERGIES TOWARD MY NEAREST AID--

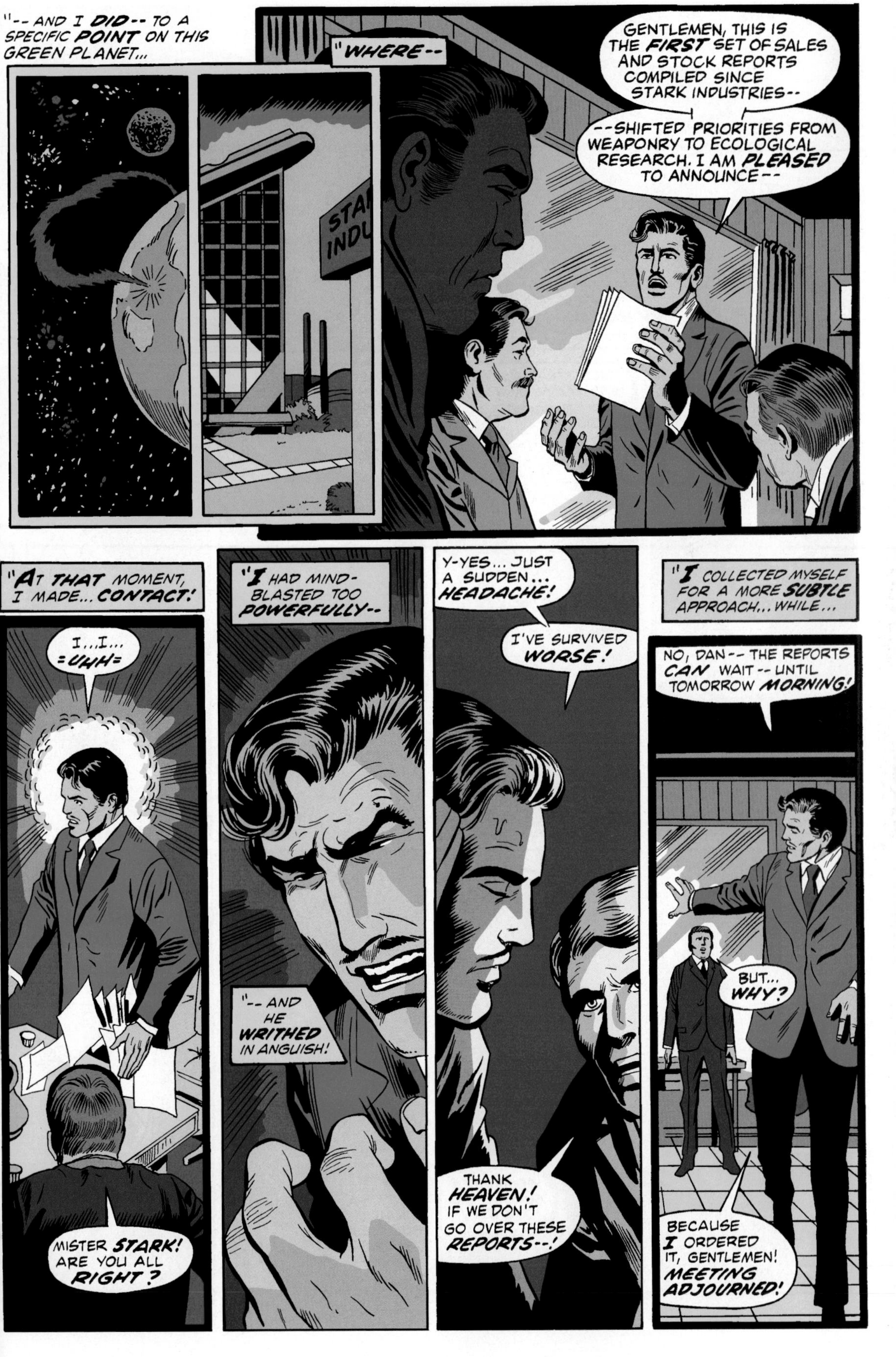
"-- AND I DID -- TO A SPECIFIC POINT ON THIS GREEN PLANET...
STA INDU
"WHERE --
GENTLEMEN, THIS IS THE FIRST SET OF SALES AND STOCK REPORTS COMPILED SINCE STARK INDUSTRIES --
-- SHIFTED PRIORITIES FROM WEAPONRY TO ECOLOGICAL RESEARCH. I AM PLEASED TO ANNOUNCE --
"AT THAT MOMENT, I MADE... CONTACT!
I...I... =UHH=
MISTER STARK! ARE YOU ALL RIGHT?
"I HAD MIND-BLASTED TOO POWERFULLY --
"-- AND HE WRITHED IN ANGUISH!
Y-YES... JUST A SUDDEN... HEADACHE!
I'VE SURVIVED WORSE!
THANK HEAVEN! IF WE DON'T GO OVER THESE REPORTS --!
"I COLLECTED MYSELF FOR A MORE SUBTLE APPROACH... WHILE...
NO, DAN -- THE REPORTS CAN WAIT -- UNTIL TOMORROW MORNING!
BUT... WHY?
BECAUSE I ORDERED IT, GENTLEMEN! MEETING ADJOURNED!

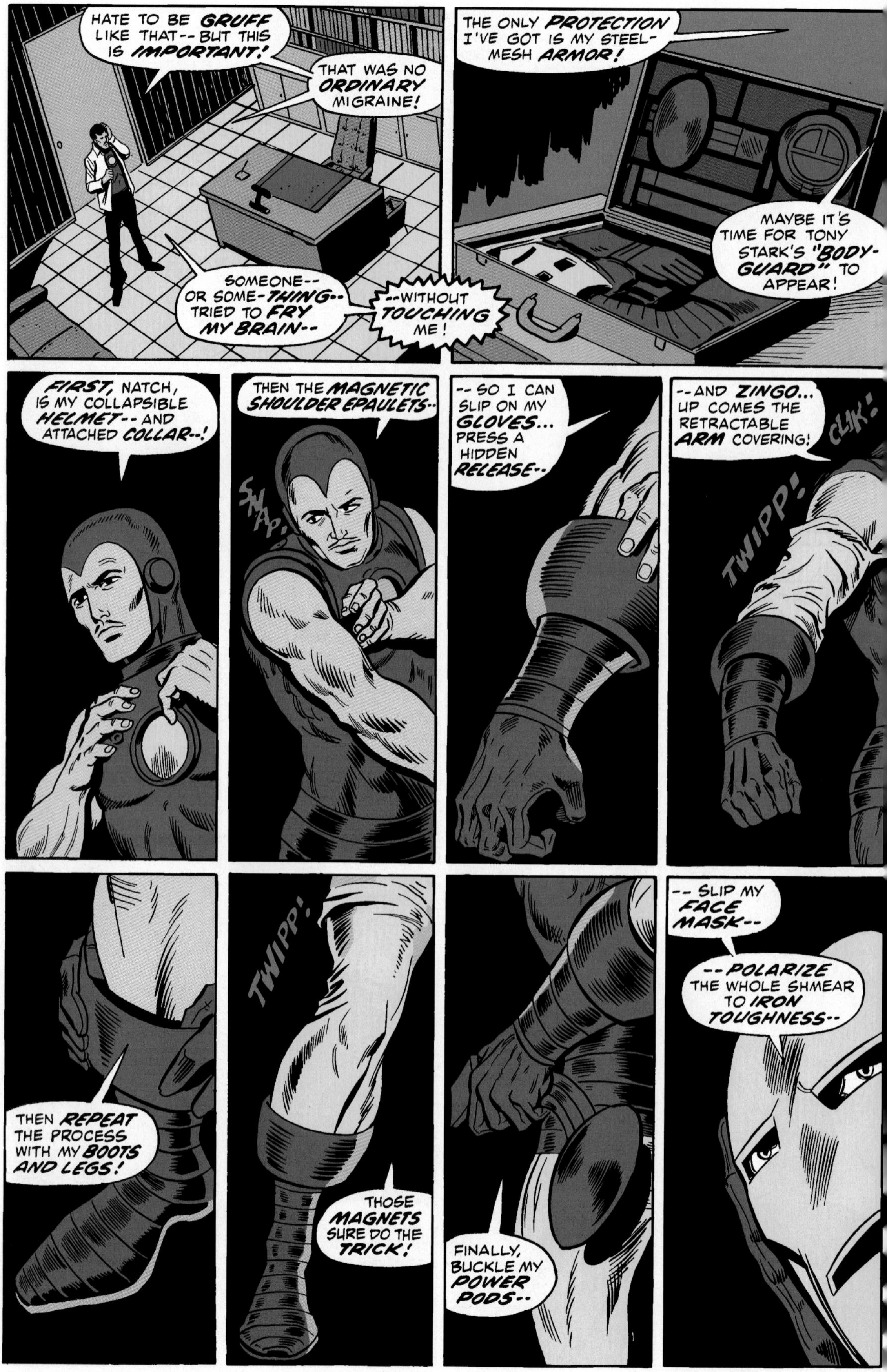

HATE TO BE GRUFF LIKE THAT-- BUT THIS IS IMPORTANT!
THAT WAS NO ORDINARY MIGRAINE!
SOMEONE-- OR SOME-THING-- TRIED TO FRY MY BRAIN--
--WITHOUT TOUCHING ME!
THE ONLY PROTECTION I'VE GOT IS MY STEEL-MESH ARMOR!
MAYBE IT'S TIME FOR TONY STARK'S "BODY-GUARD" TO APPEAR!
FIRST, NATCH, IS MY COLLAPSIBLE HELMET-- AND ATTACHED COLLAR--!
THEN THE MAGNETIC SHOULDER EPAULETS--
SNAP!
-- SO I CAN SLIP ON MY GLOVES... PRESS A HIDDEN RELEASE--
--AND ZINGO... UP COMES THE RETRACTABLE ARM COVERING!
CLIK!
TWIPP!
THEN REPEAT THE PROCESS WITH MY BOOTS AND LEGS!
TWIPP!
THOSE MAGNETS SURE DO THE TRICK!
FINALLY, BUCKLE MY POWER PODS--
-- SLIP MY FACE MASK--
--POLARIZE THE WHOLE SHMEAR TO IRON TOUGHNESS--

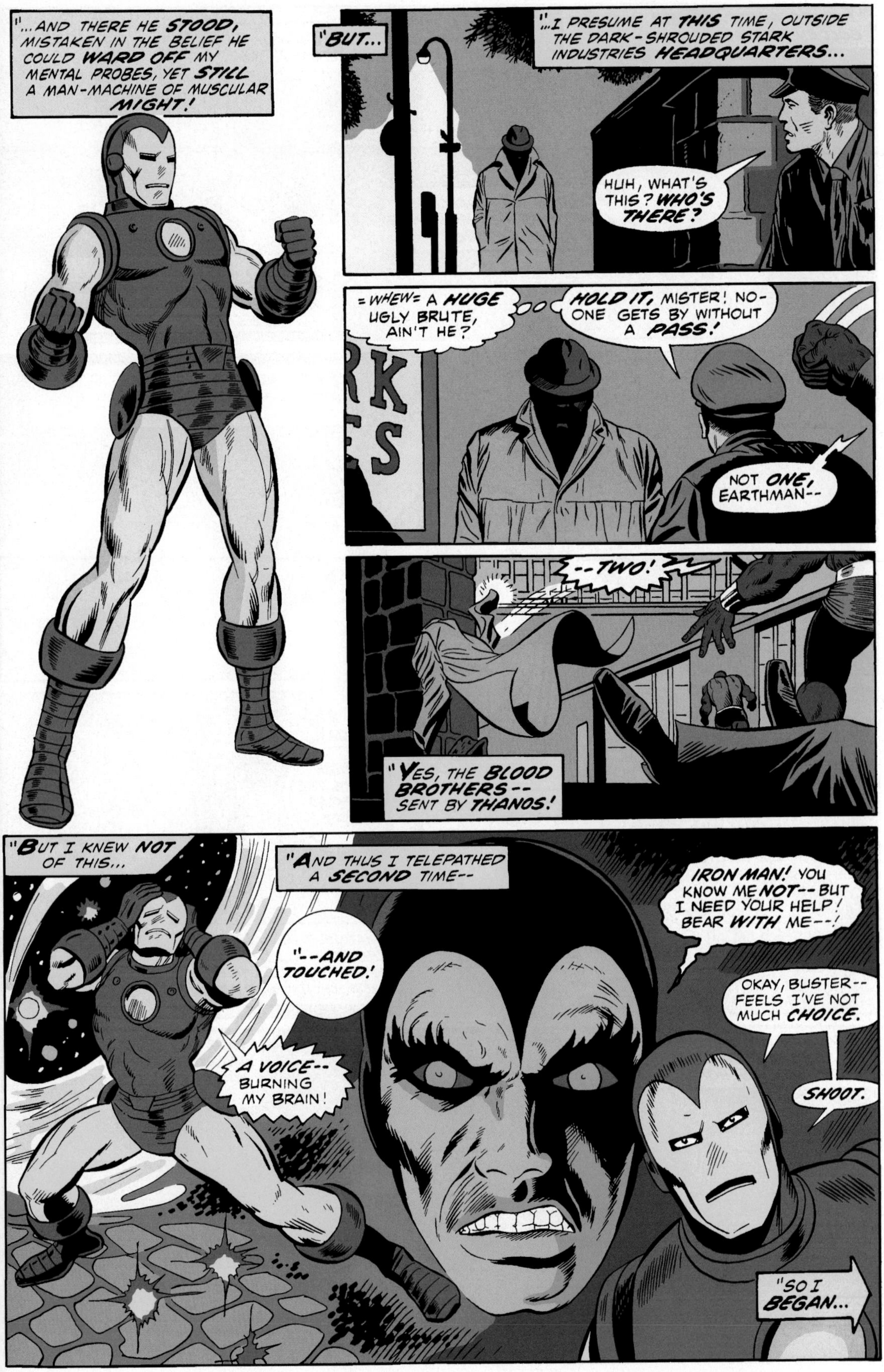
"...AND THERE HE STOOD, MISTAKEN IN THE BELIEF HE COULD WARD OFF MY MENTAL PROBES, YET STILL A MAN-MACHINE OF MUSCULAR MIGHT!
"BUT...
"...I PRESUME AT THIS TIME, OUTSIDE THE DARK-SHROUDED STARK INDUSTRIES HEADQUARTERS...
HUH, WHAT'S THIS? WHO'S THERE?
=WHEW= A HUGE UGLY BRUTE, AIN'T HE?
HOLD IT, MISTER! NO-ONE GETS BY WITHOUT A PASS!
NOT ONE, EARTHMAN--
--TWO!
"YES, THE BLOOD BROTHERS--SENT BY THANOS!
"BUT I KNEW NOT OF THIS...
"AND THUS I TELEPATHED A SECOND TIME--
"--AND TOUCHED!
A VOICE--BURNING MY BRAIN!
IRON MAN! YOU KNOW ME NOT--BUT I NEED YOUR HELP! BEAR WITH ME--!
OKAY, BUSTER--FEELS I'VE NOT MUCH CHOICE.
SHOOT.
"SO I BEGAN...

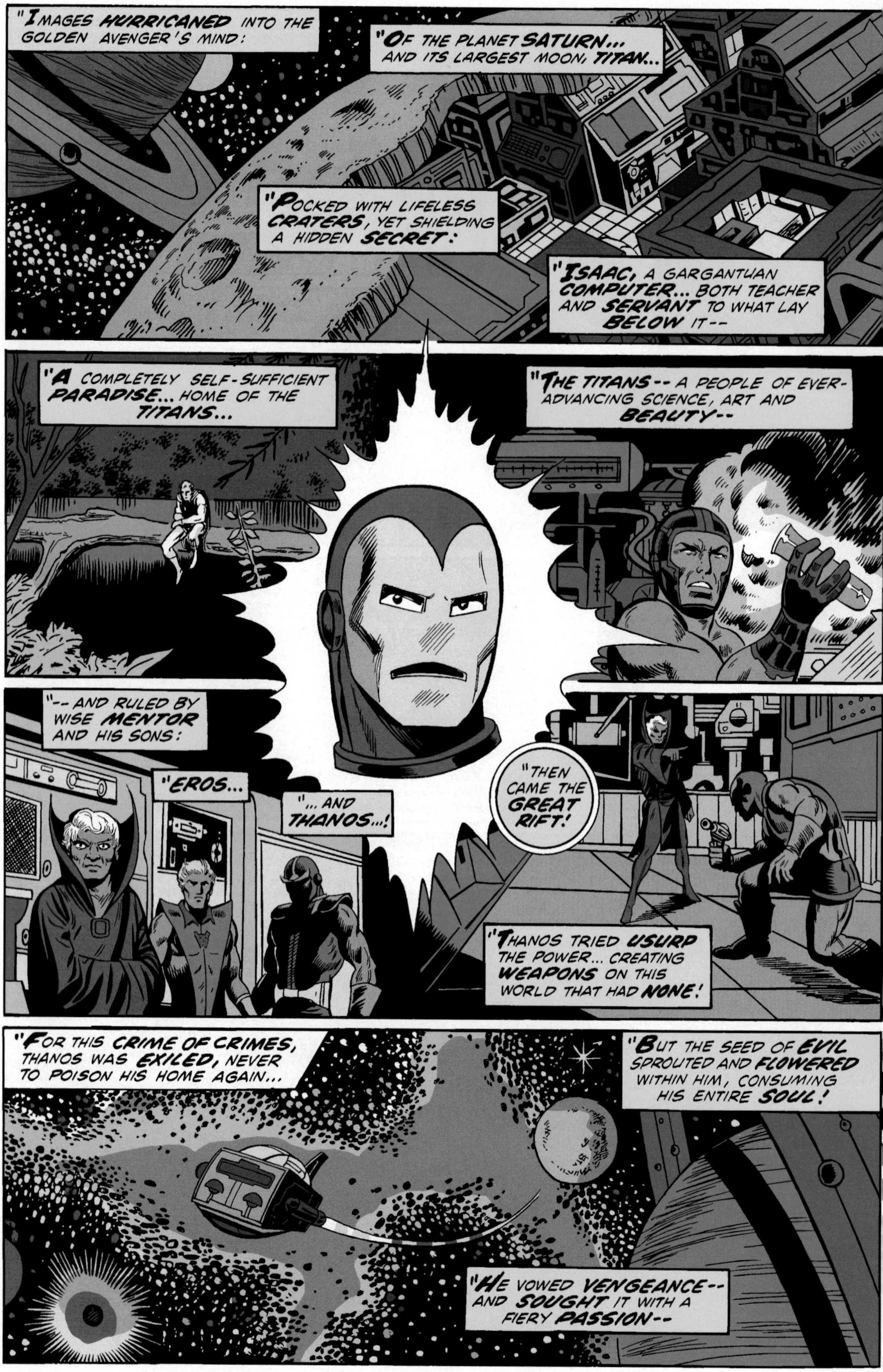
"IMAGES HURRICANED INTO THE GOLDEN AVENGER'S MIND:
"OF THE PLANET SATURN... AND ITS LARGEST MOON, TITAN...
"POCKED WITH LIFELESS CRATERS, YET SHIELDING A HIDDEN SECRET:
"ISAAC, A GARGANTUAN COMPUTER... BOTH TEACHER AND SERVANT TO WHAT LAY BELOW IT--
"A COMPLETELY SELF-SUFFICIENT PARADISE... HOME OF THE TITANS...
"THE TITANS-- A PEOPLE OF EVER-ADVANCING SCIENCE, ART AND BEAUTY--
"-- AND RULED BY WISE MENTOR AND HIS SONS:
"EROS...
"... AND THANOS...!
"THEN CAME THE GREAT RIFT!
"THANOS TRIED USURP THE POWER... CREATING WEAPONS ON THIS WORLD THAT HAD NONE!
"FOR THIS CRIME OF CRIMES, THANOS WAS EXILED, NEVER TO POISON HIS HOME AGAIN...
"BUT THE SEED OF EVIL SPROUTED AND FLOWERED WITHIN HIM, CONSUMING HIS ENTIRE SOUL!
"HE VOWED VENGEANCE-- AND SOUGHT IT WITH A FIERY PASSION--

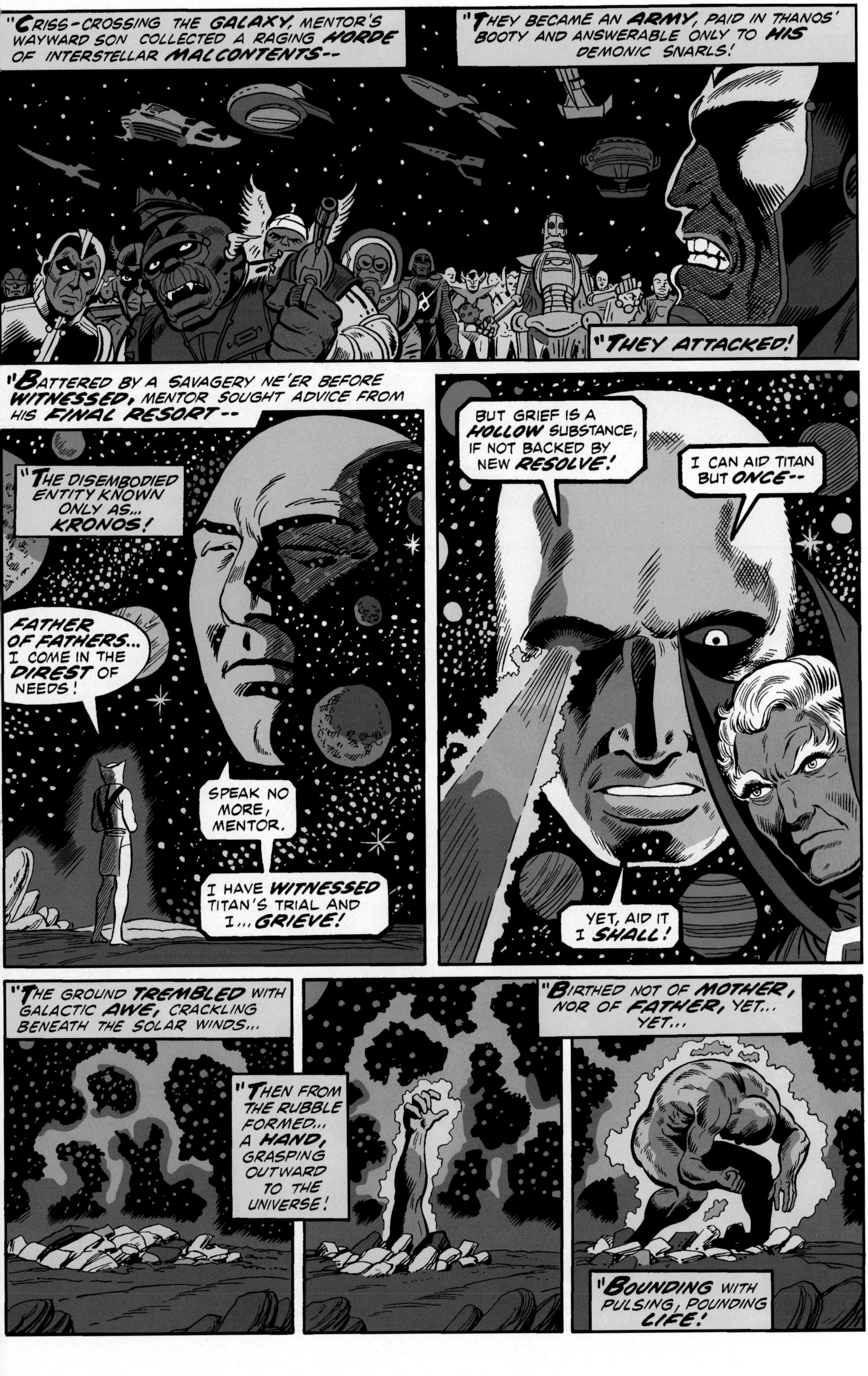
"Criss-crossing the GALAXY, Mentor's wayward son collected a raging HORDE of interstellar MALCONTENTS--
"They became an ARMY, paid in Thanos' booty and answerable only to HIS demonic snarls!
"THEY ATTACKED!
"Battered by a savagery ne'er before WITNESSED, Mentor sought advice from his FINAL RESORT--
"The disembodied entity known only as... KRONOS!
FATHER OF FATHERS... I COME IN THE DIREST OF NEEDS!
SPEAK NO MORE, MENTOR.
I HAVE WITNESSED TITAN'S TRIAL AND I... GRIEVE!
BUT GRIEF IS A HOLLOW SUBSTANCE, IF NOT BACKED BY NEW RESOLVE!
I CAN AID TITAN BUT ONCE--
YET, AID IT I SHALL!
"The ground TREMBLED with galactic AWE, crackling beneath the solar winds...
"Then from the rubble formed... a HAND, grasping outward to the universe!
"Birthed not of MOTHER, nor of FATHER, yet... yet...
"BOUNDING with pulsing, pounding LIFE!

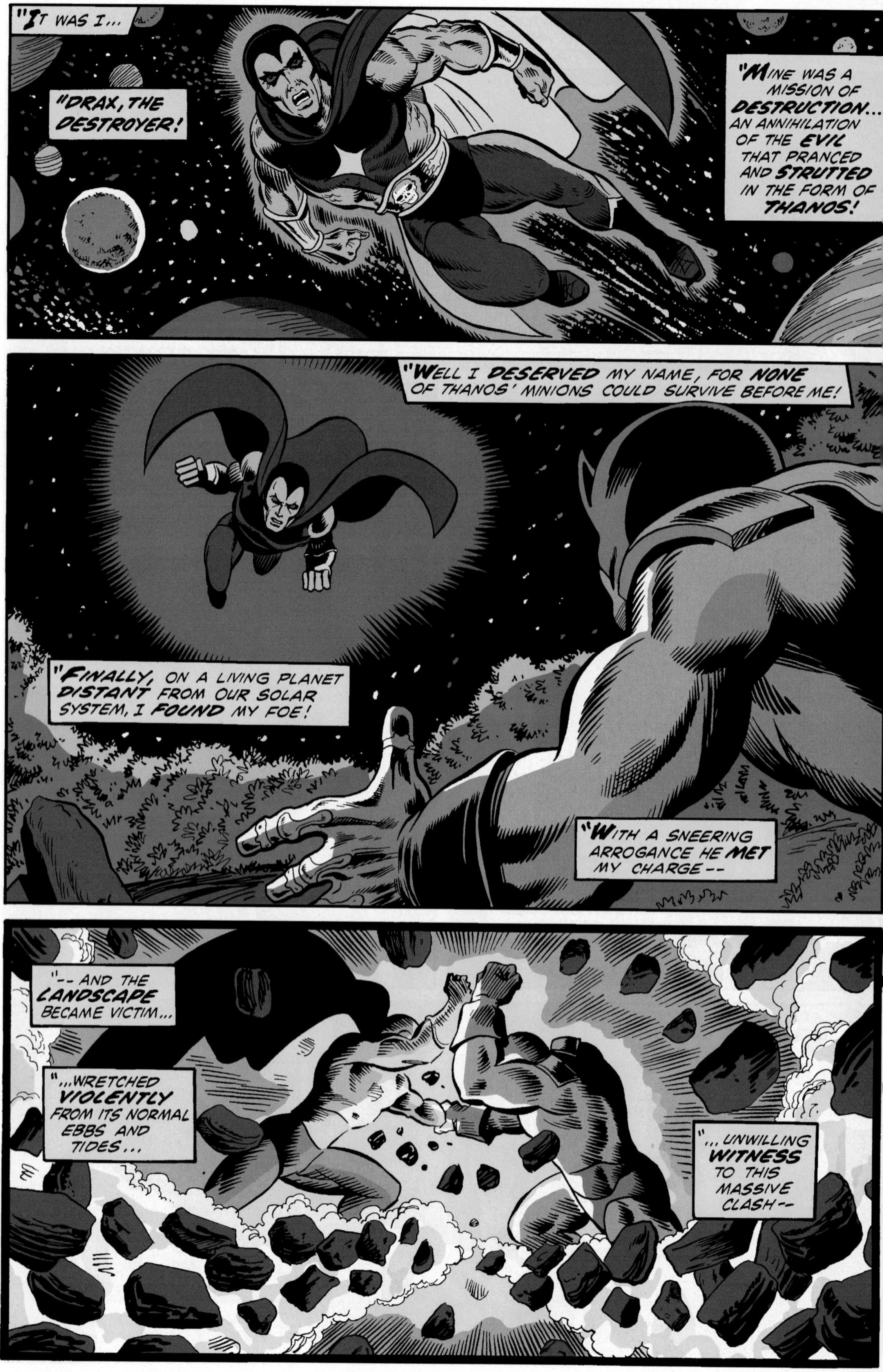
"IT WAS I...
"DRAX, THE DESTROYER!
"MINE WAS A MISSION OF DESTRUCTION... AN ANNIHILATION OF THE EVIL THAT PRANCED AND STRUTTED IN THE FORM OF THANOS!
"WELL I DESERVED MY NAME, FOR NONE OF THANOS' MINIONS COULD SURVIVE BEFORE ME!
"FINALLY, ON A LIVING PLANET DISTANT FROM OUR SOLAR SYSTEM, I FOUND MY FOE!
"WITH A SNEERING ARROGANCE HE MET MY CHARGE--
"-- AND THE LANDSCAPE BECAME VICTIM...
"...WRETCHED VIOLENTLY FROM ITS NORMAL EBBS AND TIDES...
"...UNWILLING WITNESS TO THIS MASSIVE CLASH--

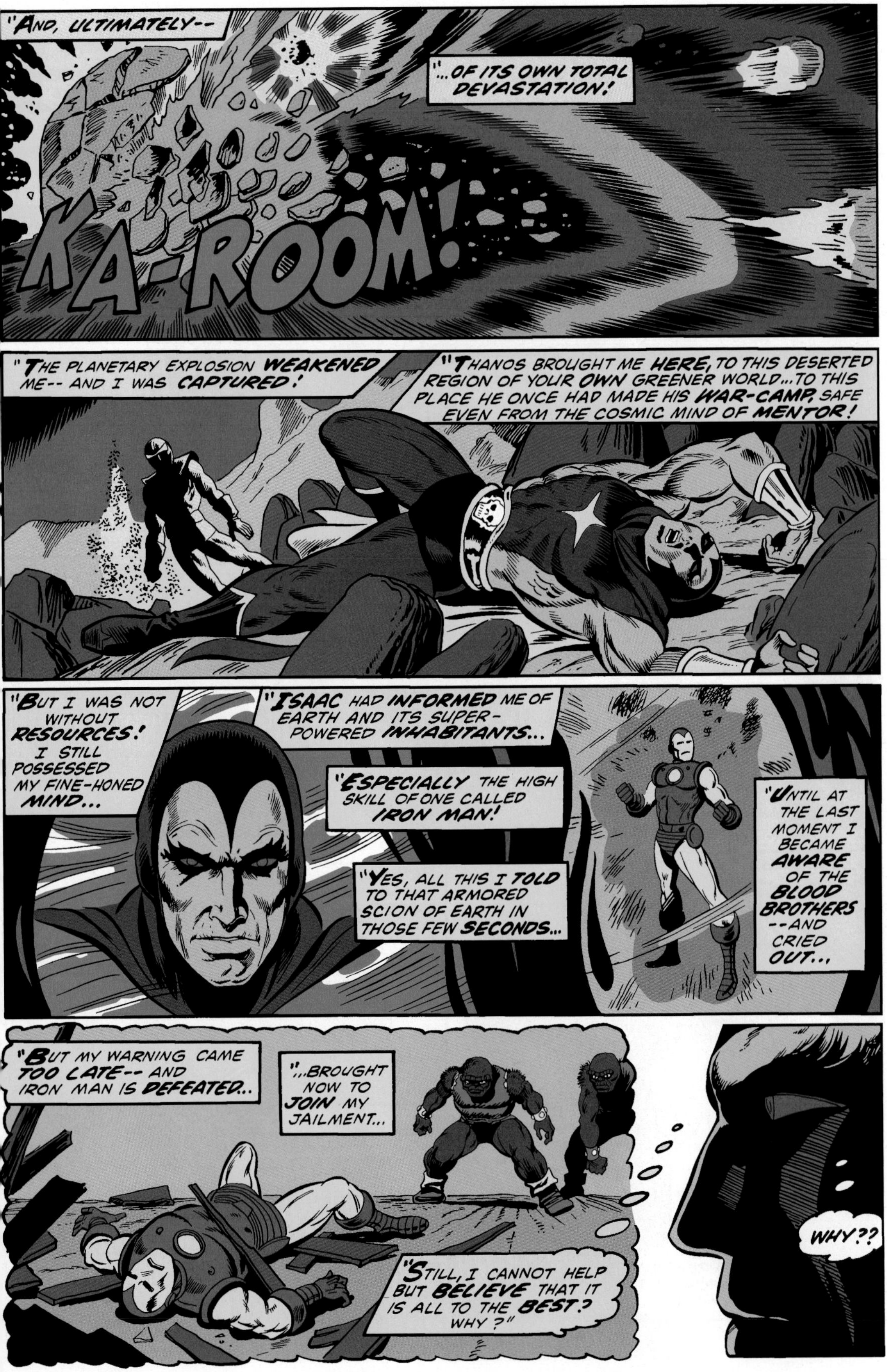
"AND, ULTIMATELY--
"...OF ITS OWN TOTAL DEVASTATION!
KA-ROOM!
"THE PLANETARY EXPLOSION WEAKENED ME-- AND I WAS CAPTURED!
"THANOS BROUGHT ME HERE, TO THIS DESERTED REGION OF YOUR OWN GREENER WORLD...TO THIS PLACE HE ONCE HAD MADE HIS WAR-CAMP, SAFE EVEN FROM THE COSMIC MIND OF MENTOR!
"BUT I WAS NOT WITHOUT RESOURCES! I STILL POSSESSED MY FINE-HONED MIND...
"ISAAC HAD INFORMED ME OF EARTH AND ITS SUPER-POWERED INHABITANTS...
"ESPECIALLY THE HIGH SKILL OF ONE CALLED IRON MAN!
"YES, ALL THIS I TOLD TO THAT ARMORED SCION OF EARTH IN THOSE FEW SECONDS...
"UNTIL AT THE LAST MOMENT I BECAME AWARE OF THE BLOOD BROTHERS --AND CRIED OUT...
"BUT MY WARNING CAME TOO LATE-- AND IRON MAN IS DEFEATED...
"...BROUGHT NOW TO JOIN MY JAILMENT...
"STILL, I CANNOT HELP BUT BELIEVE THAT IT IS ALL TO THE BEST? WHY?"
WHY??

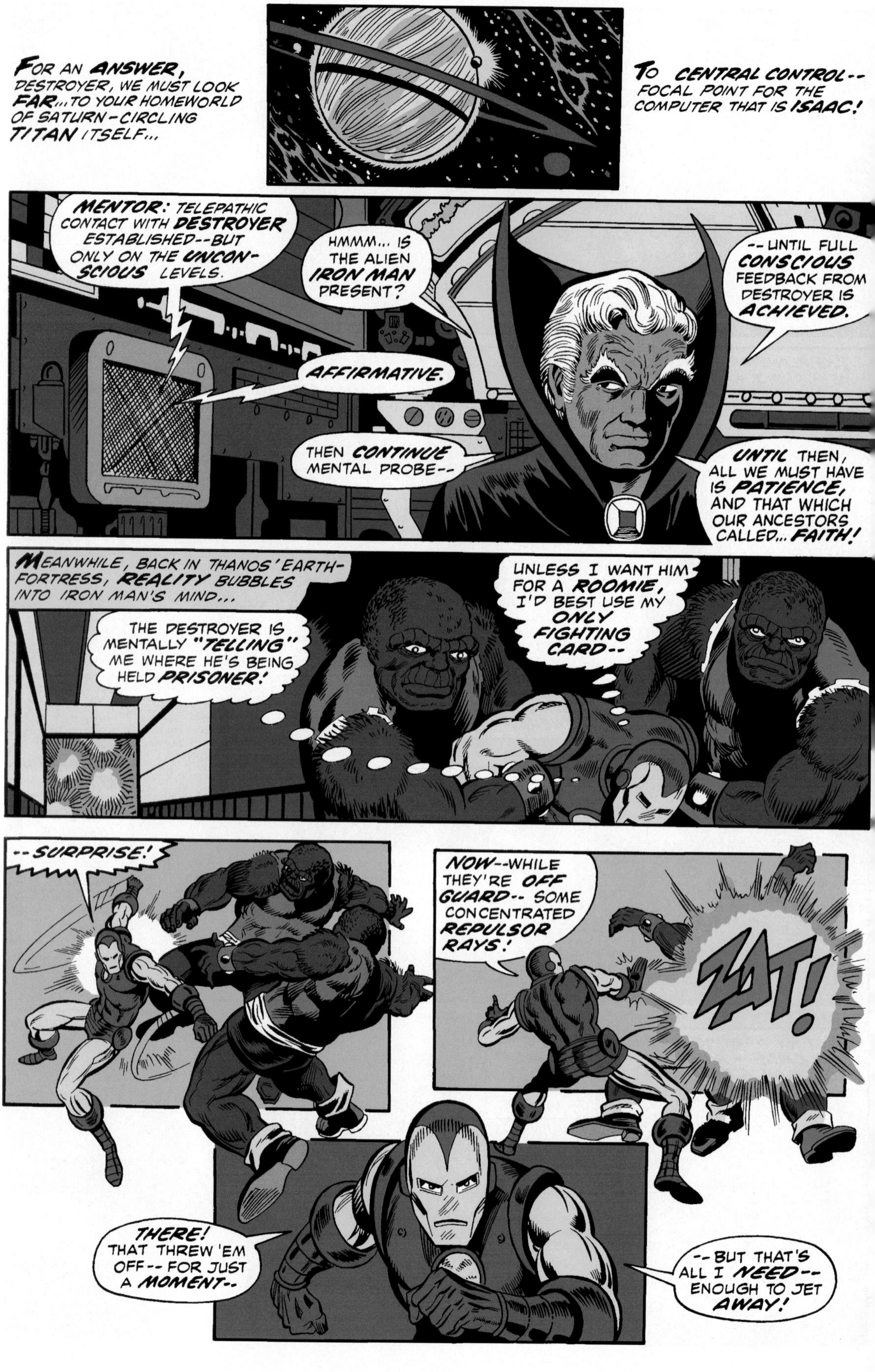

FOR AN ANSWER, DESTROYER, WE MUST LOOK FAR...TO YOUR HOMEWORLD OF SATURN-CIRCLING TITAN ITSELF...
TO CENTRAL CONTROL-- FOCAL POINT FOR THE COMPUTER THAT IS ISAAC!
MENTOR: TELEPATHIC CONTACT WITH DESTROYER ESTABLISHED--BUT ONLY ON THE UNCONSCIOUS LEVELS.
HMMM... IS THE ALIEN IRON MAN PRESENT?
AFFIRMATIVE.
THEN CONTINUE MENTAL PROBE--
--UNTIL FULL CONSCIOUS FEEDBACK FROM DESTROYER IS ACHIEVED.
UNTIL THEN, ALL WE MUST HAVE IS PATIENCE, AND THAT WHICH OUR ANCESTORS CALLED... FAITH!
MEANWHILE, BACK IN THANOS' EARTH-FORTRESS, REALITY BUBBLES INTO IRON MAN'S MIND...
THE DESTROYER IS MENTALLY "TELLING" ME WHERE HE'S BEING HELD PRISONER!
UNLESS I WANT HIM FOR A ROOMIE, I'D BEST USE MY ONLY FIGHTING CARD--
--SURPRISE!
NOW--WHILE THEY'RE OFF GUARD-- SOME CONCENTRATED REPULSOR RAYS!
ZAT!
THERE! THAT THREW 'EM OFF-- FOR JUST A MOMENT--
--BUT THAT'S ALL I NEED-- ENOUGH TO JET AWAY!

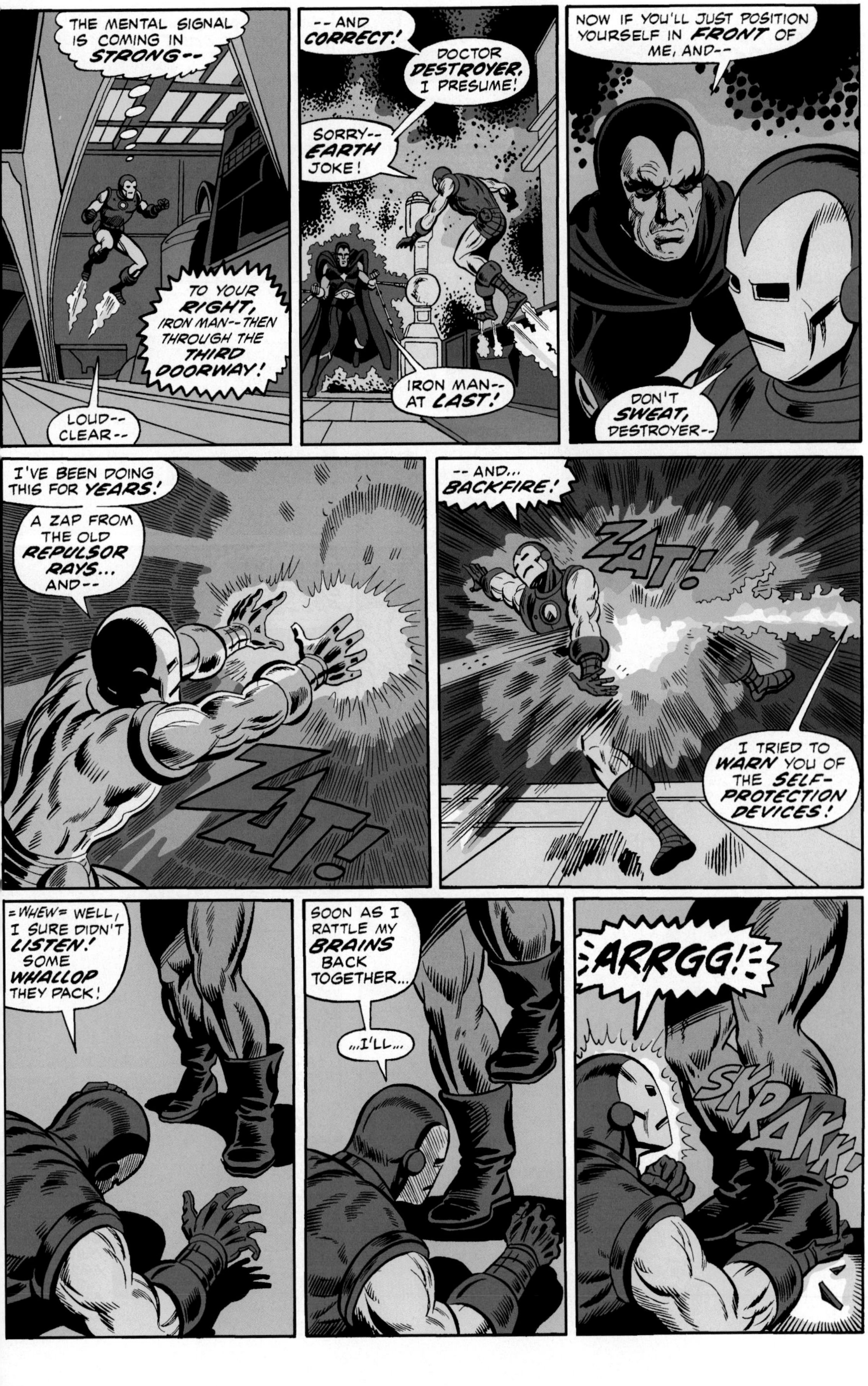
THE MENTAL SIGNAL IS COMING IN STRONG--
TO YOUR RIGHT, IRON MAN--THEN THROUGH THE THIRD DOORWAY!
LOUD--CLEAR--
--AND CORRECT!
DOCTOR DESTROYER, I PRESUME!
SORRY--EARTH JOKE!
IRON MAN--AT LAST!
NOW IF YOU'LL JUST POSITION YOURSELF IN FRONT OF ME, AND--
DON'T SWEAT, DESTROYER--
I'VE BEEN DOING THIS FOR YEARS!
A ZAP FROM THE OLD REPULSOR RAYS... AND--
ZAT!
--AND... BACKFIRE!
ZAT!
I TRIED TO WARN YOU OF THE SELF-PROTECTION DEVICES!
=WHEW= WELL, I SURE DIDN'T LISTEN! SOME WHALLOP THEY PACK!
SOON AS I RATTLE MY BRAINS BACK TOGETHER...
...I'LL...
ARRGG!
SKRAKK!

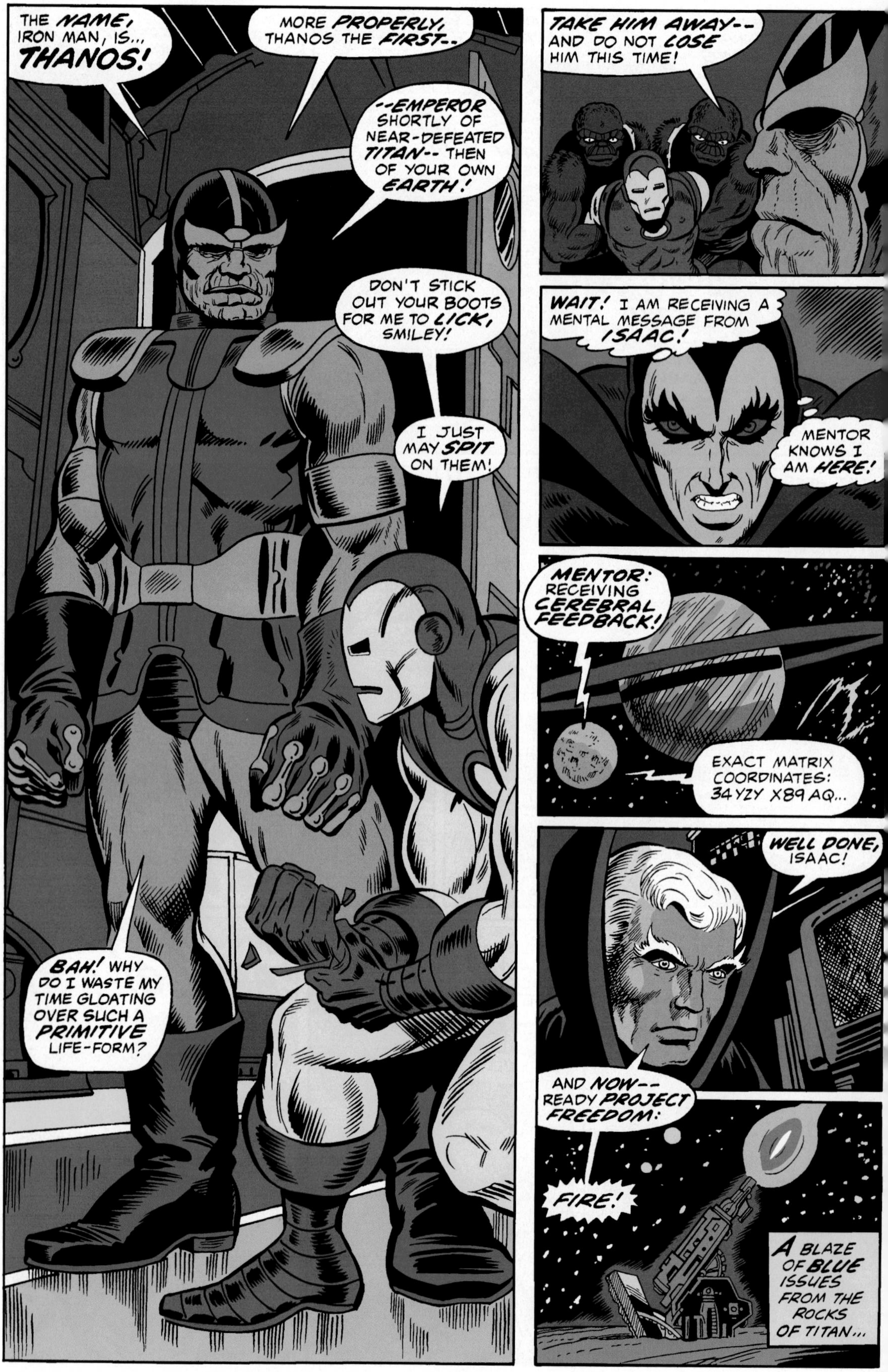
THE NAME, IRON MAN, IS... THANOS!
MORE PROPERLY, THANOS THE FIRST--
--EMPEROR SHORTLY OF NEAR-DEFEATED TITAN-- THEN OF YOUR OWN EARTH!
DON'T STICK OUT YOUR BOOTS FOR ME TO LICK, SMILEY!
I JUST MAY SPIT ON THEM!
BAH! WHY DO I WASTE MY TIME GLOATING OVER SUCH A PRIMITIVE LIFE-FORM?
TAKE HIM AWAY-- AND DO NOT COSE HIM THIS TIME!
WAIT! I AM RECEIVING A MENTAL MESSAGE FROM ISAAC!
MENTOR KNOWS I AM HERE!
MENTOR: RECEIVING CEREBRAL FEEDBACK!
EXACT MATRIX COORDINATES: 34YZY X89 AQ...
WELL DONE, ISAAC!
AND NOW-- READY PROJECT FREEDOM:
FIRE!
A BLAZE OF BLUE ISSUES FROM THE ROCKS OF TITAN...

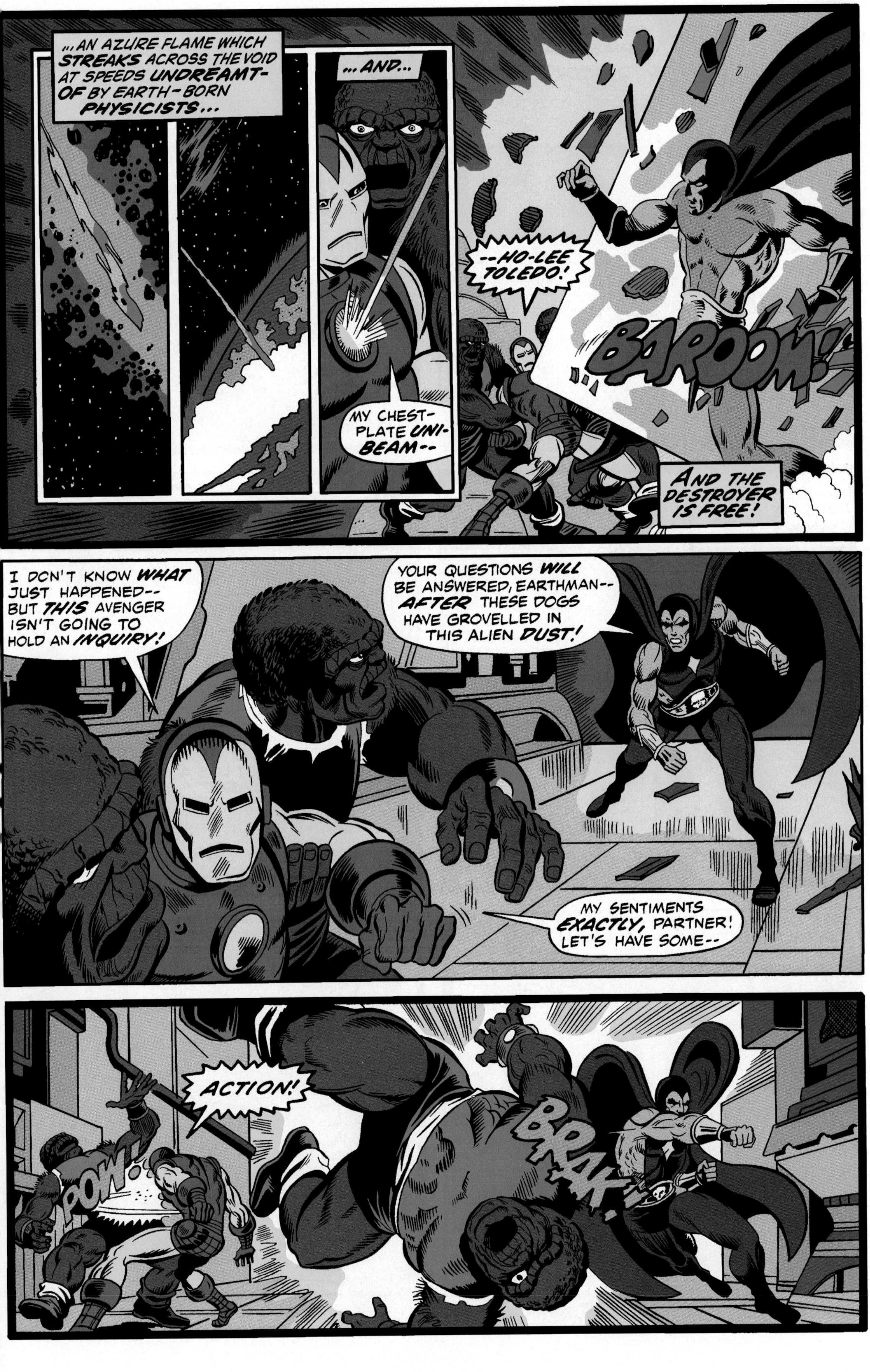
...AN AZURE FLAME WHICH STREAKS ACROSS THE VOID AT SPEEDS UNDREAMT-OF BY EARTH-BORN PHYSICISTS...
...AND...
MY CHEST-PLATE UNI-BEAM--
--HO-LEE TOLEDO!
BAROOM!
AND THE DESTROYER IS FREE!
I DON'T KNOW WHAT JUST HAPPENED-- BUT THIS AVENGER ISN'T GOING TO HOLD AN INQUIRY!
YOUR QUESTIONS WILL BE ANSWERED, EARTHMAN-- AFTER THESE DOGS HAVE GROVELLED IN THIS ALIEN DUST!
MY SENTIMENTS EXACTLY, PARTNER! LET'S HAVE SOME--
ACTION!
POW!
BRAK!

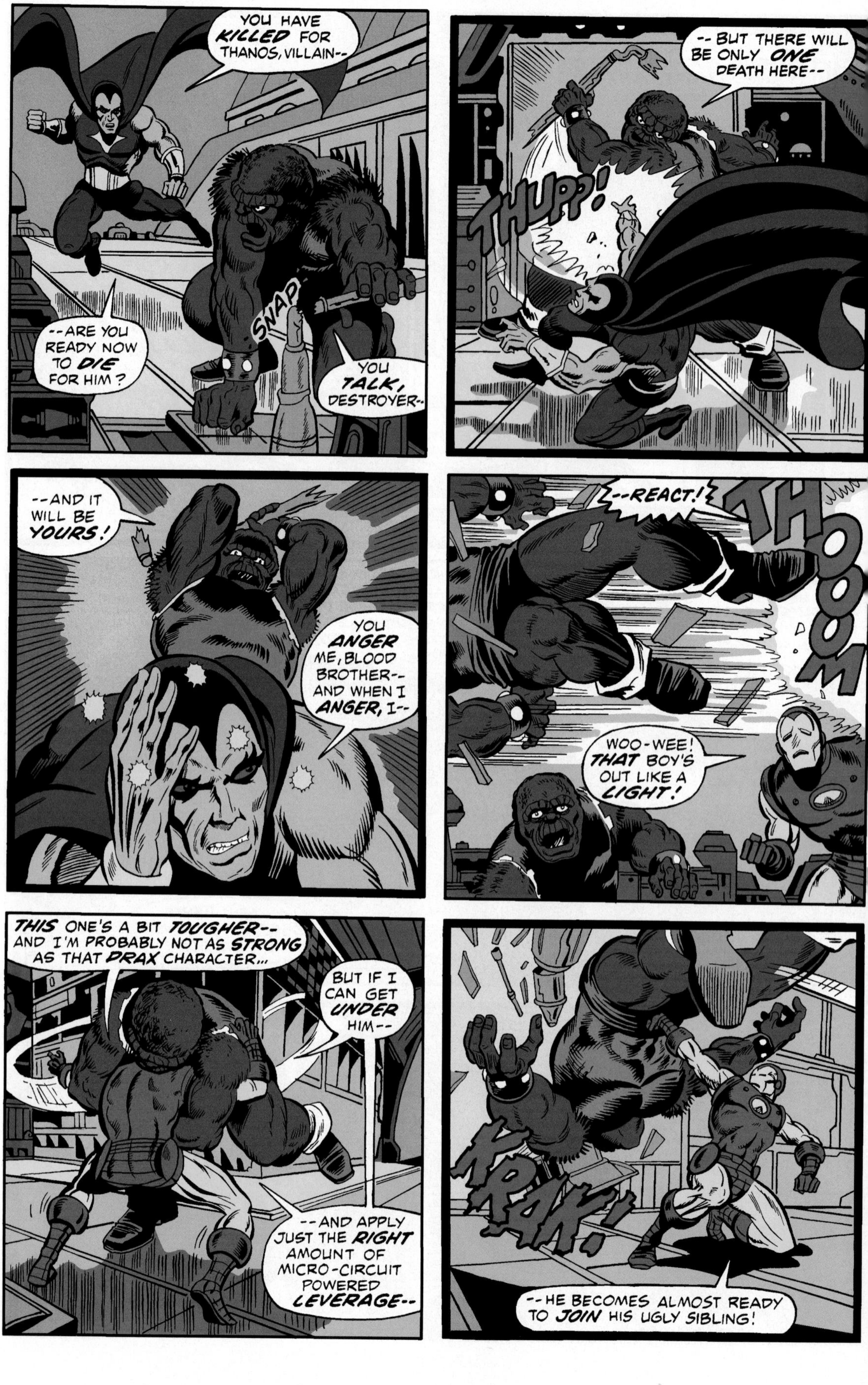
YOU HAVE KILLED FOR THANOS, VILLAIN--
--ARE YOU READY NOW TO DIE FOR HIM?
SNAP
YOU TALK, DESTROYER--
--BUT THERE WILL BE ONLY ONE DEATH HERE--
THUPP!
--AND IT WILL BE YOURS!
YOU ANGER ME, BLOOD BROTHER-- AND WHEN I ANGER, I--
--REACT!
THOOOM
WOO-WEE! THAT BOY'S OUT LIKE A LIGHT!
THIS ONE'S A BIT TOUGHER-- AND I'M PROBABLY NOT AS STRONG AS THAT DRAX CHARACTER...
BUT IF I CAN GET UNDER HIM--
--AND APPLY JUST THE RIGHT AMOUNT OF MICRO-CIRCUIT POWERED LEVERAGE--
KRAK!
--HE BECOMES ALMOST READY TO JOIN HIS UGLY SIBLING!

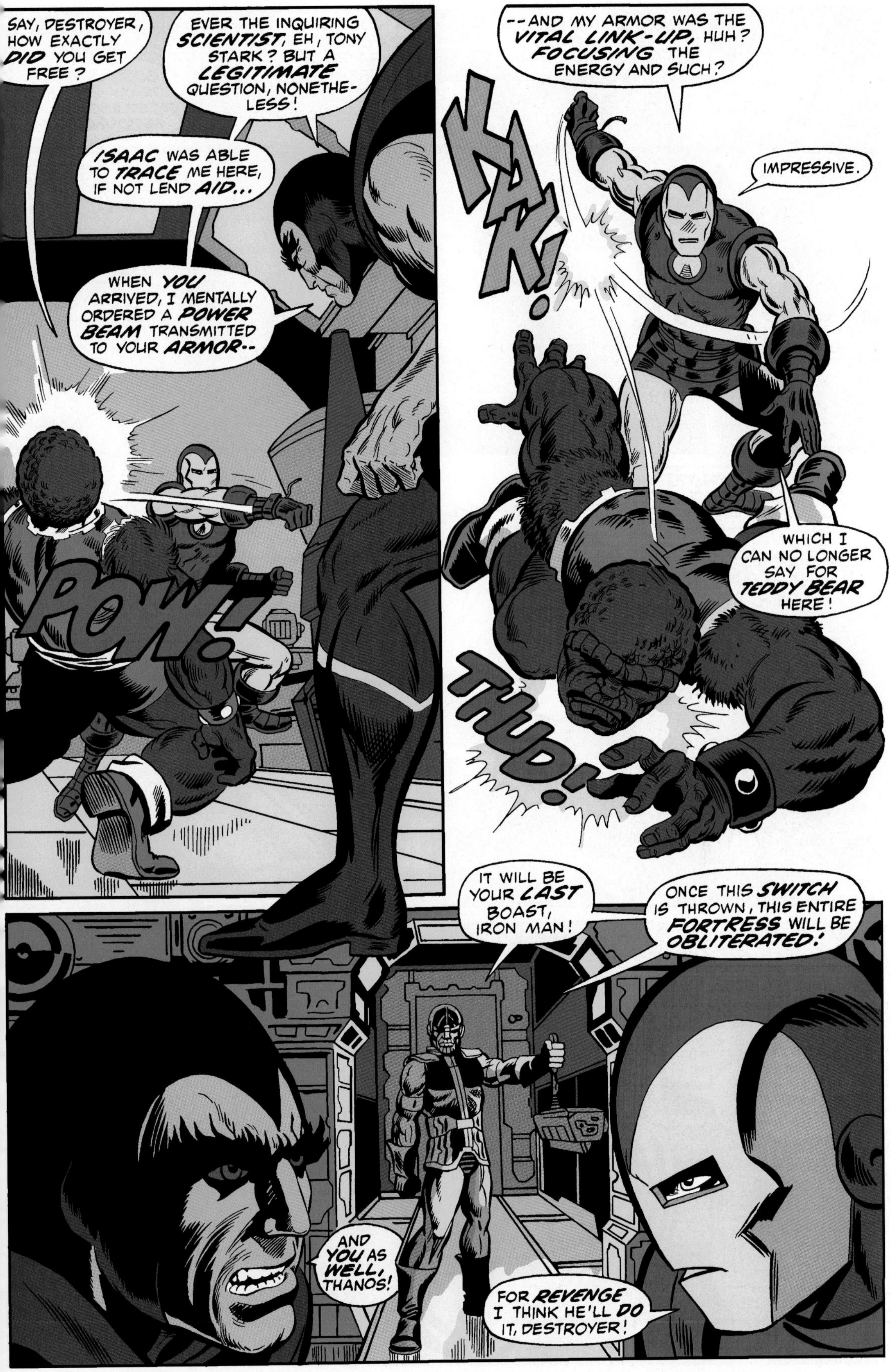
SAY, DESTROYER, HOW EXACTLY DID YOU GET FREE?
EVER THE INQUIRING SCIENTIST, EH, TONY STARK? BUT A LEGITIMATE QUESTION, NONETHE-LESS!
ISAAC WAS ABLE TO TRACE ME HERE, IF NOT LEND AID...
WHEN YOU ARRIVED, I MENTALLY ORDERED A POWER BEAM TRANSMITTED TO YOUR ARMOR--
POW!
--AND MY ARMOR WAS THE VITAL LINK-UP, HUH? FOCUSING THE ENERGY AND SUCH?
KAK!
IMPRESSIVE.
WHICH I CAN NO LONGER SAY FOR TEDDY BEAR HERE!
THUD!
IT WILL BE YOUR LAST BOAST, IRON MAN!
ONCE THIS SWITCH IS THROWN, THIS ENTIRE FORTRESS WILL BE OBLITERATED!
AND YOU AS WELL, THANOS!
FOR REVENGE I THINK HE'LL DO IT, DESTROYER!

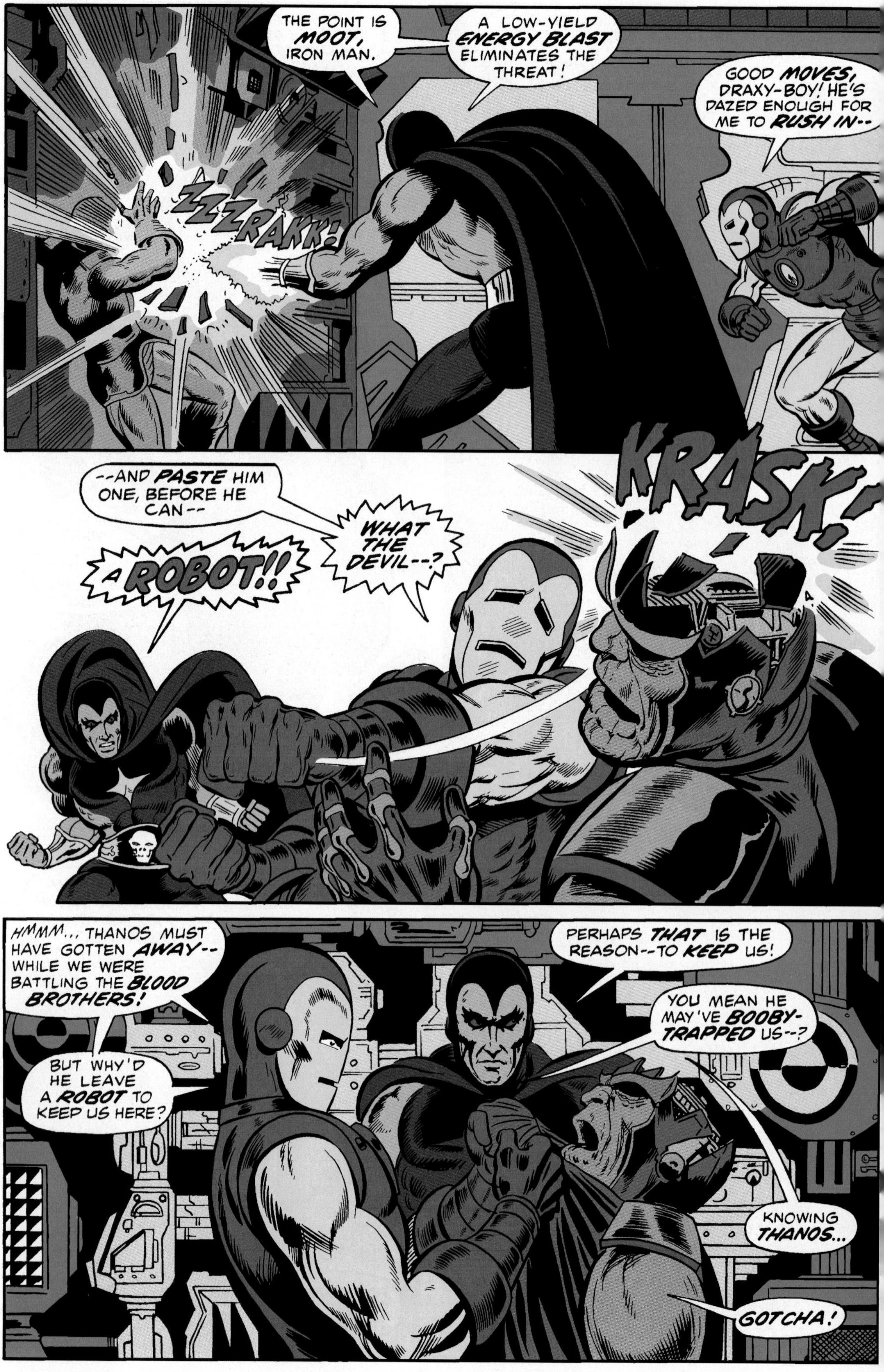
THE POINT IS MOOT, IRON MAN.
A LOW-YIELD ENERGY BLAST ELIMINATES THE THREAT!
ZZZRAKK!
GOOD MOVES, DRAXY-BOY! HE'S DAZED ENOUGH FOR ME TO RUSH IN--
--AND PASTE HIM ONE, BEFORE HE CAN--
KRASK!!
WHAT THE DEVIL--?
A ROBOT!!
HMMM.., THANOS MUST HAVE GOTTEN AWAY-- WHILE WE WERE BATTLING THE BLOOD BROTHERS!
PERHAPS THAT IS THE REASON--TO KEEP US!
BUT WHY'D HE LEAVE A ROBOT TO KEEP US HERE?
YOU MEAN HE MAY'VE BOOBY-TRAPPED US--?
KNOWING THANOS...
GOTCHA!

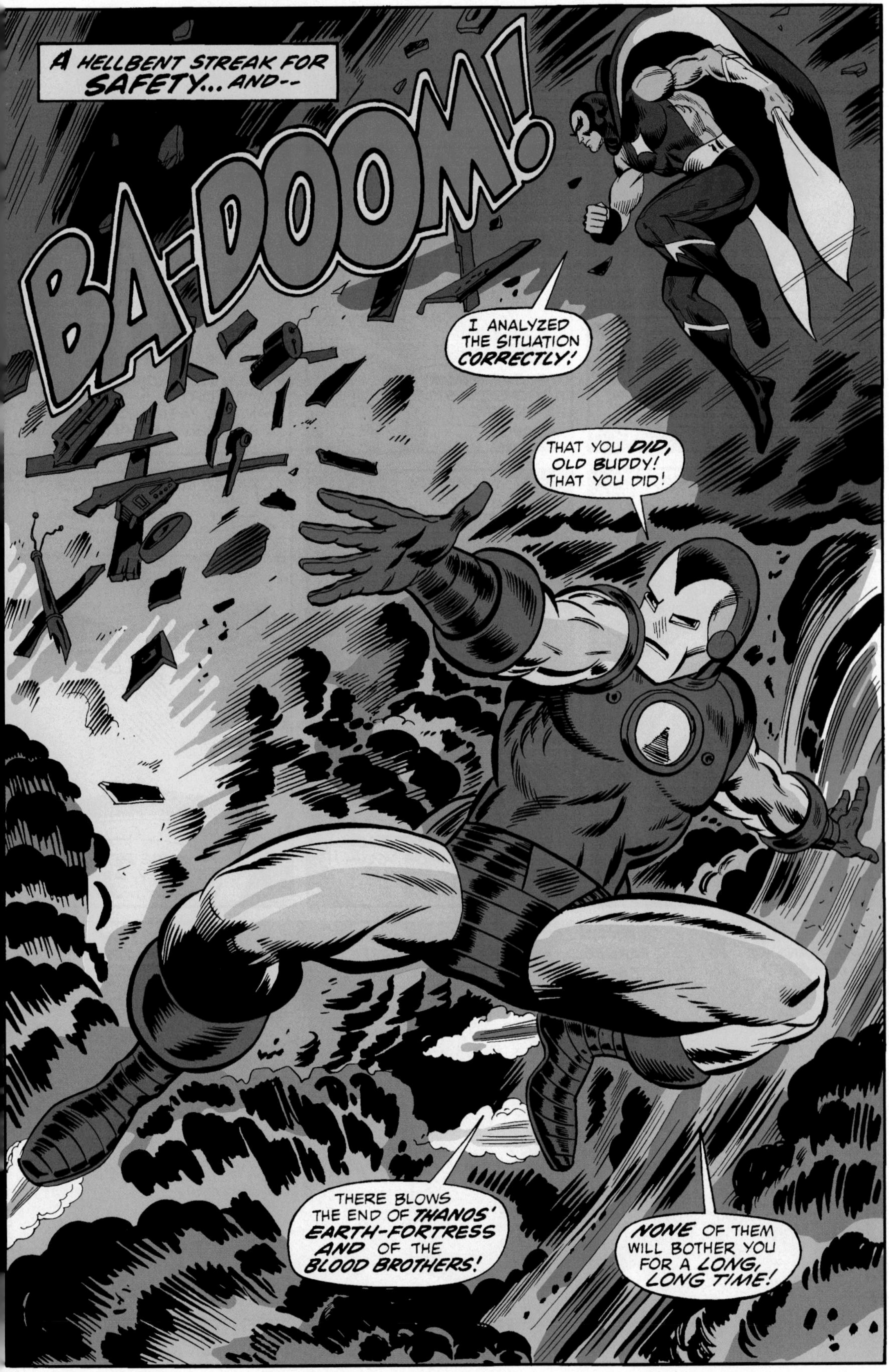
A HELLBENT STREAK FOR SAFETY... AND--
BA-DOOM!
I ANALYZED THE SITUATION CORRECTLY!
THAT YOU DID, OLD BUDDY! THAT YOU DID!
THERE BLOWS THE END OF THANOS' EARTH-FORTRESS AND OF THE BLOOD BROTHERS!
NONE OF THEM WILL BOTHER YOU FOR A LONG, LONG TIME!

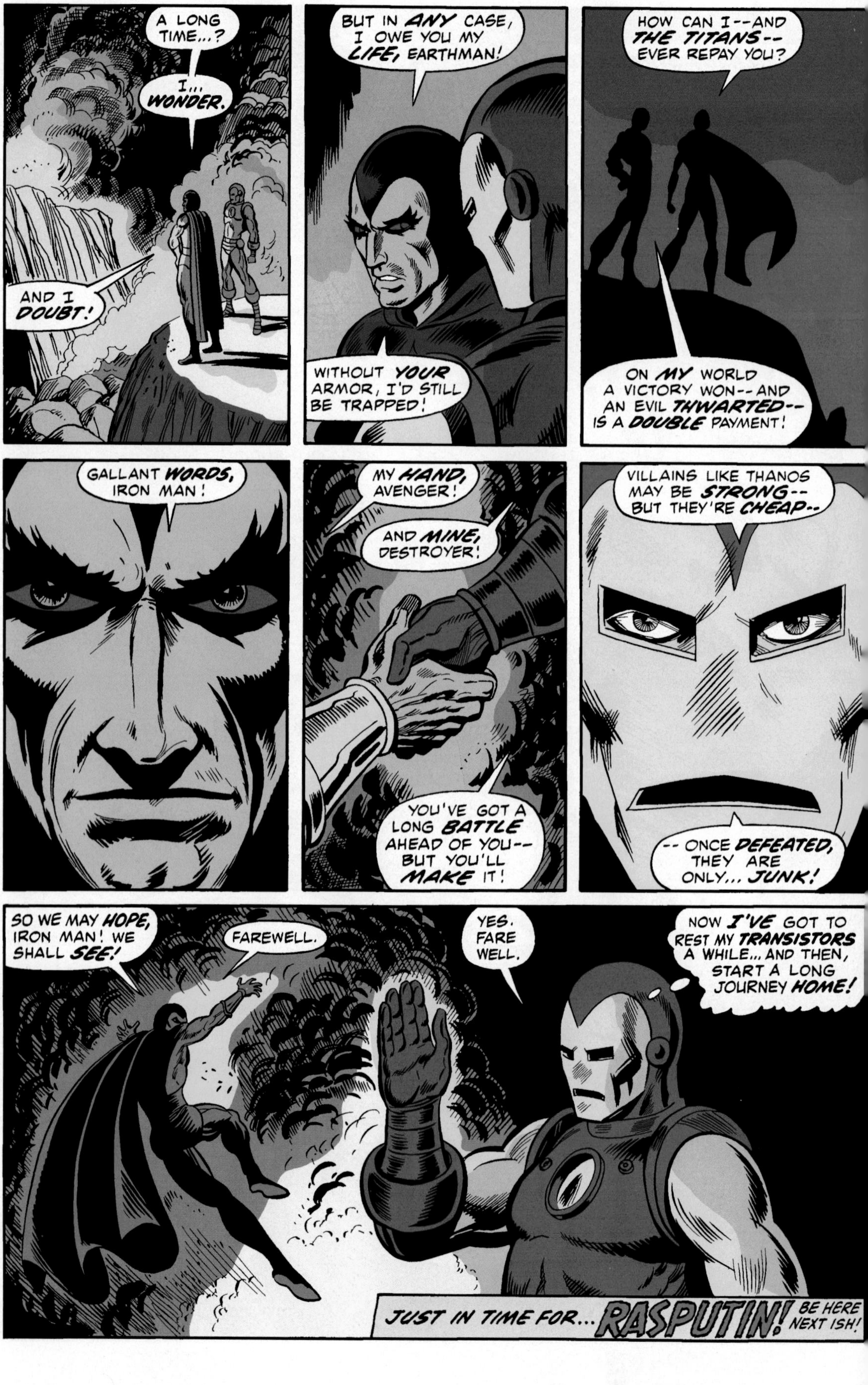
A LONG TIME...?
I... WONDER.
AND I DOUBT!
BUT IN ANY CASE, I OWE YOU MY LIFE, EARTHMAN!
WITHOUT YOUR ARMOR, I'D STILL BE TRAPPED!
HOW CAN I--AND THE TITANS--EVER REPAY YOU?
ON MY WORLD A VICTORY WON--AND AN EVIL THWARTED--IS A DOUBLE PAYMENT!
GALLANT WORDS, IRON MAN!
MY HAND, AVENGER!
AND MINE, DESTROYER!
YOU'VE GOT A LONG BATTLE AHEAD OF YOU--BUT YOU'LL MAKE IT!
VILLAINS LIKE THANOS MAY BE STRONG--BUT THEY'RE CHEAP--
--ONCE DEFEATED, THEY ARE ONLY... JUNK!
SO WE MAY HOPE, IRON MAN! WE SHALL SEE!
FAREWELL.
YES. FARE WELL.
NOW I'VE GOT TO REST MY TRANSISTORS A WHILE... AND THEN, START A LONG JOURNEY HOME!
JUST IN TIME FOR... RASPUTIN! BE HERE NEXT ISH!

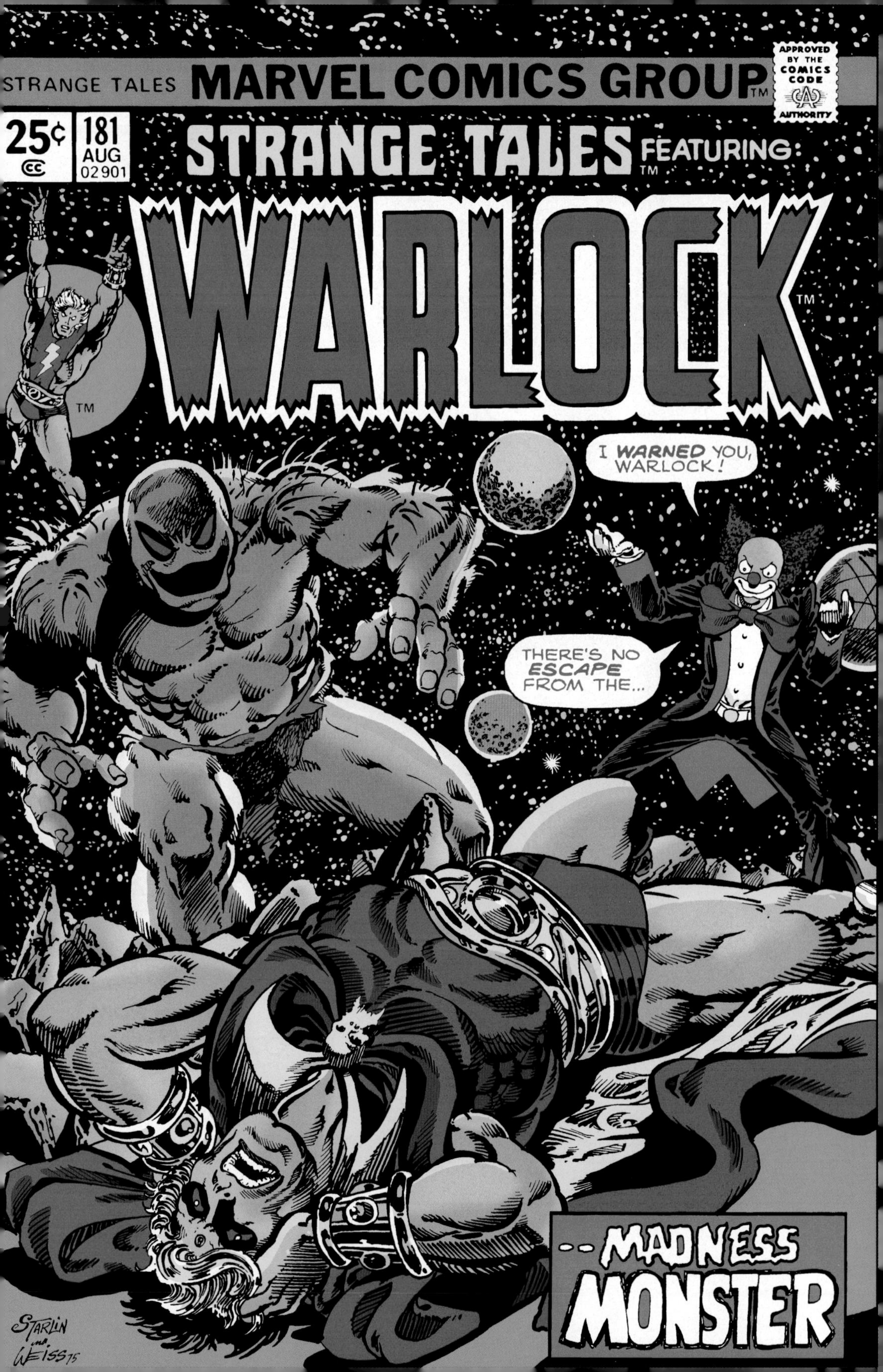

STRANGE TALES
MARVEL COMICS GROUP
APPROVED BY THE COMICS CODE AUTHORITY
25¢
181
AUG
02901
STRANGE TALES FEATURING:
WARLOCK
I WARNED YOU, WARLOCK!
THERE'S NO ESCAPE FROM THE...
..MADNESS MONSTER
STARLIN AND WEISS 75

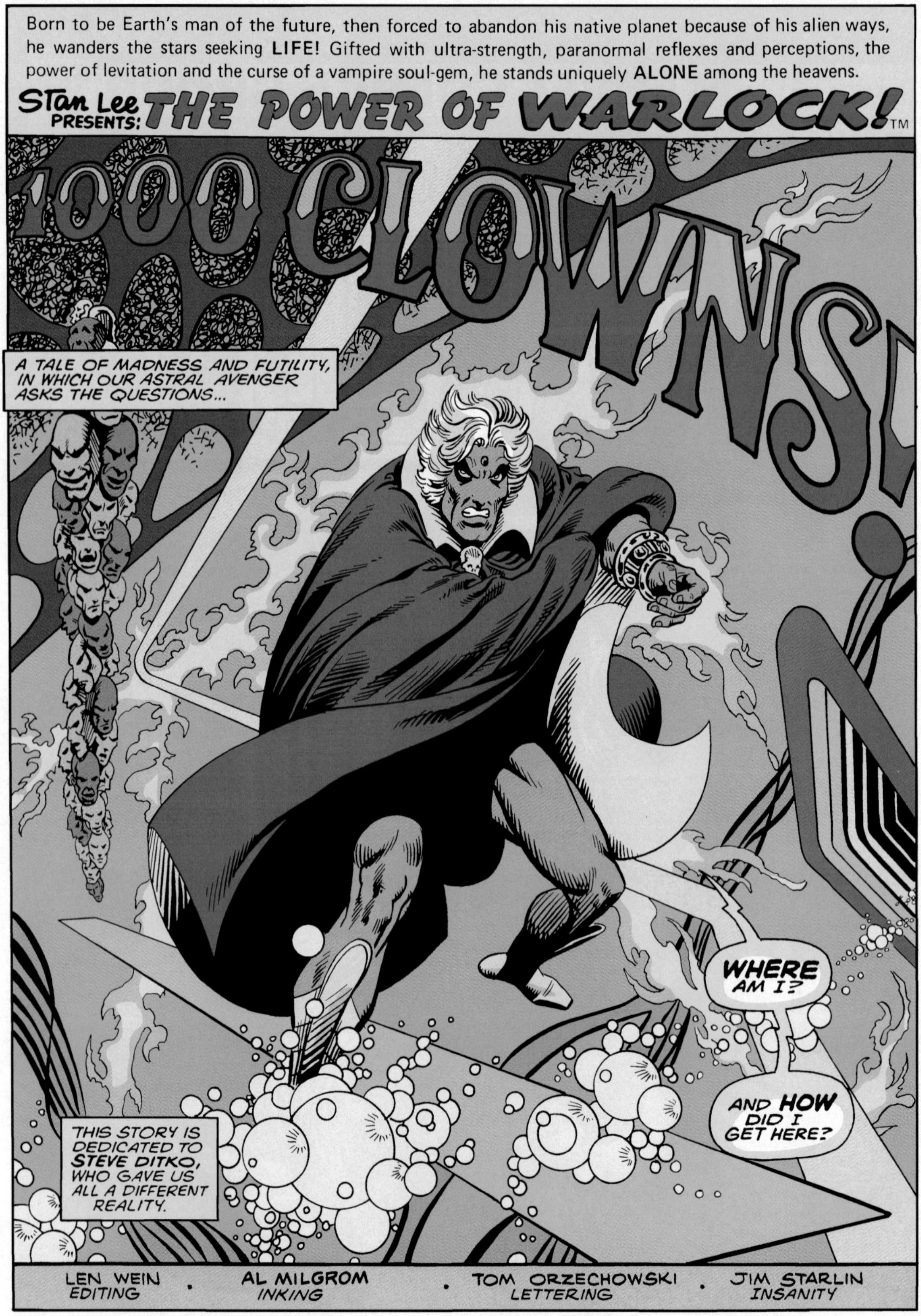
Born to be Earth's man of the future, then forced to abandon his native planet because of his alien ways, he wanders the stars seeking LIFE! Gifted with ultra-strength, paranormal reflexes and perceptions, the power of levitation and the curse of a vampire soul-gem, he stands uniquely ALONE among the heavens.
STAN LEE PRESENTS: THE POWER OF WARLOCK!™
1000 CLOWNS!
A TALE OF MADNESS AND FUTILITY, IN WHICH OUR ASTRAL AVENGER ASKS THE QUESTIONS...
WHERE AM I?
AND HOW DID I GET HERE?
THIS STORY IS DEDICATED TO STEVE DITKO, WHO GAVE US ALL A DIFFERENT REALITY.
LEN WEIN EDITING • AL MILGROM INKING • TOM ORZECHOWSKI LETTERING • JIM STARLIN INSANITY

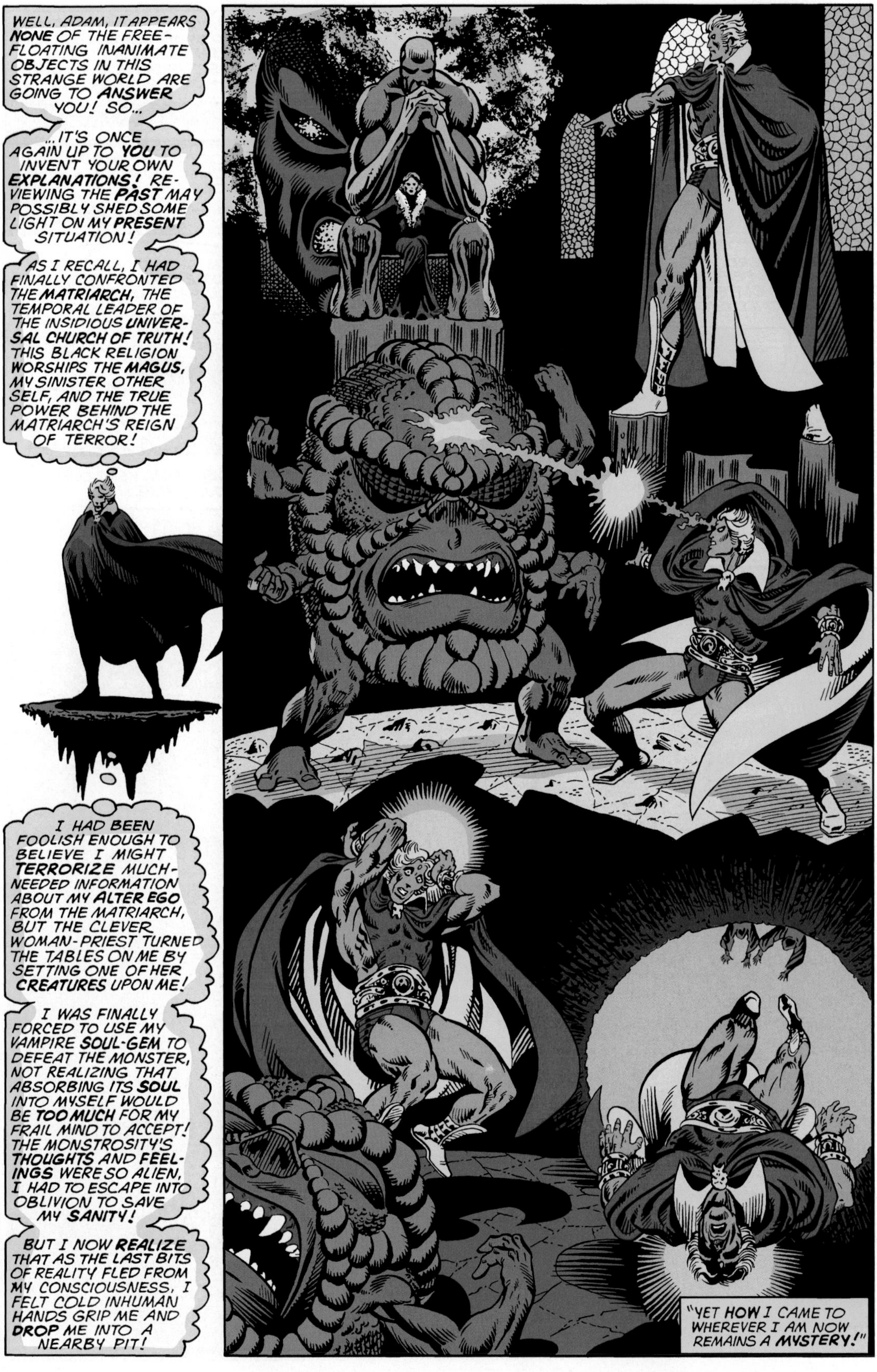
WELL, ADAM, IT APPEARS NONE OF THE FREE-FLOATING INANIMATE OBJECTS IN THIS STRANGE WORLD ARE GOING TO ANSWER YOU! SO...
...IT'S ONCE AGAIN UP TO YOU TO INVENT YOUR OWN EXPLANATIONS! REVIEWING THE PAST MAY POSSIBLY SHED SOME LIGHT ON MY PRESENT SITUATION!
AS I RECALL, I HAD FINALLY CONFRONTED THE MATRIARCH, THE TEMPORAL LEADER OF THE INSIDIOUS UNIVERSAL CHURCH OF TRUTH! THIS BLACK RELIGION WORSHIPS THE MAGUS, MY SINISTER OTHER SELF, AND THE TRUE POWER BEHIND THE MATRIARCH'S REIGN OF TERROR!
I HAD BEEN FOOLISH ENOUGH TO BELIEVE I MIGHT TERRORIZE MUCH-NEEDED INFORMATION ABOUT MY ALTER EGO FROM THE MATRIARCH, BUT THE CLEVER WOMAN-PRIEST TURNED THE TABLES ON ME BY SETTING ONE OF HER CREATURES UPON ME!
I WAS FINALLY FORCED TO USE MY VAMPIRE SOUL-GEM TO DEFEAT THE MONSTER, NOT REALIZING THAT ABSORBING ITS SOUL INTO MYSELF WOULD BE TOO MUCH FOR MY FRAIL MIND TO ACCEPT! THE MONSTROSITY'S THOUGHTS AND FEELINGS WERE SO ALIEN, I HAD TO ESCAPE INTO OBLIVION TO SAVE MY SANITY!
BUT I NOW REALIZE THAT AS THE LAST BITS OF REALITY FLED FROM MY CONSCIOUSNESS, I FELT COLD INHUMAN HANDS GRIP ME AND DROP ME INTO A NEARBY PIT!
"YET HOW I CAME TO WHEREVER I AM NOW REMAINS A MYSTERY!"

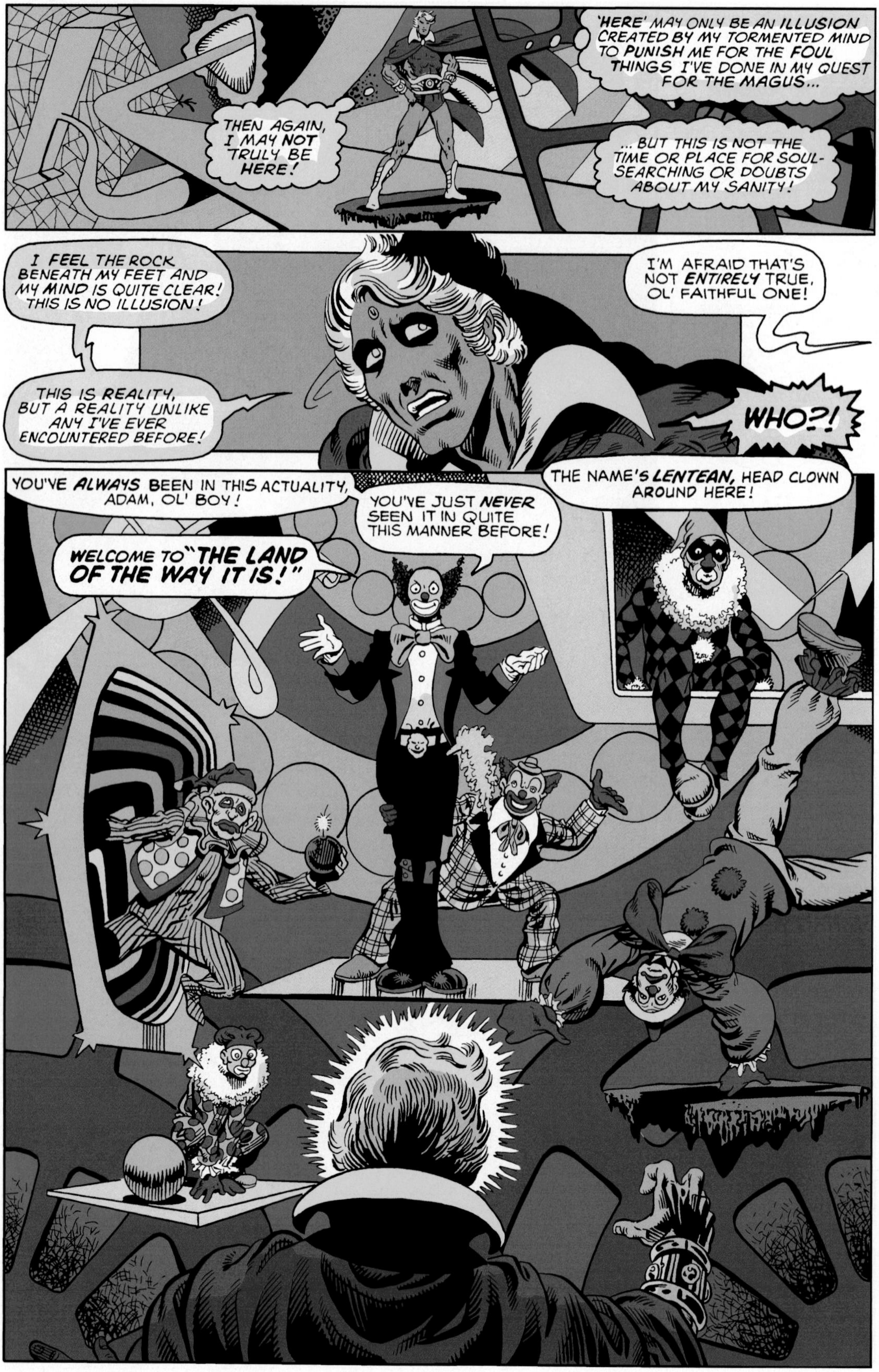
'HERE' MAY ONLY BE AN ILLUSION CREATED BY MY TORMENTED MIND TO PUNISH ME FOR THE FOUL THINGS I'VE DONE IN MY QUEST FOR THE MAGUS...
THEN AGAIN, I MAY NOT TRULY BE HERE!
... BUT THIS IS NOT THE TIME OR PLACE FOR SOUL-SEARCHING OR DOUBTS ABOUT MY SANITY!
I FEEL THE ROCK BENEATH MY FEET AND MY MIND IS QUITE CLEAR! THIS IS NO ILLUSION!
THIS IS REALITY, BUT A REALITY UNLIKE ANY I'VE EVER ENCOUNTERED BEFORE!
I'M AFRAID THAT'S NOT ENTIRELY TRUE, OL' FAITHFUL ONE!
WHO?!
YOU'VE ALWAYS BEEN IN THIS ACTUALITY, ADAM, OL' BOY!
YOU'VE JUST NEVER SEEN IT IN QUITE THIS MANNER BEFORE!
WELCOME TO "THE LAND OF THE WAY IT IS!"
THE NAME'S LENTEAN, HEAD CLOWN AROUND HERE!

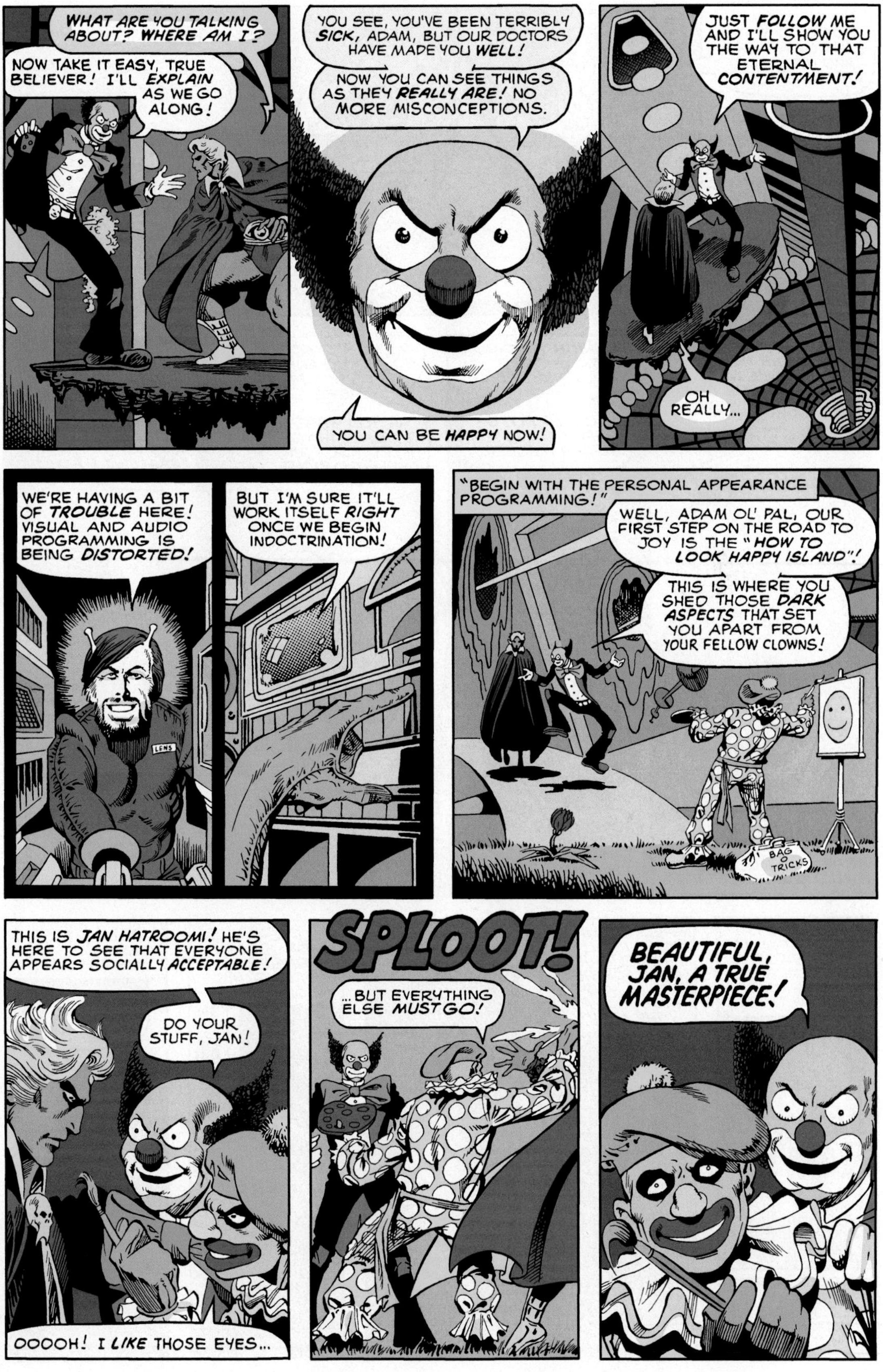
WHAT ARE YOU TALKING ABOUT? WHERE AM I?
NOW TAKE IT EASY, TRUE BELIEVER! I'LL EXPLAIN AS WE GO ALONG!
YOU SEE, YOU'VE BEEN TERRIBLY SICK, ADAM, BUT OUR DOCTORS HAVE MADE YOU WELL!
NOW YOU CAN SEE THINGS AS THEY REALLY ARE! NO MORE MISCONCEPTIONS.
YOU CAN BE HAPPY NOW!
JUST FOLLOW ME AND I'LL SHOW YOU THE WAY TO THAT ETERNAL CONTENTMENT!
OH REALLY...
WE'RE HAVING A BIT OF TROUBLE HERE! VISUAL AND AUDIO PROGRAMMING IS BEING DISTORTED!
LENS
BUT I'M SURE IT'LL WORK ITSELF RIGHT ONCE WE BEGIN INDOCTRINATION!
"BEGIN WITH THE PERSONAL APPEARANCE PROGRAMMING!"
WELL, ADAM OL' PAL, OUR FIRST STEP ON THE ROAD TO JOY IS THE "HOW TO LOOK HAPPY ISLAND"!
THIS IS WHERE YOU SHED THOSE DARK ASPECTS THAT SET YOU APART FROM YOUR FELLOW CLOWNS!
BAG O TRICKS
THIS IS JAN HATROOMI! HE'S HERE TO SEE THAT EVERYONE APPEARS SOCIALLY ACCEPTABLE!
DO YOUR STUFF, JAN!
OOOOH! I LIKE THOSE EYES...
SPLOOT!
...BUT EVERYTHING ELSE MUST GO!
BEAUTIFUL, JAN, A TRUE MASTERPIECE!

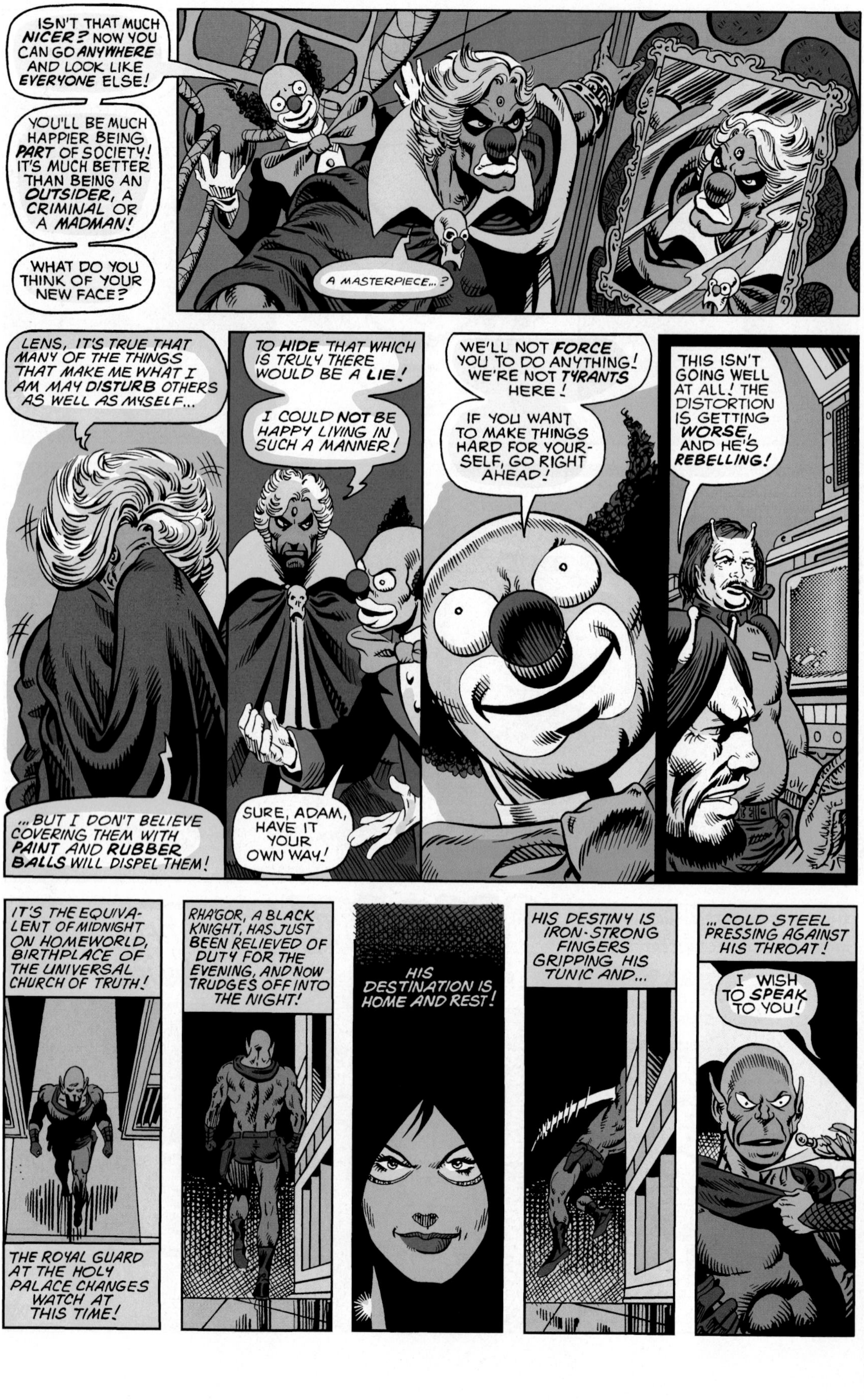

ISN'T THAT MUCH NICER? NOW YOU CAN GO ANYWHERE AND LOOK LIKE EVERYONE ELSE!
YOU'LL BE MUCH HAPPIER BEING PART OF SOCIETY! IT'S MUCH BETTER THAN BEING AN OUTSIDER, A CRIMINAL OR A MADMAN!
WHAT DO YOU THINK OF YOUR NEW FACE?
A MASTERPIECE...?
LENS, IT'S TRUE THAT MANY OF THE THINGS THAT MAKE ME WHAT I AM MAY DISTURB OTHERS AS WELL AS MYSELF...
...BUT I DON'T BELIEVE COVERING THEM WITH PAINT AND RUBBER BALLS WILL DISPEL THEM!
TO HIDE THAT WHICH IS TRULY THERE WOULD BE A LIE!
I COULD NOT BE HAPPY LIVING IN SUCH A MANNER!
SURE, ADAM, HAVE IT YOUR OWN WAY!
WE'LL NOT FORCE YOU TO DO ANYTHING! WE'RE NOT TYRANTS HERE!
IF YOU WANT TO MAKE THINGS HARD FOR YOURSELF, GO RIGHT AHEAD!
THIS ISN'T GOING WELL AT ALL! THE DISTORTION IS GETTING WORSE, AND HE'S REBELLING!
IT'S THE EQUIVALENT OF MIDNIGHT ON HOMEWORLD, BIRTHPLACE OF THE UNIVERSAL CHURCH OF TRUTH!
THE ROYAL GUARD AT THE HOLY PALACE CHANGES WATCH AT THIS TIME!
RHA'GOR, A BLACK KNIGHT, HAS JUST BEEN RELIEVED OF DUTY FOR THE EVENING, AND NOW TRUDGES OFF INTO THE NIGHT!
HIS DESTINATION IS HOME AND REST!
HIS DESTINY IS IRON-STRONG FINGERS GRIPPING HIS TUNIC AND...
...COLD STEEL PRESSING AGAINST HIS THROAT!
I WISH TO SPEAK TO YOU!

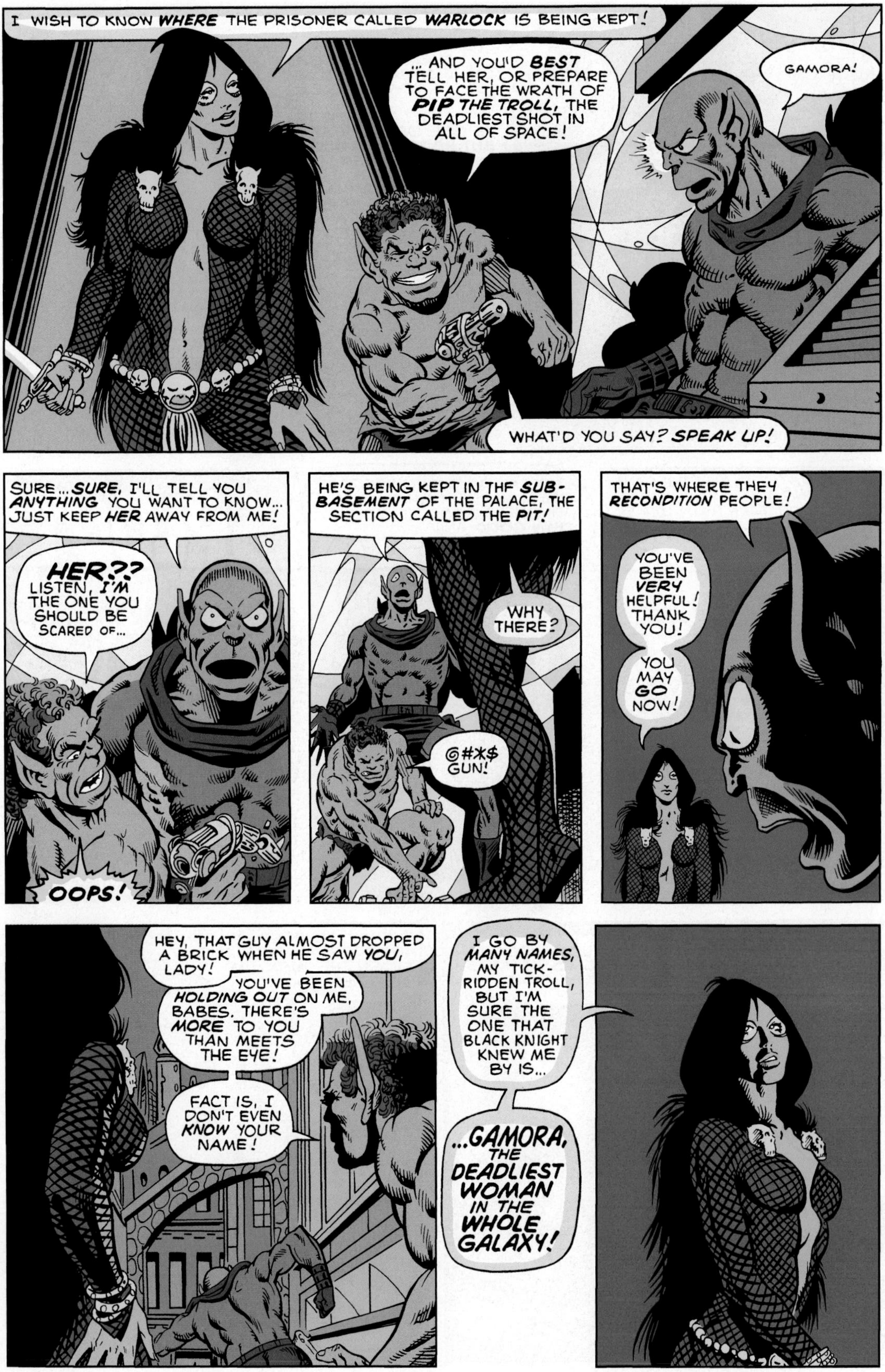
I WISH TO KNOW WHERE THE PRISONER CALLED WARLOCK IS BEING KEPT!
... AND YOU'D BEST TELL HER, OR PREPARE TO FACE THE WRATH OF PIP THE TROLL, THE DEADLIEST SHOT IN ALL OF SPACE!
GAMORA!
WHAT'D YOU SAY? SPEAK UP!
SURE... SURE, I'LL TELL YOU ANYTHING YOU WANT TO KNOW... JUST KEEP HER AWAY FROM ME!
HER?? LISTEN, I'M THE ONE YOU SHOULD BE SCARED OF...
OOPS!
HE'S BEING KEPT IN THF SUB-BASEMENT OF THE PALACE, THE SECTION CALLED THE PIT!
WHY THERE?
@#*$ GUN!
THAT'S WHERE THEY RECONDITION PEOPLE!
YOU'VE BEEN VERY HELPFUL! THANK YOU!
YOU MAY GO NOW!
HEY, THAT GUY ALMOST DROPPED A BRICK WHEN HE SAW YOU, LADY!
YOU'VE BEEN HOLDING OUT ON ME, BABES. THERE'S MORE TO YOU THAN MEETS THE EYE!
FACT IS, I DON'T EVEN KNOW YOUR NAME!
I GO BY MANY NAMES, MY TICK-RIDDEN TROLL, BUT I'M SURE THE ONE THAT BLACK KNIGHT KNEW ME BY IS...
...GAMORA, THE DEADLIEST WOMAN IN THE WHOLE GALAXY!

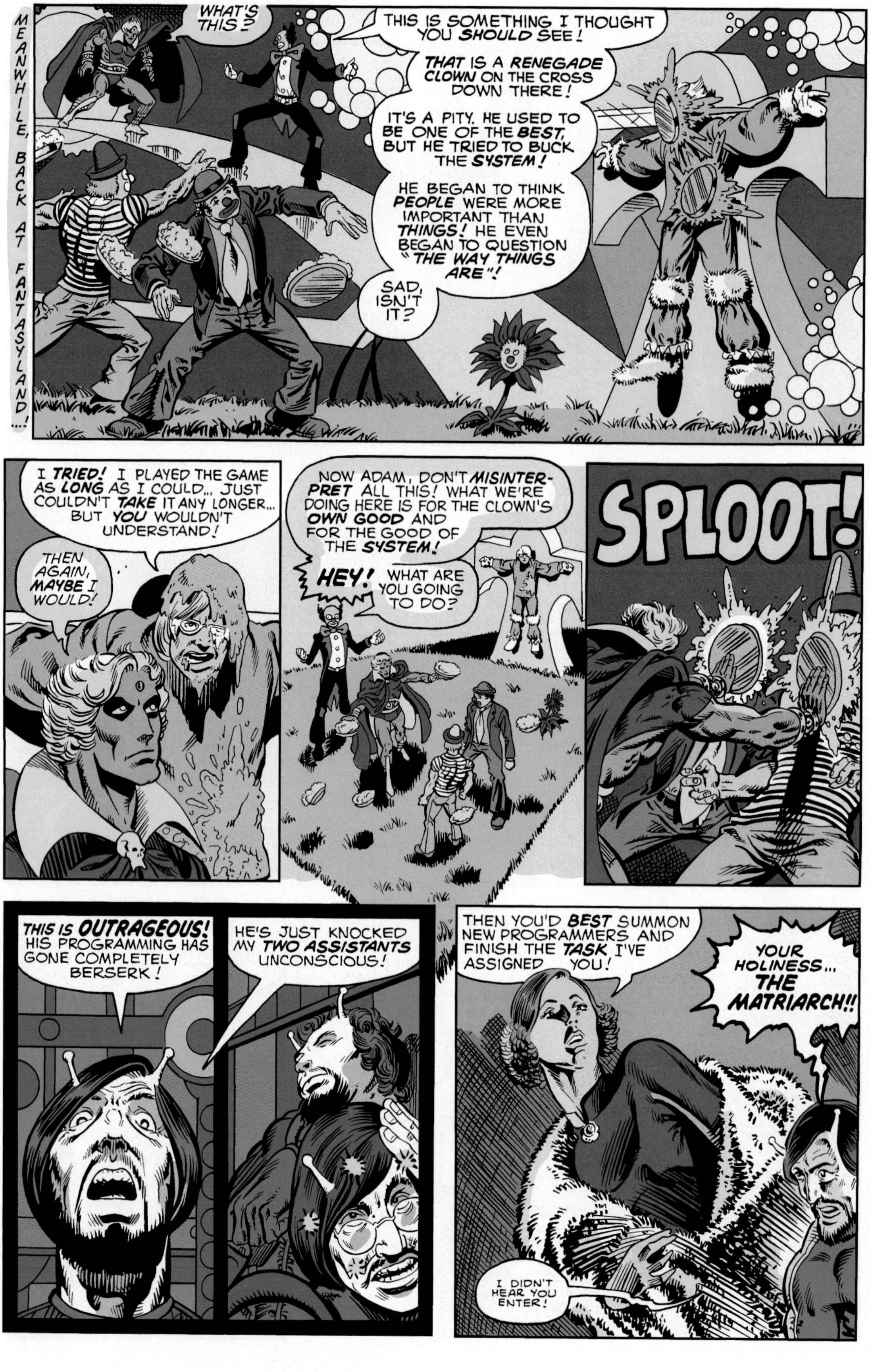

MEANWHILE, BACK AT FANTASYLAND...!
WHAT'S THIS?
THIS IS SOMETHING I THOUGHT YOU SHOULD SEE!
THAT IS A RENEGADE CLOWN ON THE CROSS DOWN THERE!
IT'S A PITY. HE USED TO BE ONE OF THE BEST, BUT HE TRIED TO BUCK THE SYSTEM!
HE BEGAN TO THINK PEOPLE WERE MORE IMPORTANT THAN THINGS! HE EVEN BEGAN TO QUESTION "THE WAY THINGS ARE"!
SAD, ISN'T IT?
I TRIED! I PLAYED THE GAME AS LONG AS I COULD... JUST COULDN'T TAKE IT ANY LONGER... BUT YOU WOULDN'T UNDERSTAND!
THEN AGAIN, MAYBE I WOULD!
NOW ADAM, DON'T MISINTERPRET ALL THIS! WHAT WE'RE DOING HERE IS FOR THE CLOWN'S OWN GOOD AND FOR THE GOOD OF THE SYSTEM!
HEY!
WHAT ARE YOU GOING TO DO?
SPLOOT!
THIS IS OUTRAGEOUS! HIS PROGRAMMING HAS GONE COMPLETELY BERSERK!
HE'S JUST KNOCKED MY TWO ASSISTANTS UNCONSCIOUS!
THEN YOU'D BEST SUMMON NEW PROGRAMMERS AND FINISH THE TASK I'VE ASSIGNED YOU!
YOUR HOLINESS... THE MATRIARCH!!
I DIDN'T HEAR YOU ENTER!

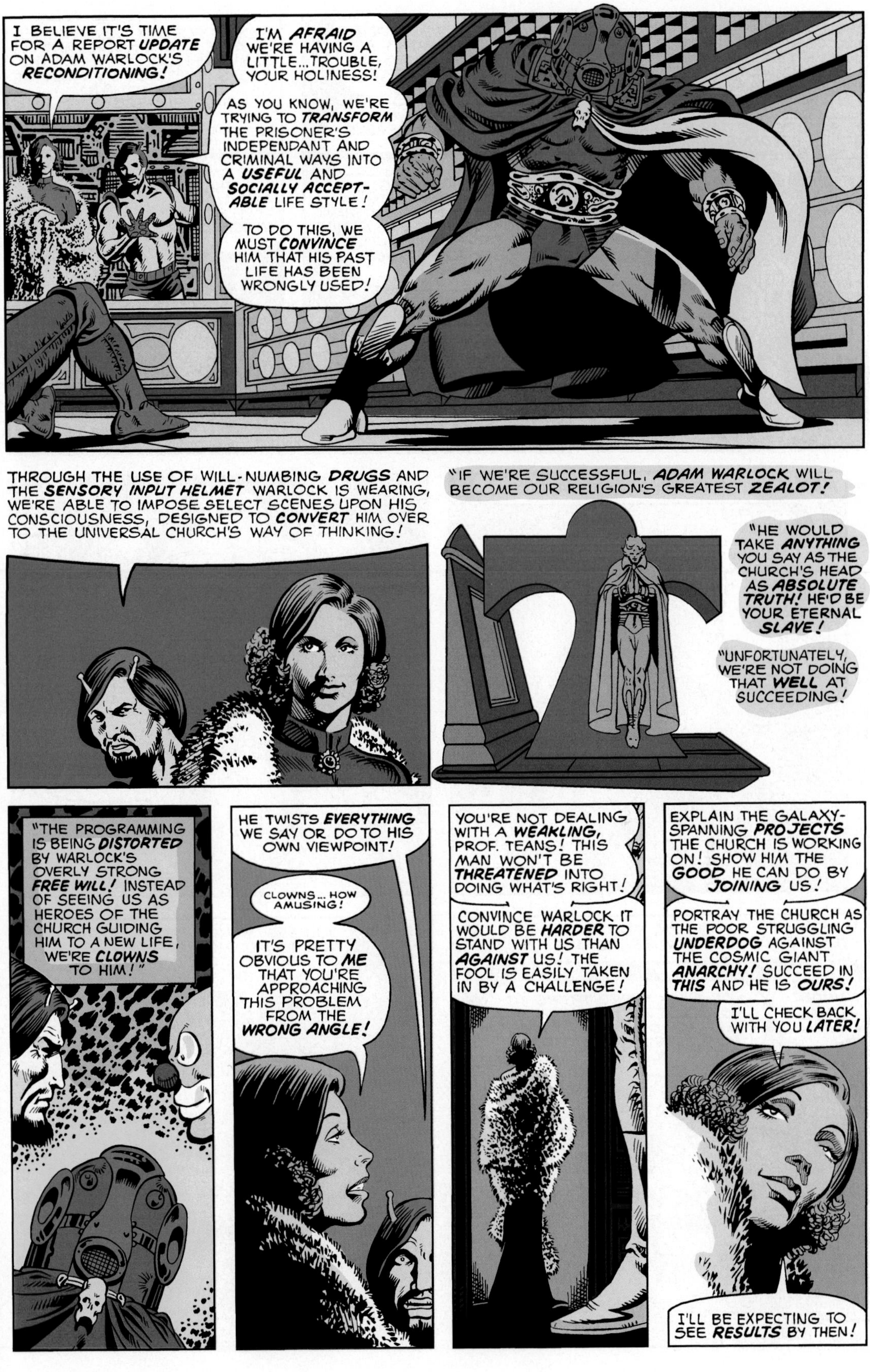
I BELIEVE IT'S TIME FOR A REPORT UPDATE ON ADAM WARLOCK'S RECONDITIONING!
I'M AFRAID WE'RE HAVING A LITTLE... TROUBLE, YOUR HOLINESS!
AS YOU KNOW, WE'RE TRYING TO TRANSFORM THE PRISONER'S INDEPENDANT AND CRIMINAL WAYS INTO A USEFUL AND SOCIALLY ACCEPT-ABLE LIFE STYLE!
TO DO THIS, WE MUST CONVINCE HIM THAT HIS PAST LIFE HAS BEEN WRONGLY USED!
THROUGH THE USE OF WILL-NUMBING DRUGS AND THE SENSORY INPUT HELMET WARLOCK IS WEARING, WE'RE ABLE TO IMPOSE SELECT SCENES UPON HIS CONSCIOUSNESS, DESIGNED TO CONVERT HIM OVER TO THE UNIVERSAL CHURCH'S WAY OF THINKING!
"IF WE'RE SUCCESSFUL, ADAM WARLOCK WILL BECOME OUR RELIGION'S GREATEST ZEALOT!
"HE WOULD TAKE ANYTHING YOU SAY AS THE CHURCH'S HEAD AS ABSOLUTE TRUTH! HE'D BE YOUR ETERNAL SLAVE!
"UNFORTUNATELY, WE'RE NOT DOING THAT WELL AT SUCCEEDING!
"THE PROGRAMMING IS BEING DISTORTED BY WARLOCK'S OVERLY STRONG FREE WILL! INSTEAD OF SEEING US AS HEROES OF THE CHURCH GUIDING HIM TO A NEW LIFE, WE'RE CLOWNS TO HIM!"
HE TWISTS EVERYTHING WE SAY OR DO TO HIS OWN VIEWPOINT!
CLOWNS... HOW AMUSING!
IT'S PRETTY OBVIOUS TO ME THAT YOU'RE APPROACHING THIS PROBLEM FROM THE WRONG ANGLE!
YOU'RE NOT DEALING WITH A WEAKLING, PROF. TEANS! THIS MAN WON'T BE THREATENED INTO DOING WHAT'S RIGHT!
CONVINCE WARLOCK IT WOULD BE HARDER TO STAND WITH US THAN AGAINST US! THE FOOL IS EASILY TAKEN IN BY A CHALLENGE!
EXPLAIN THE GALAXY-SPANNING PROJECTS THE CHURCH IS WORKING ON! SHOW HIM THE GOOD HE CAN DO BY JOINING US!
PORTRAY THE CHURCH AS THE POOR STRUGGLING UNDERDOG AGAINST THE COSMIC GIANT ANARCHY! SUCCEED IN THIS AND HE IS OURS!
I'LL CHECK BACK WITH YOU LATER!
I'LL BE EXPECTING TO SEE RESULTS BY THEN!

WELL, *THAT* SHOULD ASSURE SUCCESS! WITH THE THREAT OF MY *DISPLEASURE* HANGING OVER HIS HEAD, PROF. TEANS WILL SHATTER ADAM'S 'OVERLY STRONG FREE WILL' IN RECORD TIME!

BEFORE THE DAY BREAKS, THAT *GOLDEN GLADIATOR* WILL BE MY EVER-OBEDIANT *SERVANT*!

STILL, IN A CERTAIN WAY, I'LL BE *SAD* TO SEE THAT HAPPEN!

CLOWNS... WHAT A MIND!

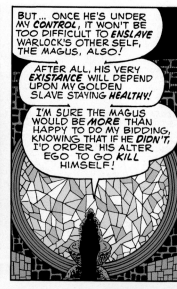

BUT... ONCE HE'S UNDER MY *CONTROL*, IT WON'T BE TOO DIFFICULT TO *ENSLAVE* WARLOCK'S OTHER SELF, THE MAGUS, ALSO!

AFTER ALL, HIS VERY *EXISTANCE* WILL DEPEND UPON MY GOLDEN SLAVE STAYING *HEALTHY*!

I'M SURE THE MAGUS WOULD BE *MORE* THAN HAPPY TO DO MY BIDDING, KNOWING THAT IF HE *DIDN'T*, I'D ORDER HIS ALTER EGO TO GO *KILL* HIMSELF!

I ONLY HOPE IT NEVER COMES TO *THAT*, FOR IF KILLING *WARLOCK* ELIMINATES ANY CHANCE OF THE *MAGUS* EXISTING... MY *KINGDOM* WILL NEVER COME INTO BEING, EITHER!

WELL, MY FINE LADY, IT'S *ALL* OR *NOTHING* THIS TIME! SO, ROLL THE *DICE* AND TO HELL WITH *TOMORROW*!

CLOWNS...

WHILE, LESS THAN A MILE AWAY...!

HEY!! WHERE WE GOING IN SUCH A HURRY?

TO *FREE* YOUR FRIEND WARLOCK!

BUT HE'S BEING HELD IN THE *HOLY PALACE*, AND THAT PLACE IS FULL OF *HUNDREDS* OF *TRIGGER-HAPPY* GUARDS!

YES, AND THEIR *FAVORITE* TARGETS ARE *TROLLS*!

STILL COMING?

SURE, RIGHT *BEHIND* YOU!

I MUST SAY, UP TO NOW YOU'VE NOT BEEN OVERLY *COOPERATIVE*, ADAM!

BUT I *UNDERSTAND* WHY!

YOU THINK WE'RE TRYING TO *MOLD* YOU INTO A DIFFERENT PERSON FOR OUR OWN *PETTY PURPOSES* RATHER THAN FOR *YOUR* OWN GOOD!

WELL, YOU'RE *WRONG*!

YOU SEE, WE'VE BEEN PREPARING *YOU* TO BECOME PART OF *THIS*... THE GREATEST *WORK FORCE* IN THE GALAXY!

WHAT ARE THOSE CLOWNS HAULING? WHY, IT LOOKS LIKE *GARBAGE*!

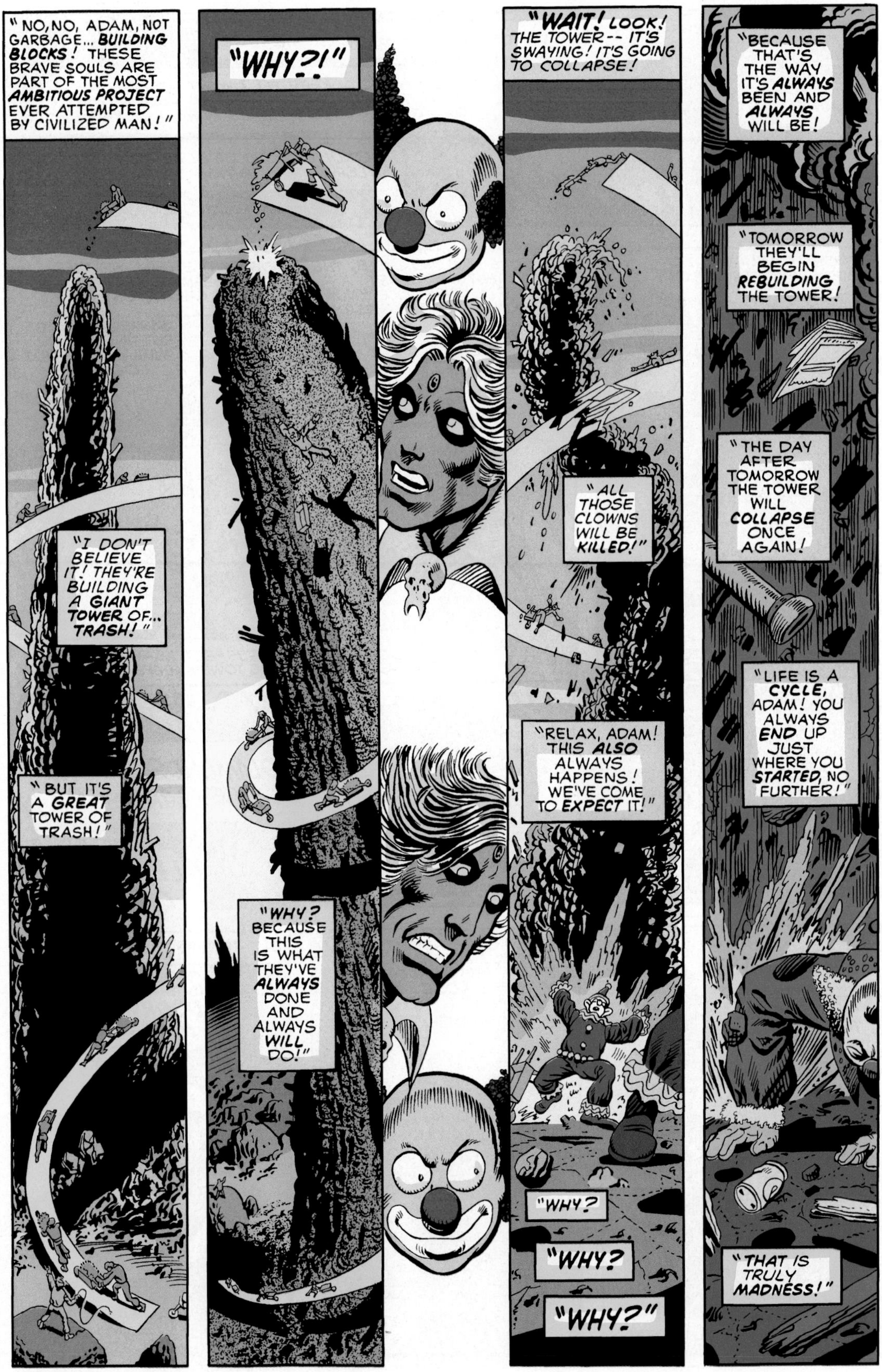
"NO, NO, ADAM, NOT GARBAGE... BUILDING BLOCKS! THESE BRAVE SOULS ARE PART OF THE MOST AMBITIOUS PROJECT EVER ATTEMPTED BY CIVILIZED MAN!"
"I DON'T BELIEVE IT! THEY'RE BUILDING A GIANT TOWER OF... TRASH!"
"BUT IT'S A GREAT TOWER OF TRASH!"
"WHY?!"
"WHY? BECAUSE THIS IS WHAT THEY'VE ALWAYS DONE AND ALWAYS WILL DO!"
"WAIT! LOOK! THE TOWER-- IT'S SWAYING! IT'S GOING TO COLLAPSE!
"ALL THOSE CLOWNS WILL BE KILLED!"
"RELAX, ADAM! THIS ALSO ALWAYS HAPPENS! WE'VE COME TO EXPECT IT!"
"WHY?
"WHY?
"WHY?"
"BECAUSE THAT'S THE WAY IT'S ALWAYS BEEN AND ALWAYS WILL BE!
"TOMORROW THEY'LL BEGIN REBUILDING THE TOWER!
"THE DAY AFTER TOMORROW THE TOWER WILL COLLAPSE ONCE AGAIN!
"LIFE IS A CYCLE, ADAM! YOU ALWAYS END UP JUST WHERE YOU STARTED, NO FURTHER!"
"THAT IS TRULY MADNESS!"

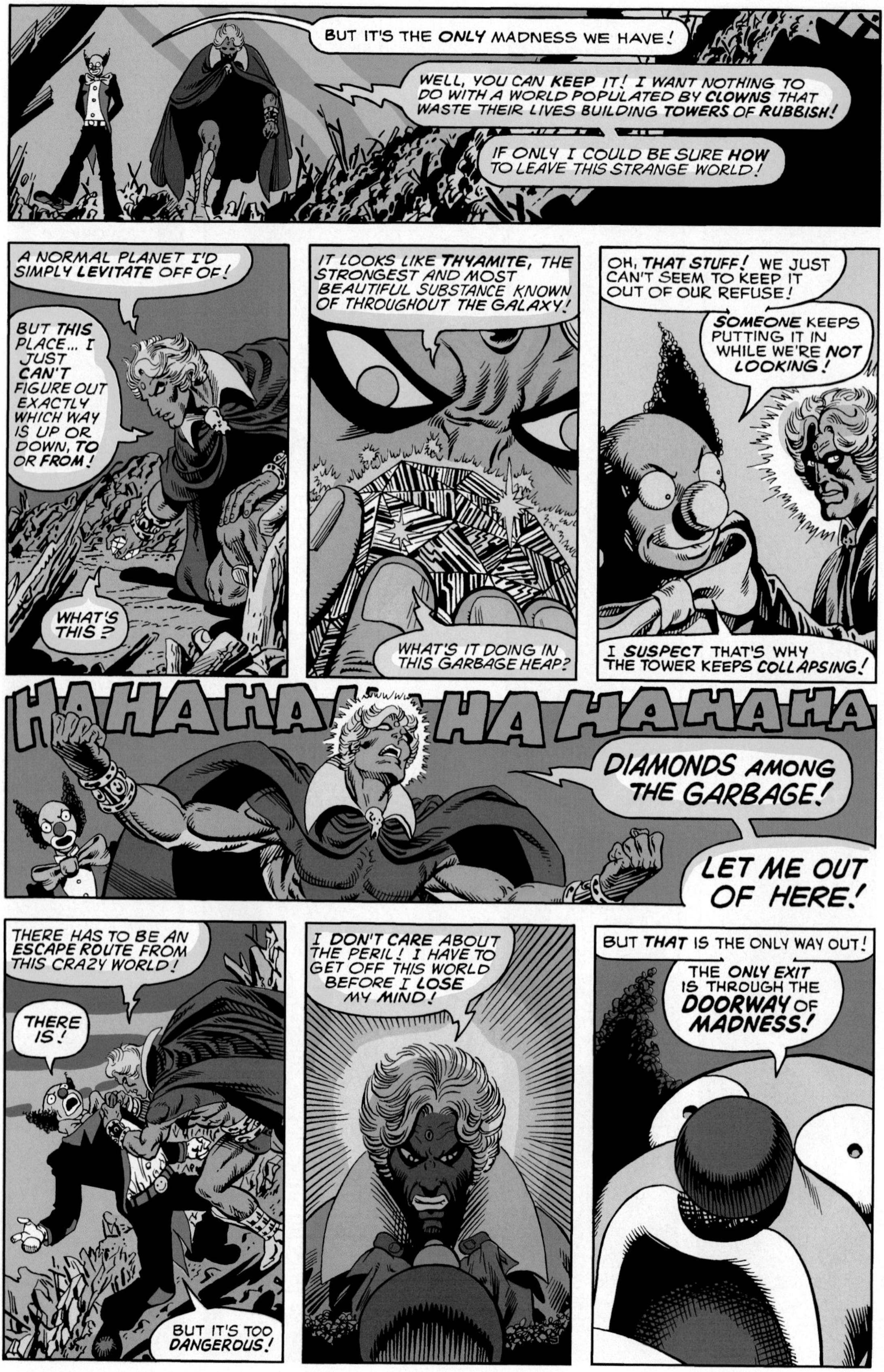
BUT IT'S THE ONLY MADNESS WE HAVE!
WELL, YOU CAN KEEP IT! I WANT NOTHING TO DO WITH A WORLD POPULATED BY CLOWNS THAT WASTE THEIR LIVES BUILDING TOWERS OF RUBBISH!
IF ONLY I COULD BE SURE HOW TO LEAVE THIS STRANGE WORLD!
A NORMAL PLANET I'D SIMPLY LEVITATE OFF OF!
BUT THIS PLACE... I JUST CAN'T FIGURE OUT EXACTLY WHICH WAY IS UP OR DOWN, TO OR FROM!
WHAT'S THIS?
IT LOOKS LIKE THYAMITE, THE STRONGEST AND MOST BEAUTIFUL SUBSTANCE KNOWN OF THROUGHOUT THE GALAXY!
WHAT'S IT DOING IN THIS GARBAGE HEAP?
OH, THAT STUFF! WE JUST CAN'T SEEM TO KEEP IT OUT OF OUR REFUSE!
SOMEONE KEEPS PUTTING IT IN WHILE WE'RE NOT LOOKING!
I SUSPECT THAT'S WHY THE TOWER KEEPS COLLAPSING!
HAHAHAHA HA HAHAHAHA
DIAMONDS AMONG THE GARBAGE!
LET ME OUT OF HERE!
THERE HAS TO BE AN ESCAPE ROUTE FROM THIS CRAZY WORLD!
THERE IS!
BUT IT'S TOO DANGEROUS!
I DON'T CARE ABOUT THE PERIL! I HAVE TO GET OFF THIS WORLD BEFORE I LOSE MY MIND!
BUT THAT IS THE ONLY WAY OUT!
THE ONLY EXIT IS THROUGH THE DOORWAY OF MADNESS!

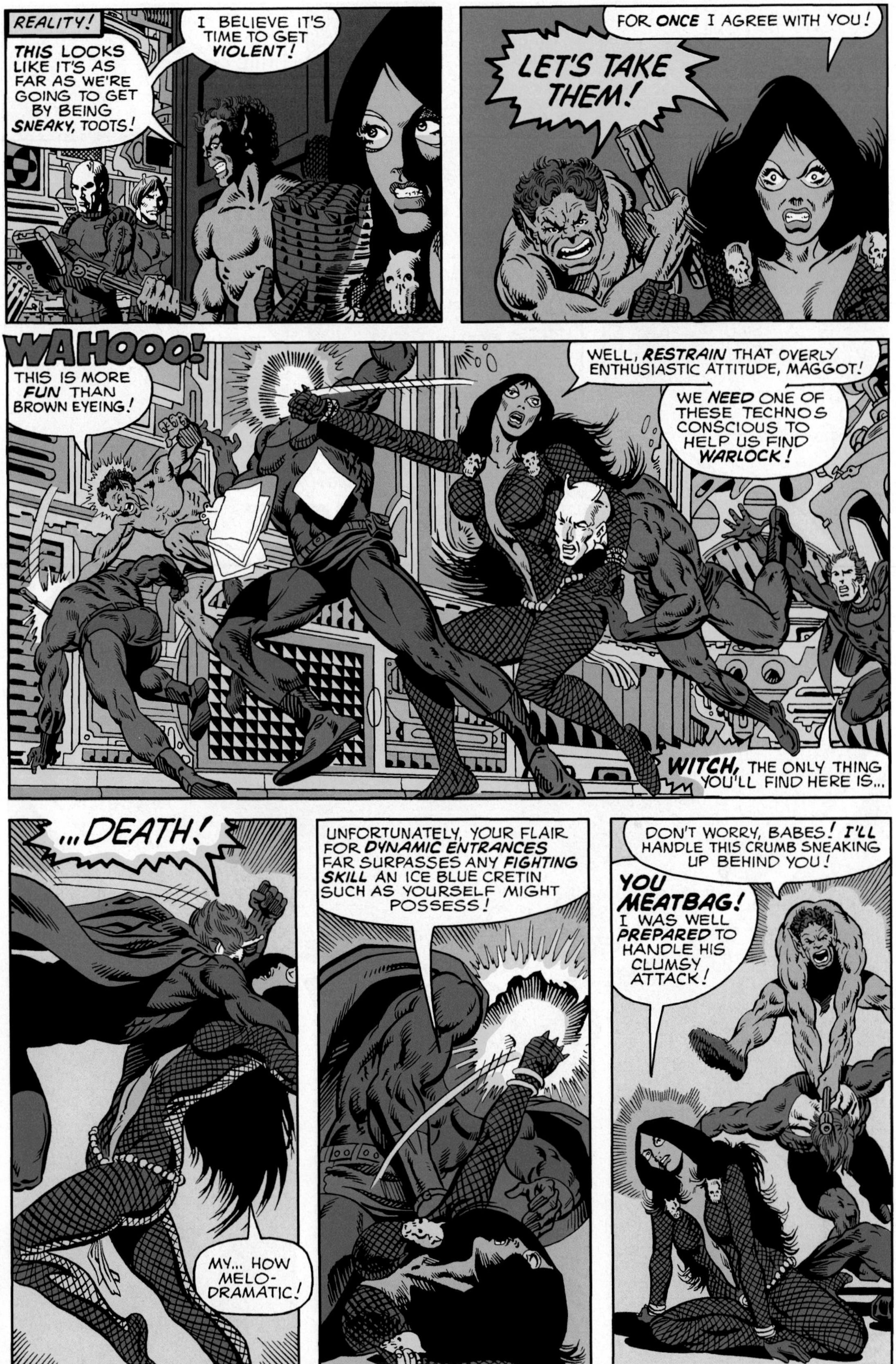
REALITY!
THIS LOOKS LIKE IT'S AS FAR AS WE'RE GOING TO GET BY BEING SNEAKY, TOOTS!
I BELIEVE IT'S TIME TO GET VIOLENT!
LET'S TAKE THEM!
FOR ONCE I AGREE WITH YOU!
WAHOOO!
THIS IS MORE FUN THAN BROWN EYEING!
WELL, RESTRAIN THAT OVERLY ENTHUSIASTIC ATTITUDE, MAGGOT!
WE NEED ONE OF THESE TECHNOS CONSCIOUS TO HELP US FIND WARLOCK!
WITCH, THE ONLY THING YOU'LL FIND HERE IS...
...DEATH!
MY... HOW MELO-DRAMATIC!
UNFORTUNATELY, YOUR FLAIR FOR DYNAMIC ENTRANCES FAR SURPASSES ANY FIGHTING SKILL AN ICE BLUE CRETIN SUCH AS YOURSELF MIGHT POSSESS!
DON'T WORRY, BABES! I'LL HANDLE THIS CRUMB SNEAKING UP BEHIND YOU!
YOU MEATBAG! I WAS WELL PREPARED TO HANDLE HIS CLUMSY ATTACK!

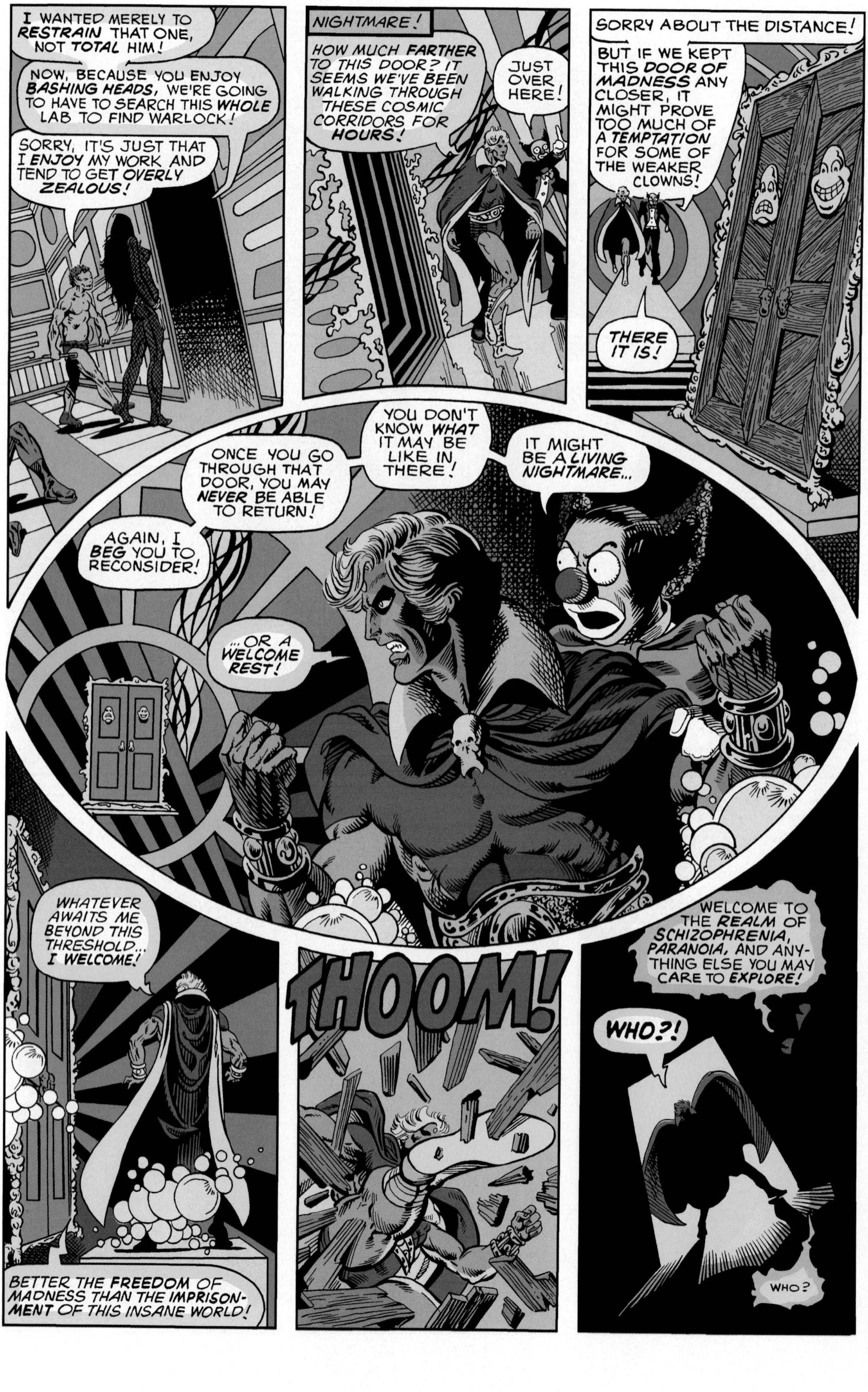
I WANTED MERELY TO RESTRAIN THAT ONE, NOT TOTAL HIM!
NOW, BECAUSE YOU ENJOY BASHING HEADS, WE'RE GOING TO HAVE TO SEARCH THIS WHOLE LAB TO FIND WARLOCK!
SORRY, IT'S JUST THAT I ENJOY MY WORK AND TEND TO GET OVERLY ZEALOUS!
NIGHTMARE!
HOW MUCH FARTHER TO THIS DOOR? IT SEEMS WE'VE BEEN WALKING THROUGH THESE COSMIC CORRIDORS FOR HOURS!
JUST OVER HERE!
SORRY ABOUT THE DISTANCE!
BUT IF WE KEPT THIS DOOR OF MADNESS ANY CLOSER, IT MIGHT PROVE TOO MUCH OF A TEMPTATION FOR SOME OF THE WEAKER CLOWNS!
THERE IT IS!
AGAIN, I BEG YOU TO RECONSIDER!
ONCE YOU GO THROUGH THAT DOOR, YOU MAY NEVER BE ABLE TO RETURN!
YOU DON'T KNOW WHAT IT MAY BE LIKE IN THERE!
IT MIGHT BE A LIVING NIGHTMARE...
...OR A WELCOME REST!
WHATEVER AWAITS ME BEYOND THIS THRESHOLD... I WELCOME!
BETTER THE FREEDOM OF MADNESS THAN THE IMPRISONMENT OF THIS INSANE WORLD!
THOOM!
WELCOME TO THE REALM OF SCHIZOPHRENIA, PARANOIA, AND ANYTHING ELSE YOU MAY CARE TO EXPLORE!
WHO?!
WHO?

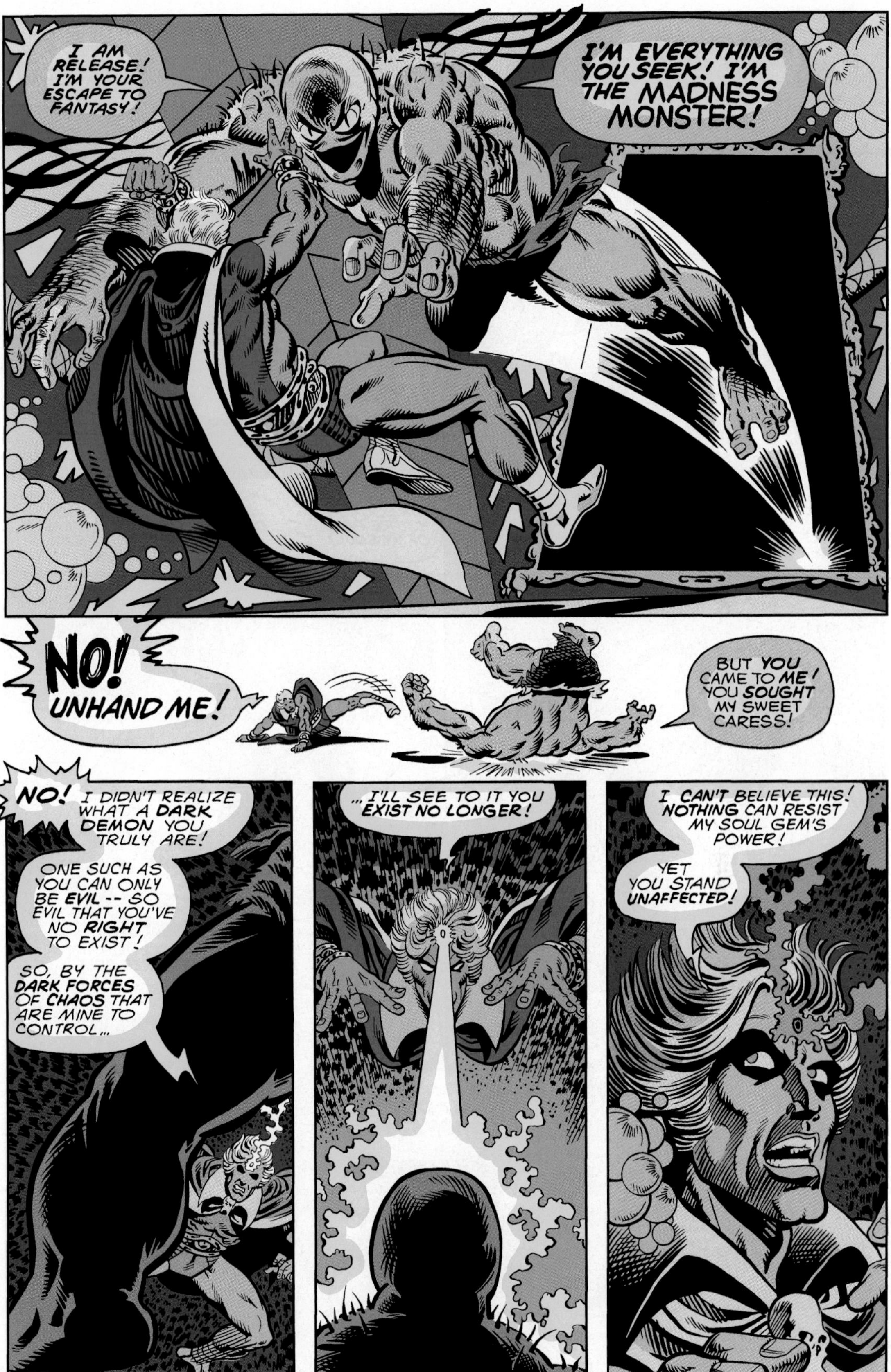
I AM RELEASE! I'M YOUR ESCAPE TO FANTASY!
I'M EVERYTHING YOU SEEK! I'M THE MADNESS MONSTER!
NO! UNHAND ME!
BUT YOU CAME TO ME! YOU SOUGHT MY SWEET CARESS!
NO! I DIDN'T REALIZE WHAT A DARK DEMON YOU TRULY ARE!
ONE SUCH AS YOU CAN ONLY BE EVIL -- SO EVIL THAT YOU'VE NO RIGHT TO EXIST!
SO, BY THE DARK FORCES OF CHAOS THAT ARE MINE TO CONTROL...
...I'LL SEE TO IT YOU EXIST NO LONGER!
I CAN'T BELIEVE THIS! NOTHING CAN RESIST MY SOUL GEM'S POWER!
YET YOU STAND UNAFFECTED!

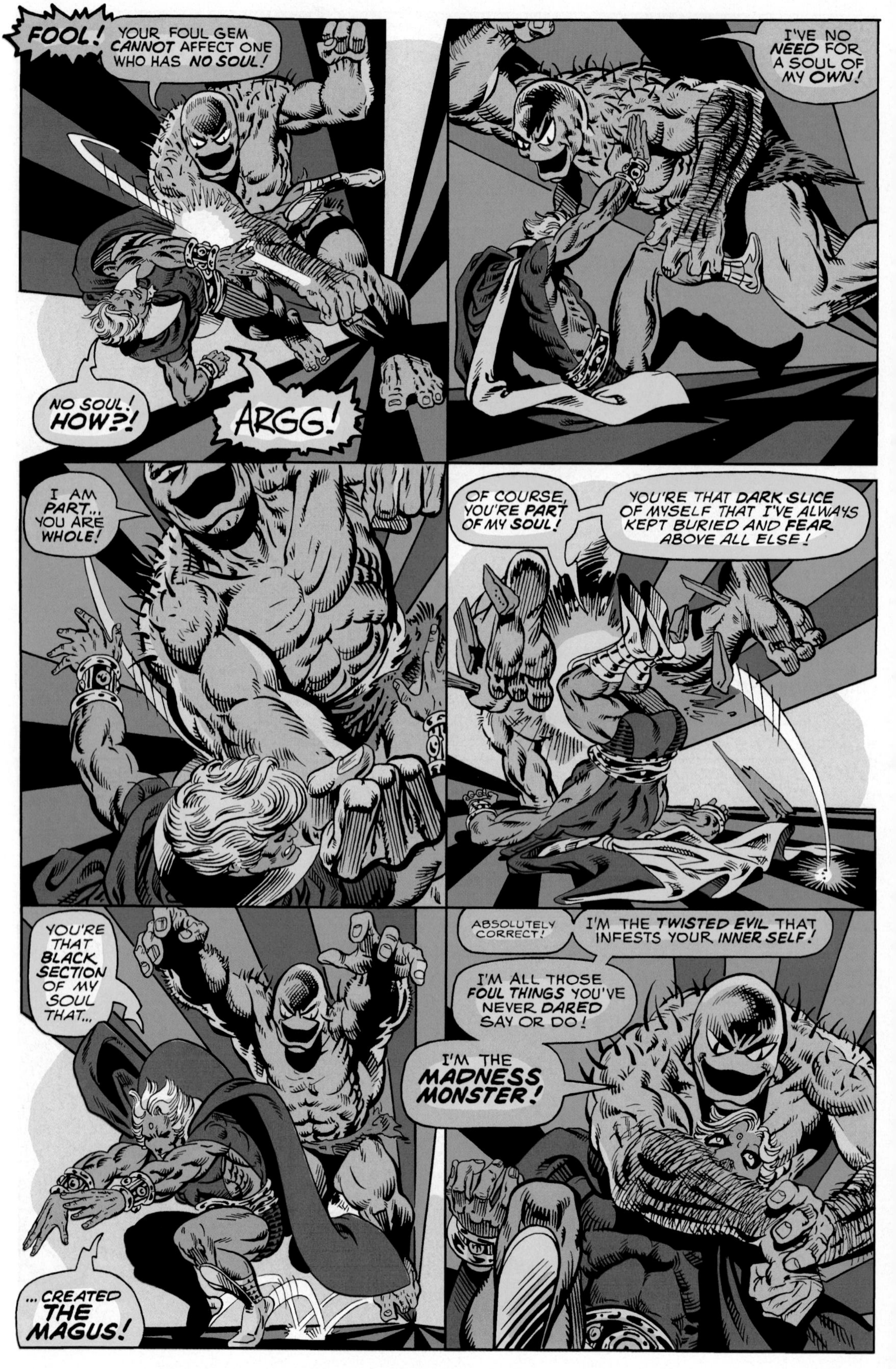

FOOL!
YOUR FOUL GEM CANNOT AFFECT ONE WHO HAS NO SOUL!
NO SOUL! HOW?!
ARGG!
I'VE NO NEED FOR A SOUL OF MY OWN!
I AM PART... YOU ARE WHOLE!
OF COURSE, YOU'RE PART OF MY SOUL!
YOU'RE THAT DARK SLICE OF MYSELF THAT I'VE ALWAYS KEPT BURIED AND FEAR ABOVE ALL ELSE!
YOU'RE THAT BLACK SECTION OF MY SOUL THAT...
...CREATED THE MAGUS!
ABSOLUTELY CORRECT!
I'M THE TWISTED EVIL THAT INFESTS YOUR INNER SELF!
I'M ALL THOSE FOUL THINGS YOU'VE NEVER DARED SAY OR DO!
I'M THE MADNESS MONSTER!

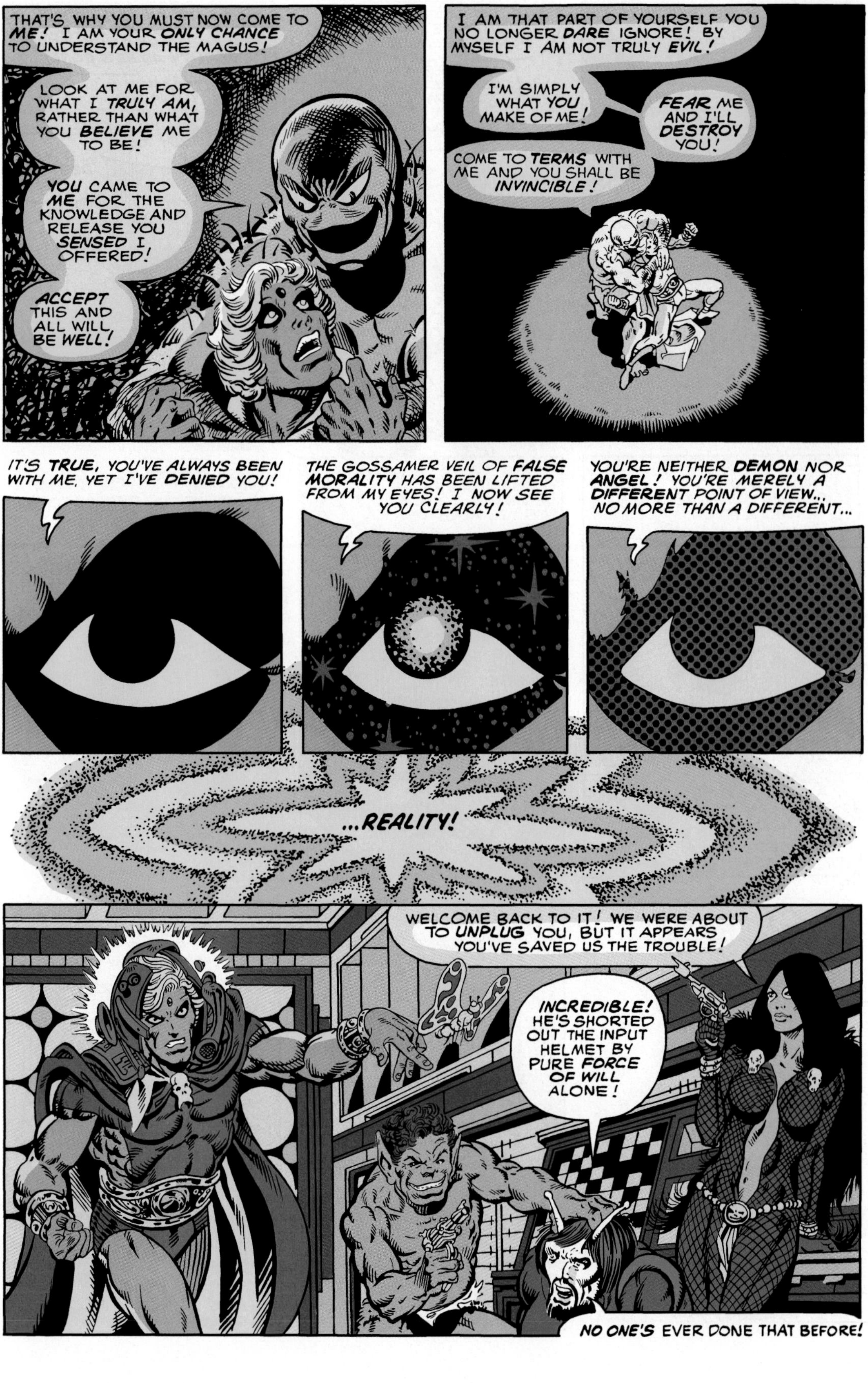

THAT'S WHY YOU MUST NOW COME TO ME! I AM YOUR ONLY CHANCE TO UNDERSTAND THE MAGUS!
LOOK AT ME FOR WHAT I TRULY AM, RATHER THAN WHAT YOU BELIEVE ME TO BE!
YOU CAME TO ME FOR THE KNOWLEDGE AND RELEASE YOU SENSED I OFFERED!
ACCEPT THIS AND ALL WILL BE WELL!
I AM THAT PART OF YOURSELF YOU NO LONGER DARE IGNORE! BY MYSELF I AM NOT TRULY EVIL!
I'M SIMPLY WHAT YOU MAKE OF ME!
FEAR ME AND I'LL DESTROY YOU!
COME TO TERMS WITH ME AND YOU SHALL BE INVINCIBLE!
IT'S TRUE, YOU'VE ALWAYS BEEN WITH ME, YET I'VE DENIED YOU!
THE GOSSAMER VEIL OF FALSE MORALITY HAS BEEN LIFTED FROM MY EYES! I NOW SEE YOU CLEARLY!
YOU'RE NEITHER DEMON NOR ANGEL! YOU'RE MERELY A DIFFERENT POINT OF VIEW... NO MORE THAN A DIFFERENT...
...REALITY!
WELCOME BACK TO IT! WE WERE ABOUT TO UNPLUG YOU, BUT IT APPEARS YOU'VE SAVED US THE TROUBLE!
INCREDIBLE! HE'S SHORTED OUT THE INPUT HELMET BY PURE FORCE OF WILL ALONE!
NO ONE'S EVER DONE THAT BEFORE!

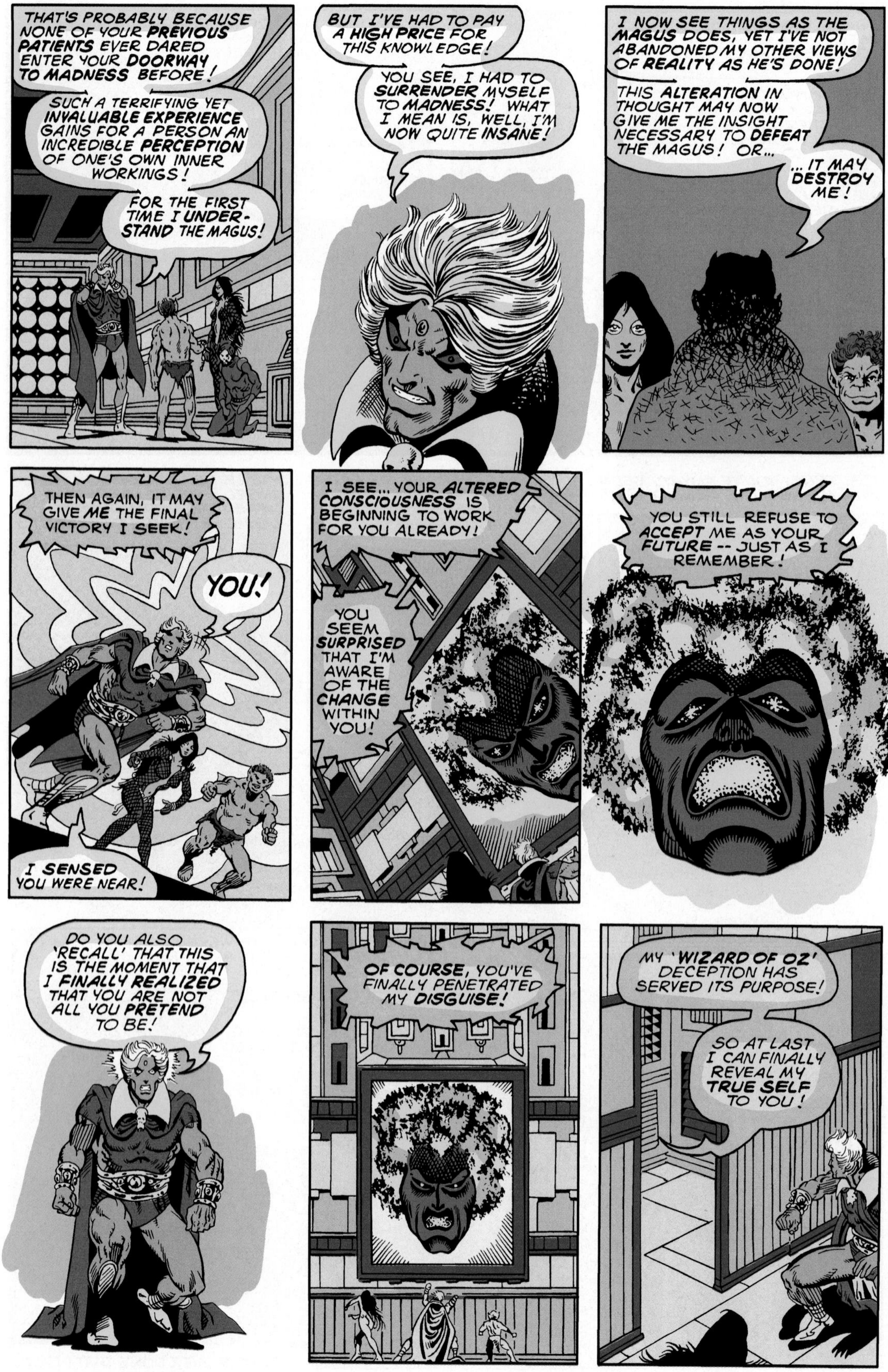

THAT'S PROBABLY BECAUSE NONE OF YOUR PREVIOUS PATIENTS EVER DARED ENTER YOUR DOORWAY TO MADNESS BEFORE!
SUCH A TERRIFYING YET INVALUABLE EXPERIENCE GAINS FOR A PERSON AN INCREDIBLE PERCEPTION OF ONE'S OWN INNER WORKINGS!
FOR THE FIRST TIME I UNDER-STAND THE MAGUS!
BUT I'VE HAD TO PAY A HIGH PRICE FOR THIS KNOWLEDGE!
YOU SEE, I HAD TO SURRENDER MYSELF TO MADNESS! WHAT I MEAN IS, WELL, I'M NOW QUITE INSANE!
I NOW SEE THINGS AS THE MAGUS DOES, YET I'VE NOT ABANDONED MY OTHER VIEWS OF REALITY AS HE'S DONE!
THIS ALTERATION IN THOUGHT MAY NOW GIVE ME THE INSIGHT NECESSARY TO DEFEAT THE MAGUS! OR...
...IT MAY DESTROY ME!
THEN AGAIN, IT MAY GIVE ME THE FINAL VICTORY I SEEK!
YOU!
I SENSED YOU WERE NEAR!
I SEE... YOUR ALTERED CONSCIOUSNESS IS BEGINNING TO WORK FOR YOU ALREADY!
YOU SEEM SURPRISED THAT I'M AWARE OF THE CHANGE WITHIN YOU!
YOU STILL REFUSE TO ACCEPT ME AS YOUR FUTURE -- JUST AS I REMEMBER!
DO YOU ALSO 'RECALL' THAT THIS IS THE MOMENT THAT I FINALLY REALIZED THAT YOU ARE NOT ALL YOU PRETEND TO BE!
OF COURSE, YOU'VE FINALLY PENETRATED MY DISGUISE!
MY 'WIZARD OF OZ' DECEPTION HAS SERVED ITS PURPOSE!
SO AT LAST I CAN FINALLY REVEAL MY TRUE SELF TO YOU!

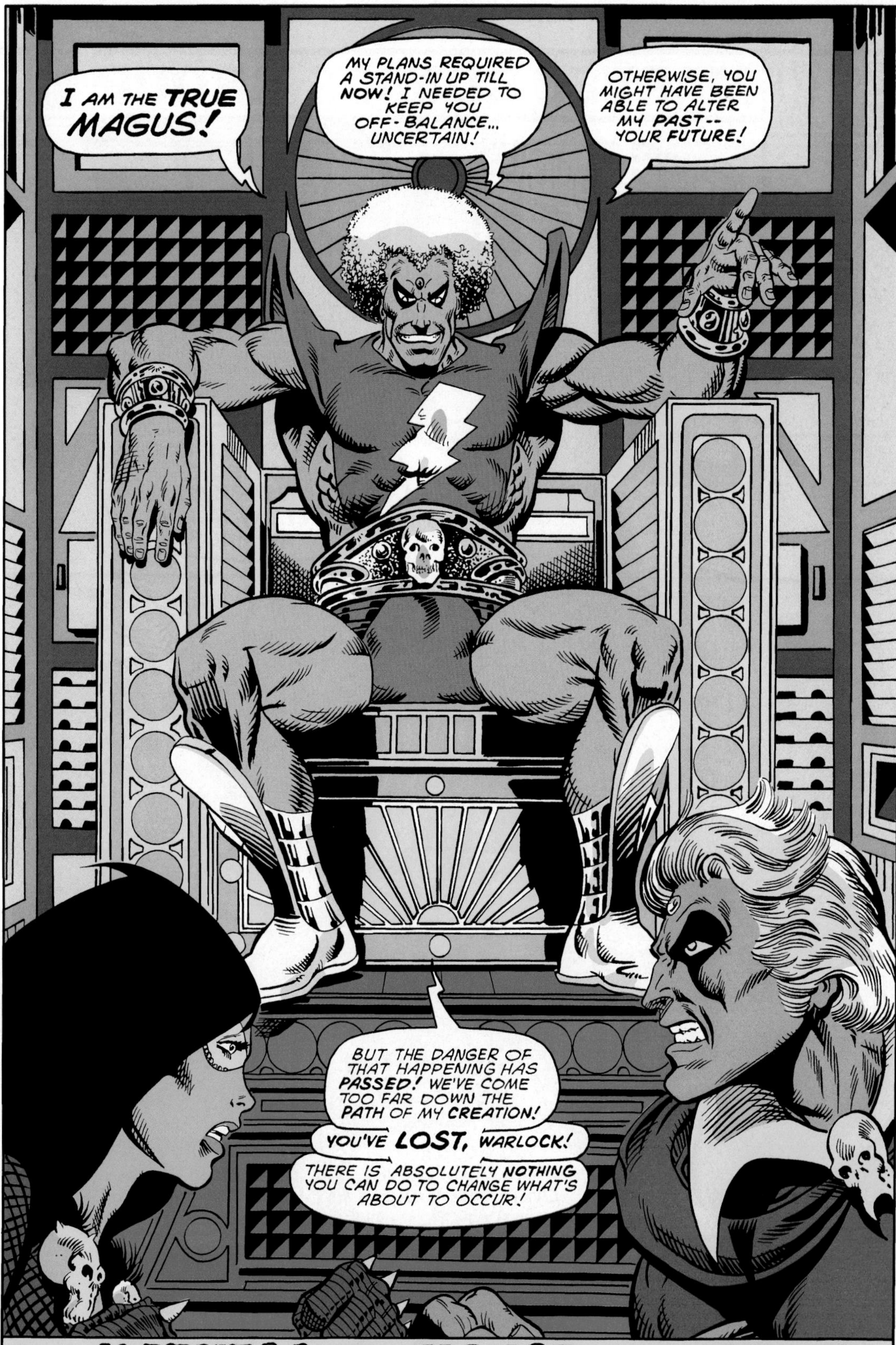
I AM THE TRUE MAGUS!
MY PLANS REQUIRED A STAND-IN UP TILL NOW! I NEEDED TO KEEP YOU OFF-BALANCE... UNCERTAIN!
OTHERWISE, YOU MIGHT HAVE BEEN ABLE TO ALTER MY PAST-- YOUR FUTURE!
BUT THE DANGER OF THAT HAPPENING HAS PASSED! WE'VE COME TOO FAR DOWN THE PATH OF MY CREATION!
YOU'VE LOST, WARLOCK!
THERE IS ABSOLUTELY NOTHING YOU CAN DO TO CHANGE WHAT'S ABOUT TO OCCUR!
NEXT: MADNESS IN THE HOUSE OF THE MAGUS!

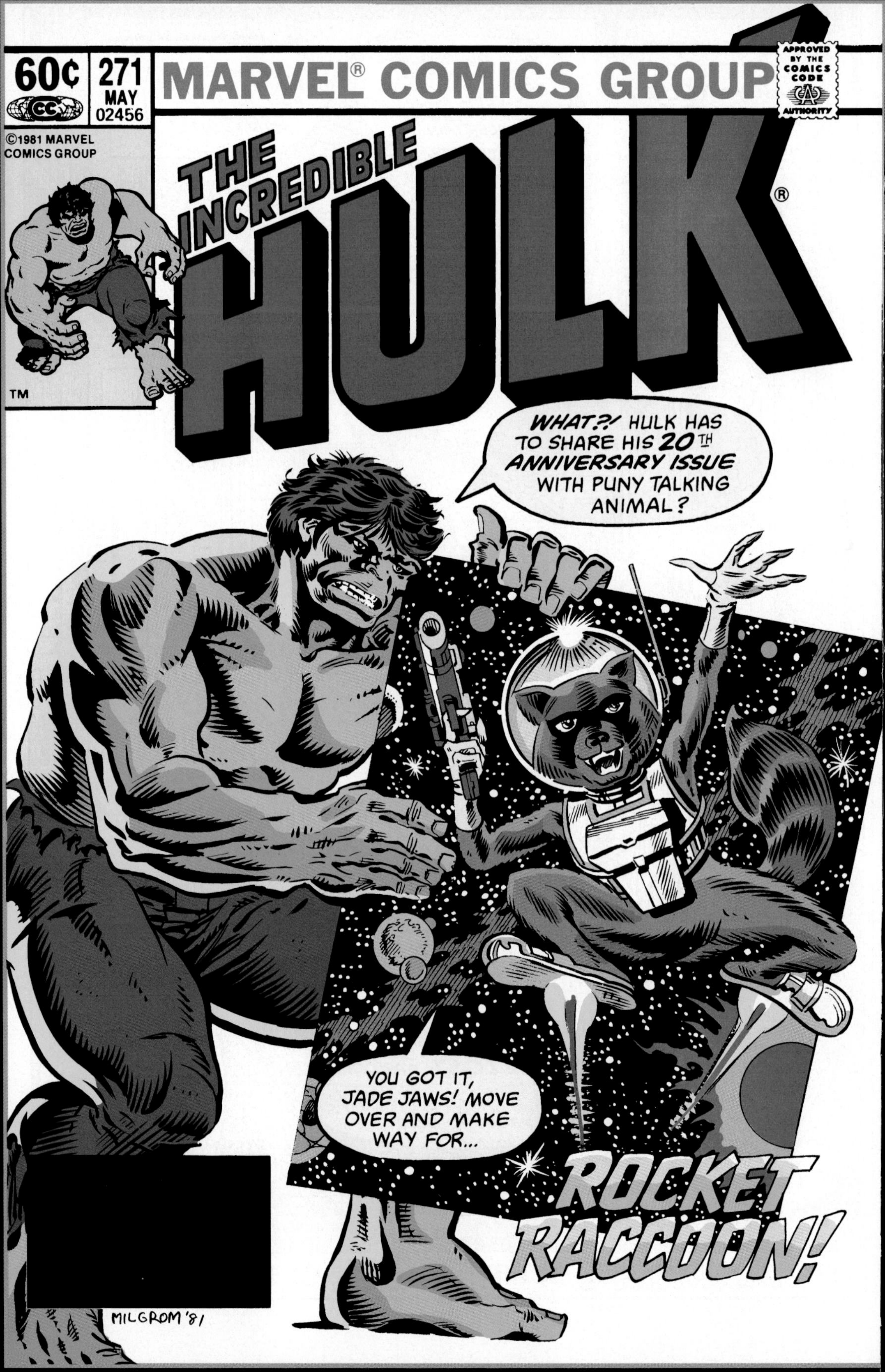
60¢
271
MAY
02456
MARVEL® COMICS GROUP
APPROVED BY THE COMICS CODE AUTHORITY
©1981 MARVEL COMICS GROUP
TM
THE INCREDIBLE HULK®
WHAT?!' HULK HAS TO SHARE HIS 20TH ANNIVERSARY ISSUE WITH PUNY TALKING ANIMAL?
YOU GOT IT, JADE JAWS! MOVE OVER AND MAKE WAY FOR...
ROCKET RACCOON!
MILGROM '81

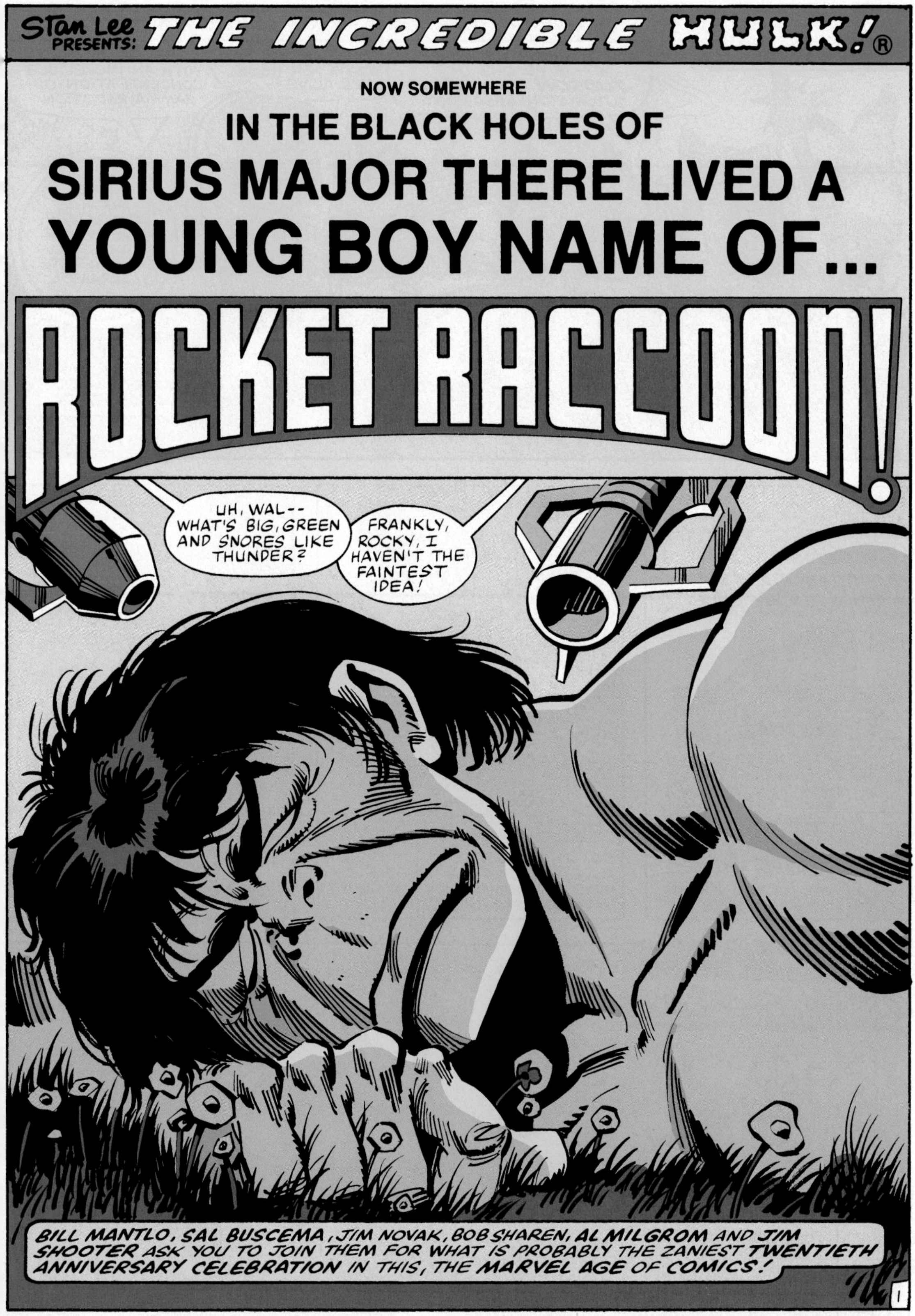
STAN LEE PRESENTS: THE INCREDIBLE HULK!®
NOW SOMEWHERE IN THE BLACK HOLES OF SIRIUS MAJOR THERE LIVED A YOUNG BOY NAME OF...
ROCKET RACCOON!
UH, WAL-- WHAT'S BIG, GREEN AND SNORES LIKE THUNDER?
FRANKLY, ROCKY, I HAVEN'T THE FAINTEST IDEA!
BILL MANTLO, SAL BUSCEMA, JIM NOVAK, BOB SHAREN, AL MILGROM AND JIM SHOOTER ASK YOU TO JOIN THEM FOR WHAT IS PROBABLY THE ZANIEST TWENTIETH ANNIVERSARY CELEBRATION IN THIS, THE MARVEL AGE OF COMICS!
1

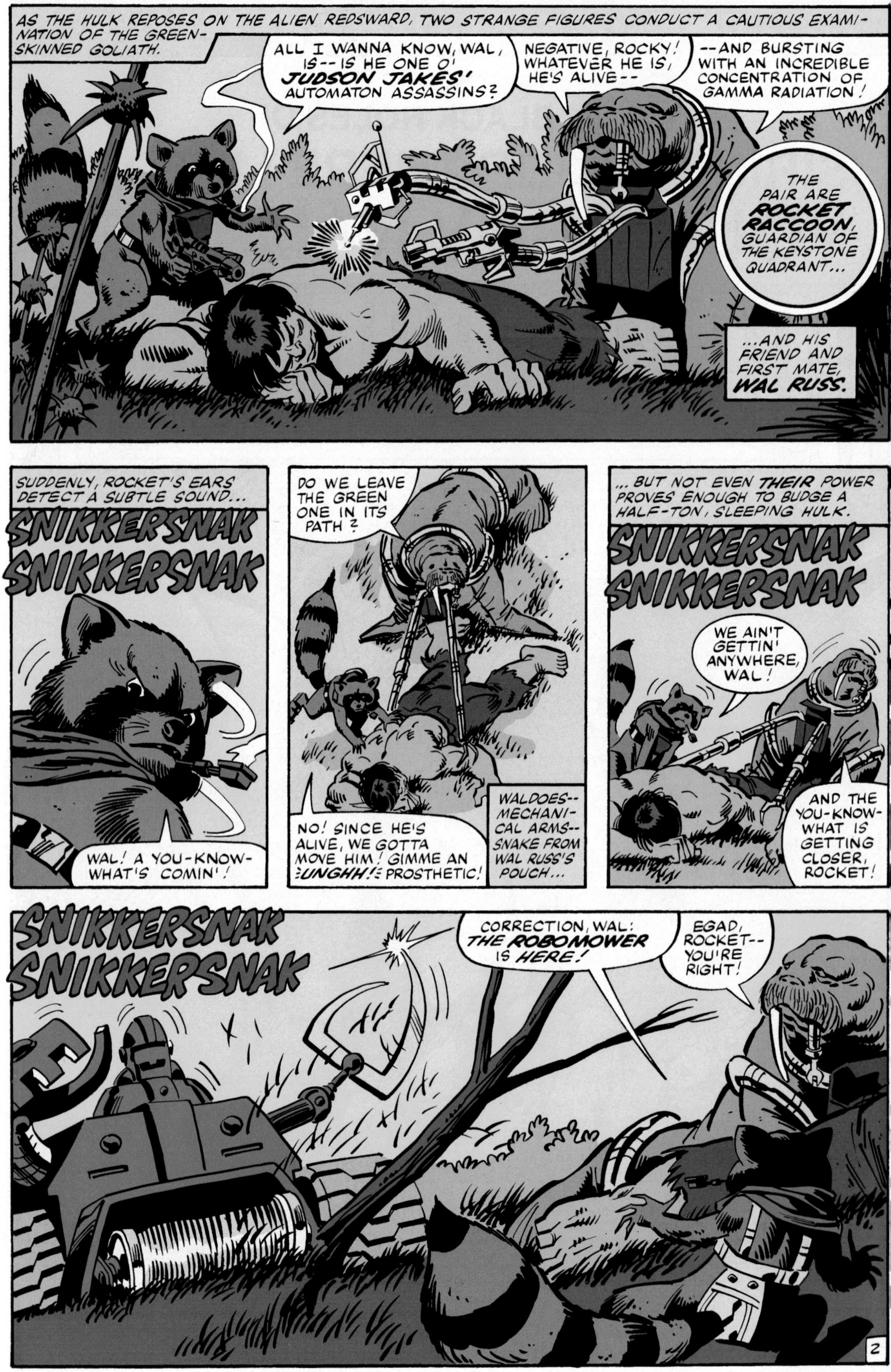
AS THE HULK REPOSES ON THE ALIEN REDSWARD, TWO STRANGE FIGURES CONDUCT A CAUTIOUS EXAMINATION OF THE GREEN-SKINNED GOLIATH.
ALL I WANNA KNOW, WAL, IS-- IS HE ONE O' JUDSON JAKES' AUTOMATON ASSASSINS?
NEGATIVE, ROCKY! WHATEVER HE IS, HE'S ALIVE--
--AND BURSTING WITH AN INCREDIBLE CONCENTRATION OF GAMMA RADIATION!
THE PAIR ARE ROCKET RACCOON, GUARDIAN OF THE KEYSTONE QUADRANT...
...AND HIS FRIEND AND FIRST MATE, WAL RUSS.
SUDDENLY, ROCKET'S EARS DETECT A SUBTLE SOUND...
SNIKKERSNAK SNIKKERSNAK
WAL! A YOU-KNOW-WHAT'S COMIN'!
DO WE LEAVE THE GREEN ONE IN ITS PATH?
NO! SINCE HE'S ALIVE, WE GOTTA MOVE HIM! GIMME AN UNGHH! PROSTHETIC!
WALDOES--MECHANICAL ARMS--SNAKE FROM WAL RUSS'S POUCH...
...BUT NOT EVEN THEIR POWER PROVES ENOUGH TO BUDGE A HALF-TON, SLEEPING HULK.
SNIKKERSNAK SNIKKERSNAK
WE AIN'T GETTIN' ANYWHERE, WAL!
AND THE YOU-KNOW-WHAT IS GETTING CLOSER, ROCKET!
SNIKKERSNAK SNIKKERSNAK
CORRECTION, WAL: THE ROBOMOWER IS HERE!
EGAD, ROCKET--YOU'RE RIGHT!

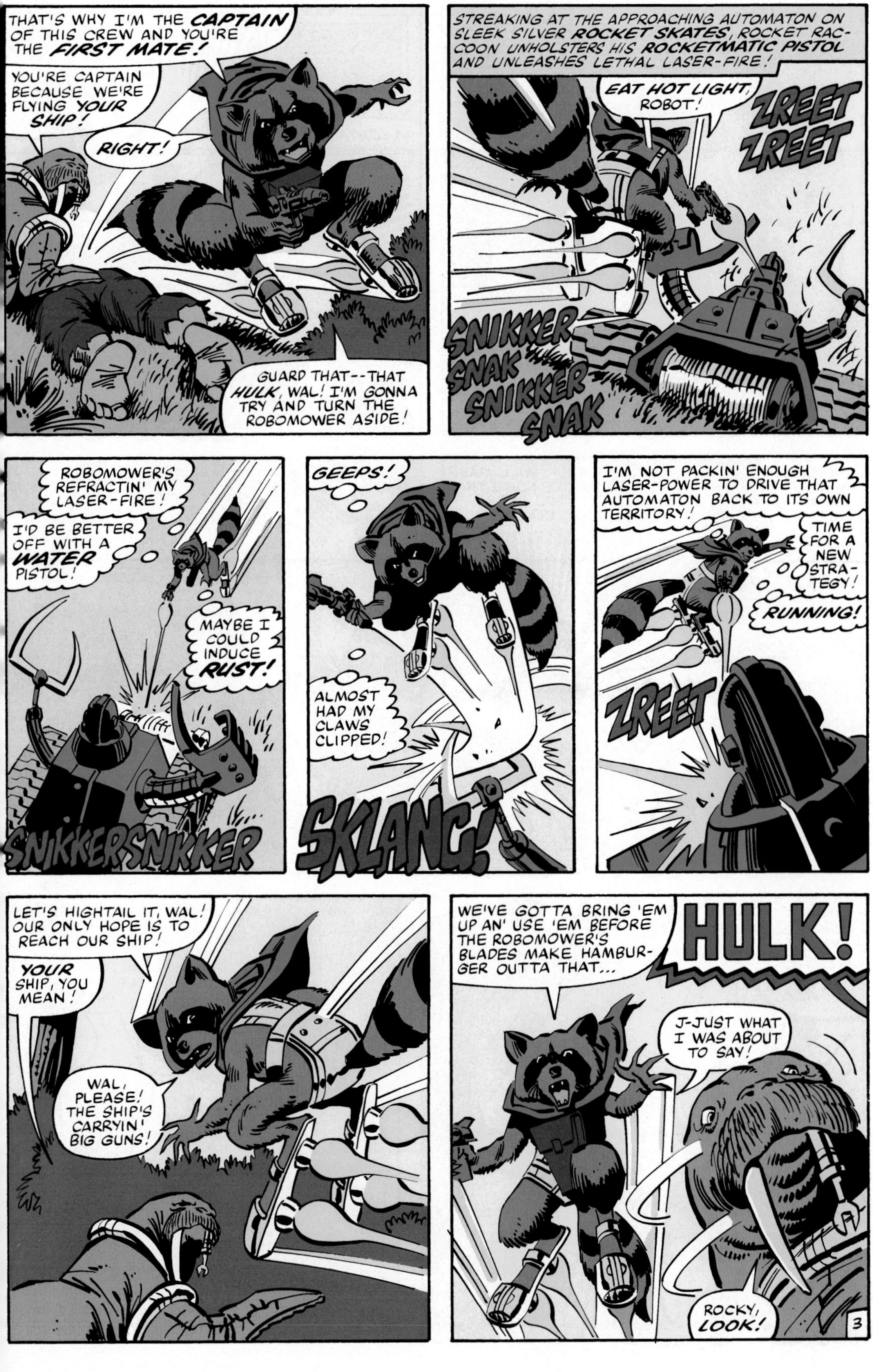
THAT'S WHY I'M THE CAPTAIN OF THIS CREW AND YOU'RE THE FIRST MATE!
YOU'RE CAPTAIN BECAUSE WE'RE FLYING YOUR SHIP!
RIGHT!
GUARD THAT--THAT HULK, WAL! I'M GONNA TRY AND TURN THE ROBOMOWER ASIDE!
STREAKING AT THE APPROACHING AUTOMATON ON SLEEK SILVER ROCKET SKATES, ROCKET RACCOON UNHOLSTERS HIS ROCKETMATIC PISTOL AND UNLEASHES LETHAL LASER-FIRE!
EAT HOT LIGHT, ROBOT!
ZREET ZREET
SNIKKER SNAK SNIKKER SNAK
ROBOMOWER'S REFRACTIN' MY LASER-FIRE!
I'D BE BETTER OFF WITH A WATER PISTOL!
MAYBE I COULD INDUCE RUST!
SNIKKERSNIKKER
GEEPS!
ALMOST HAD MY CLAWS CLIPPED!
SKLANG!
I'M NOT PACKIN' ENOUGH LASER-POWER TO DRIVE THAT AUTOMATON BACK TO ITS OWN TERRITORY!
TIME FOR A NEW STRATEGY!
RUNNING!
ZREET
LET'S HIGHTAIL IT, WAL! OUR ONLY HOPE IS TO REACH OUR SHIP!
YOUR SHIP, YOU MEAN!
WAL, PLEASE! THE SHIP'S CARRYIN' BIG GUNS!
WE'VE GOTTA BRING 'EM UP AN' USE 'EM BEFORE THE ROBOMOWER'S BLADES MAKE HAMBURGER OUTTA THAT...
HULK!
J-JUST WHAT I WAS ABOUT TO SAY!
ROCKY, LOOK!

NOISE WOKE HULK UP! HULK DIDN'T WANT TO WAKE UP! NOW HULK IS *MAD!*

WHAT DID HE SAY, ROCKY?

HE SAID HE'S MAD, WAL!

Y'KNOW, HE *LOOKS* MAD!

HE DOES, DOESN'T HE?

"BUT BEING MAD WON'T STOP A RUNAWAY ROBOMOWER!"

"YOU TELL *HIM* THAT, WAL!"

MACHINE MADE NOISE THAT WOKE HULK UP!

HULK WILL SMASH MACHINE!

SKRAKOW!

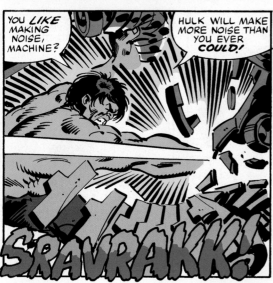

YOU *LIKE* MAKING NOISE, MACHINE?

HULK WILL MAKE MORE NOISE THAN YOU EVER *COULD!*

SRAVRAKK!

SNI-KER-SNAK-KER-SNIK-KER-SNAK-KER

GET READY, MACHINE!

HERE COMES THE BIGGEST NOISE OF ALL!

SKROOM!

HUNH! GOOD! NOISE HAS STOPPED! BUT HULK IS NOT TIRED ANYMORE!

WAL, D-DID YOU SEE WHAT HE DID?

I SAW, ROCKY, I SAW!

HE STOPPED A *ROBOMOWER* WITH HIS *BARE HANDS!*

I SAID, I SAW!

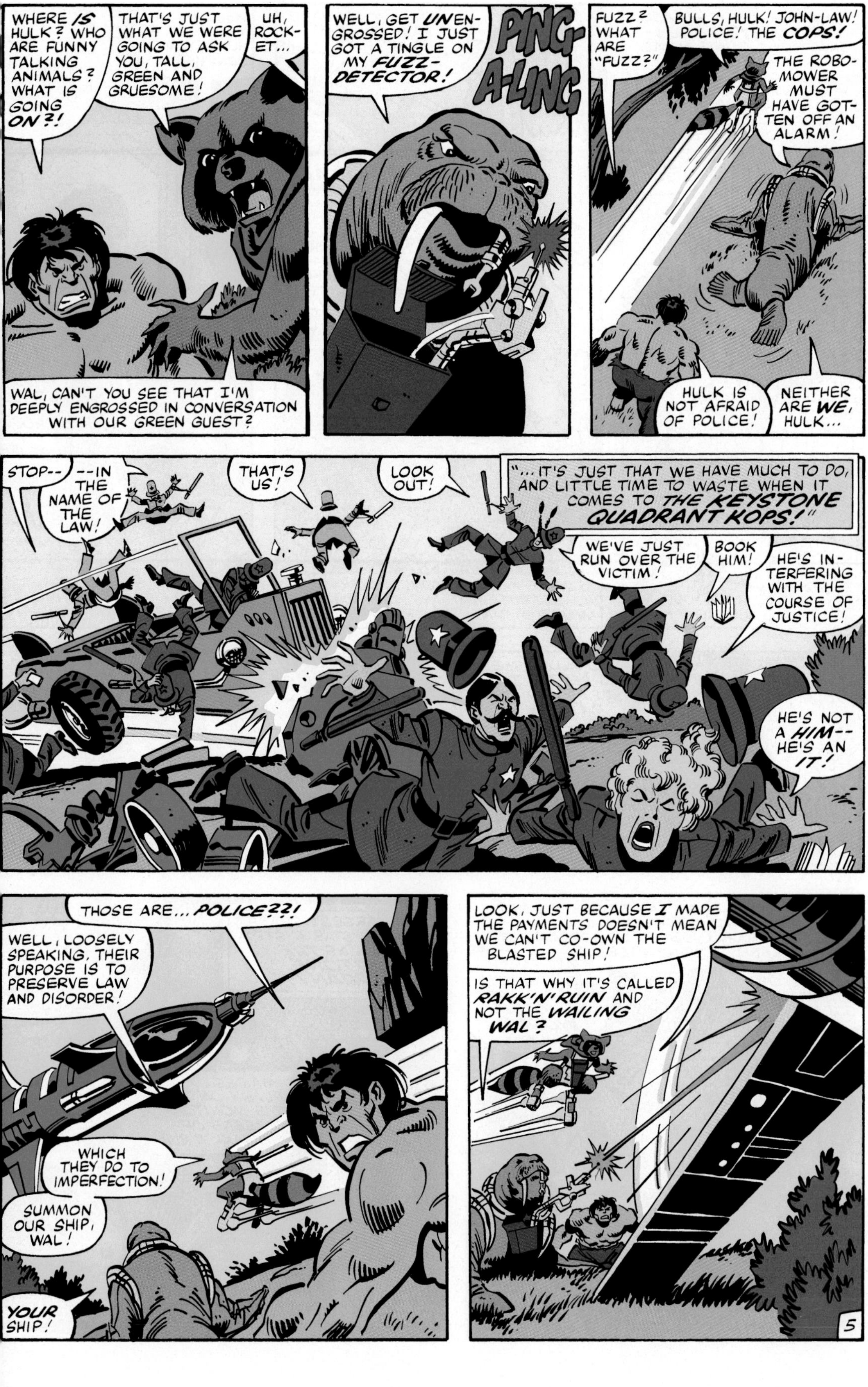

WHERE IS HULK? WHO ARE FUNNY TALKING ANIMALS? WHAT IS GOING ON?!
THAT'S JUST WHAT WE WERE GOING TO ASK YOU, TALL, GREEN AND GRUESOME!
UH, ROCKET...
WAL, CAN'T YOU SEE THAT I'M DEEPLY ENGROSSED IN CONVERSATION WITH OUR GREEN GUEST?
WELL, GET UNENGROSSED! I JUST GOT A TINGLE ON MY FUZZ-DETECTOR!
PING-A-LING
FUZZ? WHAT ARE "FUZZ?"
BULLS, HULK! JOHN-LAW! POLICE! THE COPS!
THE ROBO-MOWER MUST HAVE GOTTEN OFF AN ALARM!
HULK IS NOT AFRAID OF POLICE!
NEITHER ARE WE, HULK...
STOP--
--IN THE NAME OF THE LAW!
THAT'S US!
LOOK OUT!
"...IT'S JUST THAT WE HAVE MUCH TO DO, AND LITTLE TIME TO WASTE WHEN IT COMES TO THE KEYSTONE QUADRANT KOPS!"
WE'VE JUST RUN OVER THE VICTIM!
BOOK HIM!
HE'S INTERFERING WITH THE COURSE OF JUSTICE!
HE'S NOT A HIM-- HE'S AN IT!
THOSE ARE...POLICE??!
WELL, LOOSELY SPEAKING, THEIR PURPOSE IS TO PRESERVE LAW AND DISORDER!
WHICH THEY DO TO IMPERFECTION!
SUMMON OUR SHIP, WAL!
YOUR SHIP!
LOOK, JUST BECAUSE I MADE THE PAYMENTS DOESN'T MEAN WE CAN'T CO-OWN THE BLASTED SHIP!
IS THAT WHY IT'S CALLED RAKK'N'RUIN AND NOT THE WAILING WAL?

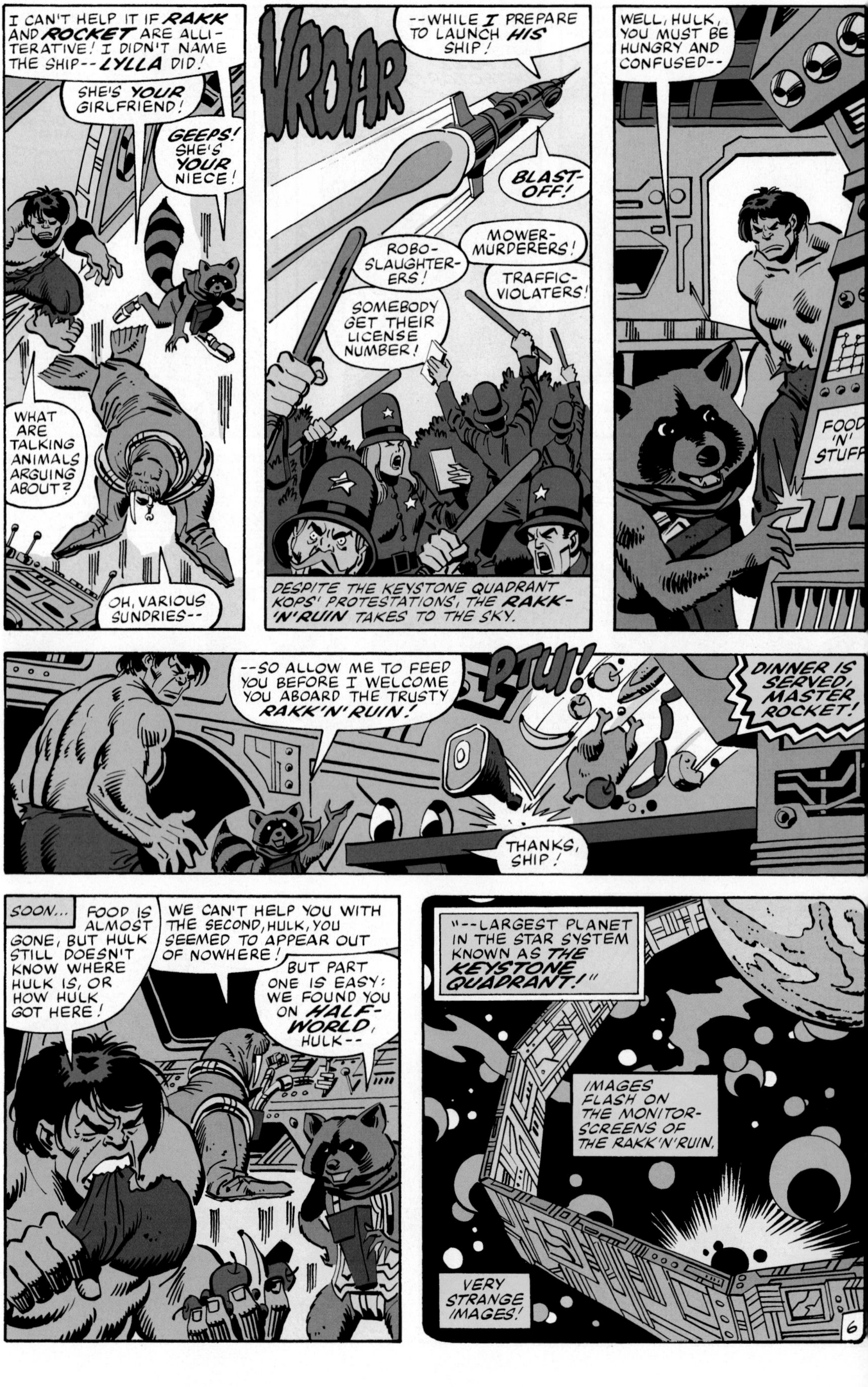

I CAN'T HELP IT IF RAKK AND ROCKET ARE ALLITERATIVE! I DIDN'T NAME THE SHIP--LYLLA DID!
SHE'S YOUR GIRLFRIEND!
GEEPS! SHE'S YOUR NIECE!
WHAT ARE TALKING ANIMALS ARGUING ABOUT?
OH, VARIOUS SUNDRIES--
VROAR
--WHILE I PREPARE TO LAUNCH HIS SHIP!
BLAST-OFF!
MOWER-MURDERERS!
ROBO-SLAUGHTERERS!
TRAFFIC-VIOLATERS!
SOMEBODY GET THEIR LICENSE NUMBER!
DESPITE THE KEYSTONE QUADRANT KOPS' PROTESTATIONS, THE RAKK-'N'RUIN TAKES TO THE SKY.
WELL, HULK, YOU MUST BE HUNGRY AND CONFUSED--
FOOD 'N' STUFF
--SO ALLOW ME TO FEED YOU BEFORE I WELCOME YOU ABOARD THE TRUSTY RAKK'N'RUIN!
PTUI!
DINNER IS SERVED, MASTER ROCKET!
THANKS, SHIP!
SOON...
FOOD IS ALMOST GONE, BUT HULK STILL DOESN'T KNOW WHERE HULK IS, OR HOW HULK GOT HERE!
WE CAN'T HELP YOU WITH THE SECOND, HULK, YOU SEEMED TO APPEAR OUT OF NOWHERE!
BUT PART ONE IS EASY: WE FOUND YOU ON HALF-WORLD, HULK--
"--LARGEST PLANET IN THE STAR SYSTEM KNOWN AS THE KEYSTONE QUADRANT!"
IMAGES FLASH ON THE MONITOR-SCREENS OF THE RAKK'N'RUIN.
VERY STRANGE IMAGES!

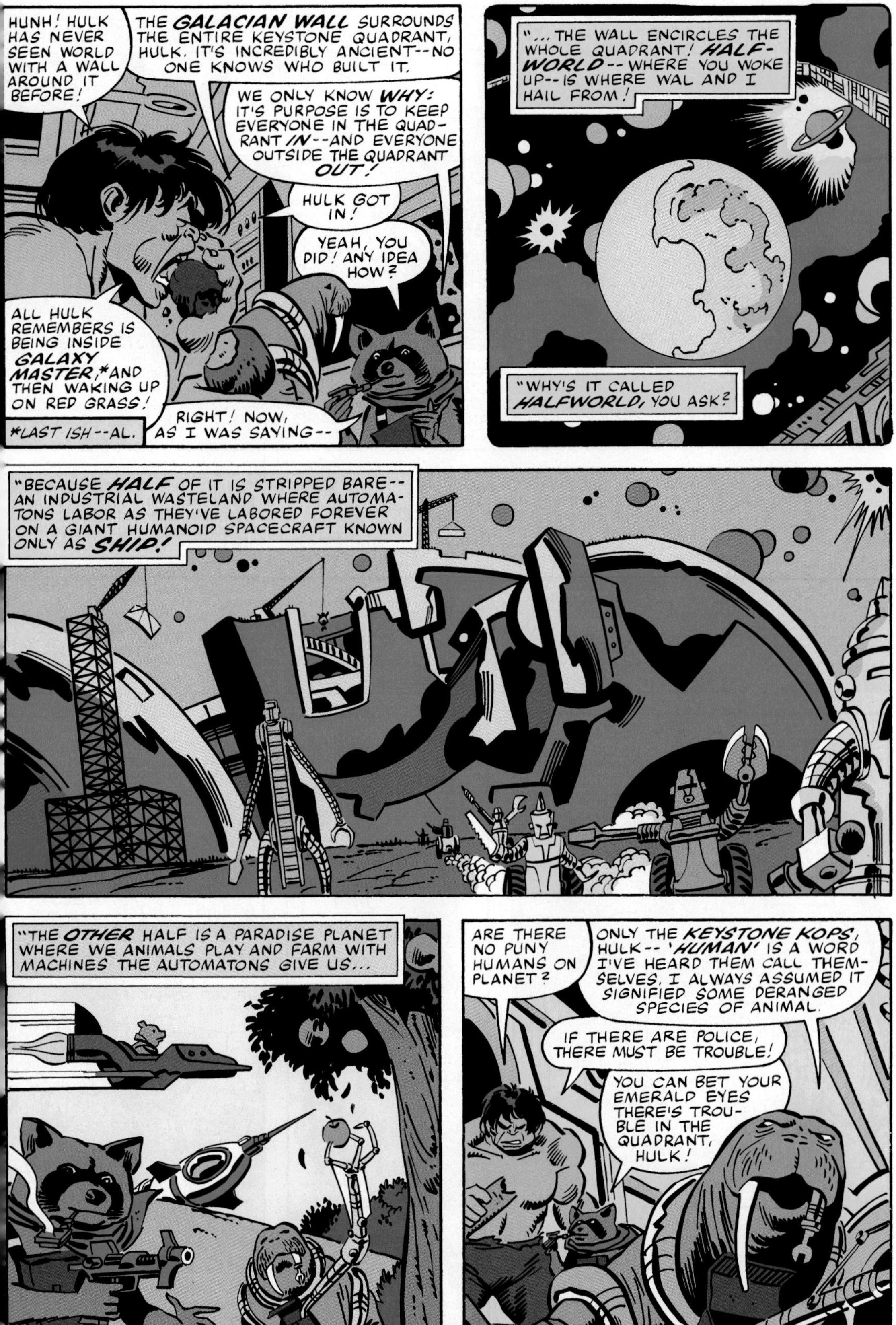
HUNH! HULK HAS NEVER SEEN WORLD WITH A WALL AROUND IT BEFORE!
THE GALACIAN WALL SURROUNDS THE ENTIRE KEYSTONE QUADRANT, HULK. IT'S INCREDIBLY ANCIENT--NO ONE KNOWS WHO BUILT IT.
WE ONLY KNOW WHY: IT'S PURPOSE IS TO KEEP EVERYONE IN THE QUADRANT IN--AND EVERYONE OUTSIDE THE QUADRANT OUT!
HULK GOT IN!
YEAH, YOU DID! ANY IDEA HOW?
ALL HULK REMEMBERS IS BEING INSIDE GALAXY MASTER,*AND THEN WAKING UP ON RED GRASS!
RIGHT! NOW, AS I WAS SAYING--
*LAST ISH--AL.
"...THE WALL ENCIRCLES THE WHOLE QUADRANT! HALF-WORLD--WHERE YOU WOKE UP--IS WHERE WAL AND I HAIL FROM!
"WHY'S IT CALLED HALFWORLD, YOU ASK?
"BECAUSE HALF OF IT IS STRIPPED BARE--AN INDUSTRIAL WASTELAND WHERE AUTOMATONS LABOR AS THEY'VE LABORED FOREVER ON A GIANT HUMANOID SPACECRAFT KNOWN ONLY AS SHIP!
"THE OTHER HALF IS A PARADISE PLANET WHERE WE ANIMALS PLAY AND FARM WITH MACHINES THE AUTOMATONS GIVE US...
"...'CAUSE THEY CAN'T HELP MAKIN' EM, AND CAN'T USE 'EM ONCE THEY DO!
ARE THERE NO PUNY HUMANS ON PLANET?
ONLY THE KEYSTONE KOPS, HULK--'HUMAN' IS A WORD I'VE HEARD THEM CALL THEMSELVES. I ALWAYS ASSUMED IT SIGNIFIED SOME DERANGED SPECIES OF ANIMAL.
IF THERE ARE POLICE, THERE MUST BE TROUBLE!
YOU CAN BET YOUR EMERALD EYES THERE'S TROUBLE IN THE QUADRANT, HULK!
7

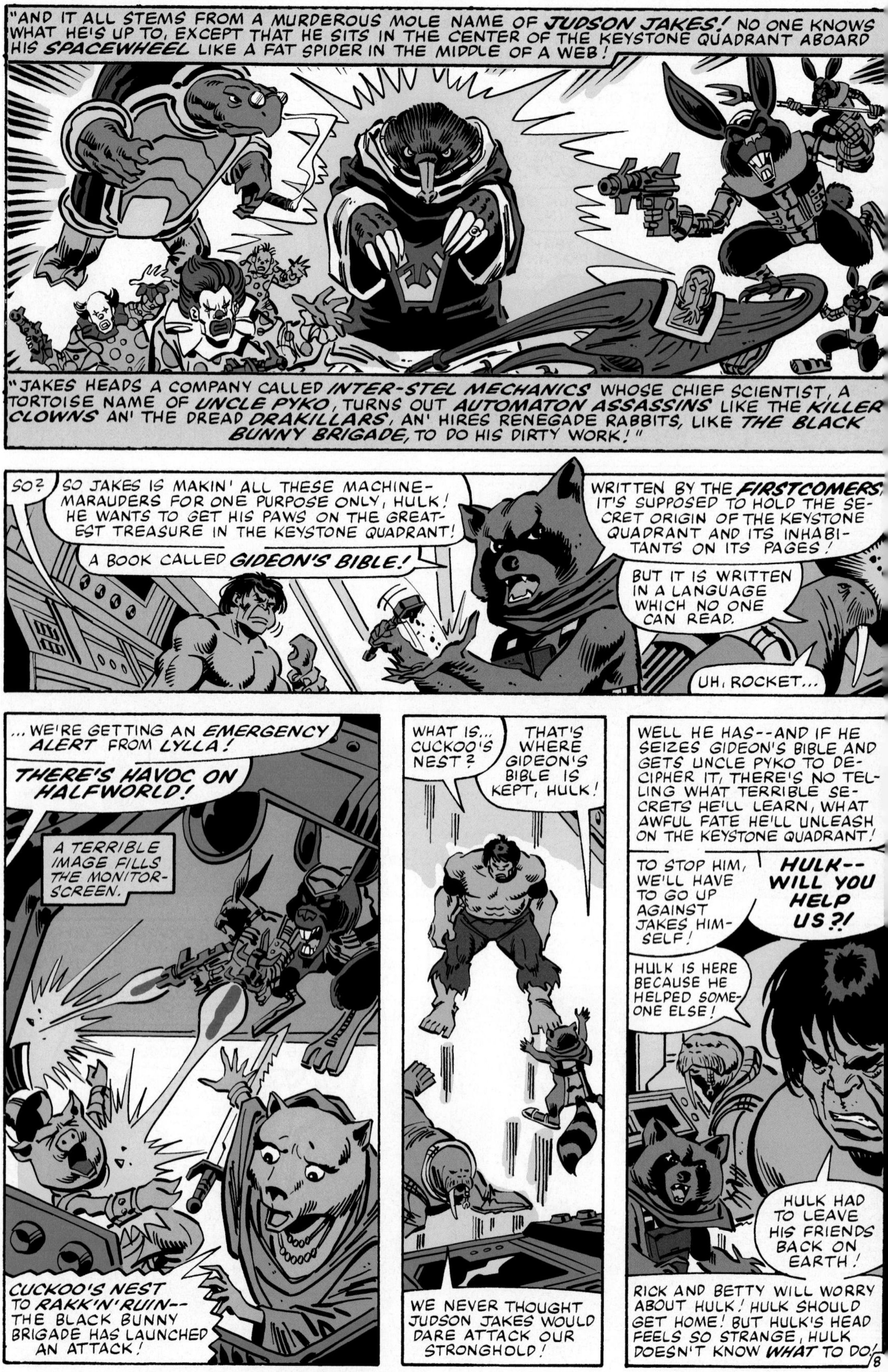
"AND IT ALL STEMS FROM A MURDEROUS MOLE NAME OF JUDSON JAKES! NO ONE KNOWS WHAT HE'S UP TO, EXCEPT THAT HE SITS IN THE CENTER OF THE KEYSTONE QUADRANT ABOARD HIS SPACEWHEEL LIKE A FAT SPIDER IN THE MIDDLE OF A WEB!
"JAKES HEADS A COMPANY CALLED INTER-STEL MECHANICS WHOSE CHIEF SCIENTIST, A TORTOISE NAME OF UNCLE PYKO, TURNS OUT AUTOMATON ASSASSINS LIKE THE KILLER CLOWNS AN' THE DREAD DRAKILLARS, AN' HIRES RENEGADE RABBITS, LIKE THE BLACK BUNNY BRIGADE, TO DO HIS DIRTY WORK!"
SO?
SO JAKES IS MAKIN' ALL THESE MACHINE-MARAUDERS FOR ONE PURPOSE ONLY, HULK! HE WANTS TO GET HIS PAWS ON THE GREATEST TREASURE IN THE KEYSTONE QUADRANT!
A BOOK CALLED GIDEON'S BIBLE!
WRITTEN BY THE FIRSTCOMERS, IT'S SUPPOSED TO HOLD THE SECRET ORIGIN OF THE KEYSTONE QUADRANT AND ITS INHABITANTS ON ITS PAGES!
BUT IT IS WRITTEN IN A LANGUAGE WHICH NO ONE CAN READ.
UH, ROCKET...
...WE'RE GETTING AN EMERGENCY ALERT FROM LYLLA!
THERE'S HAVOC ON HALFWORLD!
A TERRIBLE IMAGE FILLS THE MONITOR-SCREEN.
CUCKOO'S NEST TO RAKK'N'RUIN-- THE BLACK BUNNY BRIGADE HAS LAUNCHED AN ATTACK!
WHAT IS... CUCKOO'S NEST?
THAT'S WHERE GIDEON'S BIBLE IS KEPT, HULK!
WE NEVER THOUGHT JUDSON JAKES WOULD DARE ATTACK OUR STRONGHOLD!
WELL HE HAS--AND IF HE SEIZES GIDEON'S BIBLE AND GETS UNCLE PYKO TO DECIPHER IT, THERE'S NO TELLING WHAT TERRIBLE SECRETS HE'LL LEARN, WHAT AWFUL FATE HE'LL UNLEASH ON THE KEYSTONE QUADRANT!
TO STOP HIM, WE'LL HAVE TO GO UP AGAINST JAKES HIMSELF!
HULK-- WILL YOU HELP US?!
HULK IS HERE BECAUSE HE HELPED SOMEONE ELSE!
HULK HAD TO LEAVE HIS FRIENDS BACK ON EARTH!
RICK AND BETTY WILL WORRY ABOUT HULK! HULK SHOULD GET HOME! BUT HULK'S HEAD FEELS SO STRANGE, HULK DOESN'T KNOW WHAT TO DO!

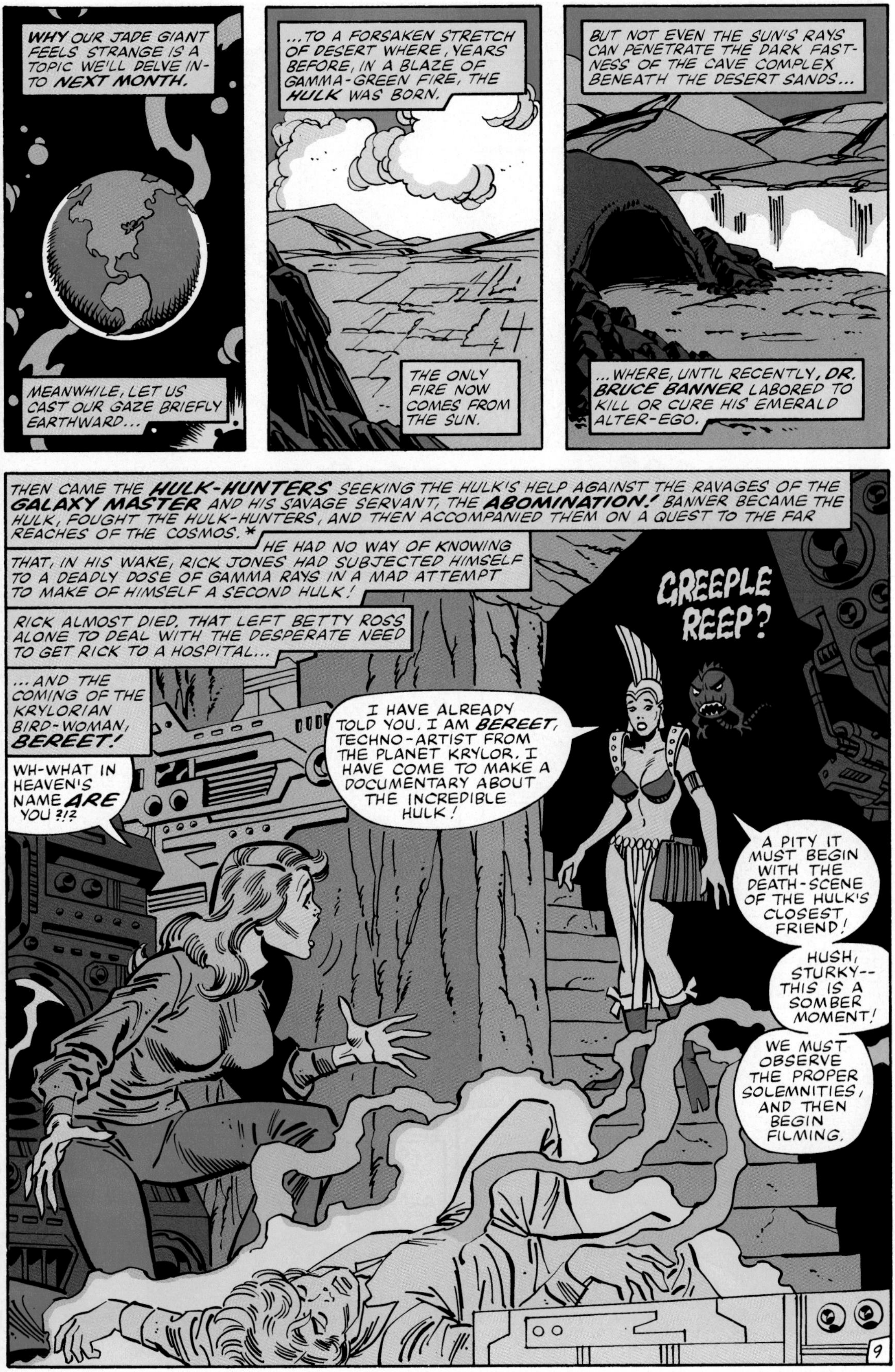
WHY OUR JADE GIANT FEELS STRANGE IS A TOPIC WE'LL DELVE INTO NEXT MONTH.
MEANWHILE, LET US CAST OUR GAZE BRIEFLY EARTHWARD...
...TO A FORSAKEN STRETCH OF DESERT WHERE, YEARS BEFORE, IN A BLAZE OF GAMMA-GREEN FIRE, THE HULK WAS BORN.
THE ONLY FIRE NOW COMES FROM THE SUN.
BUT NOT EVEN THE SUN'S RAYS CAN PENETRATE THE DARK FASTNESS OF THE CAVE COMPLEX BENEATH THE DESERT SANDS...
...WHERE, UNTIL RECENTLY, DR. BRUCE BANNER LABORED TO KILL OR CURE HIS EMERALD ALTER-EGO.
THEN CAME THE HULK-HUNTERS SEEKING THE HULK'S HELP AGAINST THE RAVAGES OF THE GALAXY MASTER AND HIS SAVAGE SERVANT, THE ABOMINATION! BANNER BECAME THE HULK, FOUGHT THE HULK-HUNTERS, AND THEN ACCOMPANIED THEM ON A QUEST TO THE FAR REACHES OF THE COSMOS.*
HE HAD NO WAY OF KNOWING THAT, IN HIS WAKE, RICK JONES HAD SUBJECTED HIMSELF TO A DEADLY DOSE OF GAMMA RAYS IN A MAD ATTEMPT TO MAKE OF HIMSELF A SECOND HULK!
RICK ALMOST DIED. THAT LEFT BETTY ROSS ALONE TO DEAL WITH THE DESPERATE NEED TO GET RICK TO A HOSPITAL...
...AND THE COMING OF THE KRYLORIAN BIRD-WOMAN, BEREET!
WH-WHAT IN HEAVEN'S NAME ARE YOU?!?
I HAVE ALREADY TOLD YOU. I AM BEREET, TECHNO-ARTIST FROM THE PLANET KRYLOR. I HAVE COME TO MAKE A DOCUMENTARY ABOUT THE INCREDIBLE HULK!
GREEPLE REEP?
A PITY IT MUST BEGIN WITH THE DEATH-SCENE OF THE HULK'S CLOSEST FRIEND!
HUSH, STURKY-- THIS IS A SOMBER MOMENT!
WE MUST OBSERVE THE PROPER SOLEMNITIES, AND THEN BEGIN FILMING.
9

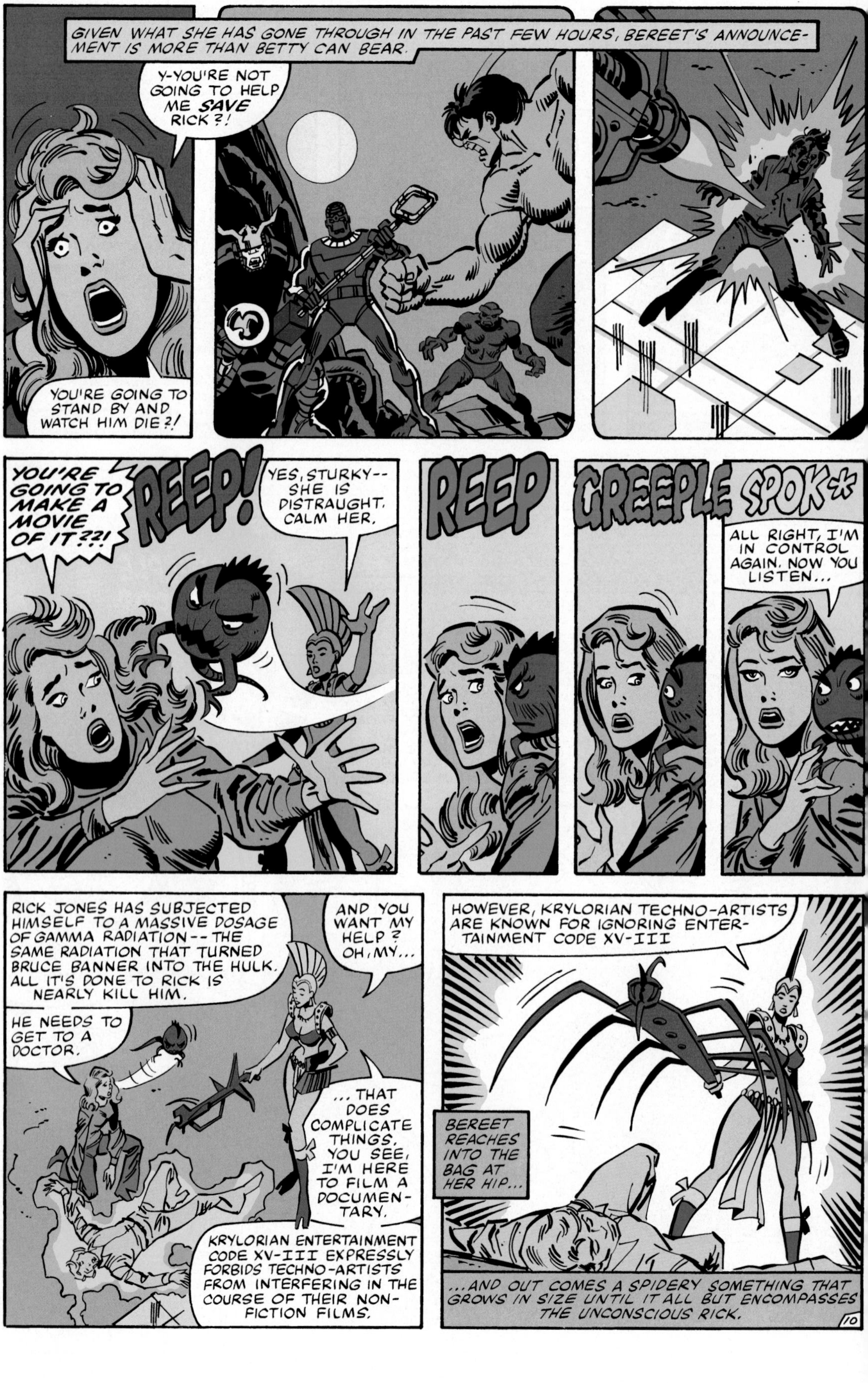
GIVEN WHAT SHE HAS GONE THROUGH IN THE PAST FEW HOURS, BEREET'S ANNOUNCEMENT IS MORE THAN BETTY CAN BEAR.
Y-YOU'RE NOT GOING TO HELP ME SAVE RICK?!
YOU'RE GOING TO STAND BY AND WATCH HIM DIE?!
YOU'RE GOING TO MAKE A MOVIE OF IT??!
REEP!
YES, STURKY-- SHE IS DISTRAUGHT. CALM HER.
REEP
GREEPLE
SPOK*
ALL RIGHT, I'M IN CONTROL AGAIN. NOW YOU LISTEN...
RICK JONES HAS SUBJECTED HIMSELF TO A MASSIVE DOSAGE OF GAMMA RADIATION -- THE SAME RADIATION THAT TURNED BRUCE BANNER INTO THE HULK. ALL IT'S DONE TO RICK IS NEARLY KILL HIM.
HE NEEDS TO GET TO A DOCTOR.
AND YOU WANT MY HELP? OH, MY...
...THAT DOES COMPLICATE THINGS. YOU SEE, I'M HERE TO FILM A DOCUMENTARY.
KRYLORIAN ENTERTAINMENT CODE XV-III EXPRESSLY FORBIDS TECHNO-ARTISTS FROM INTERFERING IN THE COURSE OF THEIR NON-FICTION FILMS.
HOWEVER, KRYLORIAN TECHNO-ARTISTS ARE KNOWN FOR IGNORING ENTERTAINMENT CODE XV-III
BEREET REACHES INTO THE BAG AT HER HIP...
...AND OUT COMES A SPIDERY SOMETHING THAT GROWS IN SIZE UNTIL IT ALL BUT ENCOMPASSES THE UNCONSCIOUS RICK.
10

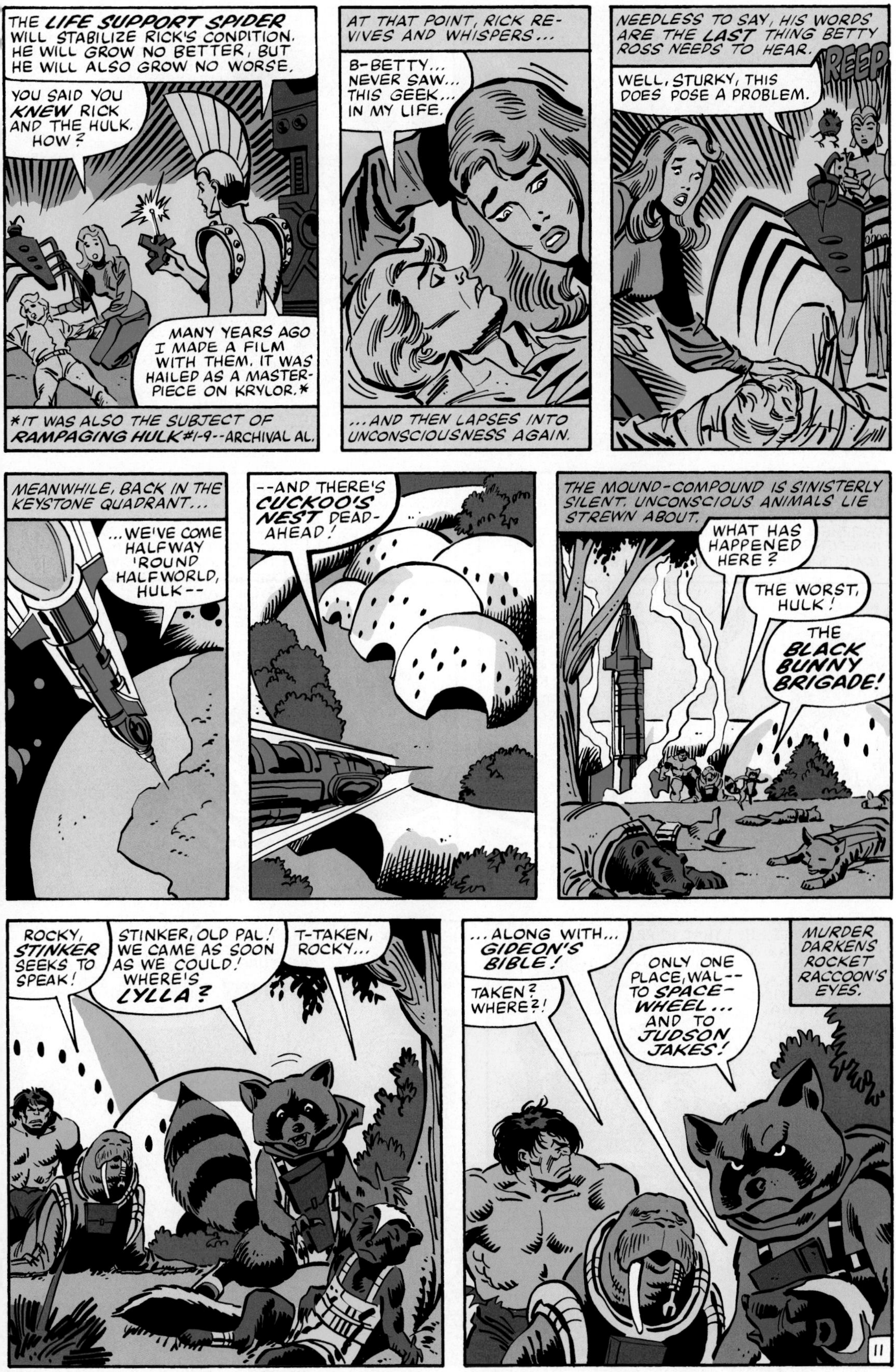
THE LIFE SUPPORT SPIDER WILL STABILIZE RICK'S CONDITION. HE WILL GROW NO BETTER, BUT HE WILL ALSO GROW NO WORSE.
YOU SAID YOU KNEW RICK AND THE HULK. HOW?
MANY YEARS AGO I MADE A FILM WITH THEM. IT WAS HAILED AS A MASTERPIECE ON KRYLOR.*
*IT WAS ALSO THE SUBJECT OF RAMPAGING HULK #1-9--ARCHIVAL AL.
AT THAT POINT, RICK REVIVES AND WHISPERS...
B-BETTY... NEVER SAW... THIS GEEK... IN MY LIFE.
...AND THEN LAPSES INTO UNCONSCIOUSNESS AGAIN.
NEEDLESS TO SAY, HIS WORDS ARE THE LAST THING BETTY ROSS NEEDS TO HEAR.
REEP
WELL, STURKY, THIS DOES POSE A PROBLEM.
MEANWHILE, BACK IN THE KEYSTONE QUADRANT...
...WE'VE COME HALFWAY 'ROUND HALFWORLD, HULK--
--AND THERE'S CUCKOO'S NEST DEAD-AHEAD!
THE MOUND-COMPOUND IS SINISTERLY SILENT. UNCONSCIOUS ANIMALS LIE STREWN ABOUT.
WHAT HAS HAPPENED HERE?
THE WORST, HULK!
THE BLACK BUNNY BRIGADE!
ROCKY, STINKER SEEKS TO SPEAK!
STINKER, OLD PAL! WE CAME AS SOON AS WE COULD! WHERE'S LYLLA?
T-TAKEN, ROCKY...
...ALONG WITH... GIDEON'S BIBLE!
TAKEN? WHERE?!
ONLY ONE PLACE, WAL-- TO SPACE-WHEEL... AND TO JUDSON JAKES!
MURDER DARKENS ROCKET RACCOON'S EYES.
11

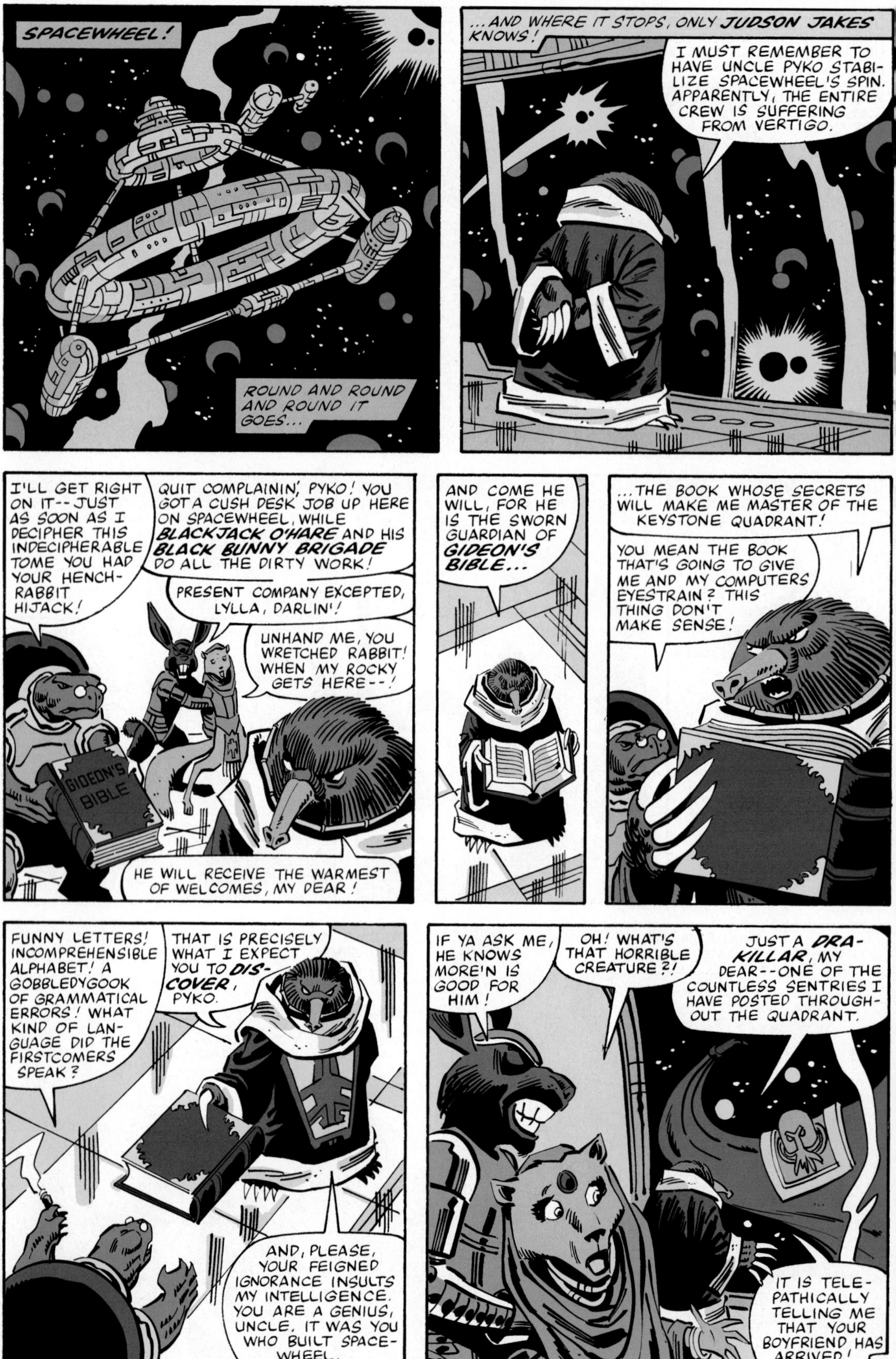
SPACEWHEEL!
ROUND AND ROUND AND ROUND IT GOES...
...AND WHERE IT STOPS, ONLY JUDSON JAKES KNOWS!
I MUST REMEMBER TO HAVE UNCLE PYKO STABILIZE SPACEWHEEL'S SPIN. APPARENTLY, THE ENTIRE CREW IS SUFFERING FROM VERTIGO.
I'LL GET RIGHT ON IT--JUST AS SOON AS I DECIPHER THIS INDECIPHERABLE TOME YOU HAD YOUR HENCH-RABBIT HIJACK!
QUIT COMPLAININ', PYKO! YOU GOT A CUSH DESK JOB UP HERE ON SPACEWHEEL, WHILE BLACKJACK O'HARE AND HIS BLACK BUNNY BRIGADE DO ALL THE DIRTY WORK!
PRESENT COMPANY EXCEPTED, LYLLA, DARLIN'!
UNHAND ME, YOU WRETCHED RABBIT! WHEN MY ROCKY GETS HERE--!
GIDEON'S BIBLE
HE WILL RECEIVE THE WARMEST OF WELCOMES, MY DEAR!
AND COME HE WILL, FOR HE IS THE SWORN GUARDIAN OF GIDEON'S BIBLE...
...THE BOOK WHOSE SECRETS WILL MAKE ME MASTER OF THE KEYSTONE QUADRANT!
YOU MEAN THE BOOK THAT'S GOING TO GIVE ME AND MY COMPUTERS EYESTRAIN? THIS THING DON'T MAKE SENSE!
FUNNY LETTERS! INCOMPREHENSIBLE ALPHABET! A GOBBLEDYGOOK OF GRAMMATICAL ERRORS! WHAT KIND OF LANGUAGE DID THE FIRSTCOMERS SPEAK?
THAT IS PRECISELY WHAT I EXPECT YOU TO DISCOVER, PYKO.
AND, PLEASE, YOUR FEIGNED IGNORANCE INSULTS MY INTELLIGENCE. YOU ARE A GENIUS, UNCLE. IT WAS YOU WHO BUILT SPACEWHEEL.
IF YA ASK ME, HE KNOWS MORE'N IS GOOD FOR HIM!
OH! WHAT'S THAT HORRIBLE CREATURE?!
JUST A DRAKILLAR, MY DEAR--ONE OF THE COUNTLESS SENTRIES I HAVE POSTED THROUGHOUT THE QUADRANT.
IT IS TELEPATHICALLY TELLING ME THAT YOUR BOYFRIEND HAS ARRIVED!

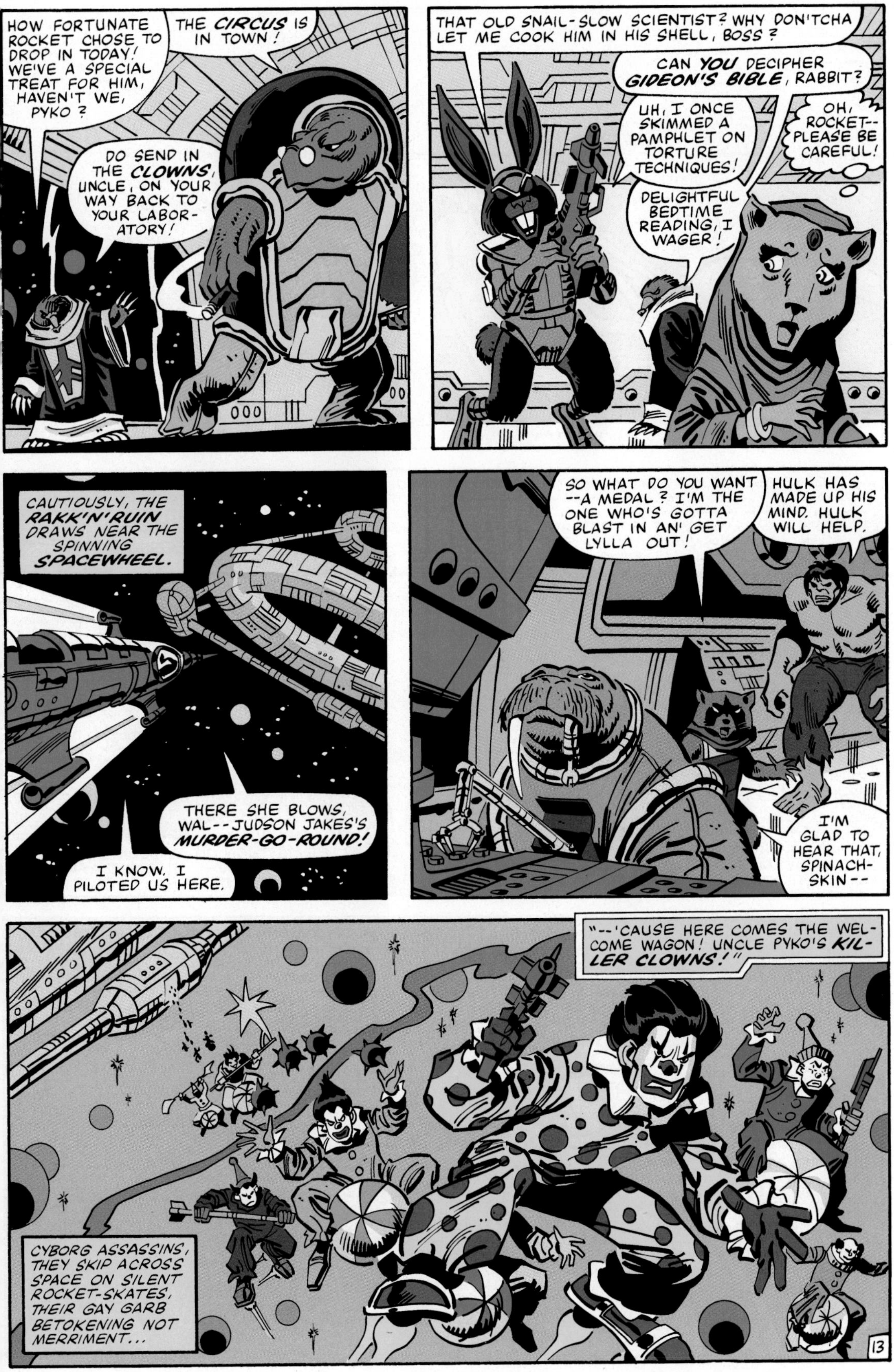
HOW FORTUNATE ROCKET CHOSE TO DROP IN TODAY! WE'VE A SPECIAL TREAT FOR HIM, HAVEN'T WE, PYKO?
THE CIRCUS IS IN TOWN!
DO SEND IN THE CLOWNS, UNCLE, ON YOUR WAY BACK TO YOUR LABOR-ATORY!
THAT OLD SNAIL-SLOW SCIENTIST? WHY DON'TCHA LET ME COOK HIM IN HIS SHELL, BOSS?
CAN YOU DECIPHER GIDEON'S BIBLE, RABBIT?
UH, I ONCE SKIMMED A PAMPHLET ON TORTURE TECHNIQUES!
DELIGHTFUL BEDTIME READING, I WAGER!
OH, ROCKET-- PLEASE BE CAREFUL!
CAUTIOUSLY, THE RAKK'N'RUIN DRAWS NEAR THE SPINNING SPACEWHEEL.
THERE SHE BLOWS, WAL--JUDSON JAKES'S MURDER-GO-ROUND!
I KNOW. I PILOTED US HERE.
SO WHAT DO YOU WANT --A MEDAL? I'M THE ONE WHO'S GOTTA BLAST IN AN' GET LYLLA OUT!
HULK HAS MADE UP HIS MIND. HULK WILL HELP.
I'M GLAD TO HEAR THAT, SPINACH-SKIN--
"--'CAUSE HERE COMES THE WEL-COME WAGON! UNCLE PYKO'S KIL-LER CLOWNS!"
CYBORG ASSASSINS, THEY SKIP ACROSS SPACE ON SILENT ROCKET-SKATES, THEIR GAY GARB BETOKENING NOT MERRIMENT...
13

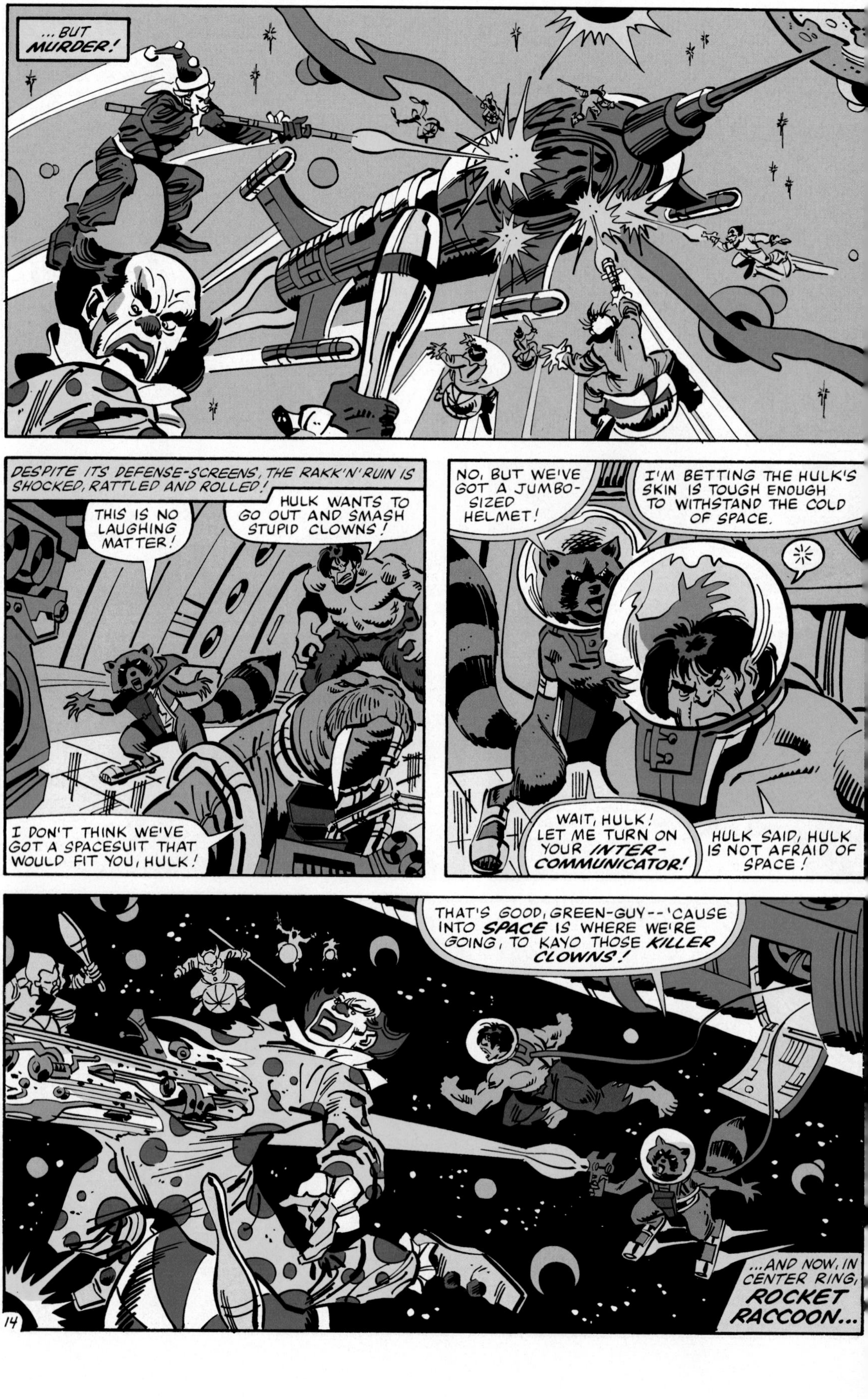
...BUT MURDER!
DESPITE ITS DEFENSE-SCREENS, THE RAKK'N'RUIN IS SHOCKED, RATTLED AND ROLLED!
THIS IS NO LAUGHING MATTER!
HULK WANTS TO GO OUT AND SMASH STUPID CLOWNS!
I DON'T THINK WE'VE GOT A SPACESUIT THAT WOULD FIT YOU, HULK!
NO, BUT WE'VE GOT A JUMBO-SIZED HELMET!
I'M BETTING THE HULK'S SKIN IS TOUGH ENOUGH TO WITHSTAND THE COLD OF SPACE.
WAIT, HULK! LET ME TURN ON YOUR INTER-COMMUNICATOR!
HULK SAID, HULK IS NOT AFRAID OF SPACE!
THAT'S GOOD, GREEN-GUY--'CAUSE INTO SPACE IS WHERE WE'RE GOING, TO KAYO THOSE KILLER CLOWNS!
...AND NOW, IN CENTER RING, ROCKET RACCOON...
14

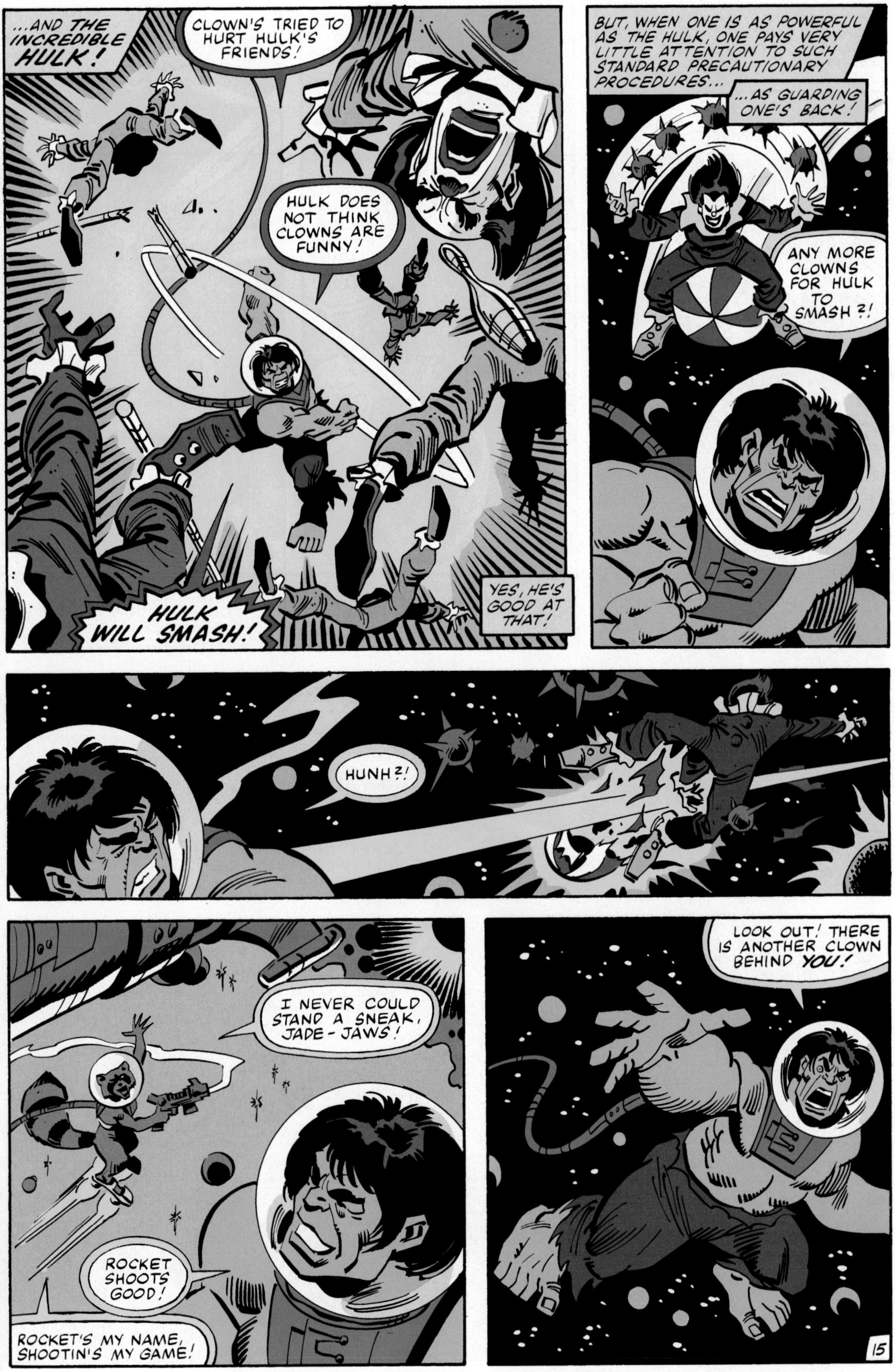
...AND THE INCREDIBLE HULK!
CLOWN'S TRIED TO HURT HULK'S FRIENDS!
HULK DOES NOT THINK CLOWNS ARE FUNNY!
HULK WILL SMASH!
YES, HE'S GOOD AT THAT!
BUT, WHEN ONE IS AS POWERFUL AS THE HULK, ONE PAYS VERY LITTLE ATTENTION TO SUCH STANDARD PRECAUTIONARY PROCEDURES...
...AS GUARDING ONE'S BACK!
ANY MORE CLOWNS FOR HULK TO SMASH?!
HUNH?!
I NEVER COULD STAND A SNEAK, JADE-JAWS!
ROCKET SHOOTS GOOD!
ROCKET'S MY NAME, SHOOTIN'S MY GAME!
LOOK OUT! THERE IS ANOTHER CLOWN BEHIND YOU!
15

THE HULK'S CRY OF WARNING COMES A TAD TOO LATE, FOR THE *LEADER* OF THE *KILLER CLOWNS* IS ALREADY UPON OUR RIGHTEOUS RACCOON!

A GREAT PRIZE AWAITS THE ONE WHO SLAYS YOU, RODENT!

THE PRIZE OF *LIFE* -- TO CEASE BEING A COLD CYBORG KILLING MACHINE...

...AND BECOME INSTEAD A *LIVING BEING!*

A LIFE FOR A DEATH, CLOWN? CUTE TRADE!

GEEPS! *LASER CONTACT-LENSES* TRYING TO OPEN MY HELMET! *HELP!!*

HELP IS AT HAND...

RAARRHH!

HULK! THANKS A LOT!

DID ROCKET THINK THAT HULK WOULD LET CLOWN KILL HIM?

TO TELL YOU THE TRUTH, GREENSKIN, RATIONAL THOUGHT GAVE WAY TO PANIC AS THOSE LASERS STARTED TO SIZZLE MY HELMET! THIS IS ONE RACCOON WHO LIKES *BREATHING!*

CLOWNS ARE ALL GONE! NOW WHAT DO HULK AND ROCKET DO?

THE JOB WE CAME FOR, SPINACH-SKIN!

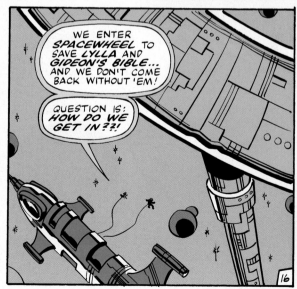

WE ENTER *SPACEWHEEL* TO SAVE *LYLLA* AND *GIDEON'S BIBLE*... AND WE DON'T COME BACK WITHOUT 'EM!

QUESTION IS: *HOW DO WE GET IN??!*

16

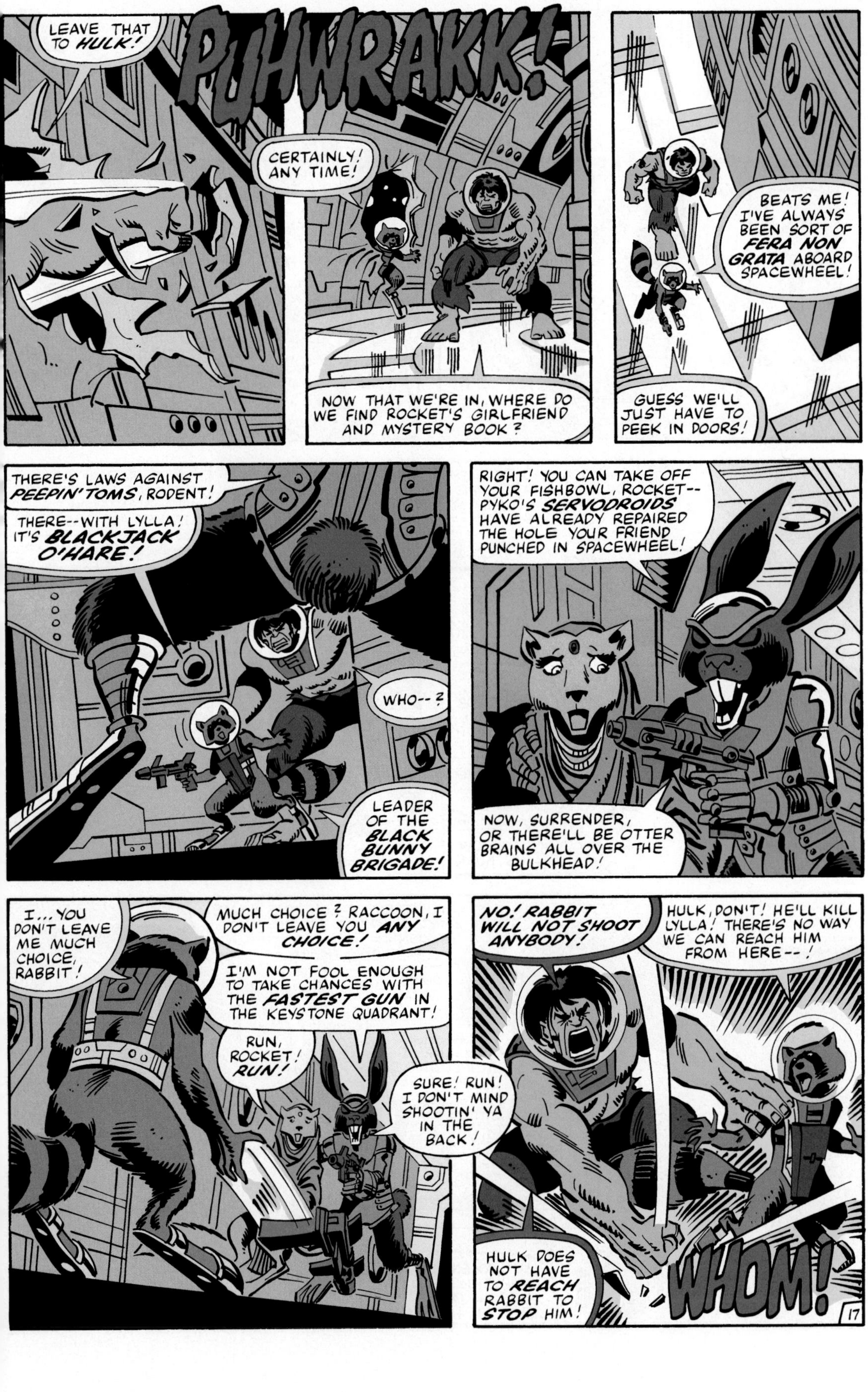
LEAVE THAT TO HULK!
PUHWRAKK!
CERTAINLY! ANY TIME!
NOW THAT WE'RE IN, WHERE DO WE FIND ROCKET'S GIRLFRIEND AND MYSTERY BOOK?
BEATS ME! I'VE ALWAYS BEEN SORT OF FERA NON GRATA ABOARD SPACEWHEEL!
GUESS WE'LL JUST HAVE TO PEEK IN DOORS!
THERE'S LAWS AGAINST PEEPIN' TOMS, RODENT!
THERE--WITH LYLLA! IT'S BLACKJACK O'HARE!
WHO--?
LEADER OF THE BLACK BUNNY BRIGADE!
RIGHT! YOU CAN TAKE OFF YOUR FISHBOWL, ROCKET-- PYKO'S SERVODROIDS HAVE ALREADY REPAIRED THE HOLE YOUR FRIEND PUNCHED IN SPACEWHEEL!
NOW, SURRENDER, OR THERE'LL BE OTTER BRAINS ALL OVER THE BULKHEAD!
I... YOU DON'T LEAVE ME MUCH CHOICE, RABBIT!
MUCH CHOICE? RACCOON, I DON'T LEAVE YOU ANY CHOICE!
I'M NOT FOOL ENOUGH TO TAKE CHANCES WITH THE FASTEST GUN IN THE KEYSTONE QUADRANT!
RUN, ROCKET! RUN!
SURE! RUN! I DON'T MIND SHOOTIN' YA IN THE BACK!
NO! RABBIT WILL NOT SHOOT ANYBODY!
HULK, DON'T! HE'LL KILL LYLLA! THERE'S NO WAY WE CAN REACH HIM FROM HERE--!
HULK DOES NOT HAVE TO REACH RABBIT TO STOP HIM!
WHOM!

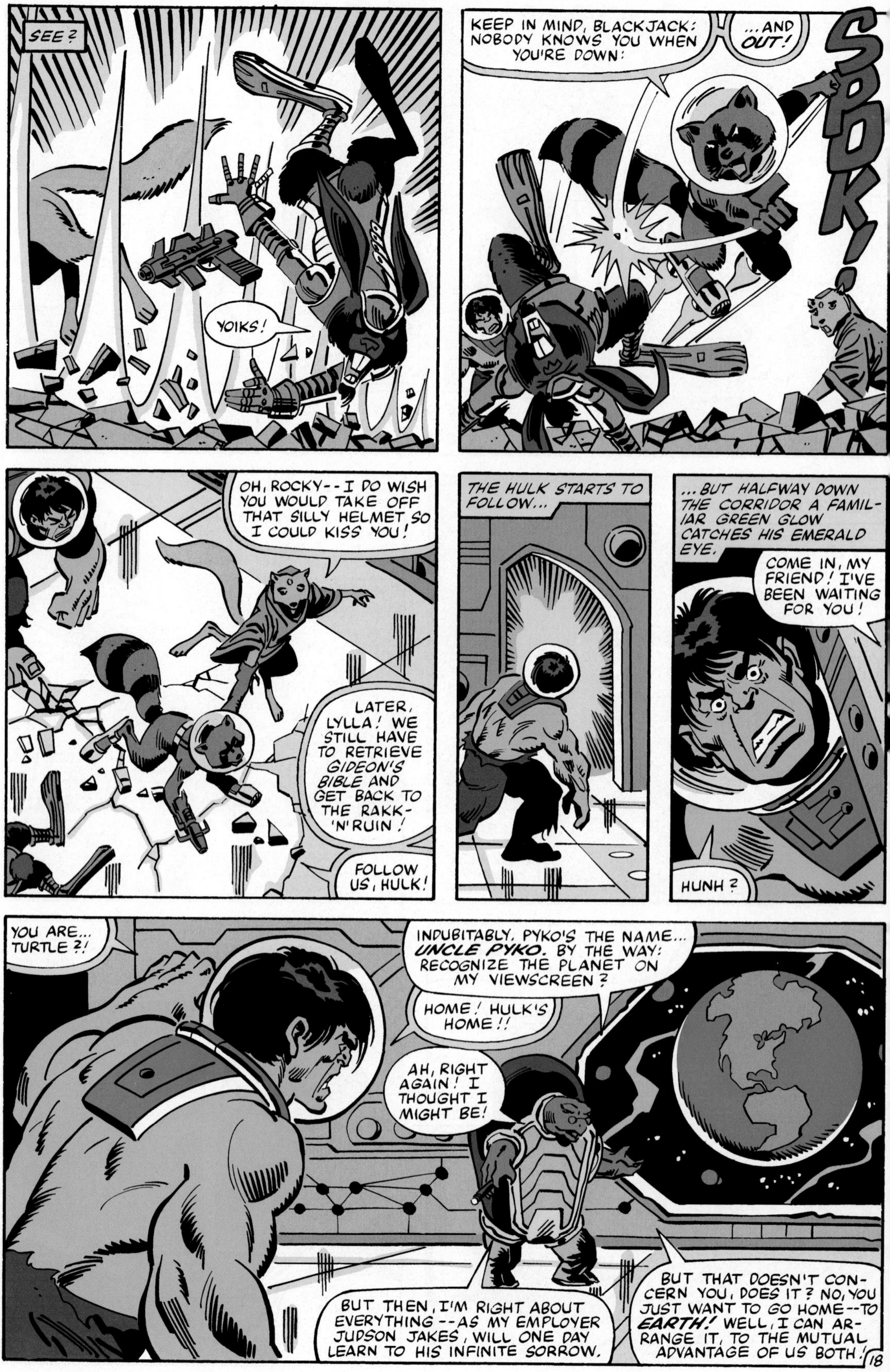

SEE?
YOIKS!
KEEP IN MIND, BLACKJACK: NOBODY KNOWS YOU WHEN YOU'RE DOWN:
...AND OUT!
SPOK!
OH, ROCKY--I DO WISH YOU WOULD TAKE OFF THAT SILLY HELMET SO I COULD KISS YOU!
LATER, LYLLA! WE STILL HAVE TO RETRIEVE GIDEON'S BIBLE AND GET BACK TO THE RAKK-'N'RUIN!
FOLLOW US, HULK!
THE HULK STARTS TO FOLLOW...
...BUT HALFWAY DOWN THE CORRIDOR A FAMILIAR GREEN GLOW CATCHES HIS EMERALD EYE.
COME IN, MY FRIEND! I'VE BEEN WAITING FOR YOU!
HUNH?
YOU ARE... TURTLE?!
INDUBITABLY. PYKO'S THE NAME... UNCLE PYKO. BY THE WAY: RECOGNIZE THE PLANET ON MY VIEWSCREEN?
HOME! HULK'S HOME!!
AH, RIGHT AGAIN! I THOUGHT I MIGHT BE!
BUT THEN, I'M RIGHT ABOUT EVERYTHING--AS MY EMPLOYER JUDSON JAKES, WILL ONE DAY LEARN TO HIS INFINITE SORROW.
BUT THAT DOESN'T CONCERN YOU, DOES IT? NO, YOU JUST WANT TO GO HOME--TO EARTH! WELL, I CAN ARRANGE IT, TO THE MUTUAL ADVANTAGE OF US BOTH!

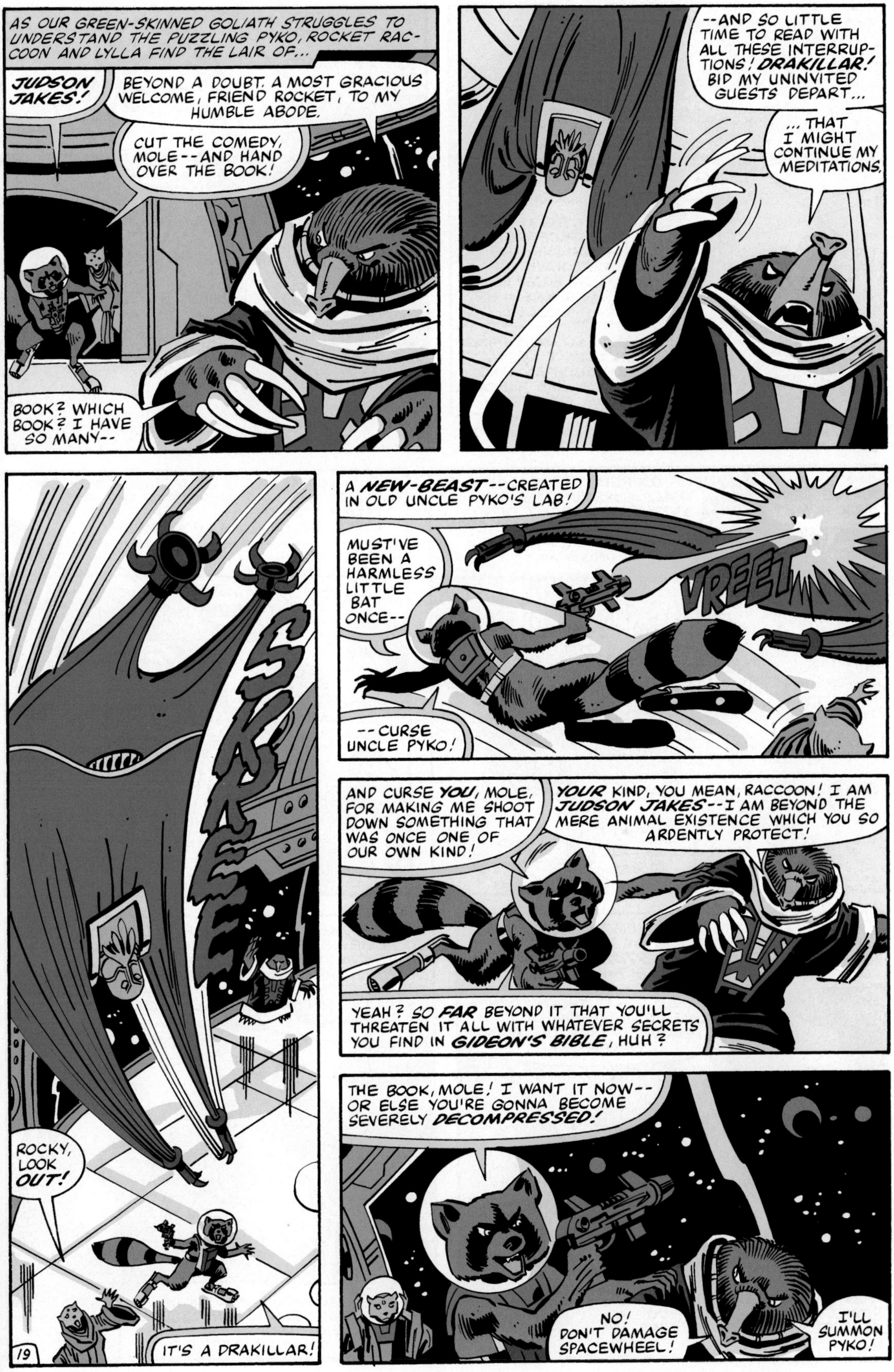
AS OUR GREEN-SKINNED GOLIATH STRUGGLES TO UNDERSTAND THE PUZZLING PYKO, ROCKET RACCOON AND LYLLA FIND THE LAIR OF...
JUDSON JAKES!
BEYOND A DOUBT, A MOST GRACIOUS WELCOME, FRIEND ROCKET, TO MY HUMBLE ABODE.
CUT THE COMEDY, MOLE--AND HAND OVER THE BOOK!
BOOK? WHICH BOOK? I HAVE SO MANY--
--AND SO LITTLE TIME TO READ WITH ALL THESE INTERRUPTIONS! DRAKILLAR! BID MY UNINVITED GUESTS DEPART...
...THAT I MIGHT CONTINUE MY MEDITATIONS.
SKREE
ROCKY, LOOK OUT!
IT'S A DRAKILLAR!
19
A NEW-BEAST--CREATED IN OLD UNCLE PYKO'S LAB!
MUST'VE BEEN A HARMLESS LITTLE BAT ONCE--
VREET
--CURSE UNCLE PYKO!
AND CURSE YOU, MOLE, FOR MAKING ME SHOOT DOWN SOMETHING THAT WAS ONCE ONE OF OUR OWN KIND!
YOUR KIND, YOU MEAN, RACCOON! I AM JUDSON JAKES--I AM BEYOND THE MERE ANIMAL EXISTENCE WHICH YOU SO ARDENTLY PROTECT!
YEAH? SO FAR BEYOND IT THAT YOU'LL THREATEN IT ALL WITH WHATEVER SECRETS YOU FIND IN GIDEON'S BIBLE, HUH?
THE BOOK, MOLE! I WANT IT NOW--OR ELSE YOU'RE GONNA BECOME SEVERELY DECOMPRESSED!
NO! DON'T DAMAGE SPACEWHEEL!
I'LL SUMMON PYKO!

AND, IN UNCLE PYKO'S LABORATORY...

BRRZZZT

AH, THE MASTER OF SPACEWHEEL SUMMONS! HE MUST HAVE ACKNOWLEDGED DEFEAT, AS I KNEW HE WOULD!

I KNOW SO MANY THINGS I SHOULDN'T KNOW, HULK--SUCH AS WHO YOU ARE, WHERE YOU CAME FROM, ETCETERA.

PLANET ON SCREEN IS EARTH, HULK'S HOME.

THAT IS WHERE HULK'S FRIENDS-- RICK AND BETTY-- WAIT FOR HULK!

CAN TALKING TURTLE SEND HULK HOME?

OF COURSE! THE GALACIAN WALL SURROUNDING THE KEYSTONE QUADRANT PREVENTS ITS INHABITANTS FROM EVER LEAVING THIS MADHOUSE UNIVERSE--

--BUT NO BARRIER IS INSUPERABLE TO ONE WHO HAS FATHOMED THE SECRETS OF THE FIRST-COMERS, TO ONE WHO COMPREHENDS THE MYSTERIES OF GIDEON'S BIBLE!

HULK THOUGHT THAT NO ONE COULD READ MYSTERY BOOK.

NO ONE BUT ME, HULK, AND EVEN I DISCOVERED HOW QUITE BY ACCIDENT...

...FROM DEEPLY-SUBMERGED MEMORIES WHICH I DREDGED FORTH ONE DAY WHEN I WAS PROBING THE ADDLED BRAIN OF A KEYSTONE COP, POOR CREATURE! HE DIDN'T SURVIVE THE PROBE!

IT SEEMS THAT THOSE LOONY-TUNE COPS ARE DIRECTLY DESCENDED FROM THE FIRST-COMERS--

--AS ARE YOU, HULK! THAT'S HOW I DEDUCED WHERE YOU CAME FROM AND HOW TO SEND YOU BACK!

20

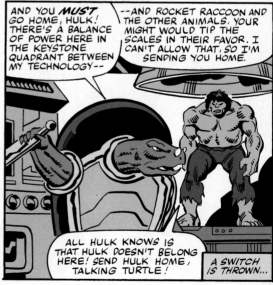

AND YOU MUST GO HOME, HULK! THERE'S A BALANCE OF POWER HERE IN THE KEYSTONE QUADRANT BETWEEN MY TECHNOLOGY--

--AND ROCKET RACCOON AND THE OTHER ANIMALS, YOUR MIGHT WOULD TIP THE SCALES IN THEIR FAVOR. I CAN'T ALLOW THAT, SO I'M SENDING YOU HOME.

ALL HULK KNOWS IS THAT HULK DOESN'T BELONG HERE! SEND HULK HOME, TALKING TURTLE!

A SWITCH IS THROWN...

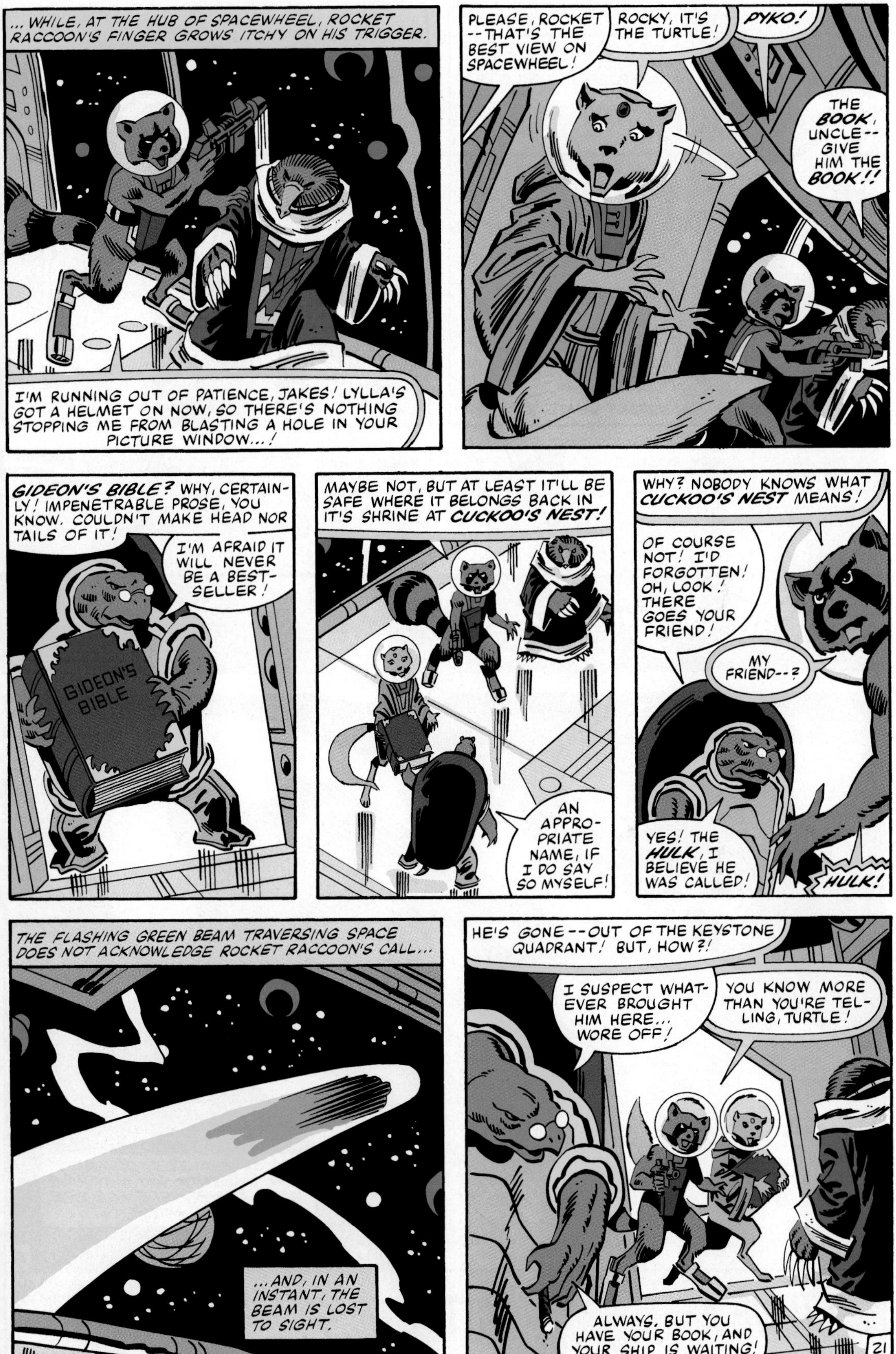
...WHILE, AT THE HUB OF SPACEWHEEL, ROCKET RACCOON'S FINGER GROWS ITCHY ON HIS TRIGGER.
I'M RUNNING OUT OF PATIENCE, JAKES! LYLLA'S GOT A HELMET ON NOW, SO THERE'S NOTHING STOPPING ME FROM BLASTING A HOLE IN YOUR PICTURE WINDOW...!
PLEASE, ROCKET --THAT'S THE BEST VIEW ON SPACEWHEEL!
ROCKY, IT'S THE TURTLE!
PYKO!
THE BOOK, UNCLE-- GIVE HIM THE BOOK!!
GIDEON'S BIBLE? WHY, CERTAINLY! IMPENETRABLE PROSE, YOU KNOW. COULDN'T MAKE HEAD NOR TAILS OF IT!
I'M AFRAID IT WILL NEVER BE A BEST-SELLER!
GIDEON'S BIBLE
MAYBE NOT, BUT AT LEAST IT'LL BE SAFE WHERE IT BELONGS BACK IN IT'S SHRINE AT CUCKOO'S NEST!
AN APPROPRIATE NAME, IF I DO SAY SO MYSELF!
WHY? NOBODY KNOWS WHAT CUCKOO'S NEST MEANS!
OF COURSE NOT! I'D FORGOTTEN! OH, LOOK! THERE GOES YOUR FRIEND!
MY FRIEND--?
YES! THE HULK, I BELIEVE HE WAS CALLED!
HULK!
THE FLASHING GREEN BEAM TRAVERSING SPACE DOES NOT ACKNOWLEDGE ROCKET RACCOON'S CALL...
...AND, IN AN INSTANT, THE BEAM IS LOST TO SIGHT.
HE'S GONE--OUT OF THE KEYSTONE QUADRANT! BUT, HOW?!
I SUSPECT WHATEVER BROUGHT HIM HERE... WORE OFF!
YOU KNOW MORE THAN YOU'RE TELLING, TURTLE!
ALWAYS, BUT YOU HAVE YOUR BOOK, AND YOUR SHIP IS WAITING!
21

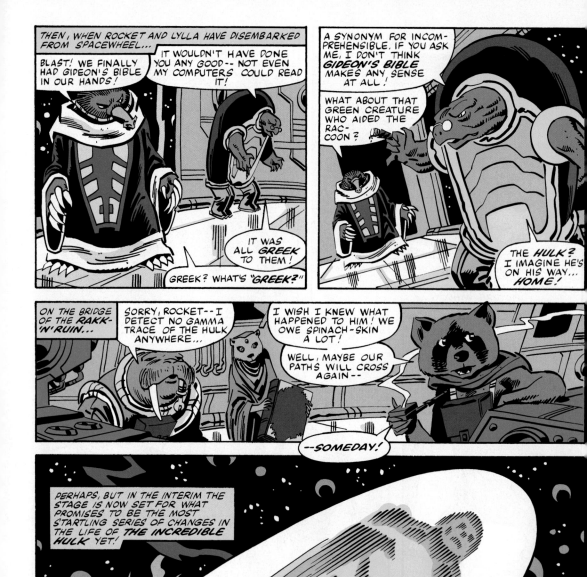

THEN, WHEN ROCKET AND LYLLA HAVE DISEMBARKED FROM SPACEWHEEL...

BLAST! WE FINALLY HAD GIDEON'S BIBLE IN OUR HANDS!

IT WOULDN'T HAVE DONE YOU ANY GOOD-- NOT EVEN MY COMPUTERS COULD READ IT!

IT WAS ALL GREEK TO THEM!

GREEK? WHAT'S "GREEK?"

A SYNONYM FOR INCOMPREHENSIBLE, IF YOU ASK ME, I DON'T THINK GIDEON'S BIBLE MAKES ANY SENSE AT ALL!

WHAT ABOUT THAT GREEN CREATURE WHO AIDED THE RACCOON?

THE HULK? I IMAGINE HE'S ON HIS WAY... HOME!

ON THE BRIDGE OF THE RAKK-'N'-RUIN...

SORRY, ROCKET-- I DETECT NO GAMMA TRACE OF THE HULK ANYWHERE...

I WISH I KNEW WHAT HAPPENED TO HIM! WE OWE SPINACH-SKIN A LOT!

WELL, MAYBE OUR PATHS WILL CROSS AGAIN--

--SOMEDAY!

PERHAPS, BUT IN THE INTERIM THE STAGE IS NOW SET FOR WHAT PROMISES TO BE THE MOST STARTLING SERIES OF CHANGES IN THE LIFE OF THE INCREDIBLE HULK YET!

CANCEL WHATEVER OTHER APPOINTMENTS YOU MAY HAVE MADE AND BE HERE FOR THE INCREDIBLE HULK #272, ENTITLED...

22

"...I HAVE A BRAIN, BUT I MUST SCREAM!"

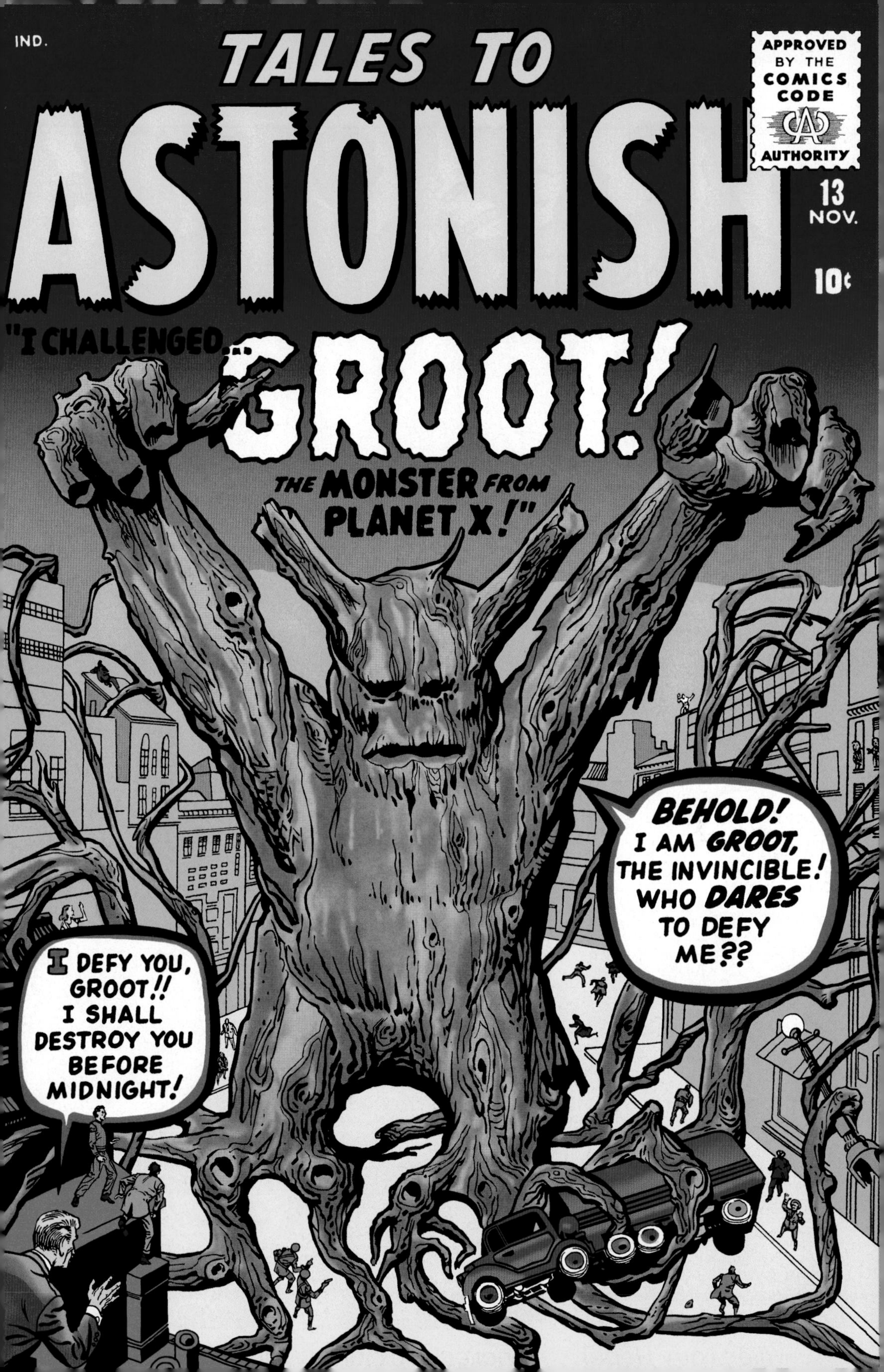
IND.
TALES TO ASTONISH
APPROVED BY THE COMICS CODE AUTHORITY
13 NOV.
10¢
"I CHALLENGED... GROOT! THE MONSTER FROM PLANET X!"
BEHOLD! I AM GROOT, THE INVINCIBLE! WHO DARES TO DEFY ME??
I DEFY YOU, GROOT!! I SHALL DESTROY YOU BEFORE MIDNIGHT!

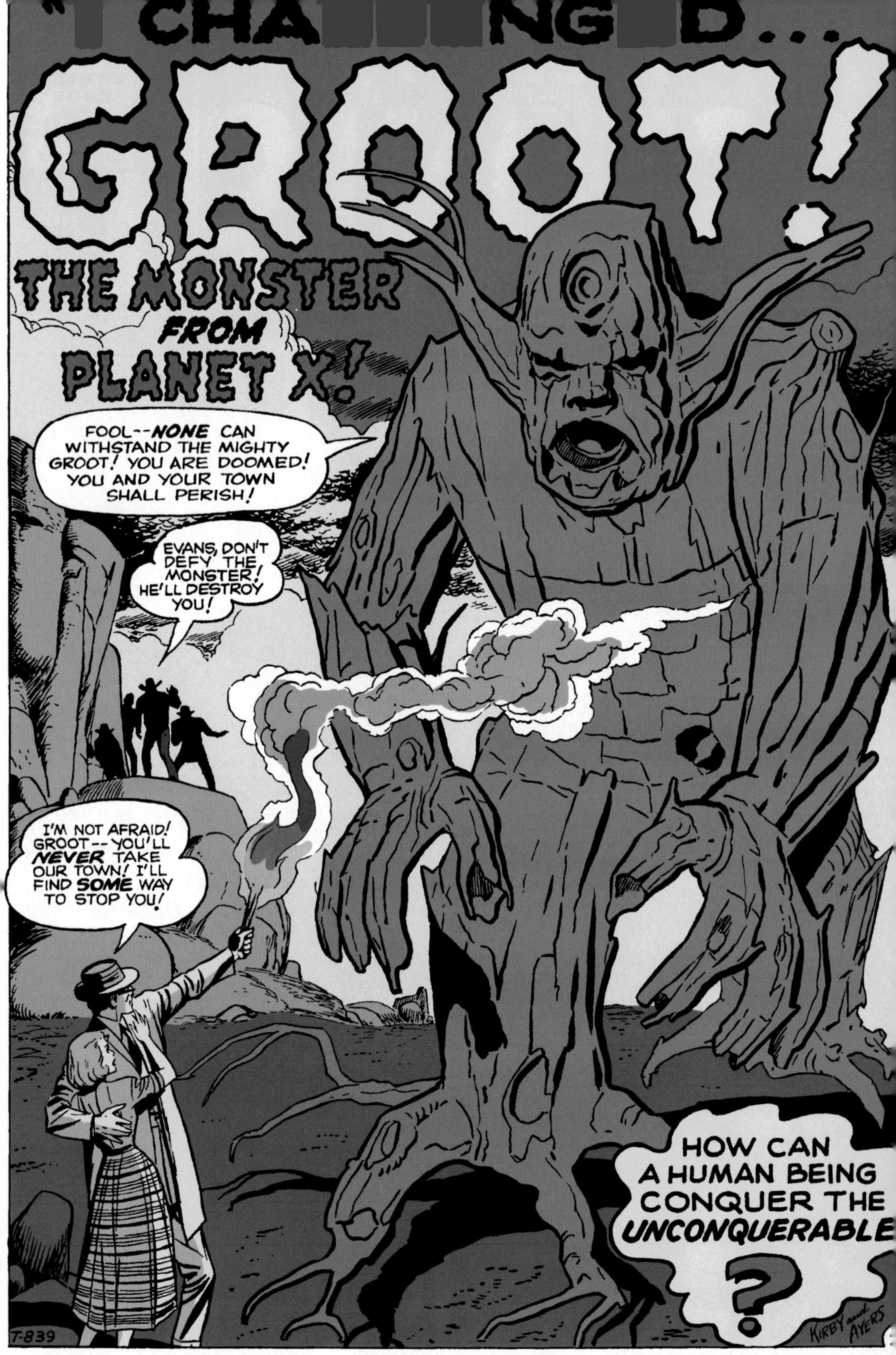
[redacted] CHA[redacted]NG[redacted]D...
GROOT!
THE MONSTER FROM PLANET X!
FOOL--NONE CAN WITHSTAND THE MIGHTY GROOT! YOU ARE DOOMED! YOU AND YOUR TOWN SHALL PERISH!
EVANS, DON'T DEFY THE MONSTER! HE'LL DESTROY YOU!
I'M NOT AFRAID! GROOT--YOU'LL NEVER TAKE OUR TOWN! I'LL FIND SOME WAY TO STOP YOU!
HOW CAN A HUMAN BEING CONQUER THE UNCONQUERABLE ?
T-839
KIRBY and AYERS

Writer: Larry Lieber Penciler: Jack Kirby Inker: Dick Ayers

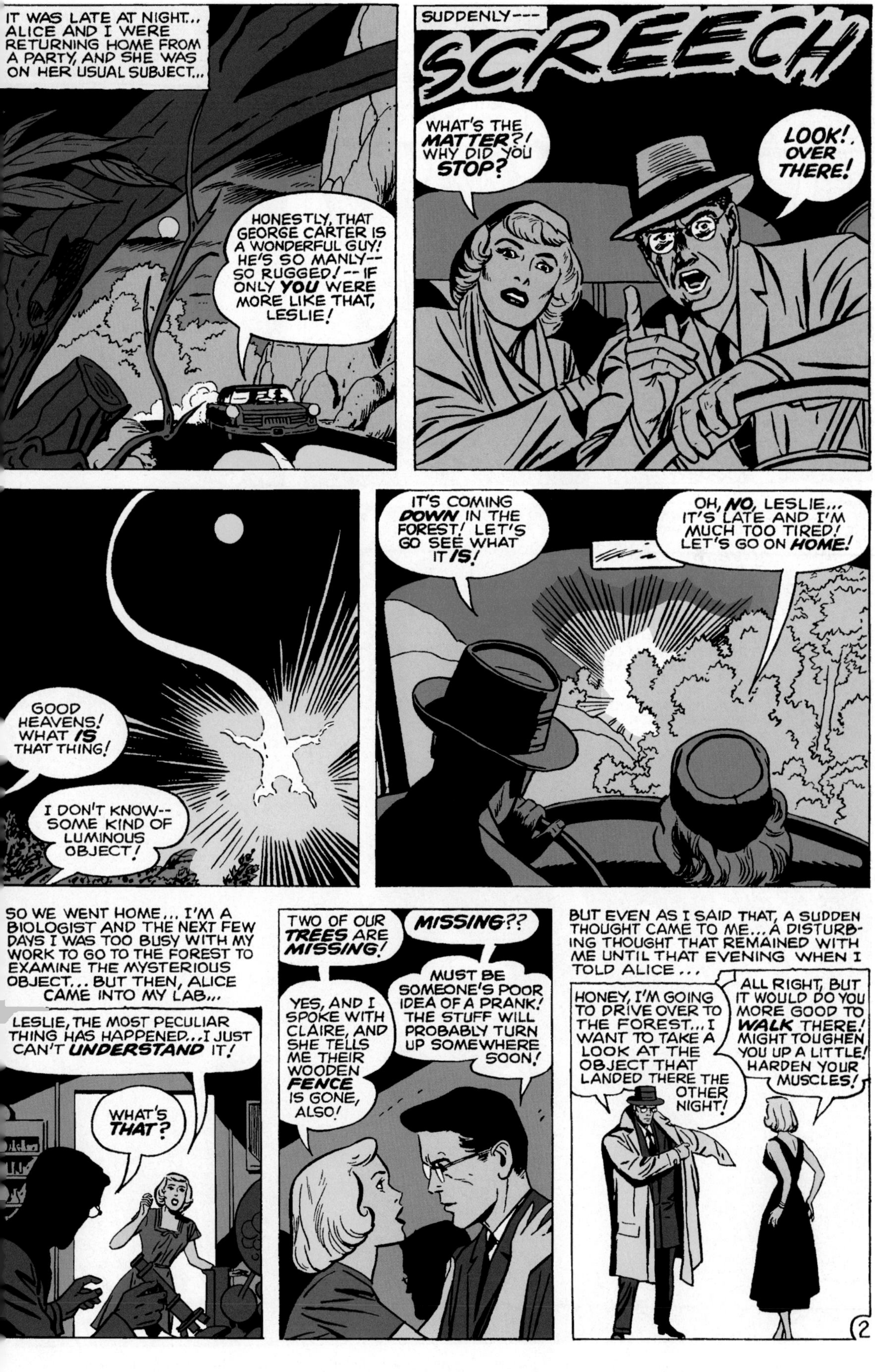
IT WAS LATE AT NIGHT... ALICE AND I WERE RETURNING HOME FROM A PARTY, AND SHE WAS ON HER USUAL SUBJECT...
HONESTLY, THAT GEORGE CARTER IS A WONDERFUL GUY! HE'S SO MANLY-- SO RUGGED! -- IF ONLY YOU WERE MORE LIKE THAT, LESLIE!
SUDDENLY---
SCREECH
WHAT'S THE MATTER?! WHY DID YOU STOP?
LOOK! OVER THERE!
GOOD HEAVENS! WHAT IS THAT THING!
I DON'T KNOW-- SOME KIND OF LUMINOUS OBJECT!
IT'S COMING DOWN IN THE FOREST! LET'S GO SEE WHAT IT IS!
OH, NO, LESLIE... IT'S LATE AND I'M MUCH TOO TIRED! LET'S GO ON HOME!
SO WE WENT HOME... I'M A BIOLOGIST AND THE NEXT FEW DAYS I WAS TOO BUSY WITH MY WORK TO GO TO THE FOREST TO EXAMINE THE MYSTERIOUS OBJECT... BUT THEN, ALICE CAME INTO MY LAB...
LESLIE, THE MOST PECULIAR THING HAS HAPPENED... I JUST CAN'T UNDERSTAND IT!
WHAT'S THAT?
TWO OF OUR TREES ARE MISSING!
MISSING??
YES, AND I SPOKE WITH CLAIRE, AND SHE TELLS ME THEIR WOODEN FENCE IS GONE, ALSO!
MUST BE SOMEONE'S POOR IDEA OF A PRANK! THE STUFF WILL PROBABLY TURN UP SOMEWHERE SOON!
BUT EVEN AS I SAID THAT, A SUDDEN THOUGHT CAME TO ME... A DISTURBING THOUGHT THAT REMAINED WITH ME UNTIL THAT EVENING WHEN I TOLD ALICE...
HONEY, I'M GOING TO DRIVE OVER TO THE FOREST... I WANT TO TAKE A LOOK AT THE OBJECT THAT LANDED THERE THE OTHER NIGHT!
ALL RIGHT, BUT IT WOULD DO YOU MORE GOOD TO WALK THERE! MIGHT TOUGHEN YOU UP A LITTLE! HARDEN YOUR MUSCLES!
2

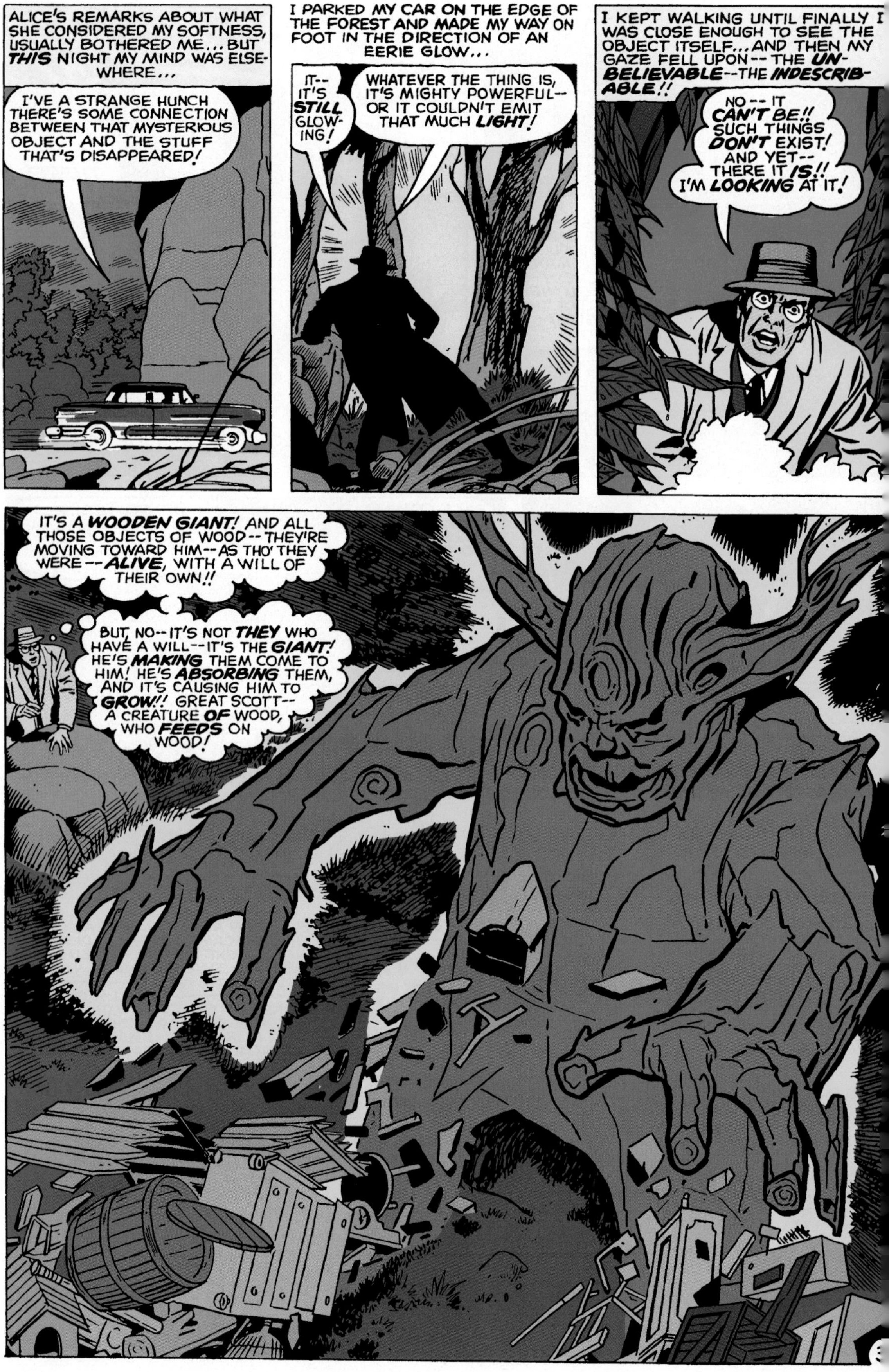
ALICE'S REMARKS ABOUT WHAT SHE CONSIDERED MY SOFTNESS, USUALLY BOTHERED ME... BUT THIS NIGHT MY MIND WAS ELSEWHERE...
I'VE A STRANGE HUNCH THERE'S SOME CONNECTION BETWEEN THAT MYSTERIOUS OBJECT AND THE STUFF THAT'S DISAPPEARED!
I PARKED MY CAR ON THE EDGE OF THE FOREST AND MADE MY WAY ON FOOT IN THE DIRECTION OF AN EERIE GLOW...
IT-- IT'S STILL GLOWING!
WHATEVER THE THING IS, IT'S MIGHTY POWERFUL-- OR IT COULDN'T EMIT THAT MUCH LIGHT!
I KEPT WALKING UNTIL FINALLY I WAS CLOSE ENOUGH TO SEE THE OBJECT ITSELF... AND THEN MY GAZE FELL UPON -- THE UNBELIEVABLE--THE INDESCRIBABLE!!
NO -- IT CAN'T BE!! SUCH THINGS DON'T EXIST! AND YET-- THERE IT IS!! I'M LOOKING AT IT!
IT'S A WOODEN GIANT! AND ALL THOSE OBJECTS OF WOOD -- THEY'RE MOVING TOWARD HIM -- AS THO' THEY WERE -- ALIVE, WITH A WILL OF THEIR OWN!!
BUT, NO-- IT'S NOT THEY WHO HAVE A WILL--IT'S THE GIANT! HE'S MAKING THEM COME TO HIM! HE'S ABSORBING THEM, AND IT'S CAUSING HIM TO GROW!! GREAT SCOTT-- A CREATURE OF WOOD, WHO FEEDS ON WOOD!

I'D BETTER GET TO TOWN **FAST!** I'VE GOT TO WARN THE SHERIFF! THIS WOOD-GIANT COULD MENACE US **ALL!!**

SOME FRANTIC MINUTES LATER, I WAS IN TOWN, TRYING TO CONVINCE THE SHERIFF I WASN'T MAD...

I TELL YOU I SAW IT WITH MY **OWN EYES!** IT WAS DEVOURING ALL KINDS OF WOODEN OBJECTS!

SHERIFF!! THERE'S A GREAT GLOWING MONSTER -- IT MUST BE AT LEAST FIFTY FEET TALL -- AND IT'S HEADING TOWARD **TOWN!**

THAT **DID** IT! THE SHERIFF AND EVERYONE ELSE WAS NOW CONVINCED -- AND THEY WENT INTO ACTION...

REMEMBER, DON'T FIRE UNTIL WE KNOW WHAT THIS THING IS **UP TO!**

RIGHT!

A BARRICADE WAS SET UP ON THE EDGE OF TOWN, AND WE ALL WAITED TENSELY -- FEARFULLY ... WE WATCHED THE APPROACH OF THE AWESOME WOOD-CREATURE...

LOOK AT THE WAY THAT MONSTER SHINES! IT--IT HURTS YOUR EYES TO **LOOK** AT IT!!

GET **READY,** MEN... THAT WALKING NIGHTMARE LOOKS LIKE IT MEANS **BUSINESS!**

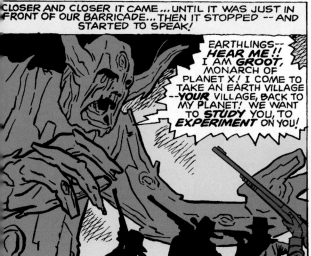

CLOSER AND CLOSER IT CAME...UNTIL IT WAS JUST IN FRONT OF OUR BARRICADE... THEN IT STOPPED -- AND STARTED TO SPEAK!

EARTHLINGS-- **HEAR ME!!** I AM **GROOT,** MONARCH OF PLANET X! I COME TO TAKE AN EARTH VILLAGE --**YOUR** VILLAGE, BACK TO MY PLANET! WE WANT TO **STUDY** YOU, TO **EXPERIMENT** ON YOU!

HE WANTS TO **KILL** US! **SHOOT HIM! SHOOT HIM !!!**

GET **OUT** OF HERE! GO BACK WHERE YOU **CAME** FROM!--BEFORE WE **BLAST YOU!**

4

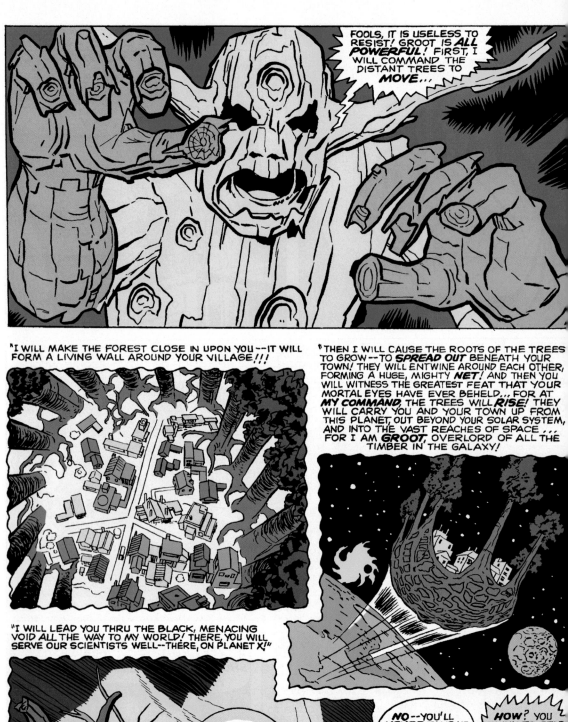

FOOLS, IT IS USELESS TO RESIST! GROOT IS *ALL POWERFUL!* FIRST, I WILL COMMAND THE DISTANT TREES TO *MOVE...*

"I WILL MAKE THE FOREST CLOSE IN UPON YOU--IT WILL FORM A LIVING WALL AROUND YOUR VILLAGE!!!

"THEN I WILL CAUSE THE ROOTS OF THE TREES TO GROW--TO *SPREAD OUT* BENEATH YOUR TOWN! THEY WILL ENTWINE AROUND EACH OTHER, FORMING A HUGE, MIGHTY *NET!* AND THEN YOU WILL WITNESS THE GREATEST FEAT THAT YOUR MORTAL EYES HAVE EVER BEHELD... FOR AT *MY COMMAND,* THE TREES WILL *RISE!* THEY WILL CARRY YOU AND YOUR TOWN UP FROM THIS PLANET, OUT BEYOND YOUR SOLAR SYSTEM, AND INTO THE VAST REACHES OF SPACE ... FOR I AM *GROOT,* OVERLORD OF ALL THE TIMBER IN THE GALAXY!

"I WILL LEAD YOU THRU THE BLACK, MENACING VOID ALL THE WAY TO MY WORLD! THERE, YOU WILL SERVE OUR SCIENTISTS WELL--THERE, ON PLANET *X!"*

NO--YOU'LL *NEVER* TAKE US OR OUR TOWN! WE'LL DESTROY *YOU* FIRST!

HOW? YOU THINK TO STOP ME WITH YOUR PUNY WEAPONS? FIRE AWAY! YOU WILL SEE HOW *USELESS* THEY ARE!

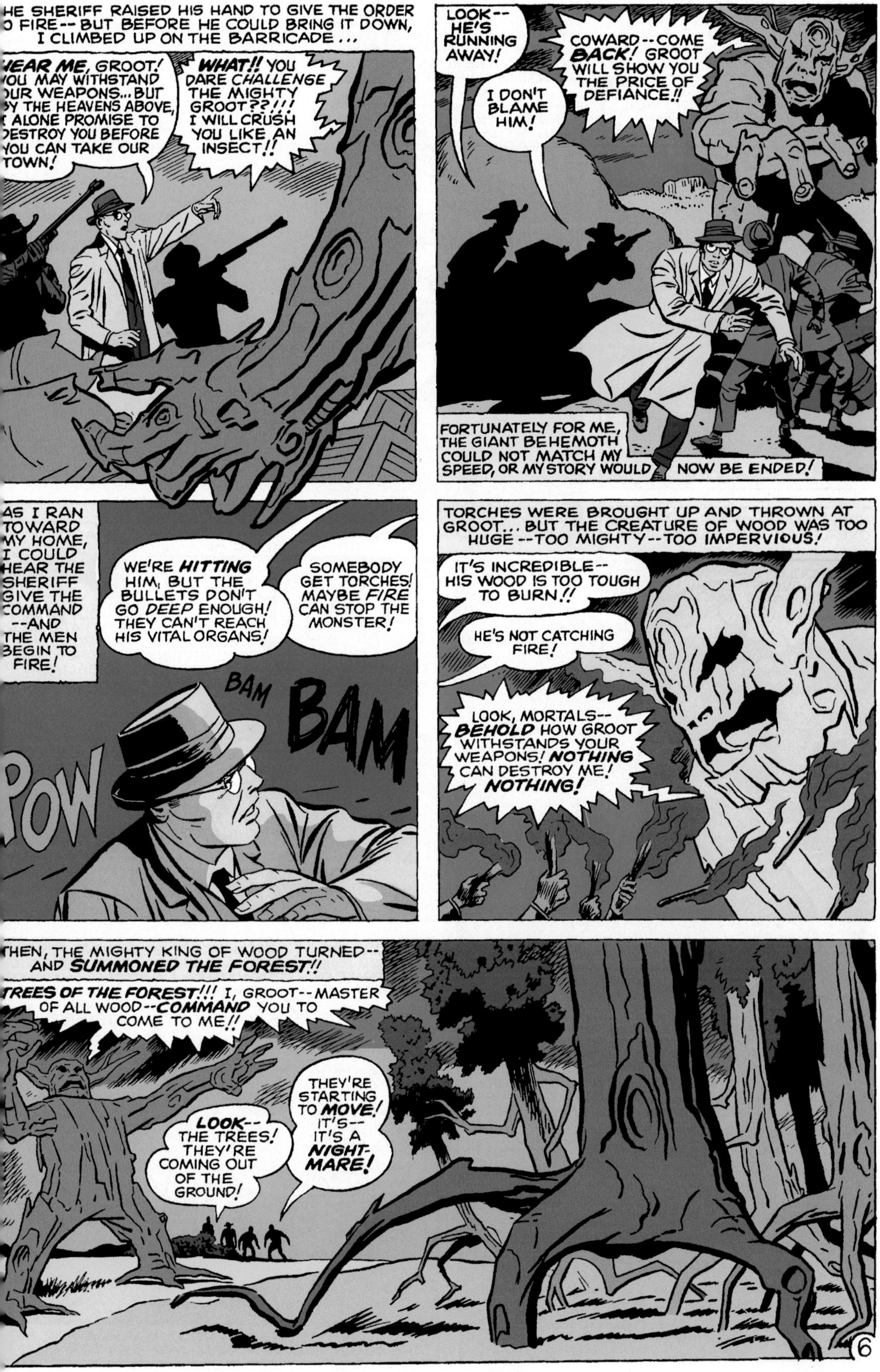

HE SHERIFF RAISED HIS HAND TO GIVE THE ORDER O FIRE-- BUT BEFORE HE COULD BRING IT DOWN, I CLIMBED UP ON THE BARRICADE...
HEAR ME, GROOT! YOU MAY WITHSTAND OUR WEAPONS... BUT BY THE HEAVENS ABOVE, I ALONE PROMISE TO DESTROY YOU BEFORE YOU CAN TAKE OUR TOWN!
WHAT!! YOU DARE CHALLENGE THE MIGHTY GROOT??!!! I WILL CRUSH YOU LIKE AN INSECT!!
LOOK-- HE'S RUNNING AWAY!
I DON'T BLAME HIM!
COWARD--COME BACK! GROOT WILL SHOW YOU THE PRICE OF DEFIANCE!!
FORTUNATELY FOR ME, THE GIANT BEHEMOTH COULD NOT MATCH MY SPEED, OR MY STORY WOULD NOW BE ENDED!
AS I RAN TOWARD MY HOME, I COULD HEAR THE SHERIFF GIVE THE COMMAND --AND THE MEN BEGIN TO FIRE!
WE'RE HITTING HIM, BUT THE BULLETS DON'T GO DEEP ENOUGH! THEY CAN'T REACH HIS VITAL ORGANS!
SOMEBODY GET TORCHES! MAYBE FIRE CAN STOP THE MONSTER!
BAM
BAM
POW
TORCHES WERE BROUGHT UP AND THROWN AT GROOT... BUT THE CREATURE OF WOOD WAS TOO HUGE--TOO MIGHTY--TOO IMPERVIOUS!
IT'S INCREDIBLE-- HIS WOOD IS TOO TOUGH TO BURN!!
HE'S NOT CATCHING FIRE!
LOOK, MORTALS-- BEHOLD HOW GROOT WITHSTANDS YOUR WEAPONS! NOTHING CAN DESTROY ME! NOTHING!
THEN, THE MIGHTY KING OF WOOD TURNED-- AND SUMMONED THE FOREST!!
TREES OF THE FOREST!!! I, GROOT--MASTER OF ALL WOOD--COMMAND YOU TO COME TO ME!!
LOOK-- THE TREES! THEY'RE COMING OUT OF THE GROUND!
THEY'RE STARTING TO MOVE! IT'S-- IT'S A NIGHT-MARE!

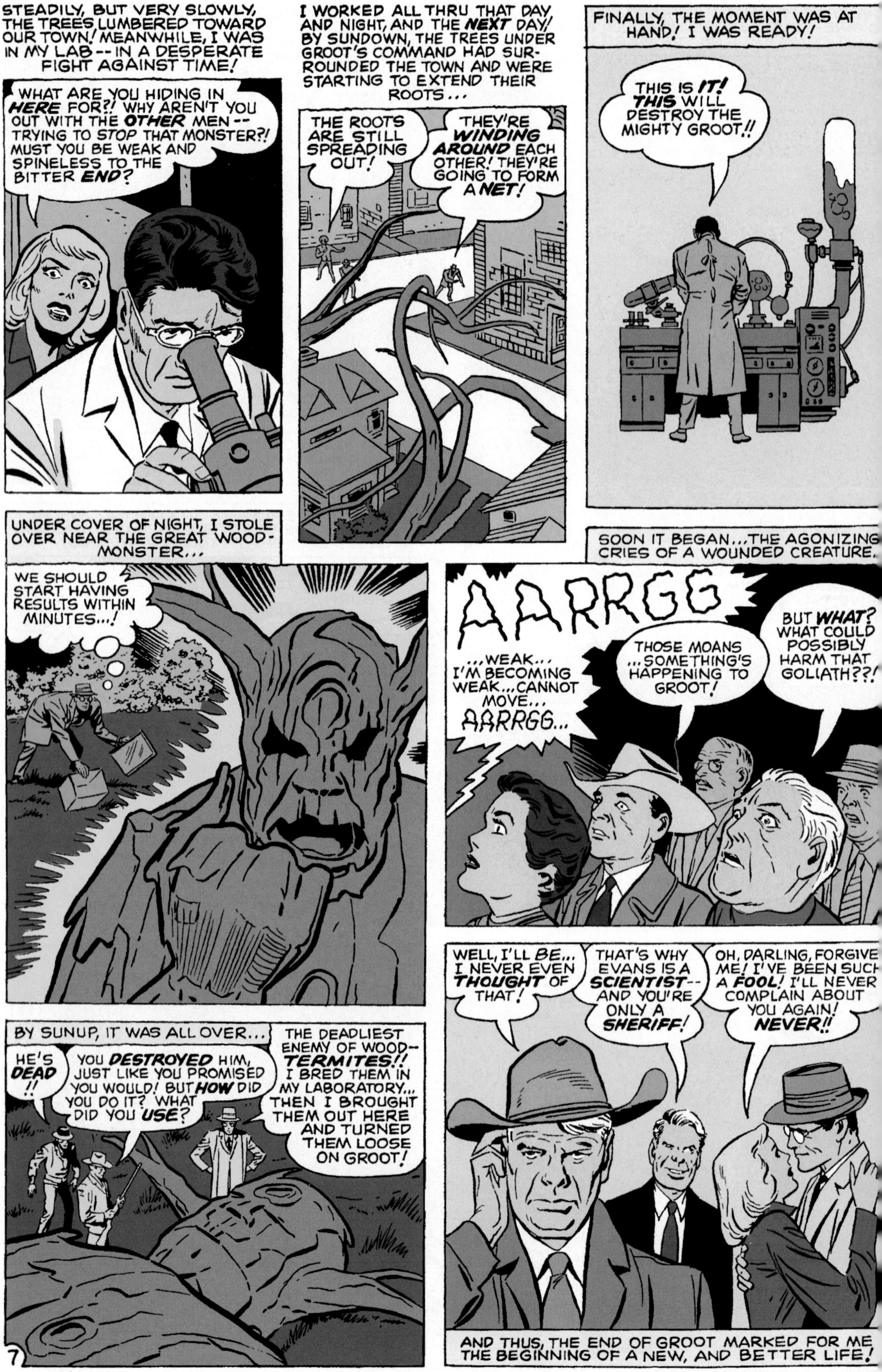

STEADILY, BUT VERY SLOWLY, THE TREES LUMBERED TOWARD OUR TOWN! MEANWHILE, I WAS IN MY LAB -- IN A DESPERATE FIGHT AGAINST TIME!
WHAT ARE YOU HIDING IN HERE FOR?! WHY AREN'T YOU OUT WITH THE OTHER MEN -- TRYING TO STOP THAT MONSTER?! MUST YOU BE WEAK AND SPINELESS TO THE BITTER END?
I WORKED ALL THRU THAT DAY AND NIGHT, AND THE NEXT DAY! BY SUNDOWN, THE TREES UNDER GROOT'S COMMAND HAD SURROUNDED THE TOWN AND WERE STARTING TO EXTEND THEIR ROOTS...
THE ROOTS ARE STILL SPREADING OUT!
THEY'RE WINDING AROUND EACH OTHER! THEY'RE GOING TO FORM A NET!
FINALLY, THE MOMENT WAS AT HAND! I WAS READY!
THIS IS IT! THIS WILL DESTROY THE MIGHTY GROOT!!
UNDER COVER OF NIGHT, I STOLE OVER NEAR THE GREAT WOOD-MONSTER...
WE SHOULD START HAVING RESULTS WITHIN MINUTES...!
SOON IT BEGAN... THE AGONIZING CRIES OF A WOUNDED CREATURE.
AARRGG
...WEAK... I'M BECOMING WEAK... CANNOT MOVE... AARRGG...
THOSE MOANS ...SOMETHING'S HAPPENING TO GROOT!
BUT WHAT? WHAT COULD POSSIBLY HARM THAT GOLIATH??!
BY SUNUP, IT WAS ALL OVER...
HE'S DEAD!!
YOU DESTROYED HIM, JUST LIKE YOU PROMISED YOU WOULD! BUT HOW DID YOU DO IT? WHAT DID YOU USE?
THE DEADLIEST ENEMY OF WOOD-- TERMITES!! I BRED THEM IN MY LABORATORY... THEN I BROUGHT THEM OUT HERE AND TURNED THEM LOOSE ON GROOT!
WELL, I'LL BE... I NEVER EVEN THOUGHT OF THAT!
THAT'S WHY EVANS IS A SCIENTIST-- AND YOU'RE ONLY A SHERIFF!
OH, DARLING, FORGIVE ME! I'VE BEEN SUCH A FOOL! I'LL NEVER COMPLAIN ABOUT YOU AGAIN! NEVER!!
AND THUS, THE END OF GROOT MARKED FOR ME THE BEGINNING OF A NEW, AND BETTER LIFE!
7

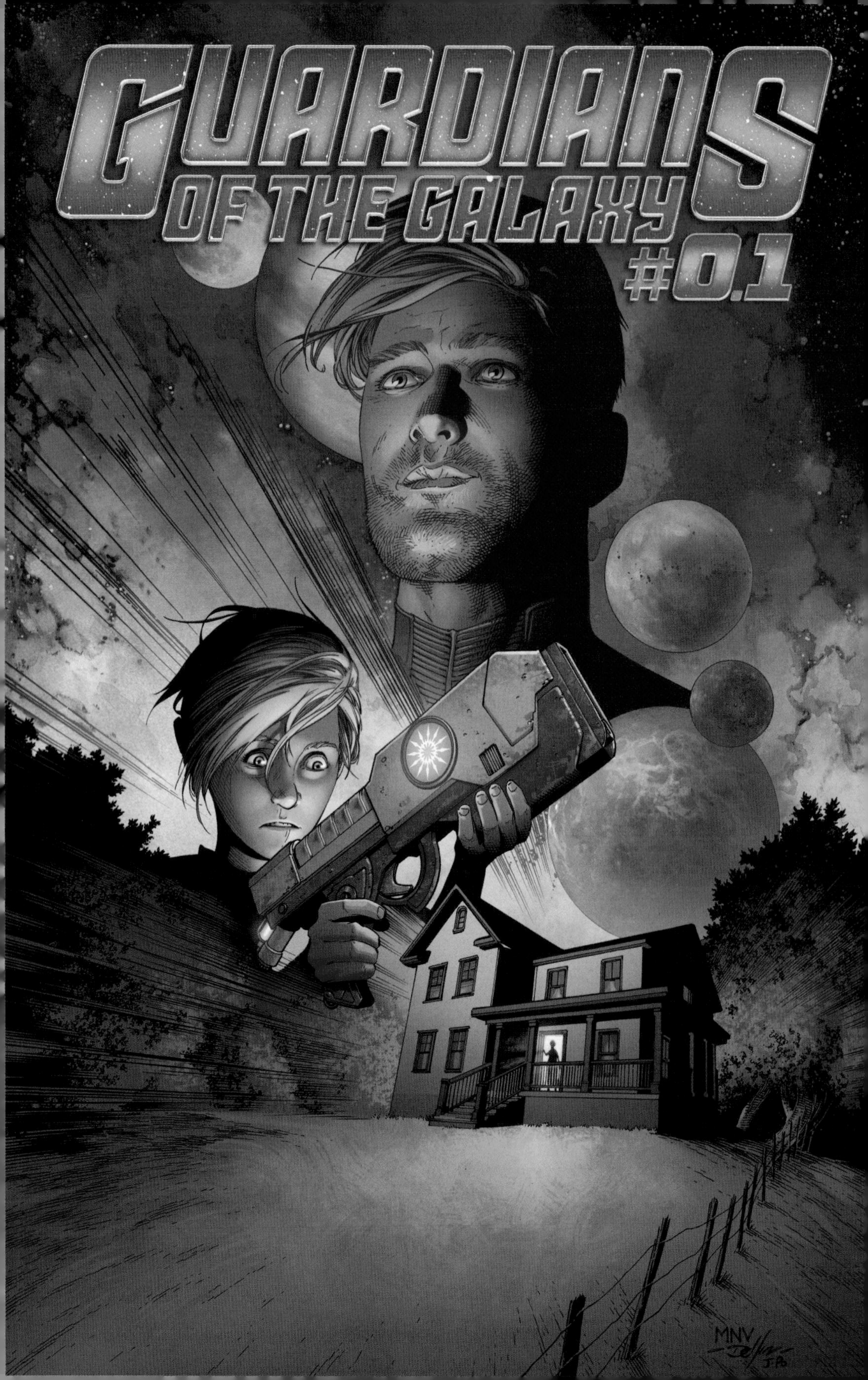
GUARDIANS
OF THE GALAXY
#0.1
MNV

30 YEARS AGO...

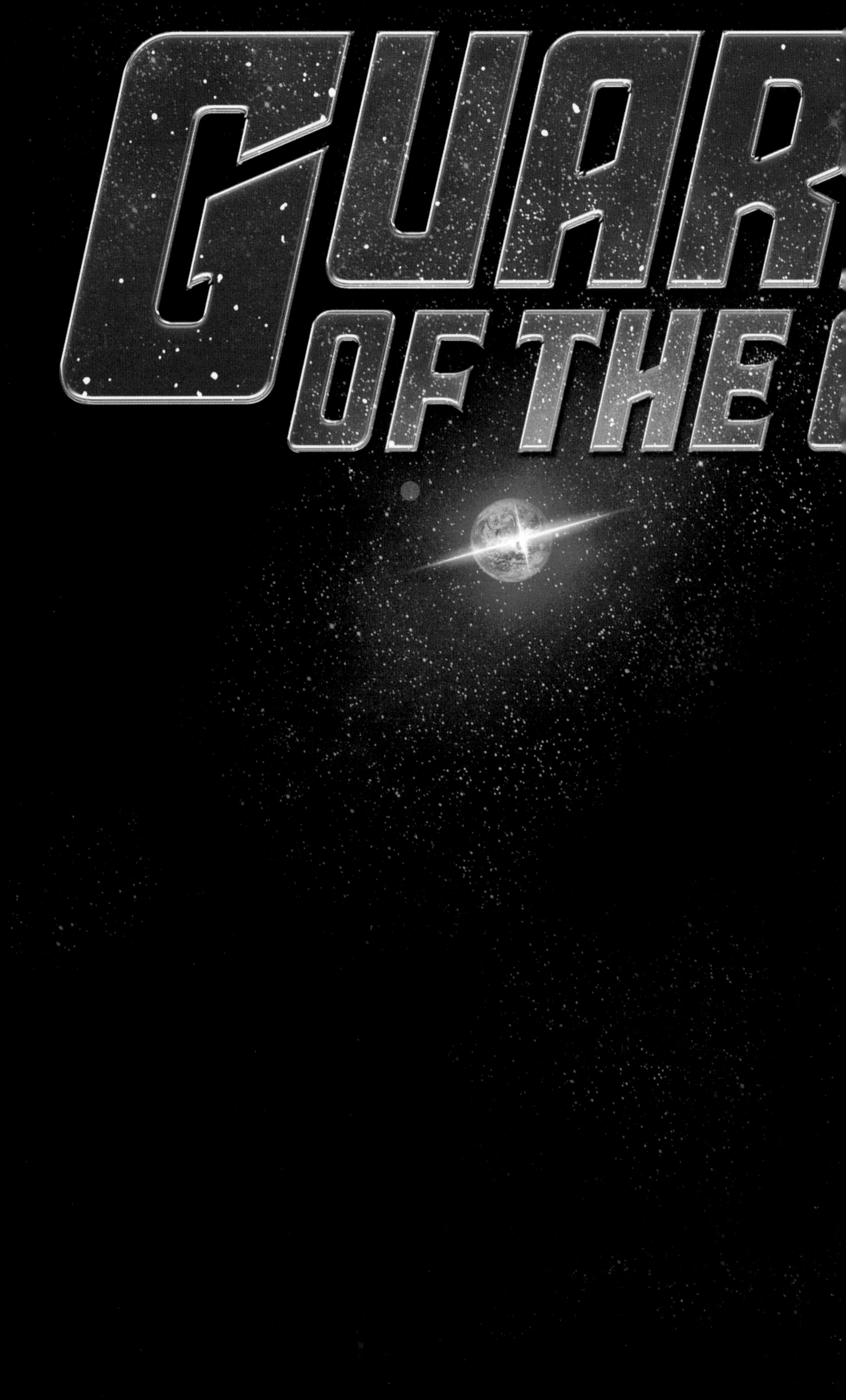
GUAR
OF THE

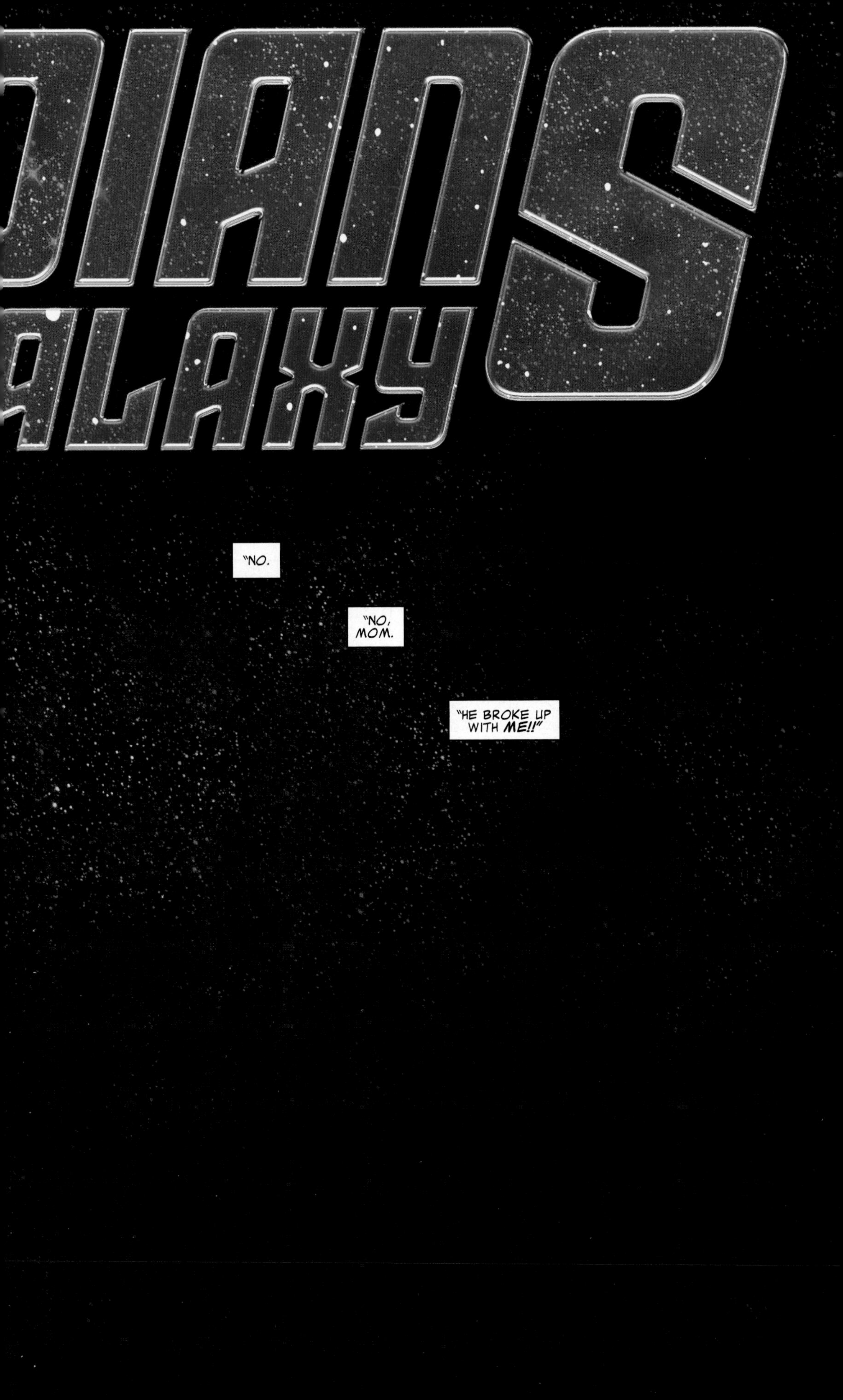
"NO.
"NO, MOM.
"HE BROKE UP WITH ME!!"

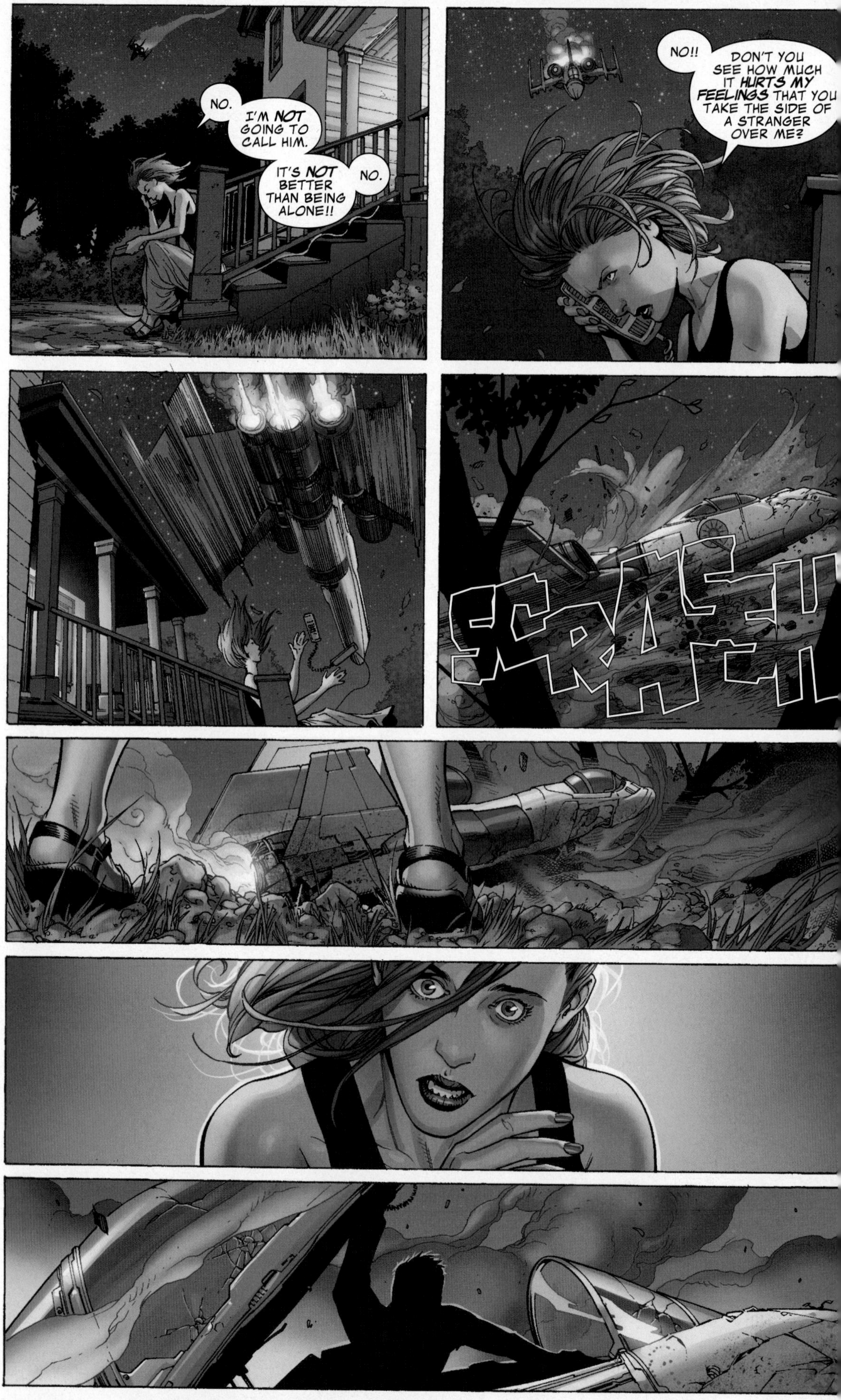
NO.
I'M **NOT** GOING TO CALL HIM.
IT'S **NOT** BETTER THAN BEING ALONE!!
NO.
NO!!
DON'T YOU SEE HOW MUCH IT **HURTS MY FEELINGS** THAT YOU TAKE THE SIDE OF A STRANGER OVER ME?

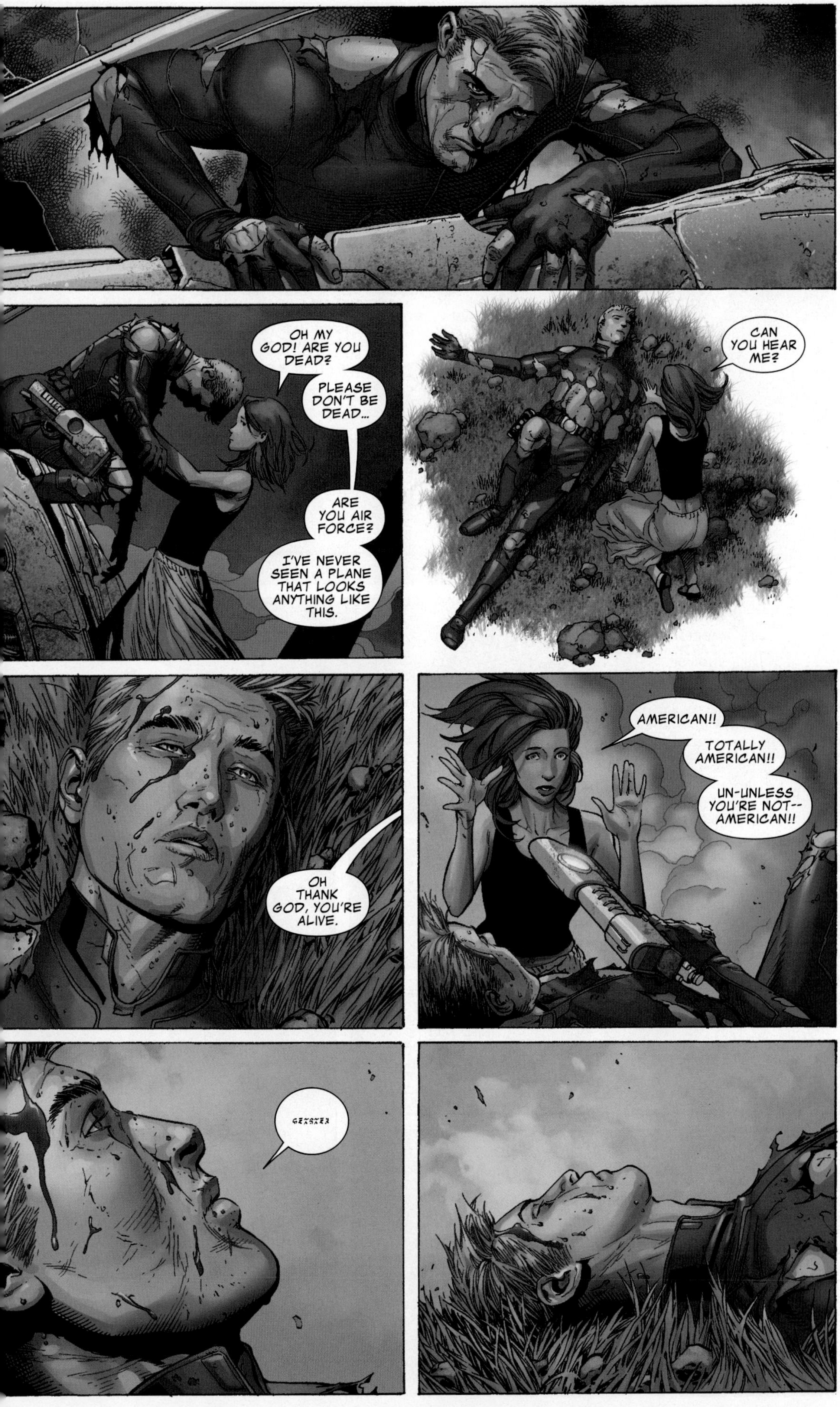
OH MY GOD! ARE YOU DEAD?
PLEASE DON'T BE DEAD...
ARE YOU AIR FORCE?
I'VE NEVER SEEN A PLANE THAT LOOKS ANYTHING LIKE THIS.
CAN YOU HEAR ME?
OH THANK GOD, YOU'RE ALIVE.
AMERICAN!!
TOTALLY AMERICAN!!
UN-UNLESS YOU'RE NOT--AMERICAN!!

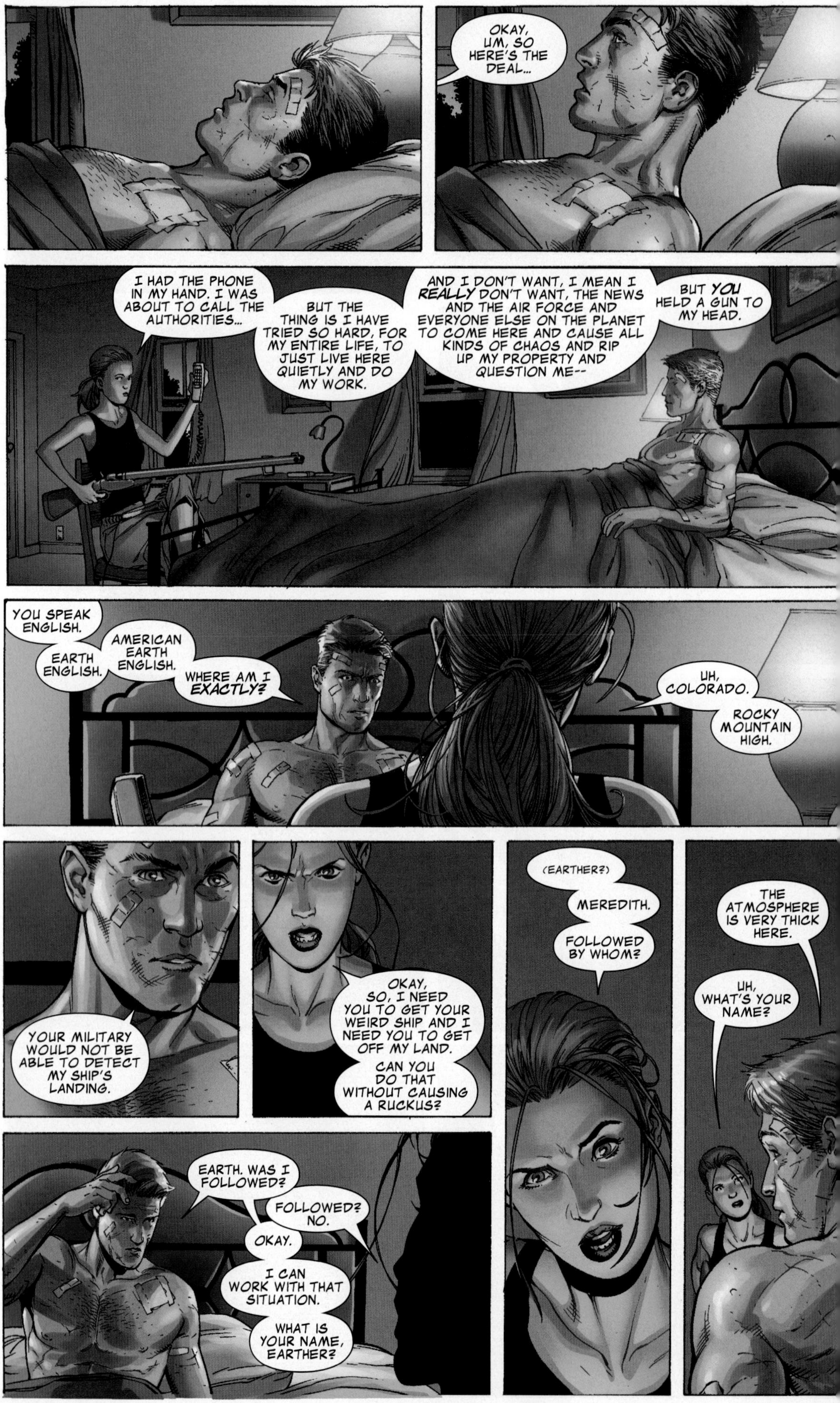
OKAY, UM, SO HERE'S THE DEAL...
I HAD THE PHONE IN MY HAND. I WAS ABOUT TO CALL THE AUTHORITIES...
BUT THE THING IS I HAVE TRIED SO HARD, FOR MY ENTIRE LIFE, TO JUST LIVE HERE QUIETLY AND DO MY WORK.
AND I DON'T WANT, I MEAN I REALLY DON'T WANT, THE NEWS AND THE AIR FORCE AND EVERYONE ELSE ON THE PLANET TO COME HERE AND CAUSE ALL KINDS OF CHAOS AND RIP UP MY PROPERTY AND QUESTION ME--
BUT YOU HELD A GUN TO MY HEAD.
YOU SPEAK ENGLISH.
EARTH ENGLISH.
AMERICAN EARTH ENGLISH.
WHERE AM I EXACTLY?
UH, COLORADO.
ROCKY MOUNTAIN HIGH.
YOUR MILITARY WOULD NOT BE ABLE TO DETECT MY SHIP'S LANDING.
OKAY, SO, I NEED YOU TO GET YOUR WEIRD SHIP AND I NEED YOU TO GET OFF MY LAND.
CAN YOU DO THAT WITHOUT CAUSING A RUCKUS?
EARTH. WAS I FOLLOWED?
FOLLOWED? NO.
OKAY.
I CAN WORK WITH THAT SITUATION.
WHAT IS YOUR NAME, EARTHER?
(EARTHER?)
MEREDITH.
FOLLOWED BY WHOM?
THE ATMOSPHERE IS VERY THICK HERE.
UH, WHAT'S YOUR NAME?

MY NAME IS J'SON OF SPARTAX. YOUR KINDNESS IS APPRECIATED.

I HOPE I WILL BE ABLE TO RETURN IT.

ARE YOU A PILOT?

IS THAT-- WHAT IS THAT?

I'M FROM SPARTAX. I AM OF THE THRONE.

I WILL NEED TO FIX MY SHIP AND GET BACK TO MY PEOPLE. I WILL TRY TO DO SO AS QUICKLY AS I CAN.

OH MY GOD. ARE YOU KIDDING ME?

ARE YOU FROM--ARE YOU FROM SPACE?

I'M FROM SPARTAX.

I'VE TOLD YOU THIS A FEW TIMES.

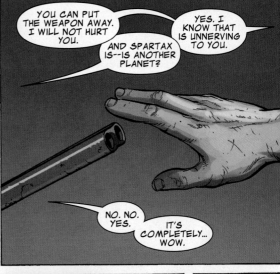

YOU CAN PUT THE WEAPON AWAY. I WILL NOT HURT YOU.

AND SPARTAX IS--IS ANOTHER PLANET?

YES. I KNOW THAT IS UNNERVING TO YOU.

NO. NO. YES.

IT'S COMPLETELY... WOW.

DO YOU-- DO YOU NEED A TOOLBOX OR--?

YOU'RE A FUNNY EARTHER.

NO. I HAVE THE TOOLS. BUT IT MAY TAKE SOME TIME.

EARTHER?

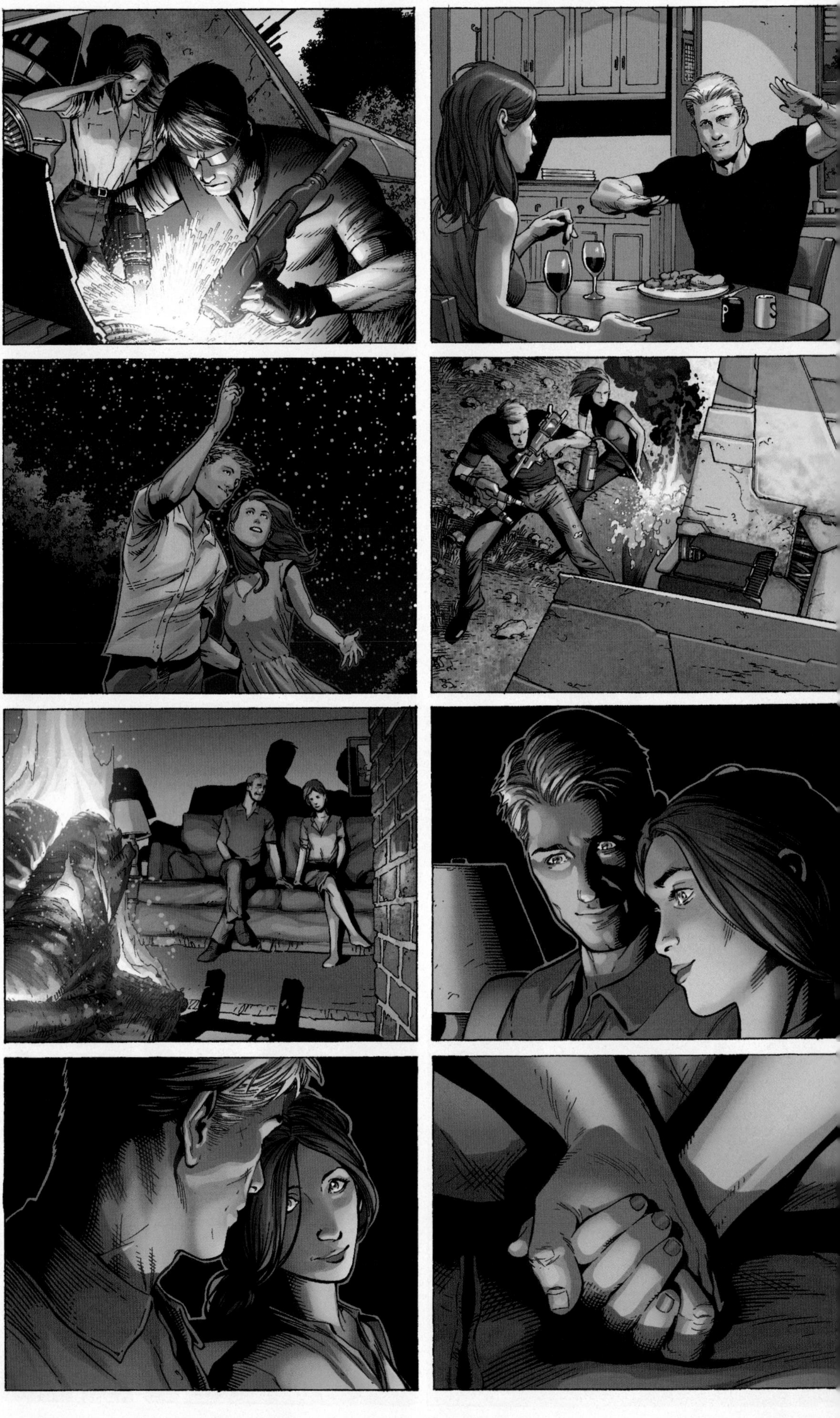

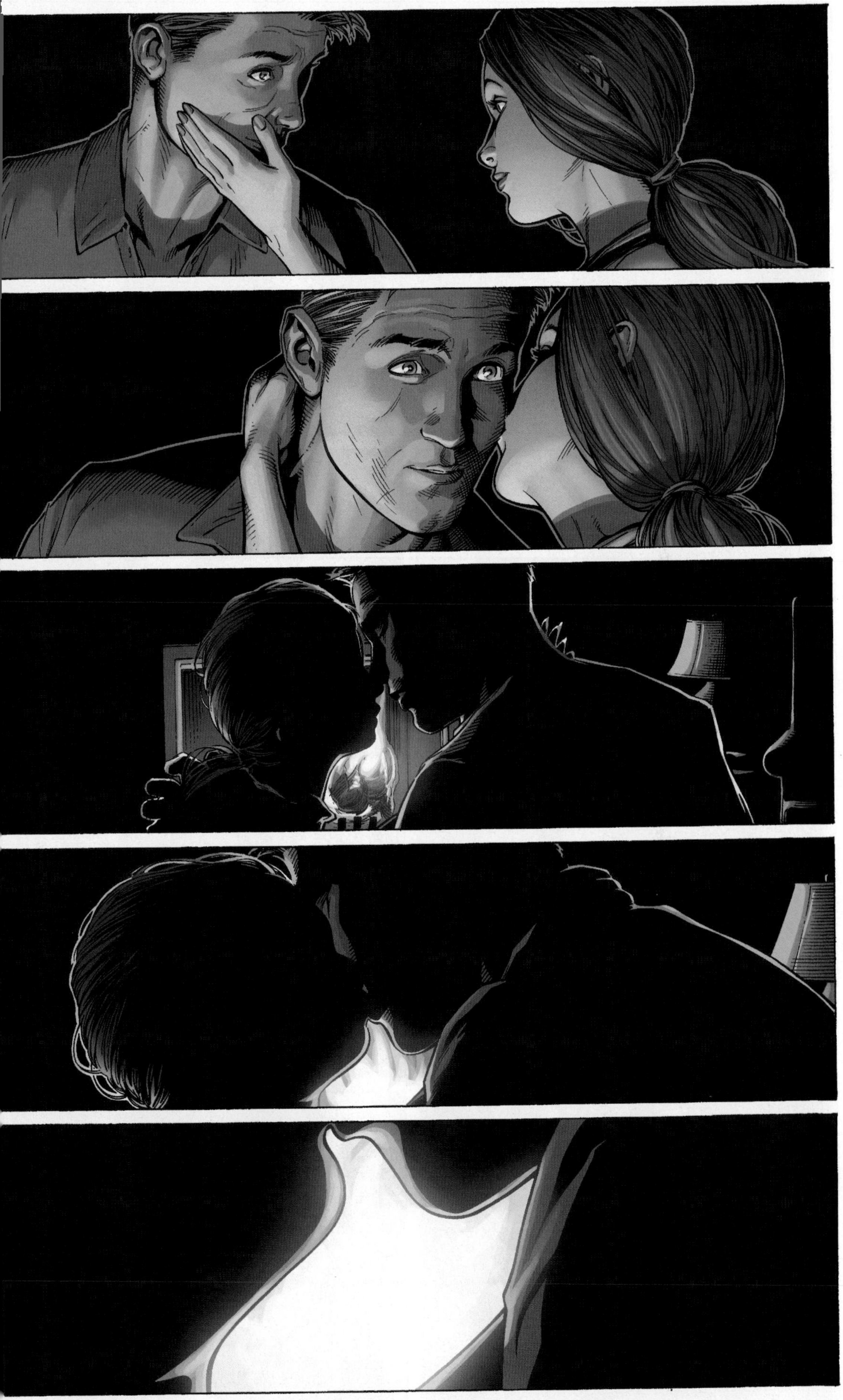

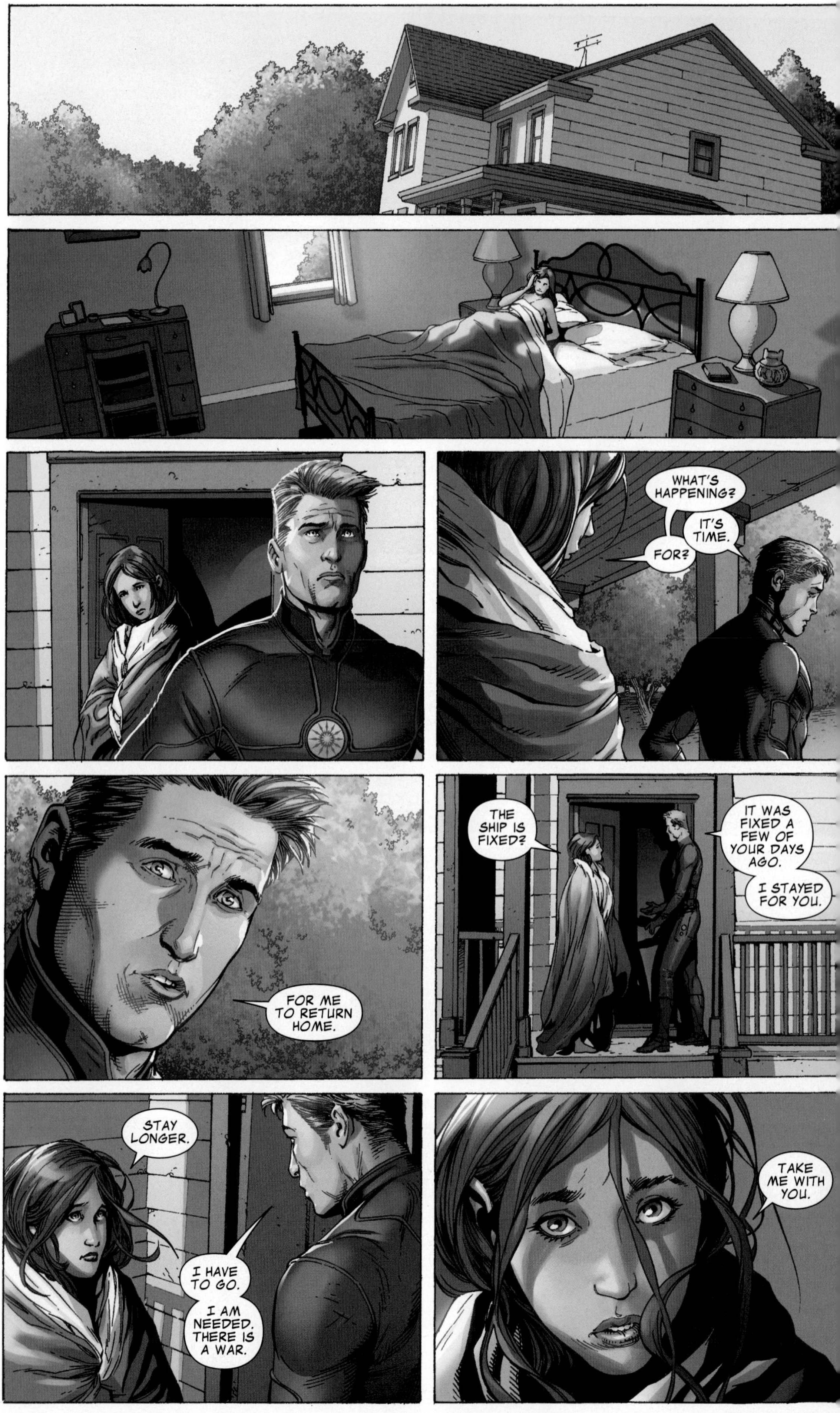
WHAT'S HAPPENING?
IT'S TIME.
FOR?
FOR ME TO RETURN HOME.
THE SHIP IS FIXED?
IT WAS FIXED A FEW OF YOUR DAYS AGO.
I STAYED FOR YOU.
STAY LONGER.
I HAVE TO GO.
I AM NEEDED. THERE IS A WAR.
TAKE ME WITH YOU.

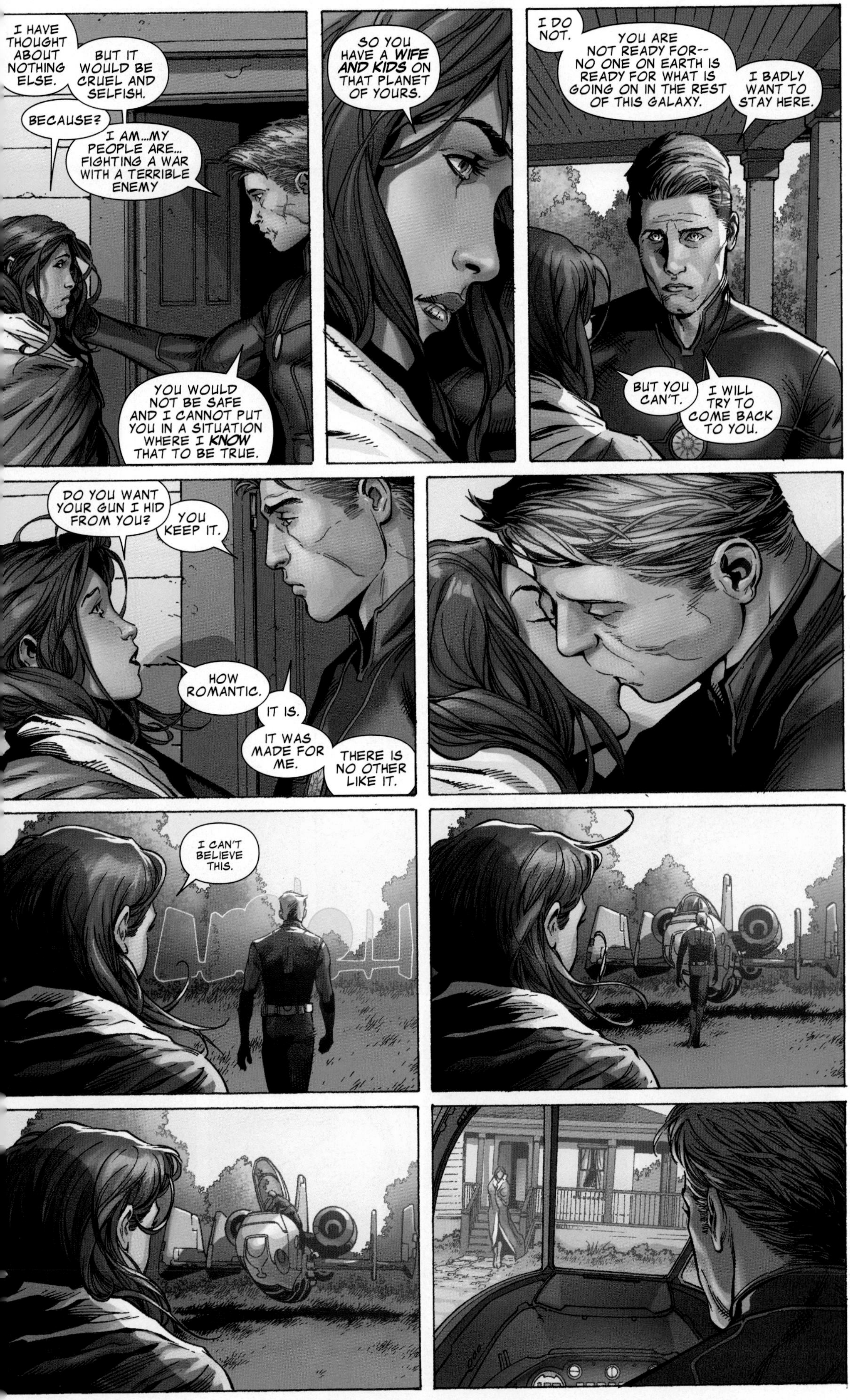
I HAVE THOUGHT ABOUT NOTHING ELSE.
BUT IT WOULD BE CRUEL AND SELFISH.
BECAUSE?
I AM...MY PEOPLE ARE... FIGHTING A WAR WITH A TERRIBLE ENEMY
YOU WOULD NOT BE SAFE AND I CANNOT PUT YOU IN A SITUATION WHERE I KNOW THAT TO BE TRUE.
SO YOU HAVE A WIFE AND KIDS ON THAT PLANET OF YOURS.
I DO NOT.
YOU ARE NOT READY FOR-- NO ONE ON EARTH IS READY FOR WHAT IS GOING ON IN THE REST OF THIS GALAXY.
I BADLY WANT TO STAY HERE.
BUT YOU CAN'T.
I WILL TRY TO COME BACK TO YOU.
DO YOU WANT YOUR GUN I HID FROM YOU?
YOU KEEP IT.
HOW ROMANTIC.
IT IS.
IT WAS MADE FOR ME.
THERE IS NO OTHER LIKE IT.
I CAN'T BELIEVE THIS.

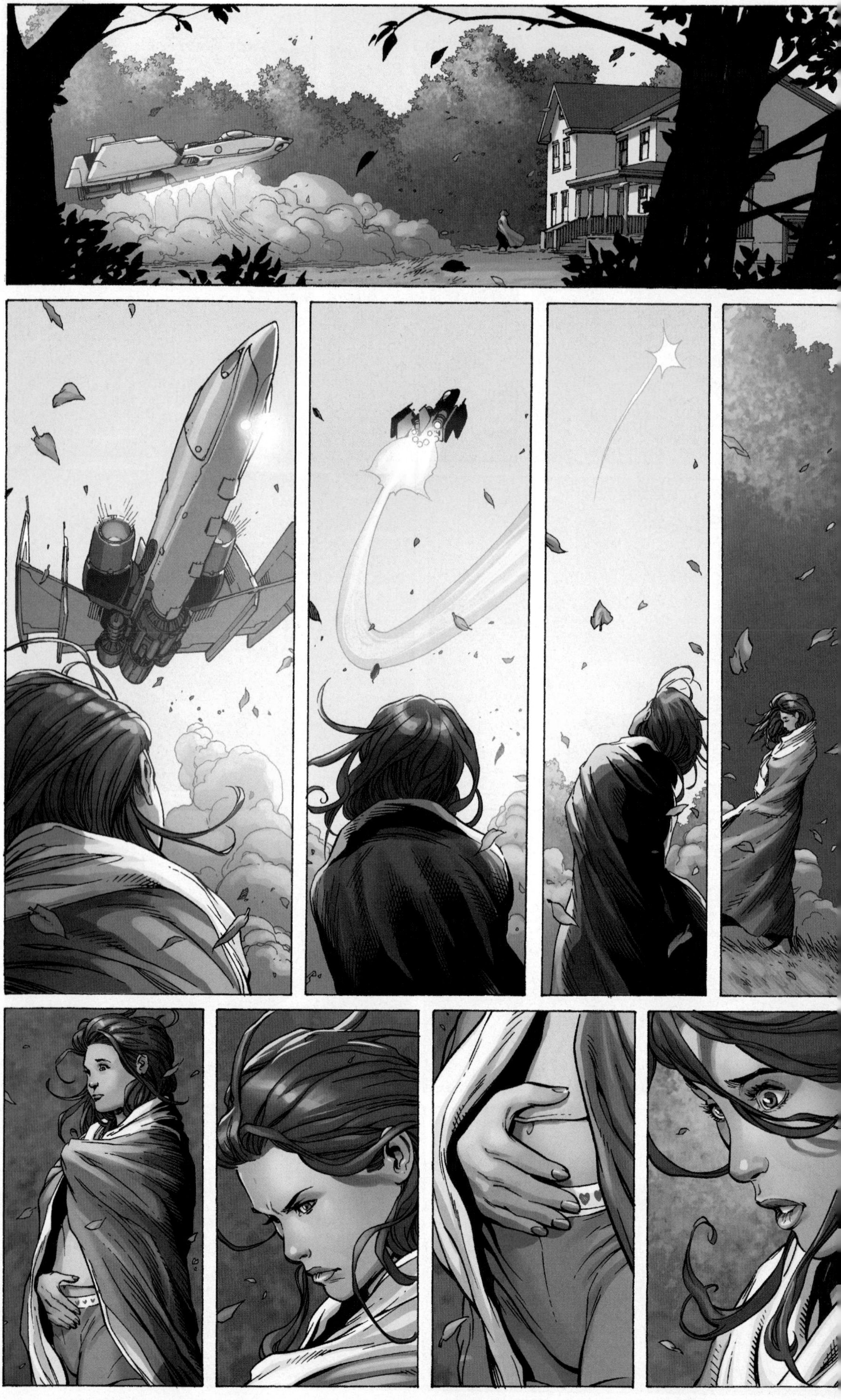

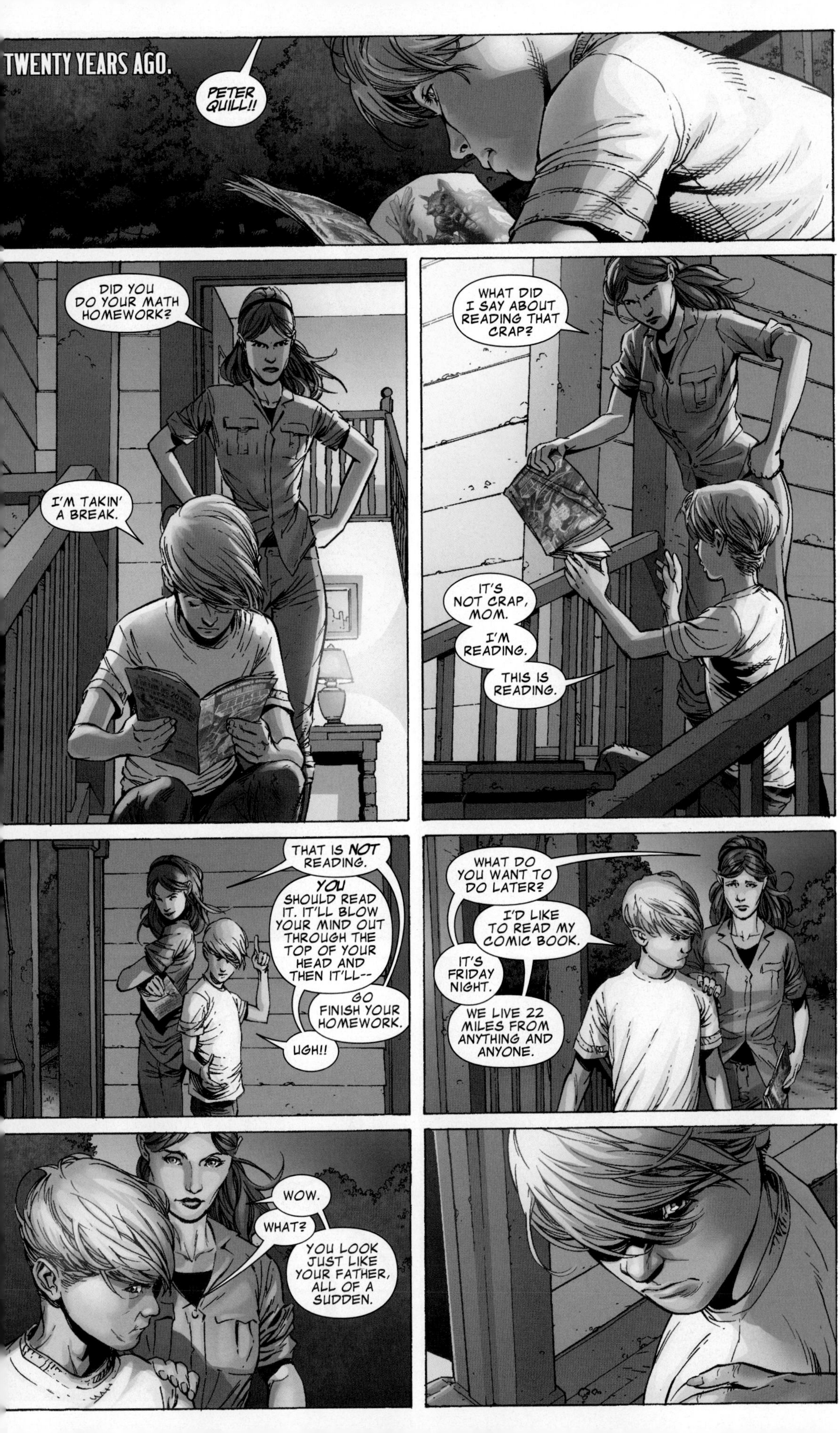

TWENTY YEARS AGO.
PETER QUILL!!
DID YOU DO YOUR MATH HOMEWORK?
I'M TAKIN' A BREAK.
WHAT DID I SAY ABOUT READING THAT CRAP?
IT'S NOT CRAP, MOM.
I'M READING.
THIS IS READING.
THAT IS NOT READING.
YOU SHOULD READ IT. IT'LL BLOW YOUR MIND OUT THROUGH THE TOP OF YOUR HEAD AND THEN IT'LL--
GO FINISH YOUR HOMEWORK.
UGH!!
WHAT DO YOU WANT TO DO LATER?
I'D LIKE TO READ MY COMIC BOOK.
IT'S FRIDAY NIGHT.
WE LIVE 22 MILES FROM ANYTHING AND ANYONE.
WOW.
WHAT?
YOU LOOK JUST LIKE YOUR FATHER, ALL OF A SUDDEN.

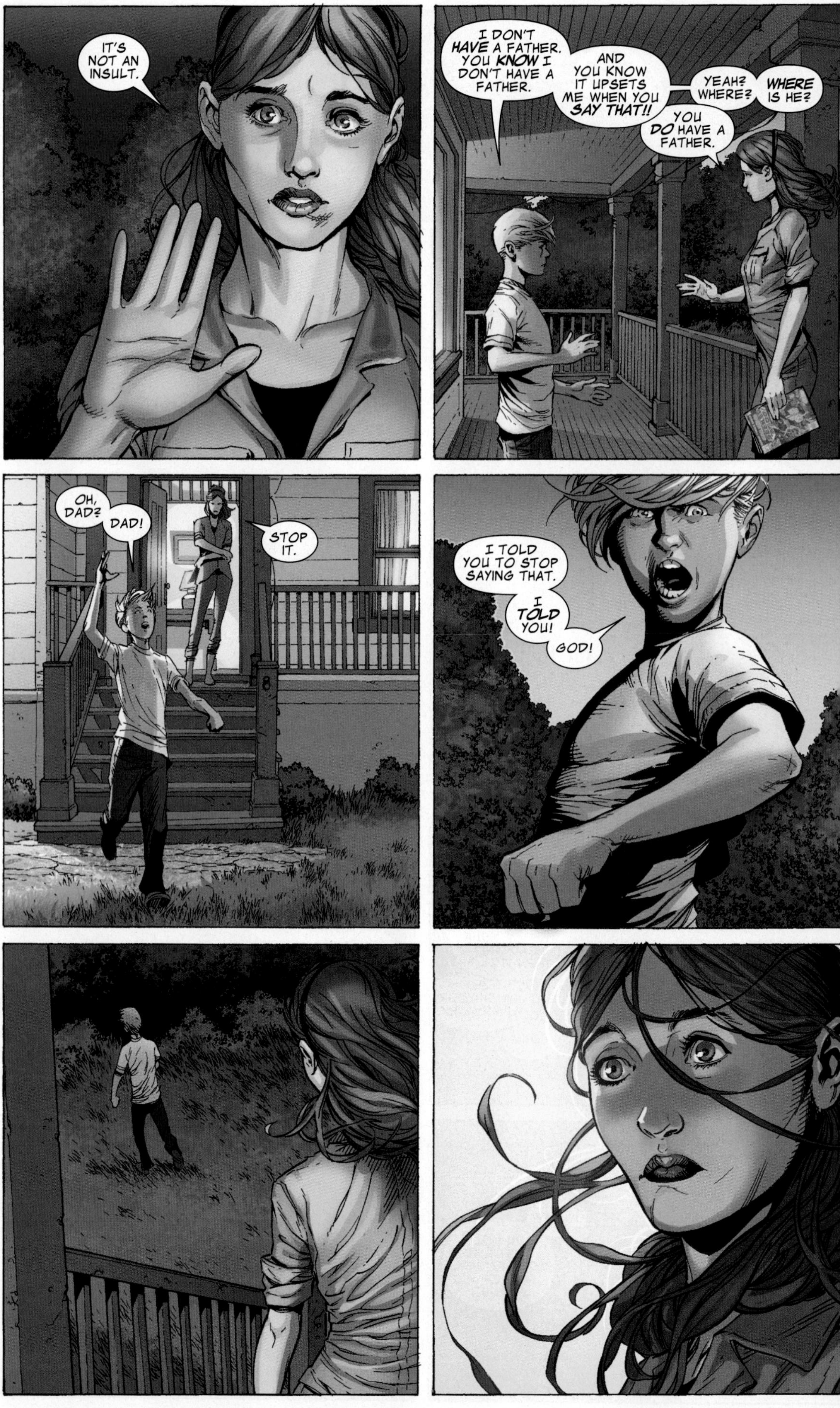
IT'S NOT AN INSULT.
I DON'T HAVE A FATHER. YOU KNOW I DON'T HAVE A FATHER.
AND YOU KNOW IT UPSETS ME WHEN YOU SAY THAT!!
YOU DO HAVE A FATHER.
YEAH? WHERE?
WHERE IS HE?
OH, DAD?
DAD!
STOP IT.
I TOLD YOU TO STOP SAYING THAT.
I TOLD YOU!
GOD!

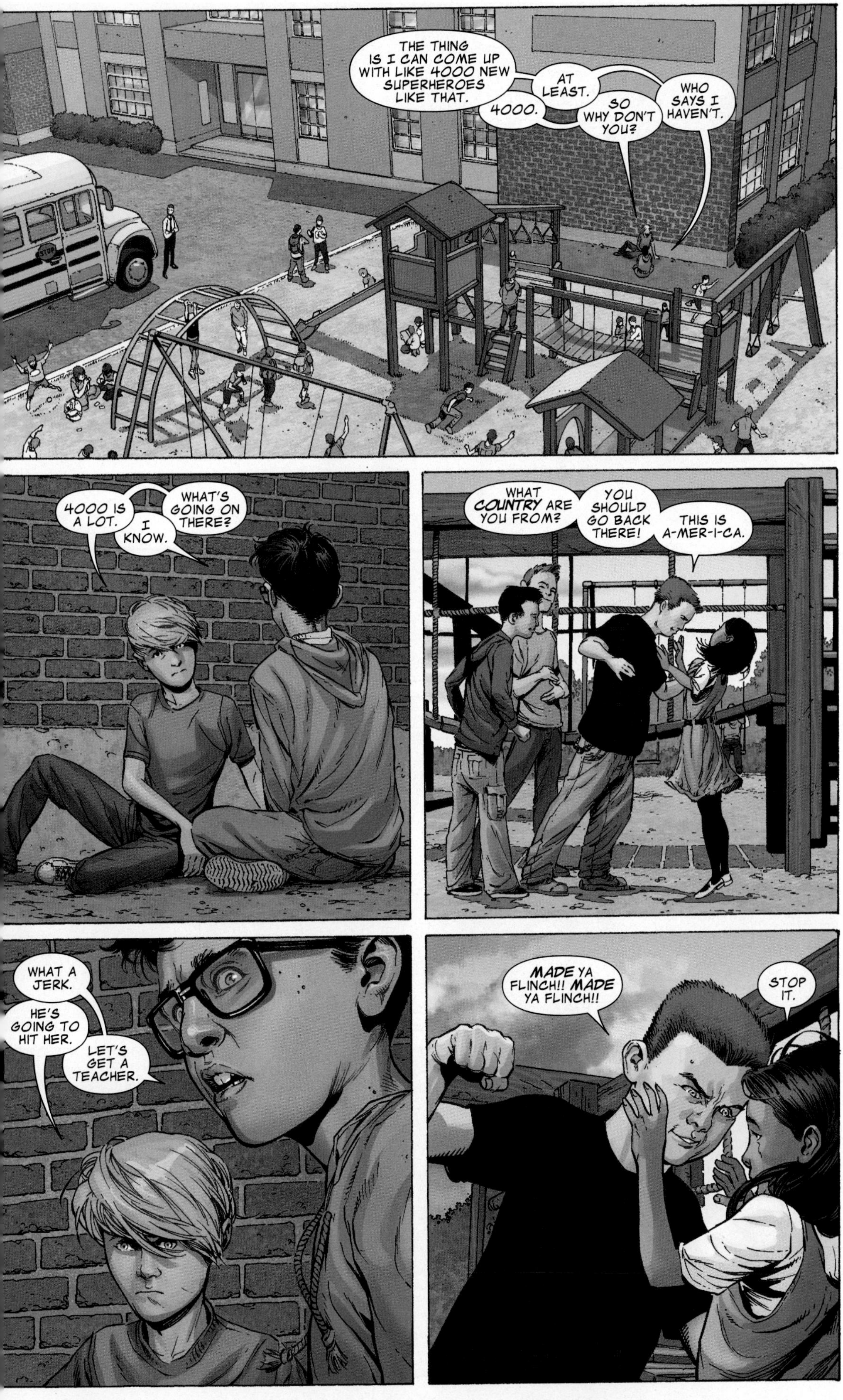
THE THING IS I CAN COME UP WITH LIKE 4000 NEW SUPERHEROES LIKE THAT.
4000.
AT LEAST.
SO WHY DON'T YOU?
WHO SAYS I HAVEN'T.
4000 IS A LOT.
WHAT'S GOING ON THERE?
I KNOW.
WHAT COUNTRY ARE YOU FROM?
YOU SHOULD GO BACK THERE!
THIS IS A-MER-I-CA.
WHAT A JERK.
HE'S GOING TO HIT HER.
LET'S GET A TEACHER.
MADE YA FLINCH!! MADE YA FLINCH!!
STOP IT.

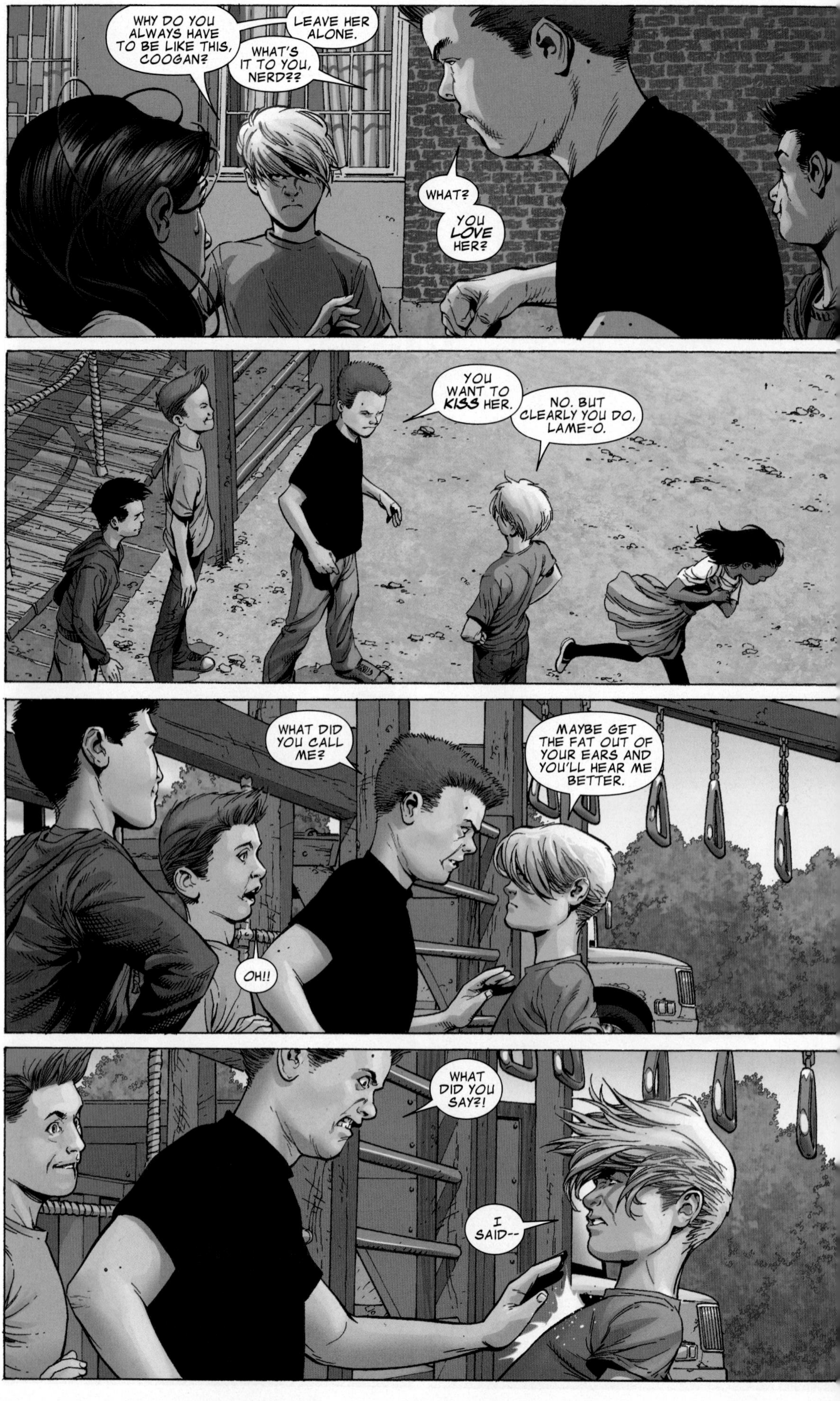
WHY DO YOU ALWAYS HAVE TO BE LIKE THIS, COOGAN?
LEAVE HER ALONE.
WHAT'S IT TO YOU, NERD??
WHAT?
YOU LOVE HER?
YOU WANT TO KISS HER.
NO. BUT CLEARLY YOU DO, LAME-O.
WHAT DID YOU CALL ME?
MAYBE GET THE FAT OUT OF YOUR EARS AND YOU'LL HEAR ME BETTER.
OH!!
WHAT DID YOU SAY?!
I SAID--

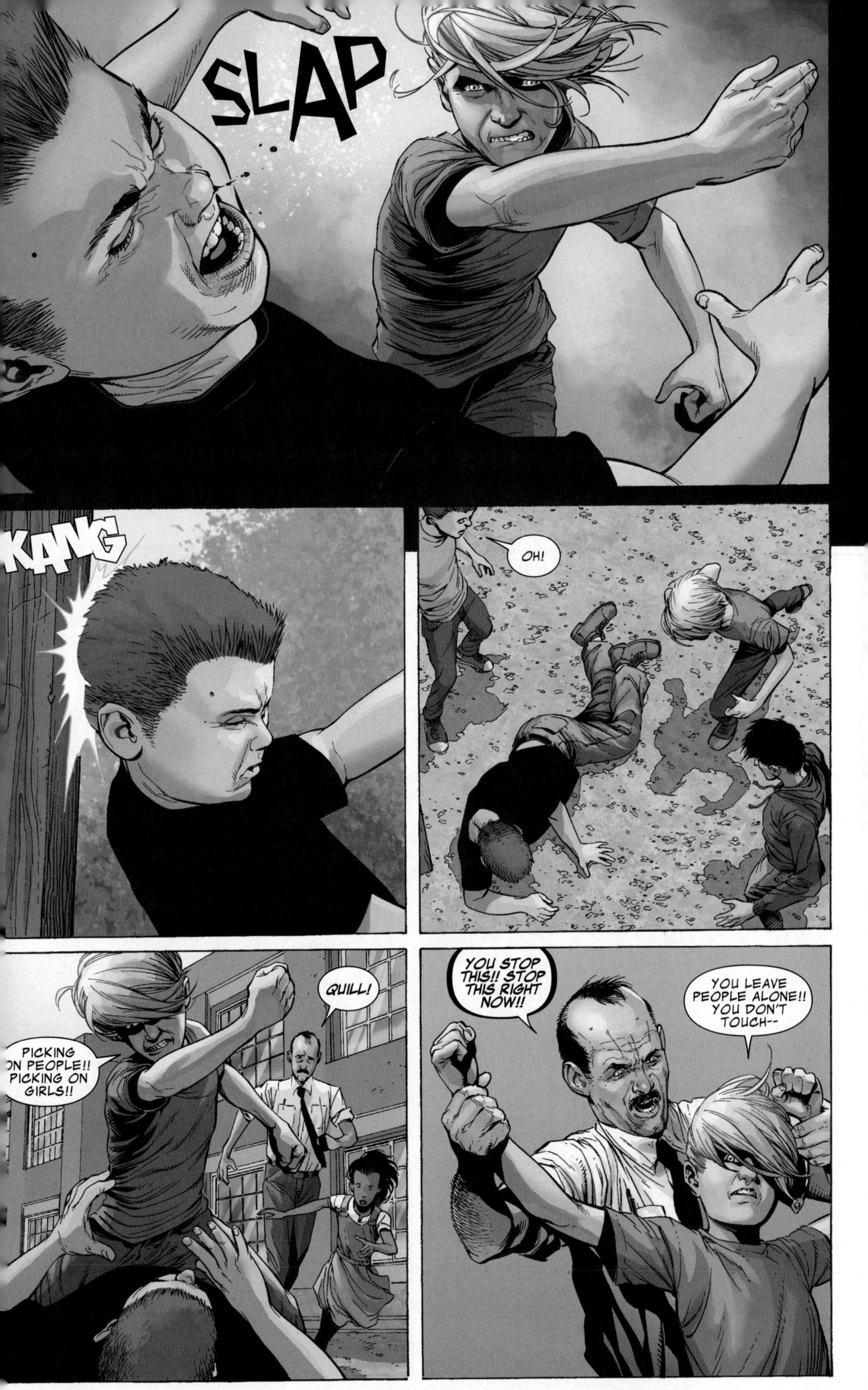
SLAP
KANG
OH!
QUILL!
PICKING ON PEOPLE!! PICKING ON GIRLS!!
YOU STOP THIS!! STOP THIS RIGHT NOW!!
YOU LEAVE PEOPLE ALONE!! YOU DON'T TOUCH--

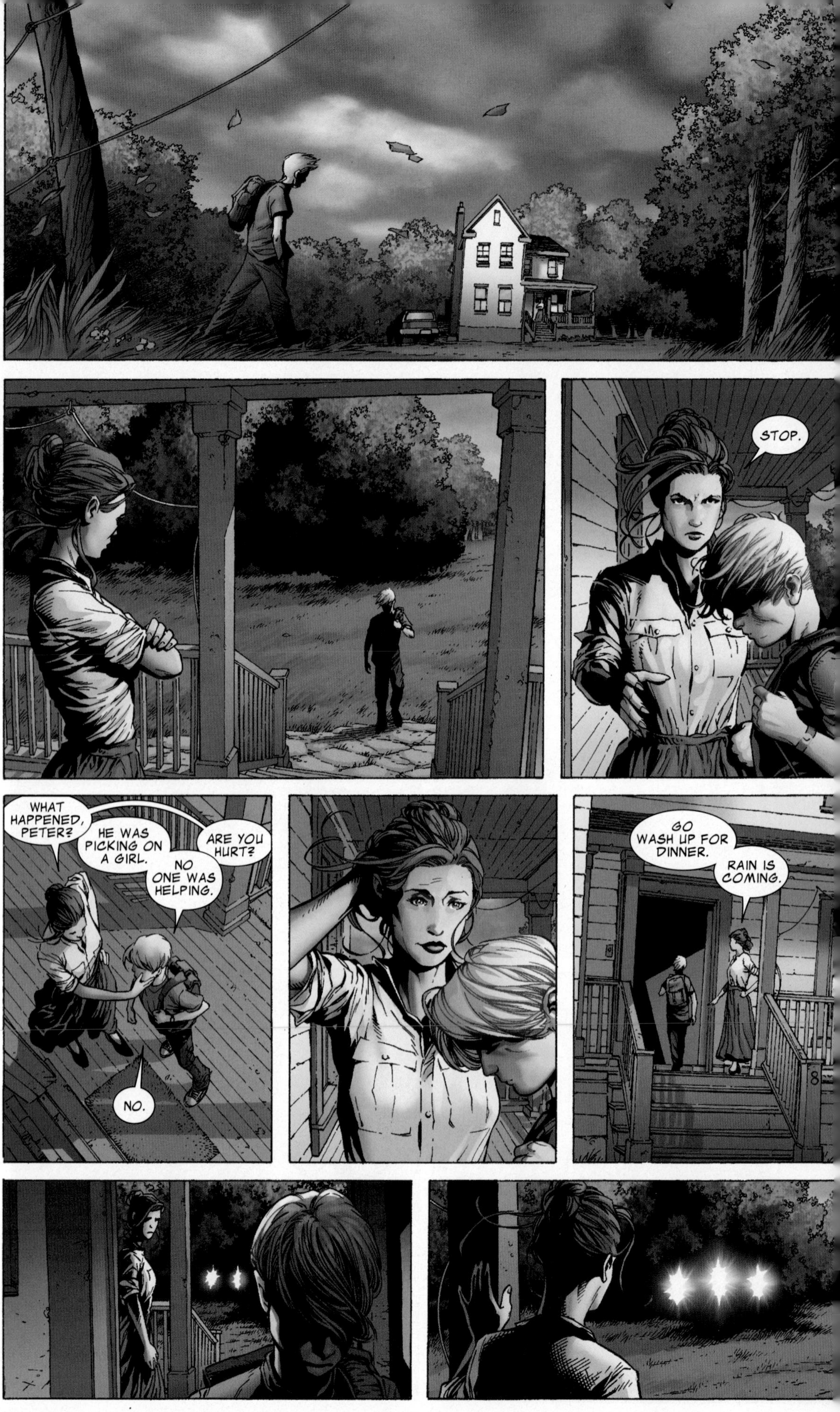

STOP.
WHAT HAPPENED, PETER?
HE WAS PICKING ON A GIRL.
ARE YOU HURT?
NO ONE WAS HELPING.
NO.
GO WASH UP FOR DINNER.
RAIN IS COMING.

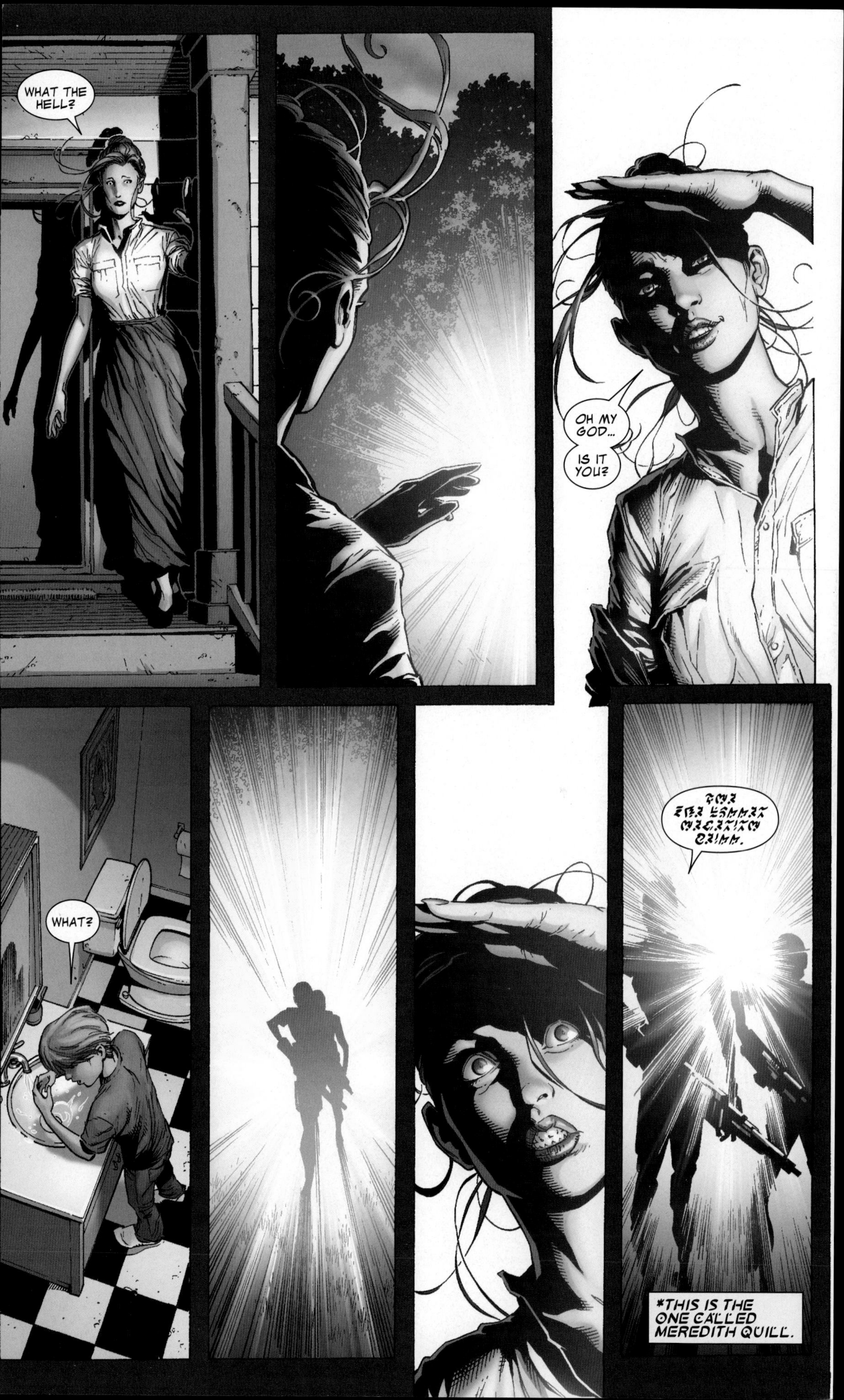
WHAT THE HELL?
OH MY GOD...
IS IT YOU?
WHAT?
*THIS IS THE ONE CALLED MEREDITH QUILL.

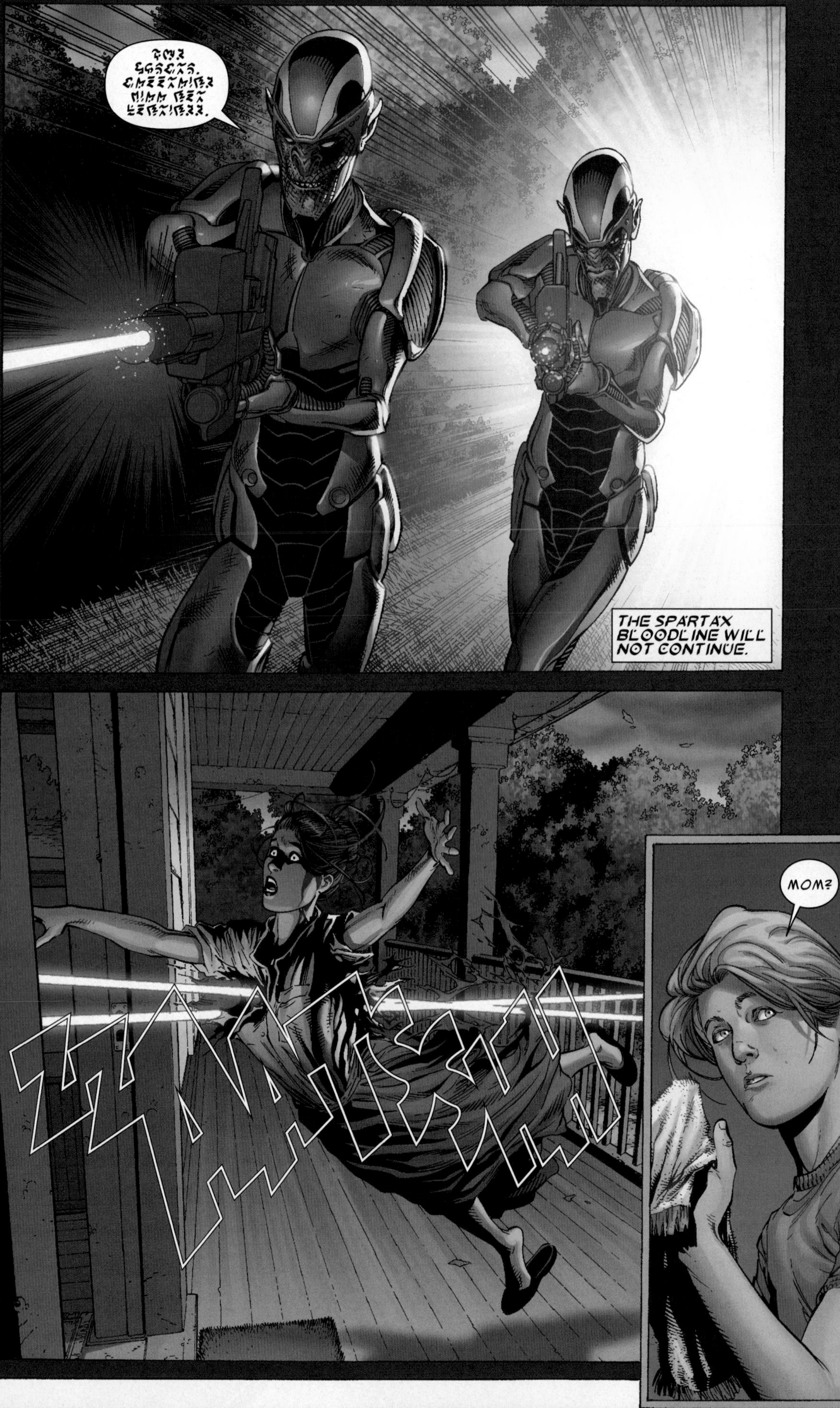
THE SPARTAX BLOODLINE WILL NOT CONTINUE.
MOM?

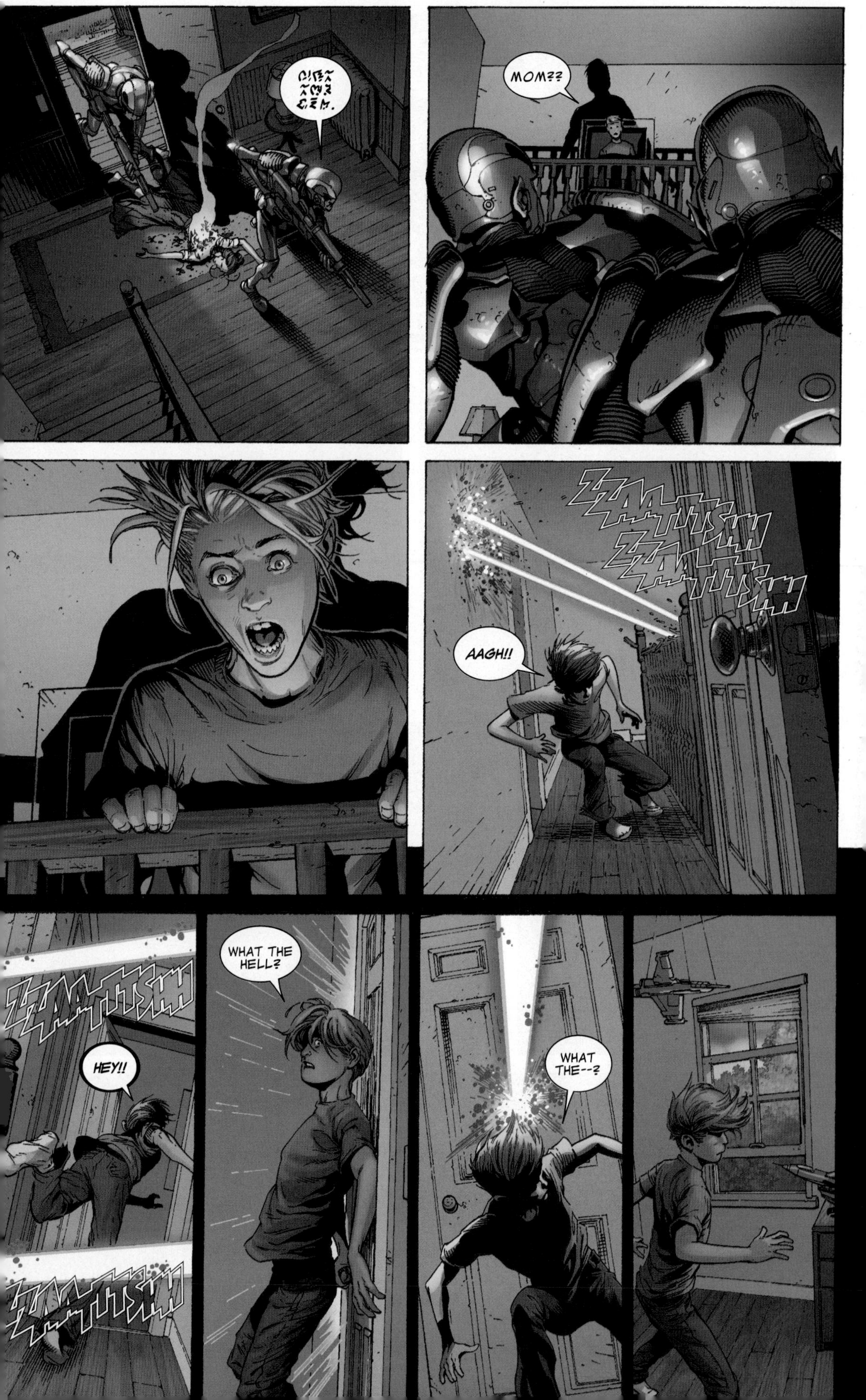
MOM??
ZZAATTTSHH
ZZAATTTSHH
AAGH!!
ZZAATTTSHH
HEY!!
ZZAATTTSHH
WHAT THE HELL?
WHAT THE--?

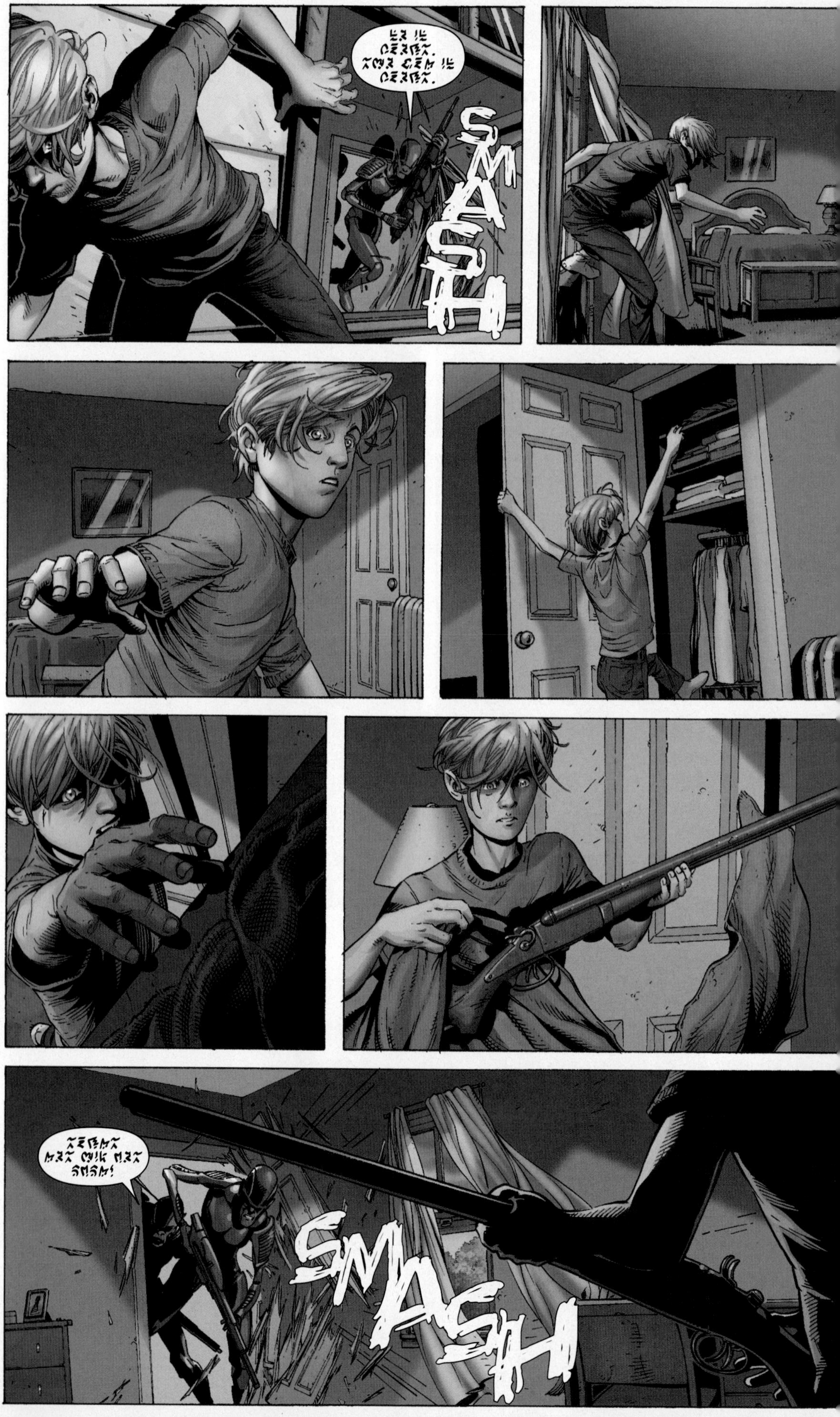
SMASH
SMASH

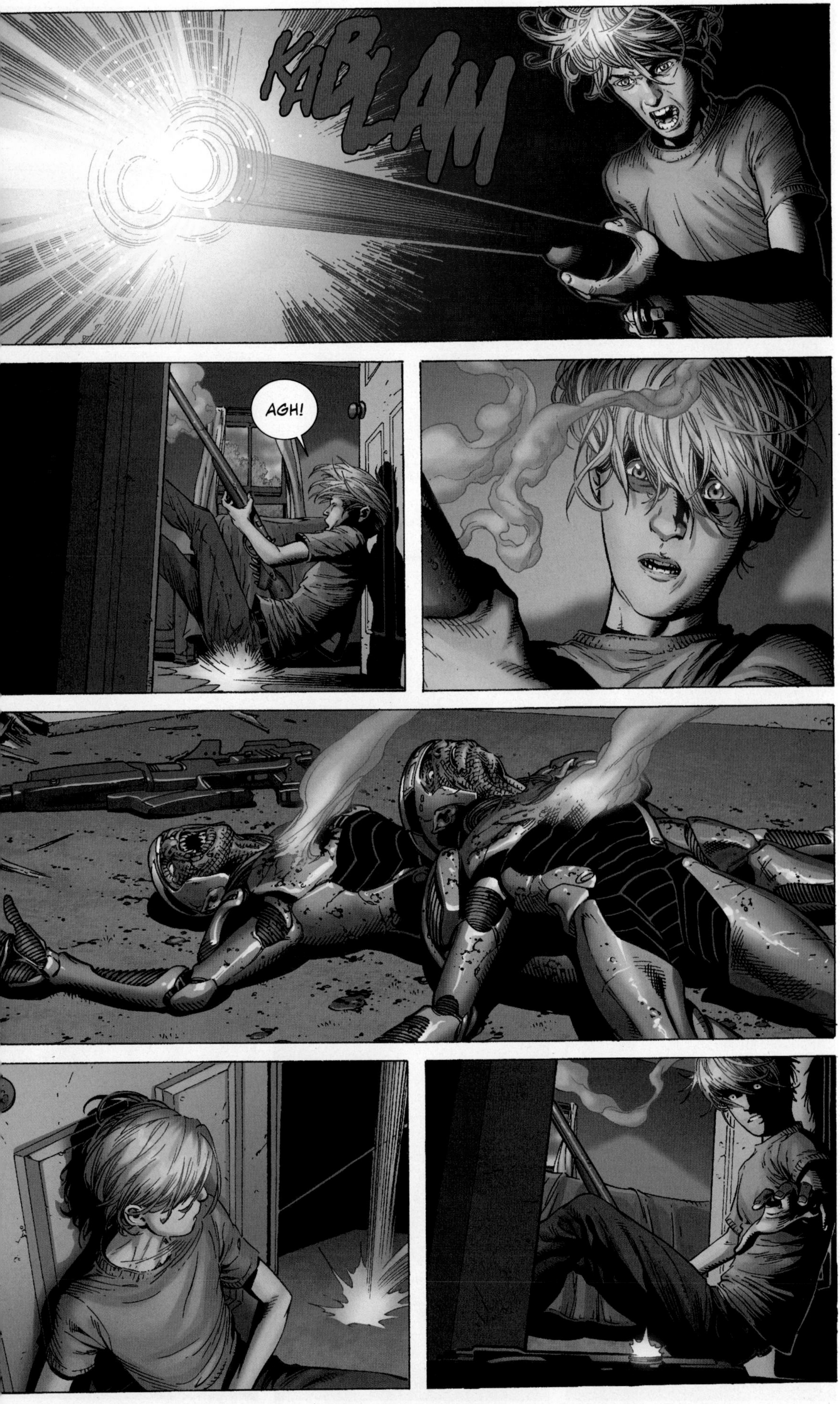
KABLAM
AGH!

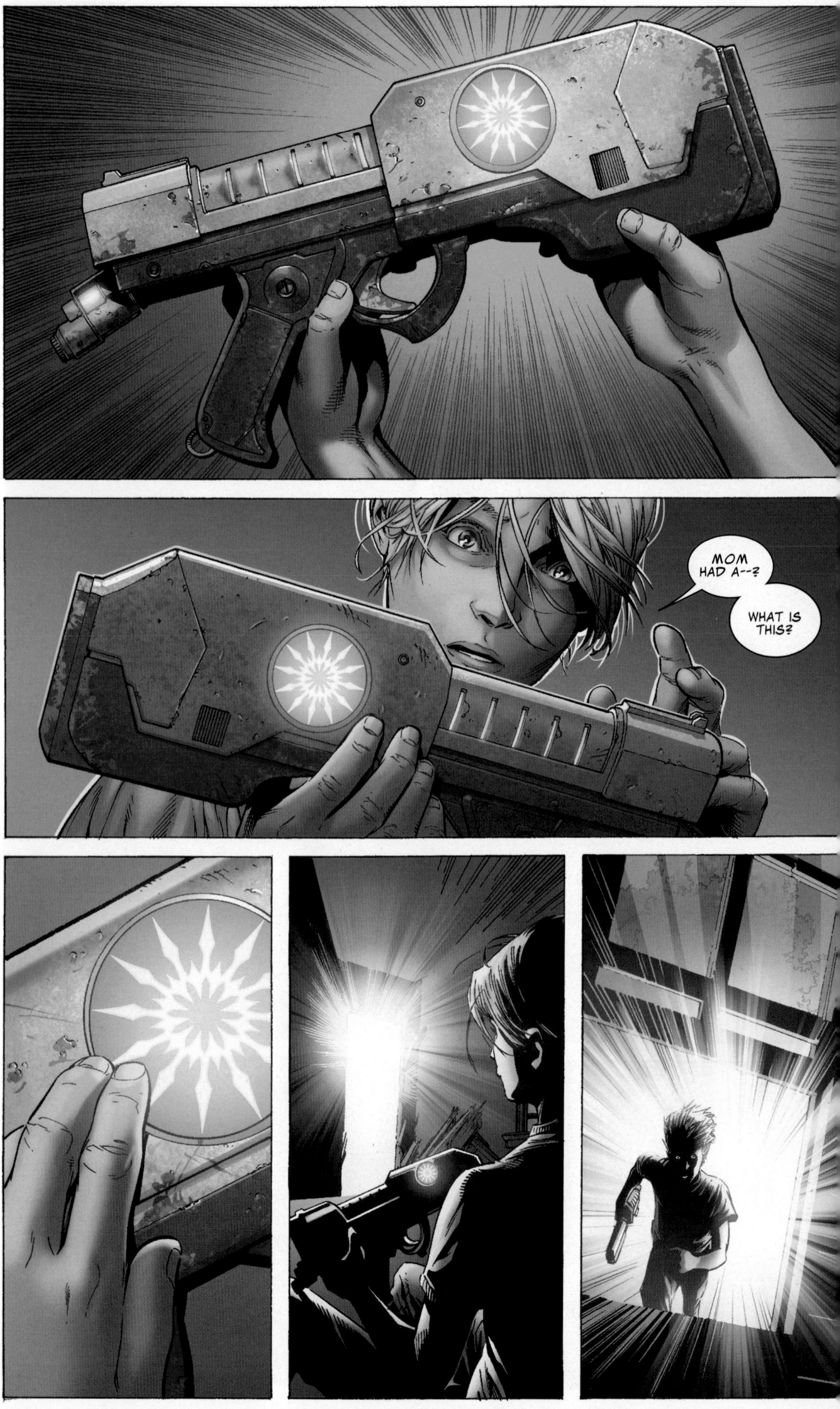
MOM HAD A--?
WHAT IS THIS?

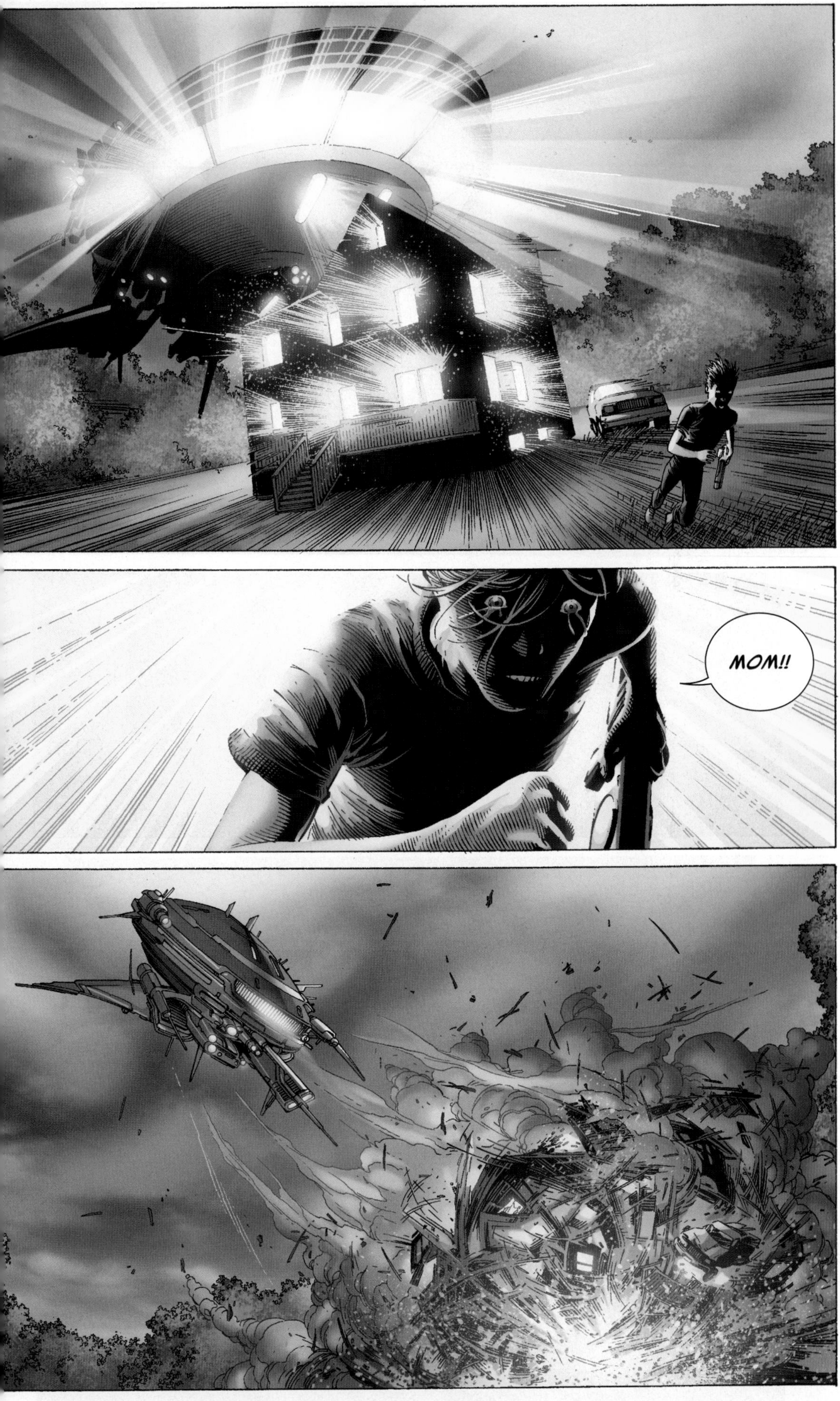
MOM!!

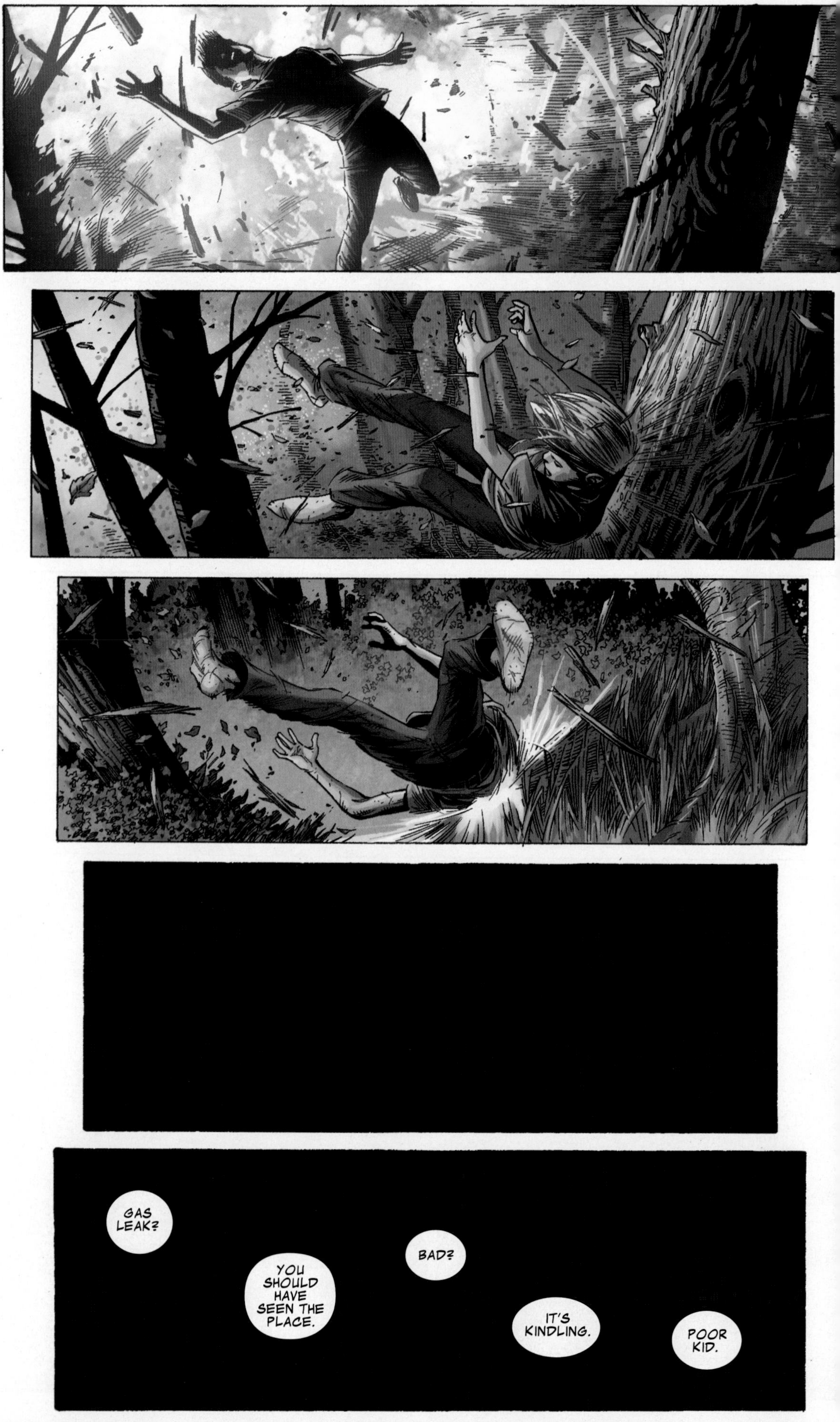
GAS LEAK?
YOU SHOULD HAVE SEEN THE PLACE.
BAD?
IT'S KINDLING.
POOR KID.

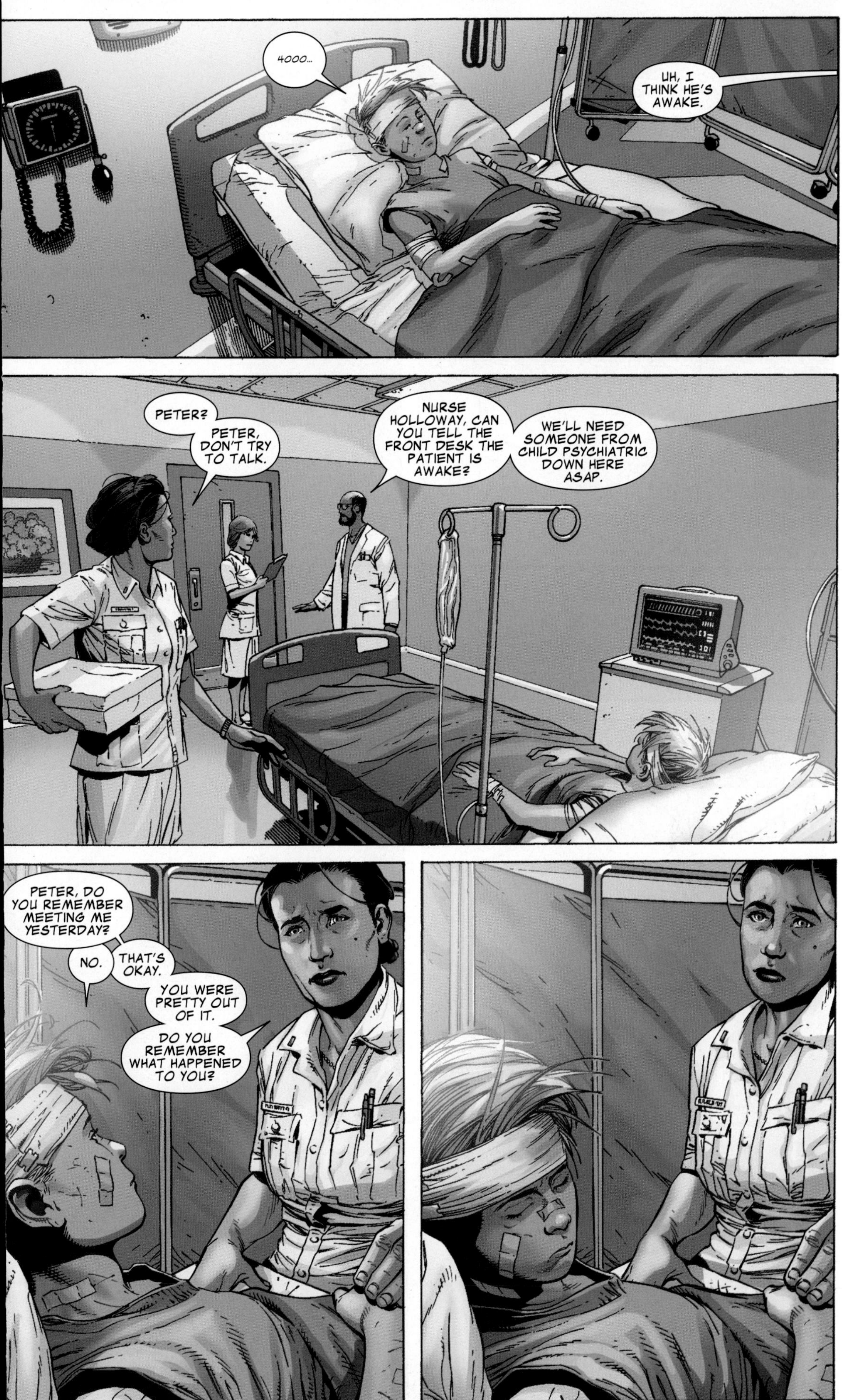

4000...
UH, I THINK HE'S AWAKE.
PETER?
PETER, DON'T TRY TO TALK.
NURSE HOLLOWAY, CAN YOU TELL THE FRONT DESK THE PATIENT IS AWAKE?
WE'LL NEED SOMEONE FROM CHILD PSYCHIATRIC DOWN HERE ASAP.
PETER, DO YOU REMEMBER MEETING ME YESTERDAY?
NO.
THAT'S OKAY.
YOU WERE PRETTY OUT OF IT.
DO YOU REMEMBER WHAT HAPPENED TO YOU?

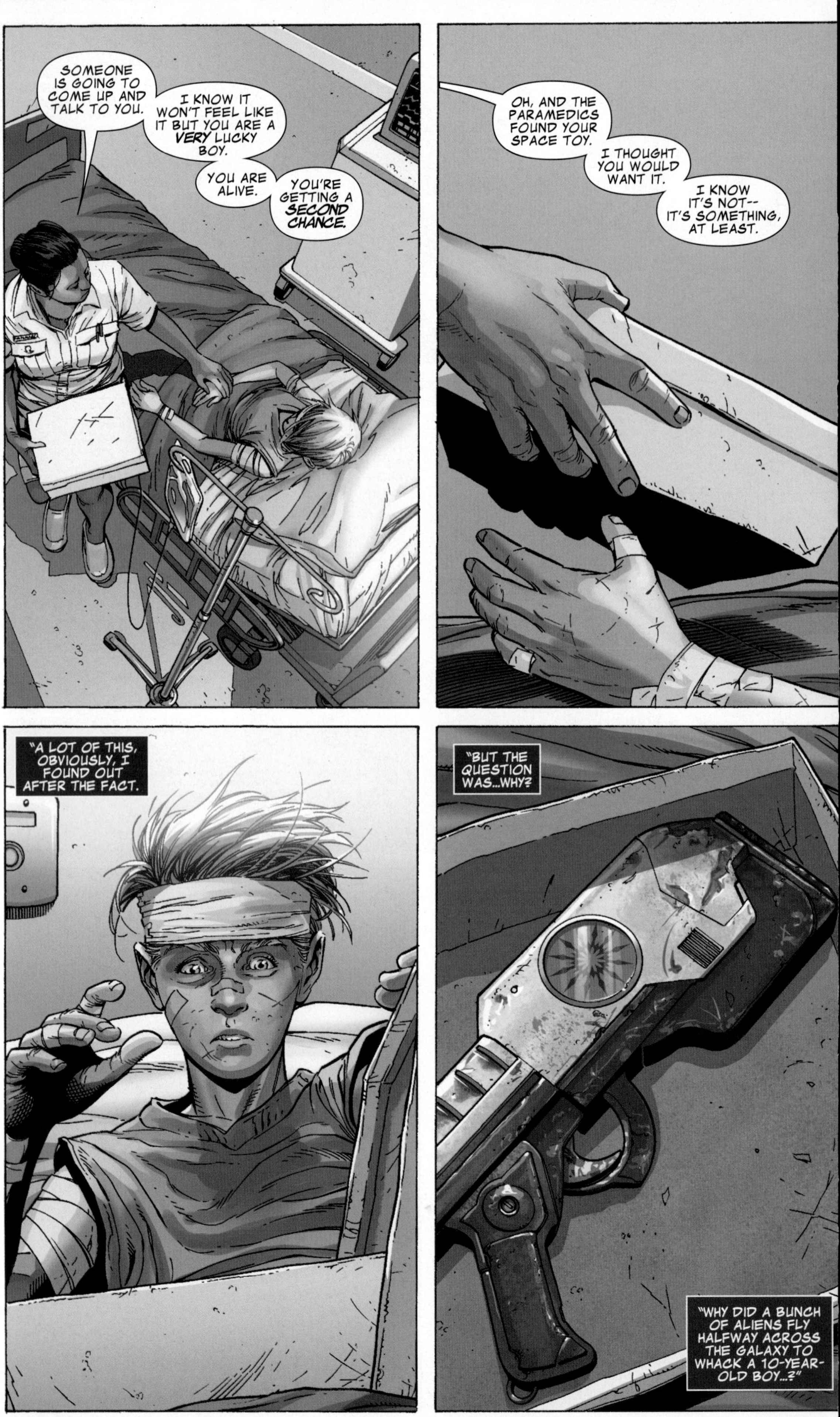
SOMEONE IS GOING TO COME UP AND TALK TO YOU.
I KNOW IT WON'T FEEL LIKE IT BUT YOU ARE A VERY LUCKY BOY.
YOU ARE ALIVE.
YOU'RE GETTING A SECOND CHANCE.
OH, AND THE PARAMEDICS FOUND YOUR SPACE TOY.
I THOUGHT YOU WOULD WANT IT.
I KNOW IT'S NOT-- IT'S SOMETHING, AT LEAST.
"A LOT OF THIS, OBVIOUSLY, I FOUND OUT AFTER THE FACT.
"BUT THE QUESTION WAS...WHY?
"WHY DID A BUNCH OF ALIENS FLY HALFWAY ACROSS THE GALAXY TO WHACK A 10-YEAR-OLD BOY...?"

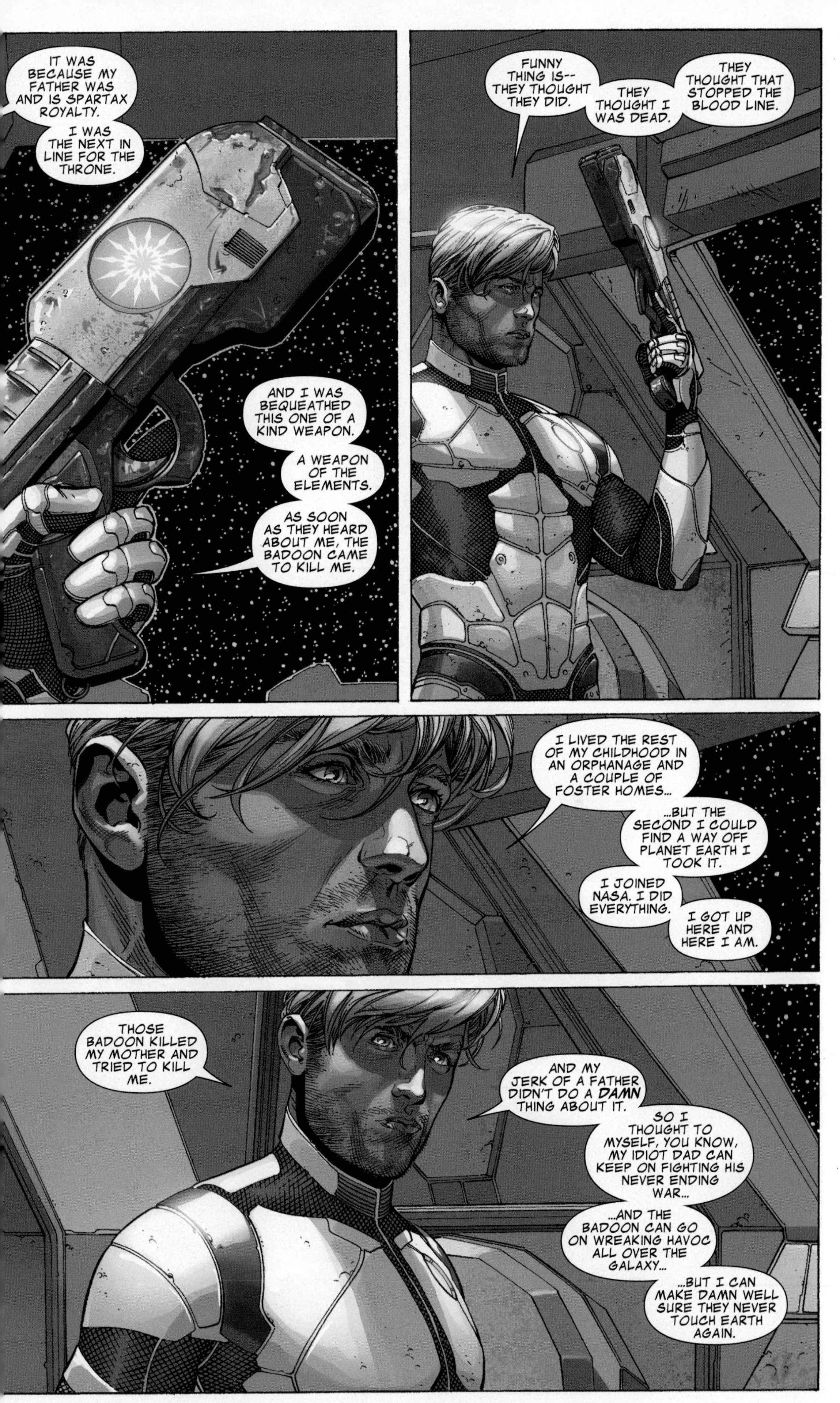
IT WAS BECAUSE MY FATHER WAS AND IS SPARTAX ROYALTY.
I WAS THE NEXT IN LINE FOR THE THRONE.
AND I WAS BEQUEATHED THIS ONE OF A KIND WEAPON.
A WEAPON OF THE ELEMENTS.
AS SOON AS THEY HEARD ABOUT ME, THE BADOON CAME TO KILL ME.
FUNNY THING IS-- THEY THOUGHT THEY DID.
THEY THOUGHT I WAS DEAD.
THEY THOUGHT THAT STOPPED THE BLOOD LINE.
I LIVED THE REST OF MY CHILDHOOD IN AN ORPHANAGE AND A COUPLE OF FOSTER HOMES...
...BUT THE SECOND I COULD FIND A WAY OFF PLANET EARTH I TOOK IT.
I JOINED NASA. I DID EVERYTHING.
I GOT UP HERE AND HERE I AM.
THOSE BADOON KILLED MY MOTHER AND TRIED TO KILL ME.
AND MY JERK OF A FATHER DIDN'T DO A *DAMN* THING ABOUT IT.
SO I THOUGHT TO MYSELF, YOU KNOW, MY IDIOT DAD CAN KEEP ON FIGHTING HIS NEVER ENDING WAR...
...AND THE BADOON CAN GO ON WREAKING HAVOC ALL OVER THE GALAXY...
...BUT I CAN MAKE DAMN WELL SURE THEY NEVER TOUCH EARTH AGAIN.

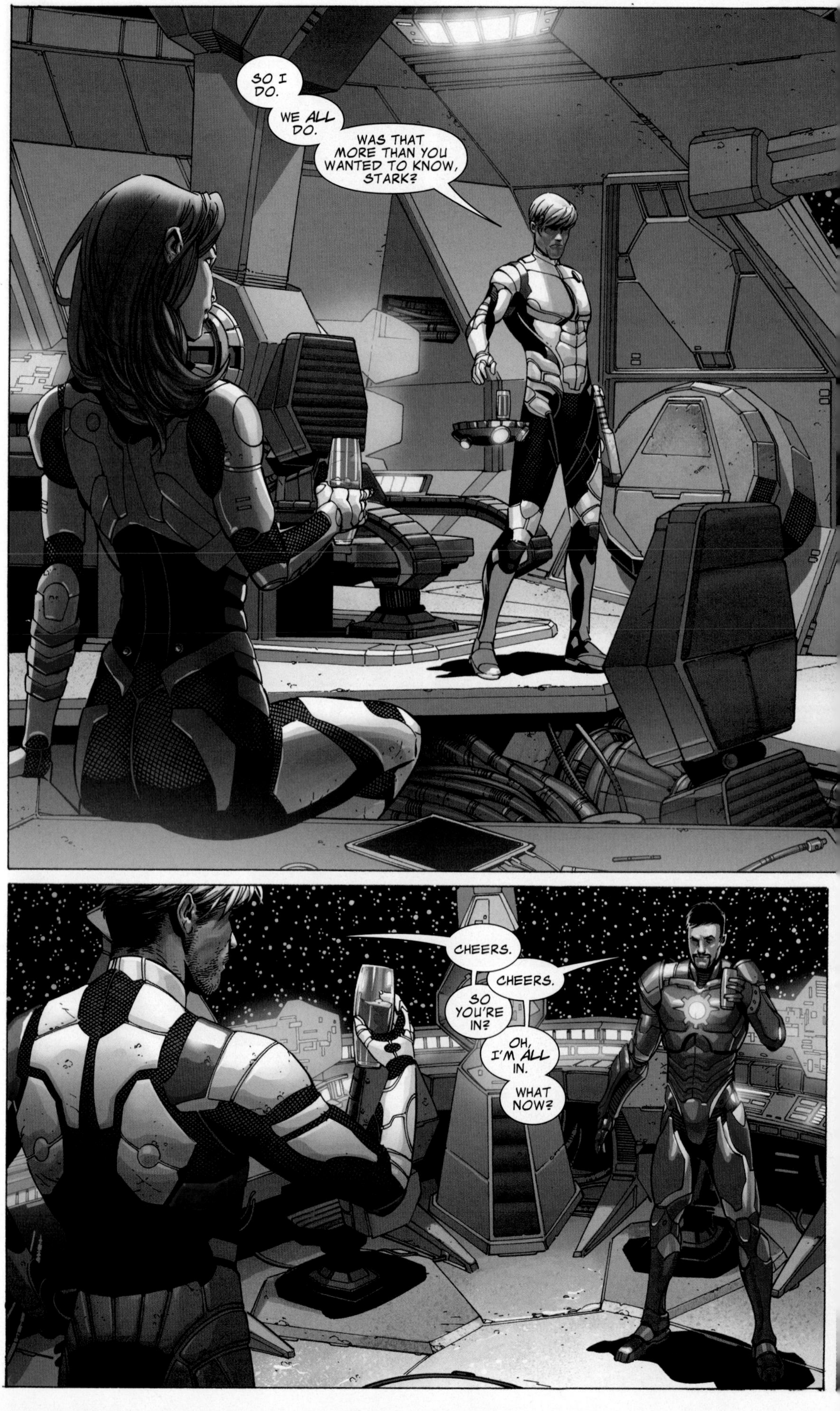
SO I DO.
WE ALL DO.
WAS THAT MORE THAN YOU WANTED TO KNOW, STARK?
CHEERS.
CHEERS.
SO YOU'RE IN?
OH, I'M ALL IN.
WHAT NOW?

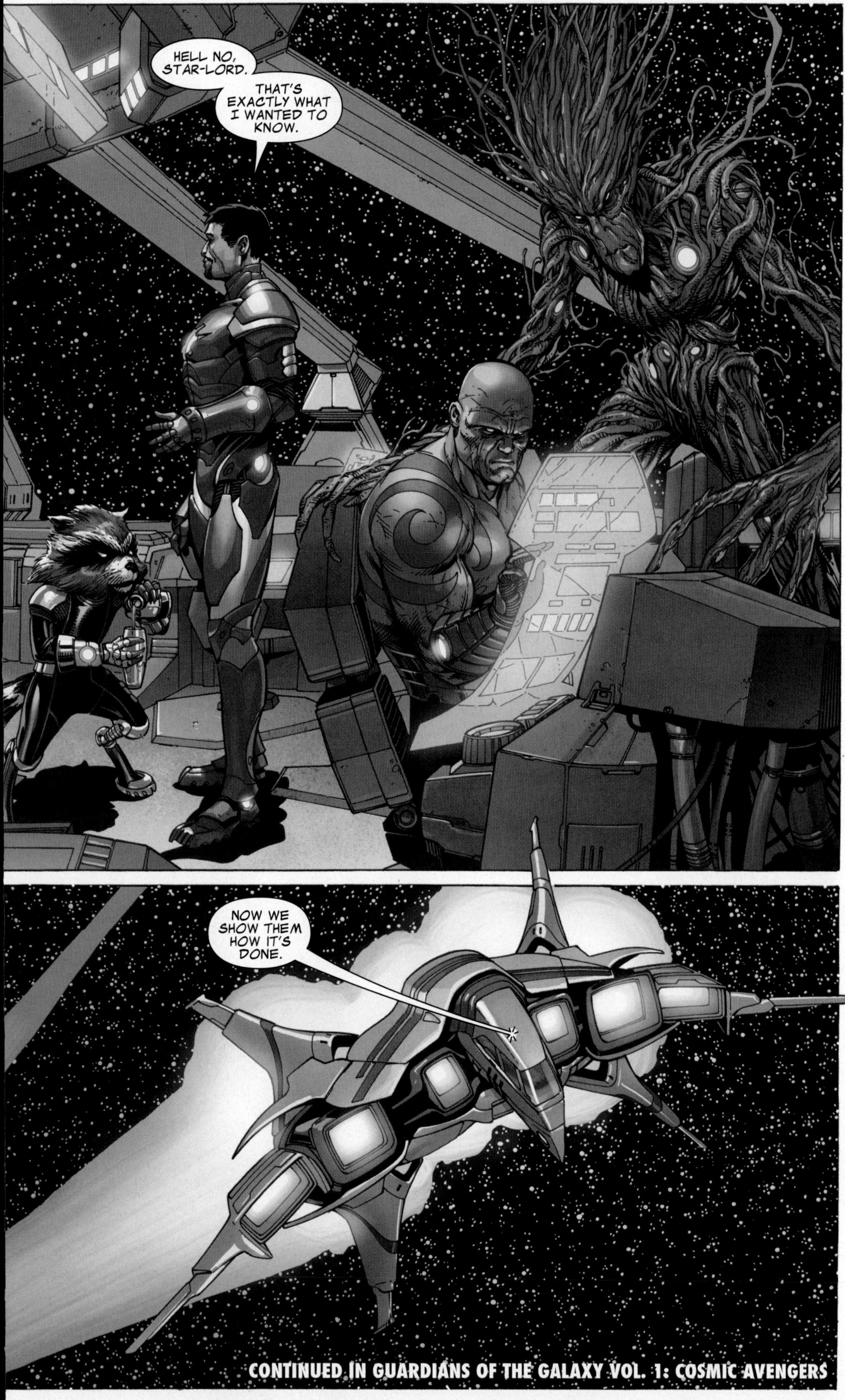
HELL NO, STAR-LORD.
THAT'S EXACTLY WHAT I WANTED TO KNOW.
NOW WE SHOW THEM HOW IT'S DONE.

CONTINUED IN GUARDIANS OF THE GALAXY VOL. 1: COSMIC AVENGERS

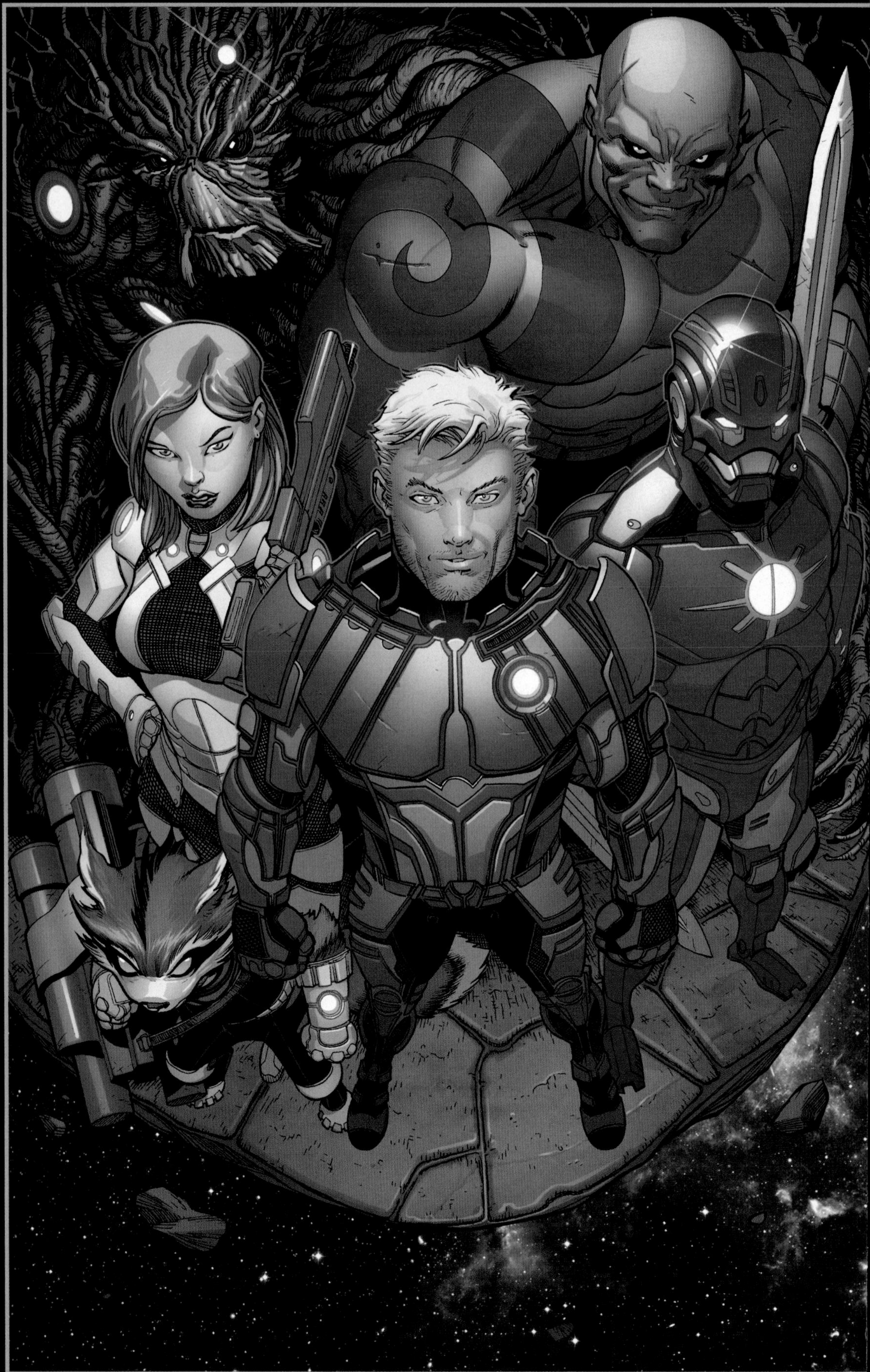

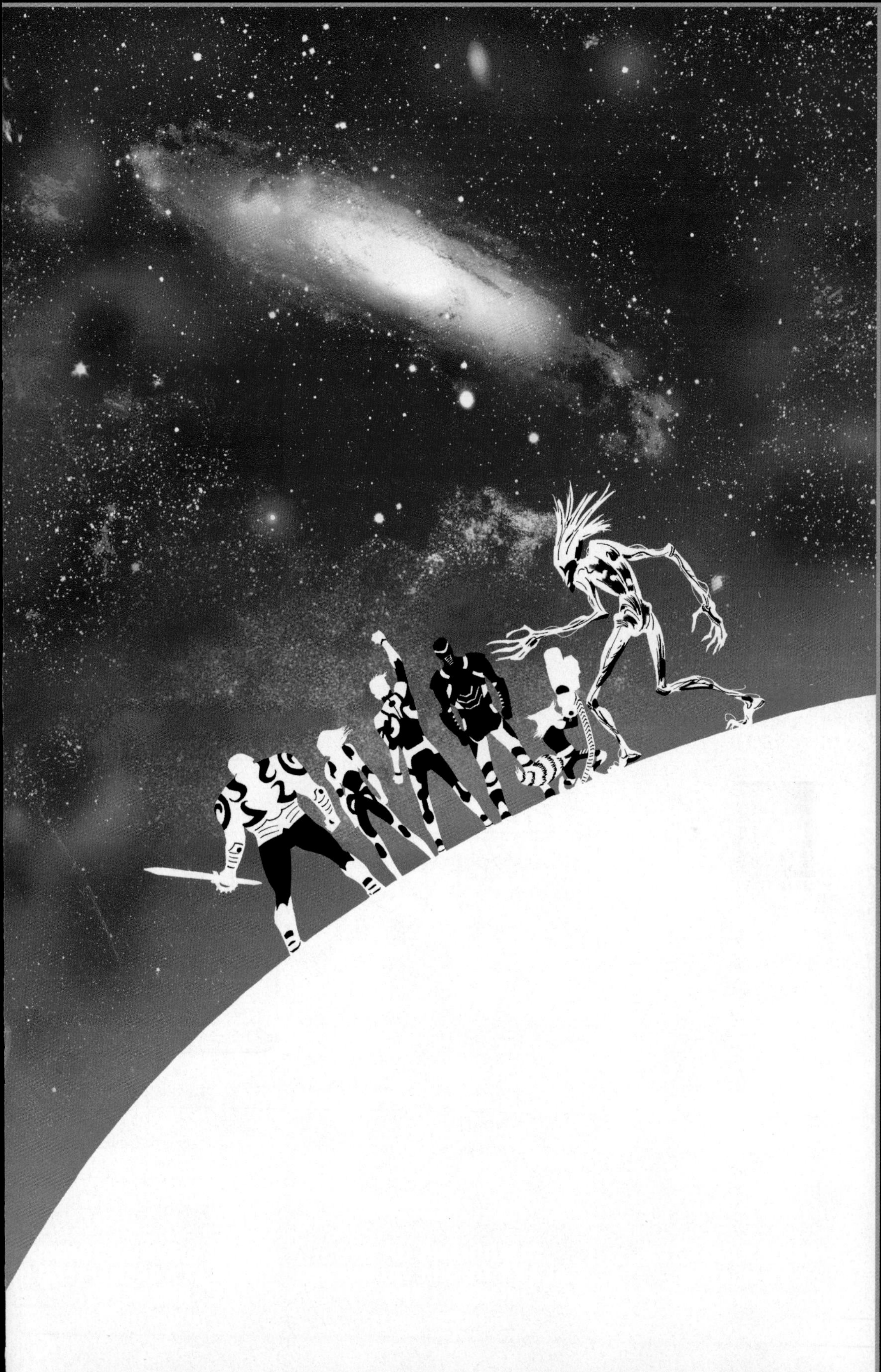

ART BY MARCOS MARTIN

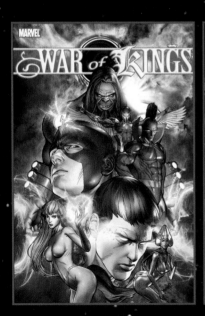